Infancy

Infancy

Second edition

J. Gavin Bremner

BLACKWELL
Oxford UK & Cambridge USA

First published 1988
Reprinted 1989, 1991, 1992
Second edition 1994
Reprinted 1994, 1995, 1997, 1998, 1999

Blackwell Publishers Ltd
108 Cowley Road
Oxford OX4 1JF, UK

Blackwell Publishers Inc
350 Main Street
Malden, Massachusetts 02148, USA

British Library Cataloguing in Publication Data
A CIP catalogue record for this book is available from the British Library

Library of Congress Cataloging in Publication Data
Bremner, J. Gavin, 1949–
Infancy/J. Gavin Bremner. — 2nd ed.
p.   cm.
Includes bibliographical references and index.
ISBN 0–631–18466–X (pbk : acid-free paper)
1. Infants—Development. 2. Infant psychology. I. Title.
RJ134.B74   1994   93–33988
305.23'2—dc20   CIP

Typeset in 10.5 on 12.5ptPhotin
by Pure Tech India Ltd., Pondicherry, India
Printed and bound in Great Britain
by MPG Books Ltd, Bodmin, Cornwall

This book is printed on acid-free paper

Contents

Preface to the second edition

When I started on this new edition of *Infancy*, I thought I would be tackling a relatively minor task. I knew that I wanted to expand the chapter on motor development and include a section on theory of mind in the chapter on social development. Other than that, however, my main aim was to bring the book up to date, a matter that I anticipated would be relatively quick. But I did not bargain with the expansion in the literature that has occurred over the past six years. So in addition to the new sections that I had planned, other expansions and new sections have led to a considerably larger book that covers over 260 further studies. I have retained the same basic structure to the book, and the theoretical analysis at the end remains much the same. However, the chapters on perception and on social development have grown more than others as a reflection of the way the literature has expanded in the last few years.

A look at the contents list does not reflect the extent of the changes in the book, since only major headings are listed there. The chapter on motor development now includes an expanded section on reaching and grasping and a section on dynamic systems theory applied to the development of walking. The chapter on perception is generally expanded but with no completely new topics. Although the chapter on cognitive development has a new section on cognitive precursors of language and an expanded section on object knowledge in early infancy, it is the substantive chapter that has grown least. The chapter on social development has grown most, due to general expansions as well as a major new section on self concept and theory of mind. The final chapter remains relatively unchanged, the main addition being the consideration of dynamic systems theory as an explanatory system in infant development.

I am indebted to Alison Mudditt of Blackwell who encouraged me to write this second edition and gathered feedback from current users. I am also grateful to Charlie Lewis for reading part of the revision and to all the people who have commented on the first edition. I hope that I have managed to respond to at least some of the comments, although I suspect that to a large extent I have done it the way I wanted.

Gavin Bremner
Lancaster

Preface to the first edition

Questions about the nature of infancy have exercised people's minds probably since the beginnings of thought about the nature of humanity. Certainly, the very earliest theories of the origins of knowledge had implications for how we should think of infancy, the case in point being the nature–nurture controversy which in one form or another has been with us since Ancient Egyptian times. Depending upon which side of the issue one favoured, the infant was viewed as either an empty receptacle for the deposit of knowledge or as an organism with all basic forms of knowledge 'built in' along with a time-clock to determine their emergence in behaviour. But it is only relatively recently that people have begun to investigate infancy empirically, a step taken none too soon since it quickly became clear from the early studies that neither of the extreme philosophical views of earlier history fitted the facts of development very well.

Jean Piaget made a major contribution to our understanding of infancy, first by showing how infancy could be studied and, secondly, by establishing a grand theory of infant development that is still a major focus of interest if not agreement today. More recently, there has been a rapid growth in the study of infancy, with the number of infant studies multiplying vastly over the past 35 years. With this growth there has come a bewildering set of findings about infant competence that seems to fit none of our past conceptions of the infant.

The aim of this book is to review the important findings that contribute to current views on infancy, and to try to fit them within a theoretical framework that does the infant justice. Consequently, there is a descriptive side to the book, particularly within the earlier chapters, that is aimed at giving the reader a fairly thorough acquaintance with accumulated knowledge about infant abilities. And there is also a more theoretical side, which builds gradually throughout the book and really takes over in the final chapter, where I attempt to give an account of infancy that can be reconciled with the body of knowledge that we currently possess.

I hope this book will appeal to a wide range of readers. On the one hand, I have tried to avoid too much obscure terminology, with a view to the book's being of use to students beginning courses in psychology, or to parents who want to know more about infancy research. On the other hand, I have aimed to tell a story about infancy that is to some extent my own, and I hope that these aspects of the book may be of interest to advanced students and even those carrying out research on infancy.

A number of people contributed to this book either directly or indirectly. Philip Carpenter of Basil Blackwell encouraged me to write it and waited patiently while the deadline came and passed. Andy Lock, Alan Slater and Val Service made constructive comments on drafts of various parts of the manuscript, and gave encouragement that helped me to keep at the task. But my greatest debt is to Maggie, Andrew and Edward who had to put up with many lost weekends and grumpy bedtimes. I dedicate the book to them, although I suspect the last thing they will want to do is read it.

Gavin Bremner
Lancaster

Acknowledgements

The author and publishers gratefully acknowledge the following for permission to reproduce copyright material: Ablex Publishing Corporation for figures 3.5, 3.7 and 3.9, first printed in *Infant Behavior and Development*; Academic Press for figures 2.3, 2.4 and 3.8, first printed in *Journal of Experimental Child Psychology*; the British Psychological Society for figures 3.1 and 3.14 from *The Psychologist*; Elsevier Science Publishers for figures 4.5 and 4.6, first printed in *Cognition*; the Society for Research in Child Development for figures 2.5, first printed in the Society's *Monographs* series, and figures 4.7 and 5.5, first printed in *Child Development*.

The publishers apologize for any errors or omissions in the above list and would be grateful to be notified of any corrections that should be incorporated in the next edition or reprint of this book.

1

Introduction

Infancy as a field of study

Psychological work on infancy has flourished over the past 30 years, and this book is largely about that research and how it has changed our images of infancy. First, though, we need to consider what period of life is treated as infancy, and what sort of image of an infant recent research has shown up as false. Although in everyday use the term 'infant' is often applied to children up to the age of seven years (e.g. 'infant school' in the UK), developmental psychologists generally think of infancy as the first two years of life. At least within the early part of this period, superficial appearances create an image of a fairly helpless and undeveloped human being. However, recent research has changed this view, presenting the infant as perceptually sophisticated and even as a competent social being right from birth.

But what is so special about the first two years? Many workers study infancy exclusively, and it is easy to think of it as a separate and unique period of development. In some respects it is; the etymological definition of infant is 'unable to speak', and this certainly marks infancy as a distinct period at least from the point of view of methodology. We cannot ask infants questions and expect sensible answers, and so our methods of investigation are more restricted. This is less of a limitation than it might seem, however, since in many areas of psychological investigation we deliberately avoid asking questions, because the answers, even those produced by adults, may not give good clues to the problem under study. What is more important is the fact that infant cognition differs from later cognition in having no linguistic basis:

Another reason for infancy being treated separately from later childhood is the strong influence of Piaget's theory, in which infancy constitutes a distinct developmental stage. According to this theory, infancy is different from later childhood because infants are unable to represent the world mentally, a limitation that sets them apart quite clearly from older children.

Nevertheless it would be misleading to present the period as if it constituted a completely separate stage of development from those following it, for there are strong continuities between infancy and later development. Also, defining infancy as the period before language is to an extent arbitrary, since first words appear during the second year without there being any apparent radical change in the child's cognitive progress as a result. Infancy is more important in the sense in which it is the very beginning of development, and a period during which development seems to be more rapid and also more mysterious than at any other time.

The importance of infancy

In any account of development, understanding of beginnings is vital. Much of developmental study involves investigation of the course of development of particular abilities, and in the extreme case if we find that a particular ability is already present at birth, then we might conclude that there was no need to study its development. Many of the more exciting findings over the past few years have been the discovery of hitherto unsuspected abilities in newborn infants, a picture that could be rather unnerving to the developmental psychologist who sees development disappearing before his eyes, to be replaced by more and more 'innate abilities'. But clearly that is not the whole story. Infants do develop, and many of the abilities attributed to newborns are specific to very precise experimental settings, or can only be detected using sophisticated techniques. These new discoveries change therefore the form that a developmental theory should take rather than make it redundant. Many of the questions are now about how, maybe over quite a long period, these early abilities (or predispositions) become translated into their mature forms.

Much of the impetus behind all these attempts to uncover very early competence comes from an age-old developmental issue, the question of the extent to which human abilities are inborn. In the pages that follow, we shall come across many examples of workers arguing that particular abilities must be inborn since they appear too early to have been learned. The controversy over the origins of human abilities, of whether they are inborn or learned from scratch, has exercised the minds of philosophers and thinkers at least since Ancient Egyptian times, long before experimental psychology came on the scene. However, early attempts to tackle the issue did have an empirical side, as an example from two centuries ago shows. Unfettered by modern day ethical constraints, James IV of Scotland set about establishing whether language was innate or learned by marooning two babies on the island of Inchkeith, with only a dumb woman to care for them. The exact outcome of this early deprivation experiment is unclear, although, to quote Lindsay of Pitscottie (1728), 'Sum sayis they spak goode hebrew . . .' But even he had his doubts.

In more recent times, the same issues underlie what is popularly known as the *nature–nurture* controversy. Historically, there were two views about the origins of human abilities. The *nativists* claimed that all abilities were inbuilt and during development simply emerged according to some pre-set plan, a theory that was later enshrined in the emerging theories of genetics. In contrast, the *empiricists* claimed that there were no such inherited abilities; instead, abilities arose through the moulding effects of the environment. On this view the infant is a kind of empty receptacle which the environment of adults gradually fills and shapes. On the face of it, the second argument might seem closer to the facts. Infants do gradually come to be able to do things that they could not do before, suggesting that they are learning from experience. And these same facts pose a problem for the nativist view. If abilities are innate why do so many of them not appear immediately? One relatively recent nativist response would have been that both the abilities *and their timetable of emergence are built into the* genetic blueprint. So when we see developmental changes, these are strictly *maturational changes* that run according to a pre-set plan, not the product of environmental influence.

Even a fairly casual look at infancy shows that both of these positions are too extreme as general statements about the origins of abilities. As we shall see, although some very early abilities appear to develop without any appreciable contribution from environmental input (the usual definition of maturation), the development of many other behaviours is either subtly or radically influenced by environmental factors. But even in these cases, the empiricist account is inadequate. Although the environmental input may be crucial for normal development, it appears that it is the infant's active use of this information that leads to development rather than the direct moulding effect of the environment.

Nowadays, few psychologists subscribe to either of these views in their extreme forms, and when the controversy reappears it is in the form of an argument about the relative contribution of environmental and genetic influences. At the very least, few would now argue that the environment can mould the individual unless the individual possesses certain characteristics from the outset that permit this moulding to be effective. Similarly, few would claim that abilities would develop irrespective of the sort of environment that the child was placed in. The physical and social environment, if not having a determining role in development, has at least a permitting one in the sense that it has to be there to nurture the developing ability.

The rise in the study of infancy

Issues such as these put an understanding of development in infancy as a high priority, so why is it that the field has taken so long to flourish? One of the main reasons was the predominant influence of behaviourism during the early half of the history of experimental psychology. Although philosophers had long entertained ideas about the structure of the infant mind, when psychologists began to study development the dominant school of thought had its roots firmly in behaviourism. According to this viewpoint in its extreme form, there was little to gain by studying infancy. Not only should the behaviour of children be governed by the same principles as the behaviour of adults, but it was evident from the infant's limited behavioural repertoire that there was little there to study. The alternative of talking about internal structure was just the form of mentalism that the behaviourists wanted to avoid. It was probably partly because they did not see infants as serious subjects of study that they underrated their abilities, and so a vicious circle was created from which an impoverished image of infancy emerged. If these early psychologists had taken time to observe infants in detail, they might have rated their behavioural capabilities much higher.

A number of factors changed the tide for infancy. First of all, in the area of cognitive development, Jean Piaget did an enormous amount to establish infancy as a respectable field of study (1952, 1954). Whatever we conclude about the current standing of his theory, his investigative methods indicated that we could find out a great deal about early development. He showed that by using the right techniques, underlying order could be detected in the limited and clumsy actions of the infant, and many of his most important findings have stood the test of more rigorous experimentation.

In addition, Freud's theorizing (1940) did much to promote the notion of infancy as an important period in emotional development. Again, however we judge his theory, the popularity of his work earlier in this century opened people's minds to the infant as an emotional being, adding to the realization that there was much to be studied in infancy if only it could be captured empirically.

Apart from providing a direct stimulus for theorizing and research, these developments probably had a strong part to play in the increasing concern for the mental welfare of infants on the part of parents and authorities. A look at child care manuals of this century shows a gradual shift from emphasis on physical care and training of habits, to greater emphasis on the styles of caring designed to nurture healthy cognitive and emotional development. John Bowlby's famous report to the World Health Organization in 1951 was another manifestation of this increased concern over emotional development. So Freud and Piaget also provided an indirect stimulus for research on infancy through arousing public concern and the multitude of applied questions that came with it.

Another reason for the shift to studying infancy was the realization by learning theorists that there were dangers in extrapolating from animal learning to human learning. One of their main reasons for studying animals had been the assumption that in animal learning were to be seen the principles of human learning in simple form; however, evidence was growing that pointed to important differences in the way different species learned. If there were differences even between animals, then there were likely to be differences between animals (particularly rats and pigeons) and humans. Thus, learning theorists eventually turned to infants and children in the hope that they would find there the evidence they sought of the principles of human learning in simple form. Unfortunately, they were to be disappointed in this respect, since learning in infants turned out to be far from simple (Papousek, 1969).

Once infancy was recognized as an important period of life and one that could be studied, the development of suitable techniques followed. As we shall see later in this chapter, some of the most productive techniques are not methodologically complex, nor do they require particularly elaborate electronic equipment. Their development waited upon the right questions being asked rather than on the development of technical knowhow. On the other hand, some methods, such as eye movement monitoring, do require sophisticated equipment, and have thus only become available through technological advance.

Central theoretical orientations in infancy

Nativism versus empiricism   As I indicated, one issue that makes the study of infancy imperative is the nature–nurture controversy. Since in one form or another this runs throughout so much of theorizing about infancy, and since in many ways the controversy has been ill formulated, it is worth taking a closer look at it.

There are two main forms of the nativist viewpoint, *preformationism*, in which the structures underlying behaviour are there from birth, and *predeterminism*, in which the structures develop during childhood through a predetermined sequence of differentiation and elaboration. While the simple fact that infants develop would lead us to favour the second form, philosophers adhering to the former version did so for reasons of logic. Their quandary was the question of how something could be created from nothing, and the only way out of this was to assume that there was something there in the first place. Also, preformationists claimed to account for developmental phenomena in terms of a rather different form of maturation, in which innate structure was only gradually reflected in behaviour once physical maturation had occurred, so both versions supposedly accounted for development. The important difference is that according to preformationists all structures were present at birth and underwent no further differentiation, whereas according to predeterminists differentiation of structures took place during development. The important similarity that places both schools firmly in the nativist camp is that both claimed that any changes in behaviour were maturational. The role of the environment, human or otherwise, in the developmental process was minimal or non-existent.

The contrasting empiricist view has given rise to a variety of theories that portray the newborn as psychologically structureless but extremely malleable. For instance, in 1628 Earle (cited by Illick, 1976) said of the newborn, 'His soul is yet a white paper unscribbled with observations of the world'. Consequently such accounts are often called 'tabula rasa' (blank slate) theories, the analogy being the infant as a blank slate upon which experience writes its story. Although this analogy gained currency largely through the work of John Locke (1690), many of the subsequent theories were a good deal more extreme than his in their denial of genetic influences. In essence, according to these theories the infant is putty in the hands of the environment. He or she is shaped entirely by his or her experience, and the shaping force in development is the environment rather than the infant. The only innate characteristic that might be admitted is the malleability that allows the environment to have the constructive effects that it has, and extreme forms of the theory give the infant no active role in development whatsoever.

This view was adopted in part by the behaviourist tradition and by the learning theorists who followed. The link between empiricism and behaviourism was not so strong that the behaviourists denied an innate component to behaviour. However, they maintained the view that changes in behaviour were the result of shaping from the environment, and child development was treated very much like any other learning task, with behavioural changes produced as a result of the reinforcement contingencies imposed by the environment. There was no question of talking of cognitive structures, innate or acquired, since these were unobservable and so were, in the behaviourist view, either beyond our reach or entirely unnecessary constructs.

The consequence of all this was two extremely polarized views: development was either innate and hence genetically determined, or due to some very restricted principles of learning. However, it soon became evident that categorizing behaviour in this way was unrealistic and, as Hinde (1983) puts it, 'It is now virtually universally accepted that a dichotomy between innate and learned behaviour is neither accurate nor heuristically valuable.' Many theorists have come to see the problem as one of assessing the relative involvement of innate and experiential factors in the development of specific abilities. No longer is it a matter of fighting out the controversy to a conclusion; writers recognize that both factors contribute towards any behaviour.

However, this way of thinking often treats genetic and environmental components as if they are separable ingredients that are somehow thrown together in particular proportions to produce an end result, and there are many ways in which this view is still too simplistic as an explanation of developmental processes. Even those behaviours that appear to be the result of environmental conditioning are in a sense just as much genetically determined as ones that seem to emerge without learning. As Gottlieb (1983) says, 'There can be no behavior without an organism and there can be no organism without genes. . . . The ability to respond to environmental factors or be affected by experience is as genetically determined as the maturation process: no more, no less.'

This leads on to the question of what it means to say that a behaviour is genetically determined. Currently, our knowledge of the pathway from genes to behaviour is sparse, but sufficient to indicate that the link must be a very complex one indeed. Also, we have learned much from embryology of late that indicates that the process by which the genes become expressed in the phenotype is not under solely internal control. As we shall see in the next chapter, the picture emerging even before birth is of development occurring at least to some extent as a result of the organism's own activities. From very early on the organism is acting within the constraints of an environment, and so just as there is never behaviour without an organism so there is never behaviour without an environment.

Of course, showing that embryonic development depends upon the organism's own behaviour is not enough in itself to demolish the old notions of genetic determination; the behaviours and their contribution to development could be viewed as part of a complex genetic plan. But from what we now know of infants, behaviour is seldom rigid in the sense of being unadaptable to changing environmental conditions, so it seems more than likely that even some embryonic behaviours are part of an active process of adaptation. In fact, one recent development has been the reinterpretation of newborn 'reflexes' and other forms of behaviour as developed adaptations to the uterine environment (Prechtl, 1984). Not only does this change our views of developmental processes; it also shifts our starting point to well before birth.

Piaget's constructionist theory Piaget's theory of development is a good example of the sort of account that we need if we are to escape from the dichotomous thinking of the nature–nurture controversy. As we shall see in more detail in chapter 4, Piaget (1952) claims that infants are born without intellectual structure, but in possession of certain innate ways of operating on the world. These modes of functioning have the result that the infant gradually constructs knowledge of the world through operating upon it. So there is a vital genetic component in the sense that without these innate ways of functioning the infant would never develop. But there is also an environmental component, since the infant needs an environment to operate upon in order to develop. Both components are very different from those implicit in early nativist and empiricist thinking. The innate component is in no sense a psychological structure, and the environmental component plays a permitting rather than a determining role in development. The important thing about Piaget's theory which brings development alive is the fact that the motive force is within the individual infant. He or she laboriously constructs a logical basis upon which to understand the world. Although in infancy this logic is based in action rather than thought, it is the vital foundation for later mental growth, and it is something that cannot be viewed as solely the product of genes or solely the product of the environment.

Piaget's approach shows that it is not enough to admit that two very different principles operate in development. We need theories that abolish the notion that development is either conditioning or is innately deter-mined, or even that it is the result of the two simply added in particular proportions. Instead we need to understand the mechanisms governing the interplay between internal and external forces in development. Once this step is taken, we can largely stop talking about genetic determination and define as 'innate' those properties that the organism possesses, not just at birth, but at any point in development.

Current developments: ecological theories Some ideas about the way in which future thinking may well proceed come from a theoretical approach in psychology that is currently gaining strength in the developmental field. The *ecological* approach to perception was advanced by J. J. Gibson (1979) as a radical alternative to traditional constructivist views of perception. This theory will be discussed in more detail in chapter 6, but it is worth pulling out a few of the principles that make the theory deserve the name 'ecological'. First, Gibson sees the unit of study not as the organism but as the organism–environment system. The organism is seen as an active information seeker in an environment the nature of which is to a large extent determined by the organism's capabilities of information extraction. Hence, neither organism nor environment are separate objective things. Possibly the best way to understand this is to think of Gibson's environ-ment as the significant surroundings for the organism. Certain aspects of the physical environment have significance for some animals and not for others, hence the two animals' environments are different in ways that relate to their normal activities in the world.

    This notion is a fascinating one when applied to development in infancy. Babies are constantly changing in their abilities to act on the world, and so their Gibsonian environment must be in a state of continuous change. However, in contrast to the way in which Piaget seems to have underrated the importance of the environment in determining development, Gibson appears to underplay the organism side of the equation, claiming that the animal need simply pick up the structures that exist ready-made in the environment. An amalgamation of both views could well produce a more balanced account, and in the final chapter I shall pick up on these notions to build a developmental model based on an interactional organism–environment system in which development becomes the product of a con-stant interplay between cognitive structure and environmental structure. Over the past few years considerable interest has been generated in dy-namic systems theory, an approach to understanding development that has the potential to add precision to the general developmental model that I wish to promote. This approach will be discussed in chapter 2 in relation to motor development, and will appear again in the final chapter.

The continuing importance of infancy Although these theoretical develop-ments cast infancy in rather a different light from the old theories based on a clear cut distinction between what was innate and what was learned, the period is as important as ever. But recent findings and theoretical advances mean that we have to rethink some of our old assumptions about development. For instance, chapter 3 is full of examples of the perceptual competence of the newborn, but in chapter 2 I shall review evidence on development before birth that indicates a need to question the assumption that newborn behaviour is 'innate' in the old sense meant by the empiricists.

Nevertheless, although we may eventually find that many aspects of behaviour undergo development before birth along similar principles to later development, there is still something vitally important in the study of the newborn. Birth marks the infant's emergence into the physical and social environment to which he or she will eventually adapt, and although there may be some small continuities between prenatal and postnatal environments (for instance in the auditory modality), the discontinuities are enormous. For instance, birth marks the infant's first opportunity for visual exploration of a patterned environment, and so in this sense it is a very definite beginning.

On the other hand, in physical terms the newborn is relatively helpless, and on the basis of what I have said so far, the reader could be forgiven for wondering if the baby is more or less an adult prisoner in an infant body. However, I hope to show that the problem is much more complex than this. Although the newborn may be perceptually sophisticated, these structures are very different from adult structures. In the study of infant development, we are faced with the fascinating task of uncovering the principles through which the newborn mind is radically reorganized during the early period of life.

Methods of studying infancy

Babies are not the easiest of individuals to study. Their manual responses often appear clumsy and random, and they are liable to withdraw their cooperation without warning and in a number of ways – by going to sleep, starting to cry, or simply by showing an interest in everything but the things the experimenter has in mind. A large part of good experimental planning is consequently devoted to producing a task that will interest infants of the age being studied. Not only do they have to be generally interested and happy with the test situation, they also have to be 'homed in' on the aspects of the task that test the ability under study. For instance, as we shall see in chapter 4, object search tasks are often used to diagnose infants' knowledge of objects and spatial relations, but we have to be cautious in our interpretation here. If an infant lifts a cover off a hidden object, does this mean that he or she is bent on obtaining the object, or was the act initially prompted by an interest in the cover itself, with interest subsequently transferred to the object that was revealed in the process? Clearly this is an important problem, but fortunately it is one that we can tackle methodologically by ensuring that the infant is interested in the object rather than the cover before testing commences. Sometimes infants do show more interest in the cover than the object, but this situation can usually be reversed by letting them play with the covers until they have lost their fascination.

Of course, another factor that affects our methodology is the fact that we are studying how abilities *change*. Hence, just as in the study of other periods of childhood, infant work carries with it the usual difficulties associated with studying developmental changes. I shall start by outlining the aspects of methodology that are general to developmental work and then go on to focus on those that are used specifically with infants.

Experimental designs in developmental psychology

Much of the work in developmental psychology conforms to some extent to the conventions of basic experimentation, that is, the experimenter manipulates a particular variable (the independent variable) and measures any effect of this on the child's performance (the dependent variable). For instance, going back to the object search example, the investigator might be interested in the infant's ability to keep track of an object hidden in several places in succession, and might guess that performance could be improved by making the places perceptually distinct. The obvious way of testing this would be to compare the performance of two groups of infants, one given the task with a set of identical hiding places, and another given the same task with the hiding places made distinct in some way. In this case the two conditions are identical apart from the visual distinctiveness factor (the independent variable) and if search performance (the dependent variable) differs significantly between groups, the experimenter deduces a causal link between independent and dependent variables.

But this type of experiment does not directly investigate developmental change; it only tells us something about performance averaged across the ages of the children in the groups. Often, this is all that the developmentalist wants to know, particularly if a developmental progression has already been established and it is known that a particular age group displays a particular phenomenon. Under such circumstances the investigator may want to pin down this age-specific phenomenon a little further, and this sort of study may do that job quite well. But at other times the worker wants to know how performance on a task varies with age rather than the conditions of presentation, and here the first step away from the conventional experiment has to take place. Age has now become the variable under study, but since you cannot manipulate age within the experiment it becomes a sampling variable. Instead of taking two similar groups of children and exposing them to different conditions, the experimenter takes two groups of children that differ in age (and, hopefully, in nothing else) and tests them under the same conditions.

Here the first problem of developmental research arises. If an experiment is well designed and carried out, the investigator can conclude fairly confidently that the experimental manipulation caused the effect (e.g. the single difference between conditions produced the difference in perform- ance), but adopting age as the variable throws up more difficulties. Sure enough, it is relatively straightforward to ensure that your different groups are composed of children falling within different age groups, but most of the problems arise because, although we often label the variable as 'age', it is rare for the investigator to be interested in age as such. One of the most basic findings in developmental psychology is that development pro- gresses at different rates for different individuals (leaving aside for the moment the more serious possibility that development proceeds along different lines between individuals). This being the case, we cannot be sure that a younger group is entirely composed of children at an earlier stage of development. This is not such a huge problem as it sounds, since we can expect the relationship between age and developmental stage to be a random one. Given a group of children of the same age, some would be more advanced than others, but as long as careful sampling is done, the average developmental level should still end up lower than that of a similar group of older children. Hence, all that this factor should do is add to the random error, making it less likely that a significant age effect would emerge. If an age effect comes out, however we are home and dry.

The next problem leaves the realm of methodology and enters that of interpretation. We shall see interpretative problems arising in infant work, although the clearest examples come a little later in development. Suppose, for example, we find that most four-year-olds cannot read whereas most five-year-olds can. One might conclude that a crucial cognitive stage had been reached around this point which permits the acquisition of reading skills. But there is also a much more down to earth interpretation, namely that most children are formally taught to read for the first time when they go to school around the age of five. These two interpretations are markedly different, in the sense that the first views the four-year-old as intrinsically different from the five-year-old while the second allows that they might be quite similar. We might be able to choose between these possibilities by looking across regions or countries in which the age of commencement of formal reading instruction differs. If the main factor determining progress is intrinsic (cognitive stage), there should be stability across cultures, whereas if it is extrinsic (teaching), progress should be closely tied to educational practice. But the chances are that the outcome would not be clear cut, with both schooling and developmental level contributing to the age at which reading competence is achieved. Just as in the pure nature– nurture debate, 'either–or' questions are rarely the right ones, and what we need are more complex models of development.

Interpretative problems of this sort usually arise in more subtle guises during infancy, since there are not the same discontinuities in learning environment that occur later. However, we need to bear in mind the fact that parents make judgements about their infant's ability that will determine to some extent the type of stimulation that they provide. This raises the possibility that particular abilities emerge at given times because parents judge that their infant is of an age to achieve them, adapting their stimulation accordingly. Here, however, it is even more likely that infants' cognitive level and parents' competence judgements interact, since the latter are likely to be influenced at least partly by the former.

In pursuing this line, I have digressed a little from the topic of methodology. However, in so doing I hope I have indicated that our problems in studying development may look like methodological ones but are often really problems of interpretation. Also, the link with methodology is still very close. The beauty of experimental methods is that, having discerned two possible interpretations of a result, we should in most cases be able to design an experiment that will provide a differential test of one explanation against another.

In experimental psychology two experimental designs are used most frequently, the independent measures design that I have discussed above, and the repeated measures design in which there are two or more experimental conditions but only one group of subjects. In the first case there is a separate group of subjects tested under each condition, whereas in the second case the same group is tested under each condition in succession. When age is our experimental variable these two designs have as their parallel cross-sectional and longitudinal methods. The cross-sectional method is the one I described above and is so called because the investigator takes a 'cross-section' of children at each of the ages under study. The longitudinal method involves testing children on a given task at a given age and then testing the same children again at a later age or ages. This design is often held up as the best method of studying developmental issues, since just like other versions of the repeated measures design it reduces sampling error. Although children in the group will differ in ability, there is only one group rather than several, and so one dimension of difference is removed.

Developmentalists like this sort of design particularly when they want to achieve a detailed picture of developmental change, maybe over a relatively short period of development. If children are tested repeatedly at fortnightly or monthly intervals a fairly precise picture of development may emerge. However, the longitudinal method shares a major problem with repeated measures studies, that is, whenever you test a subject twice on the same or even a related task there is the chance of an order effect. The subjects may learn from previous exposure or they may become bored with a repeated task. It is the former type of order effect that is probably the biggest danger in longitudinal work. If repeated testing on a particular task reveals a nice developmental picture should we conclude that we have revealed the normal pattern of development? This is often the assumption made in the developmental literature, but there is a clear possibility that in repeatedly testing children we alter their normal environment sufficiently to alter their course of development.

Fortunately there is a way around this problem. We can run a longitudinal study to obtain the detailed developmental picture, but also run cross-sectional checks, not at the same frequency as longitudinal testing, but frequently enough to check that children in the longitudinal group are developing in much the same way as comparable children who are only tested once. Sadly though, the longitudinal method, let alone this combined longitudinal/cross-sectional extension, is very time-consuming, and so despite the undoubted advantages of these methods in the pursuit of many problems, they are relatively rarely used. Most of the work discussed in this book will be of a cross-sectional nature, and indeed some of it will focus on one age alone.

Although these are the basic study designs in developmental psychology, slightly more complex ones are often used to test hypotheses about causal mechanisms in development. As I pointed out, the longitudinal study is supposedly a good means of looking at development as it occurs normally, but it carries the possibility that repeated testing actually changes the course of development. But suppose we actually started out with something like this as our hypothesis, that is, that particular experience at time A would lead to changes that could be detected at time B. We could expose infants to selected experiences at one age, and then test them at a later date on the ability that the experience was predicted to affect. Of course, we would need a comparison group at the later age to check whether the ability of the experimental group had indeed been affected. But even if this was done, and an effect emerged, we should not be completely content. Sure enough, we have seen that the earlier manipulation has in some way affected later behaviour, but it may not have done so in the way the experimenter intended. For instance, it is quite plausible that during the early sessions the infants became familiar with the experimenter or the laboratory, and so improved performance later in development might arise because they were more at ease in the test setting. This can be checked to some extent by seeing whether the enhancement is specific to certain behaviours alone, but probably the best method is to include a group given early experiences of a different sort, maybe just play sessions in the laboratory lasting the same length of time as the special experience sessions for the experimental group. What we are arriving at here is an independent measures design in which measurement of the dependent variable is delayed until a later date. Both experimental and control groups are given early experiences, but only the experimental group receives the experience predicted to affect development. Also, we might want an additional control group given no form of early experience, to provide a baseline to which performance of both other groups could be compared.

As can be seen, developmentalists are often forced into using quite complicated designs by the nature of the questions to which they seek answers. Examples of these sorts of studies will appear in the chapters that follow. All too often though, constraints of time or finance force workers into simpler designs, and when this happens a single study probably does not yield results from which clear conclusions can be reached. Instead, the investigator usually has to build a picture from comparison of results arising from different studies, for instance, by comparing longitudinal data from one laboratory with cross-sectional data from another.

Experimental techniques in infancy research

Piaget did a huge service to infancy by demonstrating that we could derive quite detailed information from very close observation of infants' behaviour. His methods were not observational in the strict sense of the observer as a non-participant bystander; he performed informal 'experiments' involving things like hiding objects or moving them across the infant's visual field. Many of the phenomena that he observed in the process have stood the test of time and experimental rigour, and today's experimentalists would do well to note the virtues of detailed observation. The trend over the past 30 years or so has been towards pinning down behavioural variables that can be reduced to numerical form for the purposes of statistical analysis, and in the process we may have lost touch with the wisdom in Piaget's statement that 'an acute observation surpasses all statistics.'

For Piaget, observation and informal experiment were the ideal methods, but present day experimentalists would at least want to add more sophisticated techniques to their repertoire. Piaget set quite high criteria for the measurement of an ability, such that the infant had to show competence in spontaneous behaviour. More recently, workers have become more sensitive to the possibility that infants have relatively well-formed mental or perceptual structures that do not show themselves in spontaneous behaviour because of motor immaturity or the like. Hence, although detailed observation may be invaluable, if it is limited to spontaneous behaviour it may underestimate the infant's ability. Although there are difficulties over what status to accord to an experimentally extracted 'ability' that is not reflected in spontaneous behaviour until much later in development, it is still vital information to have in our hands when we are theorizing about early development.

Consequently, from an experimentalist's point of view, the main problem in infant work is arriving at measurable dependent variables. On the surface, infants, particularly young ones, may appear to respond to a situation in an un-measurable way, or indeed may appear to respond not at all. For instance, the newborn may display erratic eye movements, uncoordinated movements of limbs, and little else. But over the past 30 years a range of methods has been developed to surmount these surface difficulties in one way or another.

Some of these methods involve taking simple measures of behaviour under strictly controlled circumstances. For instance, a young infant might be presented with two visual stimuli, reasonably well spaced to left and right in the visual field (figure 1.1). Although early eye movements often seem very poorly controlled, such situations often yield preferential looking; that is, if we sum up the times spent looking at the two stimuli, it often transpires that the infant looks more at one stimulus than another. Of course, it is necessary to change the positions of the two stimuli to ensure that what is being measured is not just a habit of looking in one direction. Carefully applied, this *spontaneous visual preference* method has proved invaluable as a means of going beyond surface appearances, since if one stimulus is preferentially attended to this implies that the infant can discriminate between that stimulus and the one with which it is paired.

Figure 1.1 The spontaneous visual preference technique.

This method, however, has its limitations. Although we can deduce discrimination from a preference of this sort, we cannot conclude that no preference means no discrimination. The infant might discriminate between two stimuli, but find them both equally worth looking at. Nevertheless, this is not as big a problem as it might at first appear. Every experimental method is liable to yield negative results from time to time. The visual preference technique is just more likely to do so than methods that get more directly at visual discrimination.

One method that avoids relying on spontaneous preferences is based on an important principle of infant behaviour. If we show an infant a stimulus he or she may initially spend a good deal of time looking at it, but as time goes on the infant will look at it less and less. This *habituation* phenomenon seems to be important in its own right, since habituation rate appears to relate to later intelligence (Bornstein and Sigman, 1986; Fagan and Singer, 1983). But it is also a very useful phenomenon from the point of view of the investigator, since we can use habituation to look at discrimination. The basic method is to present a stimulus until the infant has habituated to it, and then to present a new stimulus and measure looking at that. The logic linking habituation to discrimination is as follows. If infants do not discriminate between the habituated stimulus and the new stimulus, they should look no more at the new stimulus than they did at the old stimulus at the end of the habituation period. However, if infants do discriminate the new stimulus from the old, they should dishabituate, that is, they should start to look much more at the new stimulus.

A modification of this method is to present a single stimulus until habituation is achieved, and then to present the habituated stimulus paired with a novel one. The prediction is then that if the two stimuli are discriminated, the novel one should be looked at more than the habituated one. On the other hand, if the two stimuli are not discriminated, looking should be distributed equally between them. Here the habituation technique is being used to ensure that if discrimination does exist, there will be a preference for the novel stimulus over the habituated one. This variation of the technique is often known as the *habituation–novelty* technique, and versions of it have been used successfully to measure discrimination in infants only one or two days old (see chapter 3).

These methods require only a fairly crude measure of visual fixation and it is usually enough for an observer simply to judge by eye where the infant is looking. But if we want a more precise measure of fixation patterns we need to resort to more hi-tech methods. For a long time the best method available involved estimating eye movements from electrical activity picked up from surface electrodes placed near the eyes (electrooculogram). This method was largely superseded by a technique called *corneal reflection* in which invisible infra-red light beams are shone into the eye, and their reflected images picked by a television camera. It is possible to compute eye orientation from the position of the reflected beams relative to reference points on the cornea such as the iris.

In addition to these methods, which aim at measuring the few behaviours available, there is a further set of methods relying on more indirect measures such as heart rate or respiration rate. The relevance of these parameters lies in the established relationships between physiological states and psychological ones. For instance, heart rate is often used as a measure of attention on the basis of the finding that heart rate falls with increased attention. This argument can be taken a step further to link up with habituation. If habituation involves a reduction in attention over time there should be a concomitant increase in heart rate over time, something that proves to be the case. Additionally, heart rate measures are used to detect emotional change. For instance, some workers (e.g. Campos and colleagues, see chapter 4) have been interested in whether infants both detect vertical drops and show wariness of them. Their measure of wariness is heart rate change, but this time in an upward direction.

In a way, these less direct measures seem to get to a deeper level of perception. Although habituation and preference methods measure discrimination, they do not tell us anything about the significance of the stimulus from the infant's point of view. On the other hand, if we detect wariness in the infant, this suggests that the significance of the stimulus is appreciated at some level. The obvious way of going beyond discrimination to appreciation of the meaning of the stimulus would be to look for the infant making appropriate responses on presentation of stimuli, for instance, avoidance responses in the case of a threatening stimulus, or a grasp response modelled appropriately to the size of the stimulus. This, it was long assumed, was something not open to those studying young infants. However, a number of workers (particularly T. G. R. Bower and his colleagues, see chapter 2) have shown that we are not so constrained in this as had previously been assumed. Their evidence is that very young infants will make avoidance responses to approaching objects, and will make appropriate grasp attempts. Oddly enough, many of these very early behaviours seem to disappear after the first month, and probably this is part of the reason why they went previously unnoticed. But another reason is that these responses are very difficult to obtain – not only were they unlooked for, they were hard to find when workers did decide to look.

There is one other technique that has proved particularly useful in the study of perceptual development. This is the *evoked potential* method in which electrodes are taped to the scalp in the region of brain under study (typically the visual or auditory cortex), and measures of brain activity are made while different external stimuli are presented. The rationale behind this technique is that if a change in brain activity is registered as a result of a change in the stimulus, the system must have discriminated the change. Although the relationship between brain activity and perception is not well understood, particularly in infancy, this method can provide useful corroboration of behavioural measures of discrimination.

Finally, there is a whole set of experimental techniques that measure very basic visual functions, most of which we would hesitate to call behaviours in the psychological sense. For instance, there are a number of optical methods used to assess the structural and functional maturity of the eye. This work is often more the domain of the ophthalmologist than the developmental psychologist, but the findings are important for those studying early perception. Suppose, for example, we discovered that infants were better at detecting vertical lines than horizontals. We might be tempted to draw inferences about the nature of early visual processing, when in fact the phenomenon might arise because of some peculiarity in the optical properties of the immature eye. We also want to know basic things such as the degree to which young infants are capable of focusing on visual stimuli, since this may have implications for the clarity of vision. These issues can be investigated through optical techniques in which a light is shone into the eye and its angle of re-emergence measured.

As infants develop, so their behavioural repertoire expands, and so it should come as no surprise that the methods used depend very much on the age of the infant. Those that I have described above are the ones used predominantly in the study of visual perception of fairly young infants. But once the infant gets a little older, different measures can be brought into play. In particular, once infants begin to grasp and manipulate objects in everyday settings, a whole range of possibilities emerges. Here many of the experimental techniques are adaptations of the measures used by Piaget, involving such things as object search, or tasks in which a cloth has to be pulled in order to obtain an object resting on it but out of direct reach. The aim in these examples is to measure the infant's understanding of the properties of objects and the basic physics of spatial relationships, and in chapter 4 I shall review the wealth of evidence arising in particular from experimental variations of search tasks.

Observational methods in infancy

So far, I have talked almost entirely about experimental method. This is deliberate, for it sets the scene for the bulk of the work to be discussed in the following three chapters. However, I certainly do not want the reader to leave this section with the view that controlled experimental methods are the only ones that yield information about infancy. In fact, towards the end of the book, I shall argue that it is just this preoccupation with tidy controlled designs that is currently the infant investigator's main stumbling block. Potential problems are always created whenever we take people out of their familiar environment or do things with them that have no clear parallel in real life. But this is just what we have to do to satisfy some of the rigid criteria for good experimental control. There are thus good arguments in support of more naturalistic methods that involve less intervention on the part of the experimenter and less rigid control of the testing environment. Using observational methods, or perhaps going back towards Piaget's less formal experiments, promises a richness of data rarely to be found in experimental studies.

Of course, with this richness come problems of interpretation, and often the only way of resolving an ambiguous result seems to be a well-controlled experimental study. In an ideal world, research would probably proceed along at least two methodological lines, say observational and experimental, with the two informing one another. In practice, however, there seems to be a good deal more compartmentalization than this. Those who study perception and cognition usually use experimental methods, whereas those who study social factors in development are much more likely to use some form of observational method. This is partly due to the difficulty of studying social interaction in an experimental setting, but the recent preoccupation with experimental methods in the study of cognitive development is due in some part to a rebound away from Piaget's informality.

Whereas the experimentalist's main problems lie with the technicalities of method and design, most of the problems with observational methods have to do with selecting what to observe, and coding it satisfactorily. Generally, particular behavioural categories are singled out for attention, and these categorizations rest to some extent on interpretation. Hence, if we are interested in noting the incidence of pointing or reaching, we are faced with the problem of deciding which acts count as points or reaches, a process that involves a good deal of interpretation in the face of the ill formed acts of young infants. This interpretative element of observational work is often identified as a limitation, the observer's presuppositions about infancy probably colouring the way in which they interpret the subject's acts. However, it is a necessary part of a method that potentially yields much richer information than experimental methods. In a way, experimental approaches are also subject to bias from the investigator's presuppositions. Just as the observer selects particular behaviours, the experimenter selects particular issues for investigation, and in both cases the selection is based on presuppositions about the nature of infancy.

One method developed by ethologists to get around the problem of interpretative bias was to code behaviour in terms of patterns of muscular contraction (see Blurton-Jones, 1972). Thus it was hoped to arrive at a much more objective classification of behaviour by grouping those actions that showed a similar pattern of muscle contraction. Although this method has its merits, it also has its difficulties, particularly when applied to infants, whose actions are so poorly organized. The area in which this method is most clearly inadequate when used alone is social behaviour, where the significance of particular gestures is culturally agreed rather than objectively evident. So although this sort of precise method can be very useful, it usually has to be employed in conjunction with other, more interpretative, methods. For instance, with the pointing example, we might look at both the behaviour of the infant and the mother, categorizing the infant's arm and hand movements in the way described, but also looking to see if the action leads the mother to look in the indicated direction. At this level, we are at least making judgements about how the mother interprets the infant's act. At some point we have to go beyond description, and as we shall see in chapter 5, some psychologists are more willing than others to interpret infant behaviour on its face value.

Observational data can be obtained in a variety of ways. The investigator might simply sit and observe behaviour over a period, taking note of the looked for behaviours as they arise. This method can be very effective for looking at some aspects of infant behaviour and parent–infant interaction, particularly if the investigator is gathering data over a long period and hence becomes almost one of the family. However, this method has the disadvantage that no permanent record is created. If the investigator did not record a particular event, time cannot be run backwards to recapture it. For this reason, many workers prefer to record sessions on videotape. Once on tape, a session can be run as many times as the investigator wishes. Single frames can be frozen and the tape can be run faster or slower to reveal behavioural patterns that might not be evident at normal speed. An additional advantage of this method is that the infant, if not the parents, is less aware of a camera than of an additional person, so in some cases a more natural record of events may be obtained.

Observational methods are often thought of as quite separate from experimental ones. But very often, maybe after initial observation of spontaneous behaviour, experiment and observation are combined by creating contrived situations in which the infant's reactions are observed. For instance, the investigator might observe mother–infant interaction under normal conditions and under conditions in which the mother is told to be unresponsive, in order to obtain a measure of the infant's sensitivity to maternal expressions and gestures. We shall come across just such a study in chapter 5.

The structure of the book

A look at the contents list of this book indicates separate chapters devoted to most of the conventional topics in infancy. But this should not be taken as an indication that I will adhere to conventional distinctions, such as perception versus cognition, or that I believe we can study cognitive development without at the same time paying attention to social or emotional development. Indeed, an important part of the argument I shall develop throughout the book is that conventional distinctions are highly problematic for a number of reasons. The prime example is the perception–cognition distinction. The general notion is that cognition is something of a higher order than perception, involving mental structures that interpret sensory input, but it rapidly becomes difficult to draw more than a very fuzzy boundary between the two.

Even the distinction between social and cognitive development has its difficulties. A relatively conventional view would be that social development and cognitive development are separable areas of study, but that one has implications for the other. For instance, it has been argued that emotional attachments cannot be formed until the infant develops the knowledge that people, like other objects, are permanent separate entities. In fact, the general thrust of Piaget's theory is that cognitive development is the primary aspect of development, and that cognitive developments have implications for the social domain. It is not so easy to find conventional links being drawn in the opposite direction, but we will come to more radical social developmental views that give social factors a clear causal role in cognitive development. An example is the suggestion that infants only come to act intentionally because their parents interpret their earlier acts as if they were intentional (Lock, 1980).

Given this viewpoint, why have I organized this book along relatively conventional lines? The reason is that the alternatives would have been rather confusing, and readers might have found it hard to fit the material and arguments into their pre-existing ways of thinking about psychology. Thus, my strategy has been to start with a structure that fits the way psychology is generally broken down, and to build arguments throughout the book that suggest we may have to cross these conventional boundaries more often and in a more profound way than in the past if good theories are to result. These arguments will then be drawn together in the final chapter, where I shall attempt to outline the image of infancy that I believe is emerging in the light of both recent theoretical developments and the growing mass of data on infant competence.

Chapter 2 follows physical and motor development from well before birth until the end of the first year. This is often viewed as rather a dull topic, but it has very important implications for general psychological development. Most theories of development view the ability to act on the world as vital for progress, and so motor developments may constrain or even determine the course of cognitive development. Also, we tend to forget abilities like facial gestures when we think of motor development. The ability to smile has enormous implications for early social development, and we need to know whether the first smile arises simply through motor development, or through some aspect of mental development that gives the act human significance.

In chapter 3 the growing data on early perceptual competence will be reviewed. Here, the major emphasis will be on vision, reflecting the bias in the literature, but I shall emphasize the importance of studying the other senses, and particularly, the importance of investigating the degree to which the senses are integrated.

Chapter 4 will be devoted to some topics conventionally considered to be key aspects of cognitive development. In this area Piaget's theory has a dominant influence, with its claim that infants develop knowledge of the world through acting upon it. Here we will come across the first major problem of keeping different sets of findings in harmony. On the one hand, chapter 3 will have emphasized the high degree of perceptual competence of infants, while on the other hand there is plenty of evidence from Piagetian work that the infant is far from competent. I shall argue that the best way out of this problem is to conclude that the infant is well equipped with perceptual structures that are necessary but not sufficient for full competence. In this light, cognitive development involves a gradual realization of the implications for action of the environmental structures extracted by the perceptual systems. So, in an important sense, this chapter will involve putting together the subject matter of the previous two chapters.

Chapter 5 will mark a considerable shift to consideration of social and emotional development. However, it is in this chapter in particular that it will become evident how much interdependence exists between different developmental domains. As the chapter proceeds I shall bring in arguments that do not simply draw links between social, emotional, cognitive and perceptual factors as if they were separate, but treat them as inseperable in important ways. This will all lead further towards the general perspective presented in chapter 6.

2

Physical and motor development before and after birth

This chapter will serve two purposes. First, it will provide an outline of physical and motor development in infancy. Although this topic in itself might appear rather uninteresting from a psychological standpoint, there is growing evidence that motor ability is an important factor in the development of spatial understanding. So although actual description of motor development will be kept fairly brief, the ground will be laid for later discussion of the relationship between motor and cognitive development (see chapter 4). Secondly, since physical and motor developments occur on a dramatic scale in the prenatal period, the account will start before birth, and in so doing the chapter will provide a basic coverage of prenatal development.

Most developmental texts include a section on development before birth, either for completeness, or because it sets later developments in some sort of context. But the content of these sections is often primarily descriptive showing the stages in the growth of the fetus and saying little about the processes behind development. Here, the aim is to investigate the *processes* rather more than the *products* of development.

The conventional view was that the major developments we see occurring before birth are a matter of maturation under genetic control (e.g. Ausubel, 1958), a view that extended not just to bodily changes such as the development of the limbs, but to changes in neural structure and the resulting behaviours of the organism. In contrast to accounts of developmental processes occurring after birth, little role was given to environmental influences in the developmental process, except to point out that certain deficiencies in the uterine environment could lead to developmental problems. Also, little role was given to the organism's own activities as causes of development. However, there is a growing view (Gottlieb, 1976; McIlwain, 1970) that the developmental processes involve more than a simple 'unfolding' according to a predetermined plan. From very early on, the activity of the organism itself appears to have an important role in determining further development of neural and muscular systems. Indeed, in arguing for such a view, Prechtl (1981) points out that from the stance of molecular biology the genetic information possessed by the organism is insufficient on its own to determine completely the complex neural system of the young organism. Consequently, it is fair to conclude that, in common with later development, much of development before birth occurs through the organism actively adapting to the environment of the womb. As Barrett puts it, 'the fetus's own behaviour contributes to its adaptive status as a newborn' (1982, p. 280).

When we investigate these developmental processes, there is, on the one hand, considerable evidence of a continuity between developmental processes before and after birth, and so in an important sense it is vital to look at the fetus to put later developments in context. On the other hand, there is neurophysiological evidence that certain mechanisms (for instance, visual ones) are inhibited before birth, as if development in that sphere is being 'frozen' until the appropriate environment is encountered. This evidence will be outlined here and its implications for theories of perceptual development will be considered more fully in chapter 3.

Development before birth

Figure 2.1 charts the physical growth of the human organism in the prenatal period. By convention, this period is subdivided into three stages. The *germinal* stage lasts from conception until roughly ten days later when the organism is implanted in the mother's womb. This marks the beginning of the *embryonic* stage, lasting until the seventh week. At this point the first direct responses to stimulation occur, an indicator that the organism has entered the *fetal* stage, which continues until birth. What is immediately striking is the degree to which the main features of the human form have developed by the end of the embryonic stage. The eyes and ears begin to develop at the beginning of the fourth week, when the embryo is only 2 mm long, and their major features are quite well formed by the end of the seventh week. Arms begin to develop around the end of the fourth week. The fingers appear at the beginning of the seventh week and are quite well formed by the end of the embryonic stage.

Despite the impressive degree of differentiation present at the end of the embryonic stage, the seven-week fetus still looks far from human, and considerable differentiation accompanies the continuing growth occurring during the fetal months. However, the reader might wonder why a further 31 weeks on average should be required before the fetus is ready to be born. The answer is largely that in order to be viable in the outside world, the fetus must develop a whole range of complex neural systems to subserve the behavioural capacities necessary for survival. It is true that infants born prematurely can survive from as early as 24 weeks' gestation, but this is more through advances in medical science than through a natural ability to survive at that point, and we can assume that important functional development continues up to the normal point of birth at around 38 weeks. Whereas the embryo has the basics of human form, the fetus develops many aspects of human behaviour, and our primary interest here is to look at the processes underlying that development.

Development of responses to external stimuli

The first activity that can be observed in the unborn infant is the heart beat. The heart develops very early and begins to function, albeit inefficiently, in the third week. This irregular rhythmic activity initially originates within the heart itself, since the nervous system is as yet unformed. But although this is quite definitely an action, it is not of the sort usually studied by psychologists; that is, it is not a response to an external stimulus. For this sort of response to be possible, there must be some nervous system to make the link from sensation of the stimulus to execution of even the simplest response. Early studies indicated that the first evidence for true responding appeared after the seventh week when the organism enters the fetal stage. First responses take the form of movement of the head away from the site of stimulation and occur on gentle brushing of regions around the nose and lips (Hooker, 1952). Stimulation of other regions does not produce any response until about three weeks later. Over the following weeks this response increases in complexity, now including extension of arms and pelvic rotation (Humphrey, 1969). This is interesting, since the involvement of body parts distant from the site of stimulation indicates relatively extended neural organization. However, responses of this sort can only be elicited by stimulation around the nose and lips. Stimulation of other regions of the body produces only a local reaction, for instance, stimulation of the palm of the hand produces the beginnings of a grasp reflex at ten weeks (Hooker, 1952), which is well established by 18 weeks.

Development of spontaneous activity

In addition to these elicited responses, spontaneous activity increases, so that by 17 weeks the mother begins to notice the frequent vigorous movements of her child. The recent development of real time ultrasonic scanning techniques has given workers the chance to monitor fetal activity much more closely than was previously possible, and one fascinating event that can be observed through this technique is 'fetal breathing' (Dawes, 1973). Although the lungs contain amniotic fluid during this period, and the movements do not result in its expulsion or intake, the rhythmic movements of chest and abdomen show clear similarities to later breathing activity, and can be seen as early as ten weeks. These movements may be important for differentiation of lung tissue and for proper innervation of the intercostal muscles (Prechtl, 1981). Additionally, movements of head and

EMBRYONIC DEVELOPMENT

AGE days	LENGTH mm	STAGE Streeter	GROSS APPEARANCE	CNS	EYE	EAR	EXTREMITIES
4		III	Blastocyst				
8	1	IV	trophoblast embryo enometrium				
12	2	V	ectoderm amnionic sac yolk sac endoderm				
18	1	VIII	ant head fold body stalk heart	Enlargement of anterior neural plate			
22	2	X early somites	foregut allantois	Partial fusion neural folds	Optic evagination	Otic placode	
26	4	XII 21-29 somites		Closure neural tube Rhombencephalon, mesen, prosen Ganglia V VII VIII X	Optic cup	Otic invagination	Arm bud
32	7	XIV		Cerebellar plate Cervical and mesencephalic flexures	Lens invagination	Otic vesicle	Leg bud
38	11	XVI		Dorsal pontine flexure Basal lamina Cerebral evagination Neural hypophysis	Lens detached Pigmented retina	Endolymphic sac Ext auditory meatus Tubotym panic recess	Hand plate, Mesench condens Innervation
43	17	XVIII		Olfactory evagination Cerebral hemisphere	Lens fibres Migration of retinal cells Hyaloid vessels		Finger rays, Elbow
47	23	XX		Optic nerve to brain	Corneal body Mesoderm No lumen in optic stalk		Clearing, central cartil
51	28	XXII			Eyelids	Spiral cochlear duct Tragus	Shell, Tubular bone

Figure 2.1 Chart of prenatal development (from Smith, 1976).

trunk appear between eight and nine weeks, and stretching movements by ten weeks (de Vries, 1992). Even startle movements can be seen at eight weeks (de Vries), although it is not clear that they are being elicited by external stimulation.

FETAL DEVELOPMENT

AGE weeks	LENGTH cm		WT gm	GROSS APPEARANCE	CNS	EYE, EAR	UROGENITAL
	C-R	Tot					
7	2.8				Cerebral hemisphere / Infundibulum, Rathke's	Lens nearing final shape	Renal vesicles
8	3.7				Primitive cereb cortex / Olfactory lobes / Dura and pia mater	Eyelid Ear canals	Müllerian ducts fusing / Ovary distinguishable
10	6.0				Spinal cord histology / Cerebellum	Iris Ciliary body Eyelids fuse Lacrimal glands Spiral gland different	Renal excretion Bladder sac Müllerian tube into urogenital sinus Vaginal sacs Prostate
12	8.8				Cord cervical B lumbar enlarged, Cauda equina	Retina layered Eye axis forward	Seminal vesicle Regression, genital ducts
16	14				Corpora quadrigemina Cerebellum prominent Myelination begins	Scala vestibuli / Cochlear duct / Scala tympani	Typical kidney Mesonephros involuting Uterus and vagina
20						Inner ear ossified	No further collecting tubules
24	32		800		Typical layers in cerebral cortex / Cauda equina at first sacral level		
28	38.5		1100		Cerebral fissures and convolutions	Eyelids reopen Retinal layers complete Perceive light	
32	43.5		1600	Accumulation of fat		Auricular cartilage	
36	47.5		2600				Urine osmolarity continues to be relatively low
38	50		3200		Cauda equina, at L-3 Myelination within brain	Lacrimal duct canalized	
First postnatal year +					Continuing organization of axonal networks Cerebrocortical function, motor coordination Myelination continues until 2-3 years	Iris pigmented, 5 months Mastoid air cells Coordinate vision, 3-5 months Maximal vision by 5 years	

Probably the major importance of the ultrasonic technique, however, lies in the very full overall picture it gives of fetal activity. The view that emerges finally disposes of the notion of the fetus as behaviourally immature, since it reveals a pattern of coordinated activity, with the fetus turning over and over in the womb, sucking its thumb, and showing startle responses. There is growing indication that these activities can be compared directly to those of the newborn in terms of complexity and degree of coordination (Prechtl, 1984). Also, in the final weeks before birth, clear changes in these activity levels can be identified which correspond closely to the states of sleep, quiet and active wakefulness characteristic of the neonate (Nijhuis, 1992), and changes between these states follow a 24 hour rhythm (Swaab, Honnebier and Mirmiran, 1992).

These spontaneous activities may have many vital functions. One possibility that has no direct psychological significance is that these activities are maintaining the flexibility of the joints. If chick embryos are prevented from moving by infusion of drugs, their joints fuse and later movement is impossible (Oppenheim et al. 1978). However, the situation is less clear in the case of humans, since spina bifida infants are not born with fused joints despite having been unable to move them during development, and so it seems likely that human fetal movements are important in other ways (see Prechtl, 1981). In particular, as appears to be the case for fetal breathing, they may have an important role in the development of musculature and neural systems. With regard to the latter, there is a long-standing school of thought that identifies a role for activity in organizing the very neural systems that underlie it. For instance, Hebb (1949) suggested that visual activity itself leads to organization of the visual regions of the brain. And there is now a growing body of opinion that fetal activity has a role in organizing the developing nervous system, either in a direct way, through affecting the growth of parts of the motor nervous system, or less directly, through producing sensory (in particular tactile) stimulation which may in turn modify the sensory system.

Much of this thinking is fairly speculative at present, but it does open up an important set of questions. Once we admit that activity may have an effect on development, we have to begin to ask questions about environmental factors, since the sorts of activities that take place are constrained by the form of the environment. Can this modification through activity be interpreted as adaptation to an environment? While we might be happy to see it in this way once the infant is born, there are clear disadvantages to this being the process taking place in the womb, since the end result might be an organism singularly well adapted to the uterine environment and poorly adapted to the outside world. However, this is just the sort of interpretation of fetal activity that some workers now favour (Ianniruberto, 1985).

It would be wrong to assume that there are no aspects of the uterine environment worth adapting to with respect to survival in the post-uterine world. When the mother moves, the infant is exposed to the same sort of forces of acceleration and deceleration as in the outside world. The walls of the womb are solid and so yield tactile information broadly similar to objects in the environment. But here, much of the information arises from the activity of the mother rather than the infant, and to some extent the activity of the infant might lead to adaptation to a restricted world of fluid rather than air. Consequently, it is no easy task to identify the sorts of uterine information that fetuses adapt to in a way that stands them in good stead after birth.

Setting aside the issue of developments relating directly to fetal activity, the basic characteristics of one form of perceptual stimulation from the outside world appear to remain fairly constant over the transition from womb to outside world. Auditory information filters through to the womb, no doubt changed to some extent in its quality. However, as we shall see in chapter 3, recent evidence (Querleu and Renard, 1981) suggests that it is not as different in quality as we might expect, and certainly it must be unchanged in its rhythm. A good deal could be learned from this stimulation that would stand the infant in good stead later. Of course, this is only true if it can be shown that the unborn infant is capable of detecting sound stimulation. There appears little doubt that this is the case, since auditory evoked potentials are obtained from 25 weeks gestation onwards (Starr, Amlie, Martin and Sanders, 1977). Also Kisilevsky, Muir and Low (1992) found that from 26 weeks gestation onwards, fetal heart rate changes and bodily movements occur in response to vibroacoustic stimulation, and there is even some data suggesting that the fetus responds to sounds as early as 12 weeks (Hepper, 1992). Thus there is evidence for auditory detection over a lengthy period prior to birth. Given its importance, this issue will be discussed further in the section on auditory perception in chapter 3.

In summary, in many respects the ideal situation might be an organism tuned to ignore aspects of the uterine environment that are unique to it, but to adapt selectively to those aspects that are common with the external environment. This may seem fanciful, and yet there is some evidence in keeping with this within the realms of perception at least. It appears that some neural systems (e.g. the visual system) are relatively well formed prior to birth but that the cortical regions are buffered from the sense receptors until after birth (Parmelee and Sigman, 1983). One interpretation is that after birth this protects the system from the poor information provided by the immature receptors, but particularly in the case of vision it is possible that such buffering has an even more important role in protecting the system from the lack of stimulation presented by the womb. The notion here is that we are seeing the development of a system the normal functioning and further development of which depends on sensory input from the world. Consequently, it requires buffering from lack of stimulation prior to birth, a lack of stimulation that we know leads to neural damage in animals after birth (Wiesel and Hubel, 1965).

On the other hand, the organism has to survive for a considerable period in the womb, and it seems unlikely that fetal life is simply a matter of adapting to those aspects of this environment that will stand it in good stead after birth. We shall come to evidence that some newborn 'reflexes' are actually adaptations to specific aspects of the uterine environment, and an important part of adaptation to the outside world may be the casting off of these redundant behaviours.

Birth and beyond

Newborns and how they change

General appearance and state   The newborn baby weighs on average 3450 grams and is around 50 centimetres from head to toe (Illingworth, 1973). Boys are on average 100 grams heavier than girls and are also a little longer. Of course, there is considerable variation around these averages, and for some reason the range of variation is larger for boys than for girls (Illingworth, 1973). Although all body parts are well formed at birth, body proportions are markedly different from the adult. For instance, the head is very much bigger in relation to the body than in adulthood, and the limbs are shorter.

Infants differ quite markedly in activity level and state at birth. These differences relate in part to whether or not the mother has received analgesia or anaesthesia during labour, since there is some transfer of medication to the infant through the placenta, resulting in drowsiness for a period after birth. However, paediatricians are also on the lookout for more serious signs of inactivity, and for this reason infants born in British and American hospitals are given an assessment known as the *Apgar* test (Apgar, 1953) immediately after birth and then five minutes later. This test measures appearance, muscle tone and response to physical stimulus, along with pulse and respiration, and a low Apgar score (less than 3 out of 10) is a good predictor of an infant at risk (Self and Horowitz, 1979). If a problem is suspected it is likely that a more detailed behavioural assessment, such as the *Neonatal Behavioral Assessment Scale* (Brazelton, 1973) will be administered, possibly along with some form of neurological assessment (Prechtl, 1977).

At face value, the newborn's activities present the impression of uncoordinated inability. Movements of the limbs are jerky and ill coordinated, and eye movements are often rather similar, giving little impression of an individual scanning the world in a controlled fashion. Yet in both these areas we shall encounter evidence that surface appearances are deceptive. If the right techniques are applied, newborns can be shown to be responsive to objects in the world, both in terms of their visual fixations and in their manual actions (see later this chapter). And even those activities such as kicking that seem particularly random have been shown to possess elements of coordinated activity that are adapted in response to perturbations such as the addition of a weight to one leg (Thelen, Skala and Kelso, 1987).

Probably the most noticeable states of the young baby are the extremes. The highly active crying state is hard to ignore, while the sound asleep state with which it often appears to alternate may be greeted with relief by parents who have had to cope with an extended bout of lung power. Immediately we can see that the newborn is far from helpless. The galvanizing effect the cry has on parental attempts to meet the infant's needs is a striking demonstration of an adaptation that helps to ensure the infant's survival. But close observation of infant states has show that in addition to the crying state, wakefulness can be further categorized into 'activity' and 'alert inactivity' (Wolff, 1973). Initially, the transitions between these states take place very rapidly, and often quiet wakefulness lasts for a much shorter time than parents would like.

This is also something that directly concerns those who study young infants, since it is only during alert wakefulness that we can hope to measure the infant's perceptual abilities at their best. What is particularly difficult is distinguishing between wakefulness and transitions into drowsiness, and many negative results with young infants may have occurred because the infants were not particularly alert when tested. Fortunately for all, the duration of alert wakefulness extends gradually as the infant gets older.

One way of thinking of the different states of the newborn is to assume that they are simply the reflection of different levels of arousal. Thus the various states are conceived of as different levels on a continuum between sleep and alert wakefulness (Brackbill, 1971). However, Prechtl (1974) dismisses this notion, arguing on the basis of behavioural and neurophysiological evidence that states are 'distinct conditions, each having its specific properties and reflecting a particular mode of nervous function'.

A good example of a qualitative difference between states can be seen in the case of sleep. Adult sleep goes through regular cycles of quiet sleep and active sleep, the latter often being called REM (rapid eye movement) sleep. REM sleep used to be called 'paradoxical sleep', because although there is an almost complete lack of muscle tone during the phase, electroencephalogram (EEG) measures reveal brain activity comparable to the waking state. Such electrophysiological measures have been used to establish that the basic qualitative distinction between REM and quiet sleep begins to appear around the seventh fetal month (Hofer, 1981). At around 32 weeks the fetus spends about 80 per cent of time in REM sleep. This proportion falls steadily, so that only 50 per cent of time is spent in REM at birth and 30 per cent by six months, with a further fall off to 20 per cent by adulthood. The very high proportion of REM sleep in early development has led many investigators to speculate on its function. The picture of high brain activity in isolation from outside stimulation has led to the suggestion that it has a role in neural organization during development and learning (Dewan, 1969), a notion supported by the finding that the proportion of REM increases when animals (Lucero, 1970) and adult humans (Zimmerman, Stoyva and Metcalf, 1970) are exposed to circumstances requiring intensive learning or adaptation.

Rhythmic cycles of passage between states can be seen as early as the fifth fetal month, when active states begin to alternate with periods of quiet (Hofer, 1981). At birth, infants are faced with a quite new environment, so it is no surprise that a few days elapse before they settle down into a consistent sleep–wake pattern. One of the things that is new to the infant is feeding, and this event has to be fitted into the cycle. The infant seems able to adapt to different frequencies of feeding, and here parental influences may have an important effect on the length of the sleep–wake cycle that emerges. It is also worth noting that the infant's early behaviours have rhythmic properties as well. For instance, sucking occurs in a burst–pause sequence. As we shall see in chapter 5, a number of workers argue that these rhythmic properties of early behaviour are extremely important in early formation of parent–infant relationships. In particular, one notion is that the basic burst–pause cycle in feeding is the basis for the turn-taking sequence that appears in later interaction between parent and infant (Brazelton, 1979).

Individual differences in state   As already noted, there are noticeable differences between newborns on basic measures of state, differences that persist after birth. Some infants show more activity than others; some are more irritable, as indicated by the frequency with which crying results from environmental events. It appears that these differences in temperament have their origins well before birth (Eaton and Saudino, 1992) and thus do not originate in differences in parental treatment. Additionally, they appear to be quite stable over the early months. We should note, however, that measures of temperament are often based on parental reports, and on this sort of measure there is even stability in relation to parental judgements prior to birth (Mebert, 1989), suggesting that parental judgements may be highly influenced by expectations. Nevertheless, Stifter and Fox (1990) found stability between birth and five months using physiological measures and response to pacifier removal, and also found correlations between these and parental judgements at five months, so it seems clear that early stability of temperament is not simply an artifact due to parental expectations. The everyday distinction between crying and placid babies is often treated as if it were an early manifestation of personality. However, although temperament differences may indicate differences in neonatal responsiveness to the environment, so far there is little evidence that they are the direct precursors of later personality traits. Stratton (1982) concludes that neonatal individual differences show little continuity with later differences. However, this does not rule out indirect links. An irritable baby may be treated by parents in a different way from a placid baby. And these differences in treatment may in turn have effects on later personality.

Development of posture and locomotion   Figure 2.2 charts the development of postural control, showing progress towards sitting and towards locomotion. As can be seen, in both cases, newborns start with very little postural control, and only gradually gain control over head, arms and legs as they get older. Initially, even when the torso is supported, there is insufficient

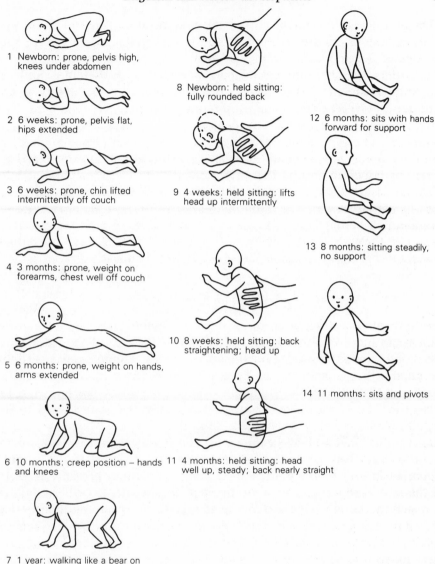

1 Newborn: prone, pelvis high, knees under abdomen

2 6 weeks: prone, pelvis flat, hips extended

3 6 weeks: prone, chin lifted intermittently off couch

4 3 months: prone, weight on forearms, chest well off couch

5 6 months: prone, weight on hands, arms extended

6 10 months: creep position – hands and knees

7 1 year: walking like a bear on soles of feet and hands

8 Newborn: held sitting: fully rounded back

9 4 weeks: held sitting: lifts head up intermittently

10 8 weeks: held sitting: back straightening; head up

11 4 months: held sitting: head well up, steady; back nearly straight

12 6 months: sits with hands forward for support

13 8 months: sitting steadily, no support

14 11 months: sits and pivots

Figure 2.2 Chart showing development of postural control during infancy (from Illingworth, 1973).

muscle control to hold the head up even for short periods. But by six or seven months, infants can sit up with use of their arms as supports. If placed prone, it is only after some time that the head can be held up and even longer before at least some of the body weight is supported on the arms. At around eight or nine months most infants begin to crawl, an achievement that often only comes after quite a period of frustration, sometimes particularly so since early attempts often lead to backwards motion away from the target instead of towards it.

The study of this gradual process of gaining motor control could easily be dismissed as of minor interest to the psychologist. However, many theories of development lay a good deal of emphasis on the importance of action in the development of perception (Held and Hein, 1963) and cognition (Piaget, 1954), so clearly the development of the ability to act is important. A recent line of research has picked up on Held and Hein's claims about the importance of locomotion for the development of space perception, and there is now growing evidence (to be discussed in chapter 4) that the infant's understanding of space is advanced through the experiences gained by crawling around the environment. I believe we should also look at the ability to sit up as a potentially important milestone, although in a slightly less direct way. Once the infant can sit upright, he or she not only commands a better view of the world, but is now in a better position to inspect it through head movements as well as through eye movements. This should extend the visual scope of the world considerably.

Newborn 'reflexes' and how they are replaced

The conventional description of newborn behaviour lists a set of 'reflexes', behaviours more or less complex that run off in a fixed sequence as the result of a specific stimulus. For instance, there are simple reflexes such as the pupil reflex to light or the knee jerk reflex. At a more complex level there is the startle reflex, involving arm flexion and triggered by a loud noise, also the Moro reflex, elicited by allowing the baby's head to drop slightly, and involving a complex sequence of arm extension with the hands closed, followed by flexion with the hands clenched. Probably the one that surprises parents most is the stepping reflex; if the infant is supported in an upright posture over a surface so that pressure is exerted on the sole of the foot, an elaborate 'step' is taken which will be followed by a step by the other leg, extending to a continuing left–right sequence if the infant is moved bodily forward. The overall effect is rather like someone walking through treacle, and it is very tempting to interpret this response sequence as a precursor of later walking.

Many of these reflexes disappear within a few weeks or months of birth, or at least appear to be progressively modified. A good example of the latter is the change in grasping pattern from initial grasp reflex in the form of a fixed sequence of finger closing triggered by stimulation of the palm, through various forms of palmar grasp becoming progressively adapted to the object, culminating in a finely tuned finger and thumb grasp under accurate visual control.

There have been various explanations of the disappearance of newborn reflexes. One argument is that they just 'drop out' through lack of use, a possibility that is in keeping with the fact that stepping persists for longer if extensive practice is given (Zelazo, 1976). Or it has been suggested that early reflexes are suppressed as the cortex develops inhibitory control over the midbrain, a notion supported by the finding that cortical damage in adults led to re-emergence of infant reflexes (Paulson and Gottlieb, 1968). Finally, a recent explanation of the disappearance of the stepping reflex is that the response becomes impossible to execute because leg muscle strength does not keep pace with increase in leg weight (Thelen and Fisher, 1982). This is rather a leveller for those seeing psychological significance in these disappearances, but none of these explanations really helps us to understand why the reflexes were there in the first place.

The conventional account in developmental texts was that these were innate forms of behaviour that had adaptive value, not necessarily in our current environment but in a past environment of evolutionary adaptation (Jersild, 1955). Within this way of thinking, the Moro reflex was interpreted as a response to regain hold of the mother, which evolved to deal with the situation in which our ancestor infants clung to their mother's belly as she travelled. The notion is that developments since then have been too rapid for evolution to keep pace, and so many of our newborn reflexes are now redundant.

These accounts of early behaviour and its modification over the first few weeks are very much in the classic tradition in which all fetal and neo-natal behaviours were assumed to be, (a) genetically specified 'hard-wired' behaviours and, (b) fixed responses to specific stimuli. But this view is not in keeping with the recent evidence on fetal activity covered in the previous section. Not only can we see spontaneous fetal activity that does not appear to be triggered by specific stimuli, it is also argued that many fetal behaviours have developed as adaptations to the womb (Prechtl, 1981).

Finding spontaneous fetal activity makes it more than likely that spontaneous behaviour is also present at birth, and we will come to the evidence on this in a page or two. However, this way of thinking about fetal activity also throws new light on some of the more fixed reflex-like neonatal activities. The new notion is that some of the behaviours we see at birth are adaptations to the uterine environment, adaptations that developed in part as a result of the fetus's own activities. For instance, the stepping reflex, instead of being seen as some innate precursor of walking, is treated as a response that allows the fetus to turn round in the womb (Prechtl, 1984). At first sight, this notion appears to be in conflict with accounts that identify a link between newborn stepping and later walking (Ferrandez and Pailhous, 1986; Thelen, 1984). However, it seems likely that the basic left–right sequence is the most effective method of gaining bipedal traction whether for walking or turning in the womb, so it is still possible to entertain the notion that the initial coordination developed as an adaptation to the womb, and has links with later walking through a common basic left–right pattern.

Prechtl's hypothesis would be more convincing if we understood the function of turning in the womb, and one explanation is that such movement is necessary to prevent adhesion to the walls of the womb. It has also been suggested that this activity is used by the fetus to turn so as to engage its head in the cervix just prior to birth (Ianniruberto, 1985). Such 'fetal collaboration in labour' may extend right through to the moment of birth, with the Moro reflex serving the function of drawing in the first lungfull of air.

An interpretation of this sort produces quite a different explanation of some early activities and why they so often disappear. First of all, it weakens the notion that what we are seeing is a set of genetically preprogrammed unlearned responses; many of them may be acquired through some form of learning process in the womb. Secondly, the rather bare notion that they die out through lack of use is modified to say that they die out or are replaced because they are no longer appropriate. This sort of interpretation has the advantage of both explaining their presence at birth and their disappearance later, although we should note that only some early reflexes fit this model well.

Of course, while this account deals with the question *Why?* it tells us less about *How?* Although considerable advances are being made in the study of how fetal behaviour may develop, we are still very much in the dark about the mechanisms that lead from the very first steps in the formation of the organism to the first behaviours. Also, we need to know far more about the processes by which behaviours disappear or are replaced by others. Probably the most widely accepted explanation is that the disappearance of reflexes is related to the growing cortical control of behaviour that occurs after birth. Initial reflexes are thought to be under the control of the earlier developed midbrain, but as the cortex develops it exerts a controlling influence on the midbrain (see Touwen, 1976), leading to the inhibition of some reflexes and the gradual modification of others. While this account seems plausible, there are a number of counts on which the story needs modification or extension.

First of all, this account, like so many others, carries with it the old notion that reflexes are fixed or 'prewired' midbrain behaviours, and this is a view that we know to be questionable. While the behaviours may be prewired if we take birth as the starting point, the fetus's activities in the womb may have been involved in the 'wiring up' process.

Secondly, this transfer of control to higher neural centres should not be seen as a 'one-off' event. At least one phenomenon in development before birth lends itself to the same sort of interpretation. Between 17 and 22 weeks the fetus shows a period of reduction in spontaneous activity accompanied by a heightening of the thresholds for elicited activity (Hofer, 1981). This is followed by a gradual re-emergence of activity of a more controlled and complex sort in the weeks that follow. A likely explanation is that this relates to the development of brain structures within the thalamus and cortex. As these structures develop, they exert an increasing inhibitory effect on lower brain centres, to be followed by a controlling effect. So instead of there being just one dramatic neural reorganization following birth, it seems much more plausible that, starting in the fetal stage, there are a series of discontinuities brought about as successively higher regions of the brain become functional.

Thirdly, if cortical inhibition is involved in the disappearance of early behaviours, we have to assume that this inhibitory effect can be counter-acted or delayed by environmental factors, given the evidence that the stepping reflex can be maintained through exercise (Zelazo, 1976).

Finally, we have to be cautious about what is involved in one region of the brain taking over the function of another. It is easy to think of the same behaviour appearing at different stages, but controlled by different brain systems. However, although early and later behaviours may show surface similarity and apparently serve the same function, in detail they may be quite different (see, for example, the development of grasping, p. 36). Hence, although the cortex may take over control of particular functions, these functions may be performed through behaviours that show marked differences. In addition, Prechtl (1981) argues that earlier and later beha-viour forms exist for a time in parallel, and so the details of how one brain system 'takes over' from another are likely to be much more complex than the simple notion of cortical inhibitory control suggests. It is here that more may be gained from analysis of the growth of skilled activity (see Connolly and Bruner, 1974) than through postulating changes in brain structure, although eventually both should come together as our understanding of the relation between brain and behaviour improves.

Despite these qualifications, when added to the arguments about adapta-tion to the womb, this discussion helps to present a fuller picture of behavioural change. While earlier adaptations are undoubtedly subserved by lower parts of the brain (since these develop earlier) their eventual replacement is tied up very closely to a take-over of function by higher regions of the brain. The fascinating question that remains is the degree to which earlier behaviours may in themselves contribute to the brain reorganization which will eventually lead to their replacement.

Tracking and reaching for objects by neonates and older infants

Just as workers tended to play down the presence of spontaneous activities in the fetus, there has long been a tendency to ignore neonatal behaviours that do not fit the 'reflex' pattern. More recent investigation has revealed a range of behaviours that look quite unlike reflexes. For instance, newborns are capable of turning their head towards the source of a sound (Field, Muir, Pilon, Sinclair and Dodwell, 1980). Such an action is goal directed, unlike a reflex which would occur in the same form whatever the location of the stimulus. Additionally, newborns have sufficient control of their eyes to both fixate interesting stationary objects and to follow moving objects (Banks and Salapatek, 1983). While their eye movements are rather sluggish and, in the case of tracking, very much less smooth than those of adults, we are quite definitely dealing with behaviours that are visually guided. Rather than running off in a fixed pattern after the initiating stimulus, these eye movements are altered more or less continuously in response to information about object position. There is much more that could be said about early visual behaviour, but since it is closely tied to the issue of early visual perception the main discussion of the evidence appears in the next chapter.

The findings on eye movement control immediately show the newborn in a new light. In the realms of visual competence at least, we have to discard the notion that we are dealing with an organism that responds in simple fixed ways to specific stimuli, and begin to view the neonate as at least partially in control of his or her actions. But some of the most surprising and contentious data relate to newborn reaching. The view in the 1960s was that visually guided reaching began to emerge during the fourth month (White, Castle and Held, 1964). However, Bower, Broughton and Moore (1970a) pointed out that young infants are often not in a position to move their arms freely. For instance, in the supine posture, when one might expect to see reaching taking place, infants use their arms to prevent rolling over. Bower's group claim that if infants a few days old are suitably supported around the torso, they will reach for objects in their visual field. What is more, this is more than simple swiping at the object, something that would be important enough in itself. The behaviour involves a reach followed by a grasp. Going even further, they claim that neonates distinguish between a real object and a two-dimensional representation of an object, reaching for the former but not the latter (Bower, Dunkeld and Wishart, 1979), and that they show surprise at not being able to touch a virtual object presented by optical means (Bower, Broughton and Moore, 1970a). Bower goes on to use this final finding in support of the notion that there is an early unity between the senses (see chapter 3).

Some workers have failed to replicate any of these findings, and question whether there is real evidence for any form of neonatal reaching (Ruff and Halton, 1978). However, it would appear that these replication failures occurred because the workers set rather high criteria for directed reaching, and other researchers. (DiFranco, Muir and Dodwell, 1978; Hofsten, 1982; Rader and Stern, 1982) have obtained evidence for crude directed reaching towards objects. Additionally, Butterworth and Hopkins (1988) obtained evidence of reaching towards the mouth by neonates, a case in which there is no visual stimulus to aim for. However, studies investigating reaching to objects found that reaches were as likely to be directed to two-dimensional representations as towards real objects. Additionally, although newborns appear to reach towards objects and show some elements of preparation for grasping, such as hand opening prior to contact, there is little evidence that they are actually capable of grasping (Hofsten, 1982). Thus the balance of evidence is that early reaching, although present, is considerably less sophisticated than Bower suggested. DiFranco, Muir and Dodwell (1978) suggest that early reaches may be ballistic movements that are simply triggered by the visual stimulus, unlike a mature reach which is under visual guidance during execution. However, the failure to find a difference in reaching to real objects and representations has more implications for early object perception than for the issue of whether newborns reach or not. Whether these early actions are ballistic or not, they appear to be important precursors of later reaching.

Like many other early behaviours, early reaching attempts appear to reduce in frequency over the first two weeks (Rader and Stern, 1982), and Bower (1982) found it very difficult to elicit them over the period four to 20 weeks. At first sight this would suggest that reaching has a common basis with other neonatal behaviours which disappear shortly after birth. But there are reasons not to equate reaching with other behaviours such as neonatal stepping. First of all, this behaviour cannot be explained as a uterine adaptation, since there is no question of visually guided behaviour in the dark confines of the womb. Consequently, we cannot explain its disappearance in the way we might in the case of the stepping reflex, that is, as the fading of a uterine adaptation. We should also note that reaching does not seem to disappear for such a long period as Bower suggested. Hofsten (1984) obtained a lower incidence of reaches to a target at seven weeks than at four weeks, but found that the incidence had risen again at ten weeks.

Bower views both stepping and reaching as early precursors of later walking and reaching respectively. In seeking an explanation of their disappearance and re-emergence he appears sympathetic with the notion that the phenomenon is due to the take-over of higher regions of the brain, but points out that the re-emerging reach at 20 weeks has been changed in the process. He claims that the neonatal reach–grasp is an undifferentiated action pattern, whereas the later behaviour has become differentiated into reach and grasp components, the second being triggered only by contact with the object. In this respect, he is in agreement with Prechtl in suggesting that we are dealing with something much more complex than a simple transfer of control of behaviour from midbrain to cortex. There is also a dramatic change in the form of the behaviour in the direction of greater differentiation into its components. In fact, Bower puts forward this principle of differentiation with great force, claiming that it is a quite general principle of early development. As we shall see in the next chapter, he argues that the very young infant is perceptually as well as motorically sophisticated, but that there is initially a lack of differentiation of experience into the separate modalities of vision, hearing and touch. Hence, the general process underlying early development is one of differentiation. Just as early actions are undifferentiated, early perception is amodal, and perceptual development is a matter of differentiation of perceptual input into different sensory modalities.

There are, however, alternative accounts of the difference between early and later reaching and the reason for the period of suppression. As already noted, Hofsten (1984) found a reduction in reaching to a target at around seven weeks. However, he also measured forward extensions of the hand when no object was present, with two main outcomes. Firstly, forward extensions were as frequent in the absence of an object as they were when one was present. This might lead us to question whether the neonatal behaviour deserves to be called reaching. However, Hofsten found that these early actions were more accurate when infants were looking at the object than when they were not. Secondly, he found no age-related reduction in forward extensions in the 'no object' condition. Thus, it appears that around the age of seven weeks the presence of a reachable object, rather than prompting reaching as one might expect, actually inhibits it. Hofsten proposes that the presence of an interesting object leads to arousal of the infant, which in seven-week-olds leads to suppression of reaching. This could be because at this age excitement leads to blocking of movements due to activation of agonist and antagonist muscles. Alternatively, the visual stimulus may produce negative arousal sufficient to prompt withdrawal, or at least inhibition of approach.

Neither of these alternatives provides a particularly convincing reason for why suppression of reaching should take place at seven weeks in particular, and a further possibility arises from another aspect of Hofsten's account. Hofsten (1982) claims that neonatal reaching is different from later reaching in the sense that the former is primarily attentive while the latter is manipulative in intent. If this is so, and if Bower is right in his claim that action systems are initially undifferentiated and proceed towards greater differentiation over time, we might conclude that initially looking and reaching might occur together because they are undifferentiated as separate attentional systems, but that once differentiated, the exercise of one might inhibit the exercise of the other. Once that point of differentiation had been achieved, re-emergence of visually guided reaching would wait upon coordination of looking and reaching as separate elements within an overall system.

Another difference between early and later reaching is pointed to by Bullinger (1990). So far, other than considering its relation to grasping, I have looked at reaching as an isolated motor ability. However, Bullinger points out that it is only possible to understand reaching fully when it is placed in the context of other motor functioning, the claim being that later reaching only becomes possible once it is coordinated with a whole set of postural adjustments. As already noted, neonatal reaching is hard to elicit unless the infant is provided with the necessary postural support. Bullinger shows that under natural conditions orientation to a stimulus involves a range of postural adjustments which occur together in a global fashion. Asymmetric postures are more stable and offer more chance for arm movement under visual regard, and Bullinger argues that well controlled visually guided reaching only becomes possible once the torso becomes stable and head movements can take place independently of other postural adjustments. Evidence in support of this position comes from work by Fontaine and Pieraut le Bonniec (1988), who found that postural maturity was a better predictor of reaching than infant age.

In effect, we are faced with two alternative explanations of the delay before accurate reaching emerges, one to do with inhibition due to arousal (Hofsten) and the other to do with the need to develop a stable postural base for visually guided reaching (Bullinger). And as my example above indicates, there are probably other ways still of interpreting the same evidence. However, it is probable that we should not be seeking to choose between Hofsten's and Bullinger's accounts, since it seems likely that both workers have identified important factors in the emergence of reaching. As we shall see in the section *A recent approach to motor development*, a current popular approach to motor development analyses the processes as the product of a complex interplay between psychological, motor and biomechanical factors. In this light, it makes perfect sense to assume that the developmental course of reaching is multiply determined.

The processes underlying later reaching   Although there is good evidence for the basics of reaching at birth, it is generally agreed that successful reaching, in which the hand at least makes contact with the target, does not emerge until the fourth month. A number of studies have gone beyond simply confirming that reaching occurs, to investigate the guidance system that infants use. In adults, it is generally assumed that a reach is commenced with a ballistic movement, in which the hand is aimed at the target location prior to commencement of the movement, and further that this movement is then modified continuously through visual feedback about the changing spatial relationship between hand and target.

In contrast, there is some controversy over the processes controlling reaching by infants. Bower (1974) claimed that four-month-old infants who misjudge a reach are unable to correct it during the movement and have to begin it over again. From this he concluded that infant reaching was ballistically guided in such a way that its direction and extent was planned prior to the movement with no possibility of modification once the movement commenced. In contrast, Hofsten and Lindhagen (1979) obtained clear evidence in four- to five-month-olds for correction of reaching during movement, although the correction movements were very crude and jerky. What was particularly striking about their results was the fact that infants seemed to be as successful in reaching for moving objects as for stationary ones, and Hofsten (1980) further investigated reaching for moving objects (see figure 2.3), concluding that correction involved a series of ballistic components. In other words, correction was only taking place at a number of points in the reach, and took the form of a 're-aiming' of a ballistic movement.

This makes infants' ability to intercept moving objects particularly striking, since it would imply that they are capable of predicting a future

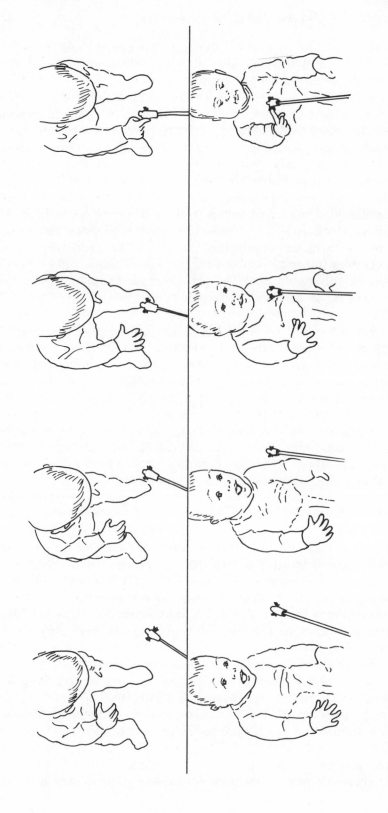

Figure 2.3 A well aimed reach for a moving target by a 21-week-old infant (from Hofsten, 1980). Each frame gives a view from above and in front of the infant.

position of the object, an impressive spatial ability. However, there is some doubt about whether prediction is really involved, apart from maybe in a very crude form. Mathew and Cook (1990) question Hofsten's (1990) conclusion about the ballistic nature of infants' reaches, pointing out that his data measurement is founded on the assumption of a ballistic basis for reaching and thus is not well suited to detect evidence for continuous correction of movement. If infants are capable of monitoring the relationship between hand and target and of making appropriate corrections, it is not clear that prediction of object position is required, since all they need to do is work continuously to bring hand and target together. What makes it difficult to pin down the system in use, is the fact that the functioning of a continuous monitoring system may be concealed by relatively crude motor control. Thus movements might be jerky for basic reasons of control rather than because a ballistic system is in use. It certainly appears that some form of visual guidance is used, since McDonnell (1975) found that infants from four months upwards were capable of directed reaching while wearing offsetting prisms. For this to be possible it is necessary to assume that infants are using information about the relationship between hand and target, since this is undistorted by the prisms. In contrast, a ballistic reach uncorrected by feedback about hand position would be offset due to the distortion of vision provided by the prisms. On the basis of evidence from a finer grained analysis of movement correction, Mathew and Cook favour the notion that the later components of infant reaching are controlled by a continuous correction system that uses information about the position of the hand relative to the target. However, there is still relatively little research on this issue, so the case is far from closed.

Preparation for grasping   Although reaches by neonates are accompanied by hand opening, there is little evidence that this results in successful grasping, and even contact with the object is not guaranteed. It is generally concluded (Bower, 1974; Hofsten, 1982; 1984) that this form of hand adjustment is an undifferentiated part of the reaching movement. Additionally, despite Bower's (1974) claims about successful reaching in neonates, subsequent research has revealed little evidence of adjustment to the size or distance of the object. However, Bruner and Koslowski (1972) obtained evidence suggesting that eight-week-olds were to some extent responsive to the visible characteristics of the object, finding that they made more arm movements towards the midline when a graspable ball was presented there than when the ball was too large to grasp.

In later months, the grasp appears to be differentiated from the reach as a separate act. Working with five-, nine-, and 13-month-old infants, Hofsten and Rönnqvist (1988) investigated both the degree to which reaching and grasping were integrated and the extent to which hand opening was adjusted to object size. At all ages, reach and grasp were well integrated, the grasp beginning during the reach and hand closing commencing prior

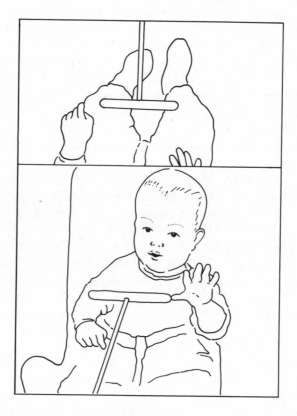

Figure 2.4 An example of a task in which correct hand orientation is important for sucessful grasping (from Hofsten and Fazel–Zandy, 1984). View from above and in front of the infant.

to contact with the object. Younger infants began hand closure later than older ones, but this still occurred prior to contact with the object. At no age was there evidence that infants separated the two acts in time by reaching and then grasping. However, only nine- and 13-month-old infants showed adjustment of hand opening to different object sizes.

Apart from adjusting the grasp to suit the size of object, it is often necessary to align the hand to the orientation of elongated objects if grasping is to be successful (see figure 2.4). Lockman, Ashmead and Bushnell (1984) investigated the ability of five- and nine-month-olds to align their hand so as to grasp a stick. They found that whereas nine-month-olds rotated their hand progressively during the reach, five-month-olds carried out most of the adjustment after contact with the stick. Five-month-olds did make some hand rotation in the appropriate direction prior to contact, but it was not sufficiently marked to reach significance. However, it appears that this negative result may have arisen because measurement of hand rotation was too gross in this study since, using a more sensitive measure, Hofsten and Fazel-Zandy (1984) obtained evidence that even 4.5-month-olds made some rotational adjustment prior to target contact.

Finally, it appears that by eight months, infants have learned how to coordinate reaching with forward leaning, and use the two together only when the distance of the object demands (McKenzie, Skouteris, Day, Hartman and Yonas, 1993). This was not simply a case of infants reaching and then leaning on finding that they had not reached the object, since both reaching and leaning were commenced together, indicating a pre-planned integrated sequence. Also, by twelve months, infants were capable of using a mechanical aid to extend their reach. In addition to their implications for coordination of actions, these findings can be assumed to provide indications about the infant's understanding of distance in space (see chapter 4).

Object manipulation   It would be inappropriate to leave this section without commenting on object manipulation, since this generally follows on from a successful reach. It should be noted, however, that object manipulation begins well before successful reaching is achieved. If two-month-old infants are presented with an object they will manipulate it manually (Rochat, 1989). However, this takes the form of fingering the object by the hand that holds it, and at this stage manual manipulation may be no more important than oral manipulation, since the object is commonly trans-ported to the mouth. At around four months, a new form of bimanual manipulation emerges in which one hand holds the object and the other fingers it. This activity appears to be related closely to visual exploration, since its frequency reduces considerably when the object is presented in the dark. Still, however, these actions appear relatively crude to adult eyes, and further important progress occurs around nine months with the emergence of the finger and thumb (pincer) grasp.

Despite its relatively crude appearance, early manipulation is clearly organized in relation to the object under investigation. For instance, Ruff found that infants from six months upwards presented with a series of objects differing in texture engaged in a high frequency of fingering activity, suggesting investigation of texture. On the other hand, if they were presented with objects differing in shape there was a high frequency of transfer from one hand to the other, suggesting more gross exploration of shape. Palmer (1989) also found differential actions depending on object properties and found additionally that the nature of the table surface affected the frequency of particular actions. For instance, infants banged a silent bell more often when the table surface was solid than when it was padded, in which case there was a higher frequency of waving. Palmer concludes that infants tailor their actions increasingly skilfully to the properties of both objects and the surfaces that they are presented on. Although these effects were more marked at nine months, differential activity was also evident at six months. And there is even some evidence for differential activity by neonates. Rochat (1987) found that they applied different types of manual pressure to balls depending upon whether they were hard or soft.

These findings suggest that, even at birth, infants are using manipulation to extract information about the objects manipulated. In particular, Rochat notes that from four months onwards, manual manipulation is increasingly coordinated with oral manipulation and visual exploration, and suggests that the whole process is important in the extraction of intermodal correspondences. Thus there is a close potential link between the material discussed here and the research on intermodal perception (chapter 3).

A recent approach to motor development: the dynamic systems approach applied to development of walking

Although there is now an extensive body of literature describing the development of a range of motor abilities during the early months of infancy, our understanding of the processes through which these developments take place is far from complete, and there is a tendency in some of the literature to rely on explanatory principles that appear somewhat dated. In particular, many accounts still rely on the nativist concept of *maturation*, a process through which abilities emerge according to a predetermined plan and without influence from the environment. Early accounts relied heavily on the concept of maturation to explain the uniformities in the sequence of motor development across children. For instance, McGraw (1945) was a primary proponent of the notion, mentioned earlier, that newborn reflexes were controlled by midbrain centres and that their suppression and subsequent replacement by more sophisticated behaviours was the result of increasing influence of cortical centres as they matured. This type of account has proved remarkably resilient and is still central to much of contemporary theorizing. Probably in part this is because motor skills are often treated as fairly low level and consequently suitable for explanation in this way. For the same reason, there is a strong tendency to adopt explanations in terms of brain development, and for some reason, whenever psychologists adopt a neurophysiological account of development, there is a tendency for the level of developmental theorizing to drop several notches.

It is, of course, perfectly sensible to draw links between behavioural development and parallel developments in the brain. It would be surprising indeed if there were not developments in the brain accompanying developments in behaviour, and onset of cortical control may be an important aspect of what is happening. The problem is, however, that many of these accounts treat the brain changes as maturational processes when there is no reason to assume that they necessarily are. Later in the book, I shall discuss evidence indicating that development of brain function is influenced by specific environmental input (Blakemore and Cooper, 1970). Once this is recognized, it becomes clear that identification of parallels between brain development and mental development should not be taken as evidence for maturational processes. Rather the problem becomes one of seeing how brain development can be accounted for within theories in which development is viewed as the outcome of a complex interaction between environmental and individual factors.

Esther Thelen and her colleagues adopt an approach to motor development which takes to the extreme the notion that development is a product of interplay between infant and environment. In their *dynamic systems* approach (Thelen and Ulrich, 1991) they claim that in order to understand development we have to understand that complex systems are self organizing: they 'prefer' certain states of equilibrium. However, they can be pushed towards new states of equilibrium by particular forces, acting from within the organism or from the external environment. Thus development is understood as a progression through a series of stable states. This approach is radical since it does not identify the developmental driving force as either within the environment or within the individual, treating the self-organization process as the outcome of cooperative interaction between subsystems within an overall system that encompasses both infant and environment. Additionally, it claims that changes in quite low level variables can have a radical effect on the system as a whole, by pushing it to a new stable state.

They apply this analysis primarily to the case of development of walking. As I have already indicated, Thelen interprets the disappearance of the newborn stepping response as due to leg weight increasing more rapidly than muscle strength. This raises the possibility that, rather than being inhibited by growing cortical control, the basic stepping pattern remains intact but simply cannot be exercised under normal circumstances. In support of this notion, Thelen, Skala and Kelso (1987) showed that alternating leg movements were present in the spontaneous kicking of young infants. But an even more convincing demonstration comes from their series of studies on stepping with the aid of a treadmill (see figure 2.5). If infants are supported above a moving belt, some show stepping movements in the first month and there is an increase in stepping thereafter, with stepping continuing right through the period prior to the onset of proper walking. This is striking evidence that aspects of the stepping pattern continue to exist during the period in which it does not occur spontaneously, and that the pattern can be triggered by presentation of appropriate environmental supports.

It would be wrong to conclude, however, that the stepping pattern is present throughout infancy in its fully developed form. Initially, left–right alternation is not very reliably elicited even in the few infants who show it, and all infants showed a clear increase in left–right stepping between their third and sixth month. Additionally, the pattern becomes increasingly stable with age. Thelen and her colleagues investigated a number of variables liable to influence this change, and conclude that a major factor

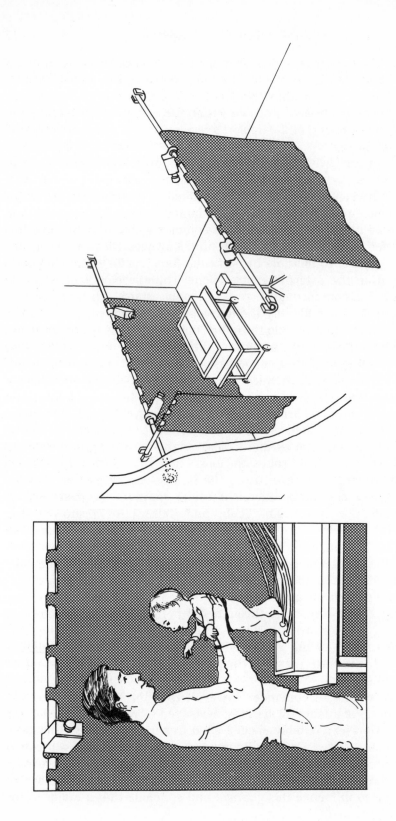

Figure 2.5 Measurement of treadmill stepping in infancy (from Thelen and Ulrich, 1991).

is the decrease in dominance of flexor muscles over extensor muscles. Again, a relatively simple change in a component of the system leads to important changes in the dynamics of the whole system.

Of course, such an account does not exclude neurophysiological accounts of development of walking. Rather it casts them in an entirely new light. Oddly enough, the essential point was put very well by the Russian psychologist Bernstein back in 1940 (reprinted in Whiting, 1984). As he puts it, '. . . the reorganisation of the movement begins with its biomechanics . . . this biomechanical reorganisation sets new problems for the central nervous system, to which it gradually adapts.' (Whiting, 1984, p. 197). In other words, changes in locomotor organization do not come as a result of developments within the brain. Instead, the opposite occurs, with changes in peripheral biomechanical organization leading to changes in the brain as it adapts to the new features of the biomechanical system under its control.

Although I have outlined the dynamic systems approach only as it applies to development of walking, it is clear that it can be applied to other motor developments. Consider, for example, the agreement between dynamic systems theory and Bullinger's claim that reaching can only be understood in the context of postural adjustments as a whole. Also, at an empirical level, there is a suggestive parallel between the finding that stepping can be elicited with the 'support' of a treadmill and the fact that early reaching is only reliably obtained when direct postural support is provided. It appears that both forms of external support can be seen as ways of circumventing physical constraints that would normally prevent the successful practice of the behaviour in question. Additionally, however, it is claimed that dynamic systems analysis can be usefully applied to any area of psychological development, including development of social interaction and communication (Fogel and Thelen, 1987). While radical in many ways, the approach has a certain amount in common with other recent theories of development, and in the final chapter I consider possible relations between this approach and other forms of developmental theorizing.

The development of the smile

Finally, we move briefly to a motor ability with strong social implications. The smile is an extremely potent social signal. Parents who have seen their infant smile at them immediately feel gratification, and the amount of time they want to spend with their infant rises once smiling has begun (Newson and Newson, 1963). But there is considerable controversy, both among practitioners and parents, as to when smiling begins. Some claim that early smiles are not directed to people, the popular notion being that they are a response to wind. Others dismiss this notion, claiming that infants smile socially from birth. As someone once put it, 'Would you smile if you had wind?'

Certainly, something that looks like smiling can be detected at birth and has also been observed before birth (Prechtl, 1984). But the facial movements involved are often one-sided, and involve the mouth but not the eyes. Also, they seem to be spontaneous, as opposed to later smiling which is elicited by specific stimuli. It is these findings that have led some to suggest we are simply seeing a response to an internal state of discomfort, in fact, that we are seeing a grimace rather than a smile, and in this light the question in the paragraph above appears more in fun than as a serious point. However, many would claim that the action is more like a smile than a grimace, and Prechtl (1984) argues for a direct link between neonatal smiles and later social smiling. Also, Bower (1982) claims that smiling occurs less rather than more at times when the infant is likely to be suffering from wind. It seems that the wind explanation is more a product of our view that newborns cannot really be smiling than a conclusion based on good evidence.

That does not mean, however, that smiling is used socially from birth. As already noted, at first it seems to be a spontaneous occurrence rather than a response to social stimuli. At around three weeks smiles begin to be elicited in response to the human voice, particularly the female voice, and by six weeks the human face, particularly the eye region, has become a very potent trigger for the smile (Wolff, 1963). But, even when smiling has begun to be directed at people, there are reasons to doubt whether it is smiling as we know it. It turns out that presentation of a two-dimensional schematic face is enough to trigger a smile, and the eyes in particular seem to be the important features, since smiling still takes place when other features are omitted (Ahrens, 1954). Furthermore, smiling is elicited more effectively if many pairs of eyes are presented at once. Drawing on the ethologists' work in innate behaviour in animals, some have suggested that the eyes are a 'releasing stimulus' for smiling as an innate social response (Spitz, 1965). In contrast, Bower suggests that smiling relates more to the degree of contrast within a visual stimulus. As we shall see in the next chapter, infants look more at stimuli containing more elements, and the smile might relate to the 'satisfaction' of viewing a 'preferred stimulus'. Bower (1982) extends this argument by pointing out that infants will smile when they have learned the relationship between their acts and some visual event. Again the notion is that smiling reflects satisfaction, this time at mastery of an action–event contingency. So although smiling may be a good indicator of the infant's emotional state, in Bower's view it should not be taken as a specifically social gesture in the early months. Later in infancy, it becomes possible to differentiate between social smiling directed to another person and smiling directed to an interesting object. Although the latter tends to be labelled non-social, it may often take place during joint attention to an object, and hence may be considered to be social in its basis. However, at eighteen months, smiling takes place predominantly to the mother or another responsive adult rather than towards objects, even

in a situation in which the infant is engaged in non-social play w
object rather than in close interaction with the adult. But smiling to
in this situation is reduced in cases when mother or adult are unresp
(Jones and Raag, 1989). The fact that these observations arose during
non-social play, indicates that by this age smiling cannot simply be an
effect of social stimulation. It thus seems clear that at least by the second
year infants use smiling as a means of transmitting positive emotion and
that they are sensitive to the receptive state of the receiver.

Links with later chapters

Discussion of the smile brings us very close to a number of issues that arise
in the chapters that follow. Before we can conclude that a smile is directed
at people, we need to know about the infant's ability to perceive people.
Possibly smiling is a newborn social response that is initially generalized to
many stimuli because of the infant's limited ability to make visual discriminations. More specifically, we might suppose that social responses can only
occur once the infant can identify people, and here person perception
would be a prerequisite for social responsiveness. The issue of perceptual
development is discussed in chapter 3, and its relation to social perception
is dealt with in chapter 5. An alternative view is that it matters not
whether the infant initially smiles socially or asocially. What matters is that
parents interpret their infant's smiles as social gestures, and it is this that leads
to their eventually becoming such. This line of thought is an important aspect
of one contemporary theory of the social bases of development, discussed
in chapter 5.

In addition, a number of issues emerged earlier in this chapter that have
implications for the discussion that follows. First, there was the indication
that we should not take birth as the starting point for psychological development. As we shall see in chapter 3, this is particularly true in the case of
auditory perception, with evidence that infants perceive and learn about the
human voice before they are born. Secondly, there is the general issue of
the relation between motor development and the development of perception
and cognition. This crops us again in chapter 3 as the methodological issue of
how we test perceptual abilities when the infant's abilities to respond are
limited. But it also appears in a more theoretical light: to what extent should
a perceptual capacity to be treated as a psychological ability if the infant is
unable to act in accordance with perception? Finally, back at the empirical
level, we shall encounter evidence in chapter 4 which suggests that specific
motor developments such as the ability to crawl have important implications
for the infant's understanding of space. In an important sense, therefore,
this chapter has prepared the ground for those that follow.

3

Perceptual development

Everyone who has spent time with babies must now and then have wondered what sense they make of their world. Some of the questions that come to mind are quite basic ones, such as how well can they see or hear? Other questions are more socially oriented, for instance, are they capable of recognizing their parents' faces or voices? Once we start asking questions at this level, we begin to uncover complex issues. What does it mean, for example, to say that a baby recognizes his or her mother? Are we talking simply about recognition of a visual or auditory pattern, or is it more a matter of recognizing a person 'out there', carrying with it knowledge that the visual or auditory sensations originate from an external object, animate rather than inanimate, human rather than non-human, female rather than male, and so on? All these different levels of inquiry are quite legitimate, and in the next two chapters I shall be reviewing evidence that spans the full range from the very simplest of questions about perception to more complex ones about the infant's understanding.

I have adopted the conventional pattern of devoting one chapter to perceptual development and following it with one on cognitive development. In general, the term 'perception' is used to describe more basic processing of sensory information, while the term 'cognition' describes capacities that in one way or another go beyond direct processing of sensory input to extract meaning or understanding. However, in practice it is often hard to draw a clear line between perceptual and cognitive processes, particularly in the light of theories such as J. J. Gibson's (1979) in which perception is supposed to supply objective information about the world directly and without need for interpretation. This issue will be raised again in chapter 4.

This chapter addresses three main topics – visual perception, auditory perception and intersensory coordination. I shall say most about vision, less about hearing and very little about the other senses, a pattern of selectivity that reflects the general emphasis in the literature. Most work on infant perception concentrates on vision, and very little indeed is done on taste and smell for instance. The reasoning behind this is that vision is the most important sense, a conclusion that seems quite reasonable, particularly when we note how sophisticated human vision is in comparison vision in some other species that rely more on hearing or smell. although there are good arguments to back psychologists' preoccupa with vision, the reader should be careful not to forget the other senses, ev the ones that seem least important. There is evidence, for example, th infants only a few days old discriminate between their mother and other through their sense of smell (Cernoch and Porter, 1985; Macfarlane, 1975). This finding has relevance for theories of person perception in infancy, and in turn may have implications for theories of infant–parent attachment, topics that are covered in chapter 5. Additionally, newborns discriminate between sour, bitter, salty and sweet tastes, producing different facial expressions for each (Rosenstein and Oster, 1988).

Within the sections on vision and hearing, I shall start by discussing basic measures of sensory capacity that, on the face of it, do not seem obviously related to infant psychology. However, I hope I shall convince the reader that a knowledge at this level is important both for our interpretation of more complex perceptual activities, and for its contribution to our understanding of developmental mechanisms in early perception.

Visual perception of two-dimensional stimuli

Since the pioneering work of Robert Fantz in the 60s, interest in infant visual perception has grown rapidly so that there are now many workers generating large volumes of data on various aspects of visual perception in quite young babies. In general the work concentrates on the first six months of life, since most workers are attempting to find out just how much infants can perceive and how early they can do it. Various levels of analysis are adopted, from questions about the optics of the newborn's eye, to ones about detection of size and shape constancy and whether infants can use visual information to control their posture. As a consequence, quite different methods of investigation are used, ranging from ophthalmic measures, through measures of brain activity, to detection of motor responses to complex visual stimuli. Some methods, however, are quite versatile and are used to tackle questions at a number of levels of analysis. The best examples here are the spontaneous visual preference technique, and the habituation–dishabituation method.

Basic measures of visual function

People have always suspected that young infants' vision is not as good as adults', indeed it was not so long ago that there was a widespread belief that babies were born blind and only gradually became able to see. Although we now know that this is far from the truth, we do know that the newborn's vision falls far short of adult standards. There are several

with
But
ion
en
at

is might be so. First, the optics of the eye might be
e is about half the size of the adult's and the optical
ange during development. So one possibility is that
ast in part from optical imperfections. Second, the
be due to deficits in *visual accommodation*. When
objects at different distances, the curvature of the
the visual image focused on the retina. The popular
ast was that newborns were incapable of visual accom-
t they were very near-sighted, only seeing clearly things
distance of about nine inches (McGurk, 1974). Third, we
der *retinal acuity*. There is little benefit from having a well-
age if the retina is not sufficiently developed to encode it in
m. Fourth, acuity deficits could be located at higher neural levels.
image could be cast on the retina, and it could be neurally encoded
e receptors with little loss of resolution, but the visual cortex might be
ufficiently developed to process this information.

Not surprisingly, a number of methods, some of them fairly technical, have been used to measure young infants' basic visual functioning and to identify which of the above factors contribute to the limitations that emerge.

Optical maturity of the infant's eyes The optical state of the eye can be measured by techniques such as *dynamic retinoscopy* (Haynes, White and Held, 1965) and, more recently, *photorefraction* (Braddick et al., 1979), in which a light is shone into the eye, and reflections that re-emerge are measured to assess the refractive state of the eye. Current evidence suggests that despite differences in the size and shape of the newborn's eye, its optical properties are really quite good. Although errors such as astigmatism are more prevalent in infants than in older subjects (Banks, 1980a), they are generally of insufficient severity to impose major limitations on visual perception.

Accommodation As I mentioned, a common claim is that newborns are incapable of visual accommodation. This notion arises from the work of Haynes, White and Held (1965), who used dynamic retinoscopy to measure changes in the focusing of the eye as the distance of a stimulus was varied. They found no evidence for visual accommodation in infants less than a month old, but noted a sharp rise in accommodation in the second month and a continuing rise to near the adult level by four months. However, more recent studies (Banks, 1980b; Brookman, 1980) indicate a more positive picture for young infants. Brookman, for example, showed accommodation at roughly one-third the adult level in two-week-old infants. It may be that Hayne's group (1965) obtained an underestimate of young infants' ability because their test stimulus was too small. As we shall see, limits on visual acuity in early infancy mean that some patterns are not resolved even if a sharp image is cast on the retina, and the stimulus used in Haynes's study may not have been optimal in this respect.

Acuity Acuity is the basic measure of the visual pattern analysis. If adults are shown a grating of vertical lines whose thickness and separation are gradually reduced, a point is reached at which this ceases to be seen as a set of lines and becomes a uniform grey. Minimum separable acuity is defined in terms of the angle subtended at the eye by adjacent lines at the point when they are just resolved as separate, and in adults this is about half a minute of arc. In neonates, the figure is about 30 times larger, that is, lines in a grating have to be 30 times thicker and further apart if they are to be seen as separate lines. An alternative method of measuring acuity is in terms of spatial frequencies. If we take the grating that can just be resolved and count the number of stripes, or light–dark cycles per degree of visual angle we gain a measure of the number of cycles per degree in the stimulus, defined as its spatial frequency. In this case, the higher the spatial frequency resolved the higher is acuity. But the main point is that we are measuring the same thing in both cases, and figure 3.1 illustrates how much information is lost to the newborn through acuity limitations.

Figure 3.1 Newborn acuity limitations. The left hand image shows what the newborn is capable of extracting from an image, in comparison with the adult capacity shown on the right (from Slater, 1990). © British Psychological Society.

Three main methods have been used to assess visual acuity in infancy. First, Fantz, Ordy and Udelf (1962) harnessed the phenomenon of *opto-kinetic nystagmus* (OKN). This is an involuntary response occurring in the presence of a moving field, taking the form of tracking movements interspersed with reverse saccades (rapid shifts of fixation, see p. 50). (A good way to observe the phenomenon is to watch a person's eyes as they look out of the window of a moving train.) OKN also occurs when infants are presented with a moving patterned surface, and an estimate of acuity can be gained by reducing the separation and thickness of lines in a moving grating until OKN ceases. The rationale here is that OKN only occurs when there is a detectable moving pattern to lock on to, so when it drops out we have reached the point where the visual system no longer resolves the grating separation.

Secondly, we can use a method that I described in chapter 1, the spontaneous visual preference technique. The rationale here derives from the finding that infants prefer to look at patterned stimuli rather than plain ones. Thus, if we present them with a linear grating paired with a plain grey stimulus (matched in terms of overall brightness) they will look more at the grating, but only so long as they can resolve the grating pattern. So by reducing the grating separation to a point at which a preference is no longer shown, we can reach an estimate of the infants' acuity. Tests of acuity generally use a variant of this method known as the *forced choice preferential looking* technique, in which on each presentation the observer is unaware of the locus of the patterned stimulus, and must use the infant's behaviour to decide where it is. The location of the patterned stimulus is varied at random, the observers are given feedback on whether they were correct on each trial, and their degree of success is used as a measure of the infant's discrimination. Use of this method (Allen, 1978; Mohn and van Hof-van Duin, 1985) yields similar acuity estimates to those obtained through OKN by Fantz, Ordy and Udelf (1962), with acuity starting at around one-thirtieth of adult levels but improving by a factor of three or four by the fifth month (for a review, see Atkinson and Braddick, 1981).

A third method of estimating acuity is based on measurement of relatively localized brain activity in response to a changing visual stimulus (visual evoked potentials: VEP). As mentioned in chapter 1, the rationale here is that if a change in the stimulus produces a change in brain activity, we have evidence of discrimination. So if we presented a black and white grating in which the regions of black and white were periodically reversed, a change in VEP would indicate that the change had been detected and hence that the grating separation fell within the bounds of the subject's acuity. This method often yields slightly higher estimates of acuity than either the OKN or visual preference techniques (Norcia and Tyler, 1985; Sokol, 1978).

It is not clear why this disparity arises, or which measure gives the best estimate of infants' everyday visual functioning. On the one hand, it is easy to suggest that the visual preference technique is conservative since infants may detect a difference between stimuli without showing a preference for one over the other. Note, however, that the OKN method does not have this limitation, since an involuntary response is involved. Additionally, using an habituation technique, Adams (1987) obtained very similar acuity estimates to those arising from preferential looking studies. As indicated in chapter 1, habituation techniques avoid the need to assume a preference and hence should not be conservative in this respect. On the other hand, the presence of a response in the visual cortex does not tell us anything directly about the quality of vision that the infant experiences. The link between neural activity and perception is much too tenuous for that. Some clarification is, however, provided by Suter, Suter and Crow (1991), who measured heart rate change to presentation of gratings of various spacings. This method yielded similar acuity estimates to VEP studies. The assumption is that the heart rate change is an indicator of arousal controlled by higher cortical centres. Thus, Suter et al. (1991) suggest that visual information is processed beyond the visual cortex, and further suggest that the more conservative estimates gathered from studies based on directed looking arise because the cortical system controlling directed looking lags behind other systems in its acuity tuning. This, however, does not explain the disparity between OKN and VEP methods, so there is still much to be learned in this area.

The next problem is to identify the level within the visual system that imposes the constraint on visual acuity. Poor optics or poor visual accommodation could both lead to decrements in visual acuity through limits on the quality of the retinal image. But we know that the infant's visual optics are well developed. In addition, measures of acuity do not vary with stimulus distance (Salapatek, Bechtold and Bushnell, 1976), a finding that suggests that neither optical nor accommodative errors account for acuity limits. The issue then becomes one of whether the limits lie at retinal or cortical level. Here, there is plenty of evidence that the main constraint may be imposed by retinal immaturity. Evidence from monkeys indicates that although no new retinal receptors are developed after birth, the newborn retina does not have the normal concentration of cones (the receptors associated with high acuity vision in adults) in the central (foveal) region. This dense packing in central vision comes about only gradually, apparently due to migration of cones towards the centre and of rods (associated with low acuity vision) towards the periphery (Hendrickson and Kupfer, 1976). Banks and Salapatek (1983) suggest that the increase in acuity between infancy and adulthood may largely be accounted for by an increase in the density of foveal cones by a factor of about 20. This is an attractively simple explanation, but is probably not the whole story. For instance, on its basis one would predict that infant peripheral acuity would be as good or even better than adult peripheral acuity, due to the higher density of cones in the periphery early in development. However, testing one- to three-month-olds, Courage and Adams (1990) showed that peripheral acuity was very poor at one month but improved rapidly in the second and third month. Thus, although the cone migration must play a part in development of acuity, it appears that other factors must be involved. As Banks and Salapatek note, knowledge of the state of the retina does not indicate anything about the resolution capability of the visual cortex. Although a general principle emerging from animal work is that central mechanisms develop somewhat in advance of peripheral mechanisms (Parmelee and Sigman, 1983), the fine tuning of these mechanisms may depend on the delivery of relatively high acuity input. Hence in quite a complex way retinal and cortical development may go hand in hand.

Contrast sensitivity   So far, I have considered the case of perception of very clear cut stimuli composed of black and white sectors with very sharp boundaries between them. However, everyday perception involves detection of patterns that may contain both sharp contours and gradual variations in brightness. Another factor that determines the effectiveness of visual perception is the degree to which the system is capable of detecting small differences in brightness, a factor known as contrast sensitivity. Adults show very high contrast sensitivity, being able to detect brightness contrasts of as little as 1% of the contrast between pure black and pure white. Newborns, on the other hand, only detect contrasts greater than 30–40%, although this improves to near adult levels during the first year (Atkinson and Braddick, 1981).

As one might expect, adult contrast sensitivity shows a relationship to the spatial frequency or spacing of the contrast, with subjects showing greater sensitivity to contrasts over a moderate spatial range than to contrasts that take place over a large spatial range. However, this difference is not present in newborns, and we must assume that the improvement in contrast sensitivity during infancy is greatest for moderate spatial frequencies.

Depth of focus: a link between acuity and accommodation   To summarize so far, we know that both accommodation and acuity improve with age. What is more, it looks as if limits of acuity are imposed by neural factors at retinal or cortical level rather than by poor retinal images due to accommodative error. But there is an apparent paradox here that the reader may have spotted already. The relatively large accommodative errors recorded with young infants would suggest that objects or patterns should be seen more clearly at some distances than at others, yet the acuity studies do not indicate a relationship between acuity and stimulus distance.

Banks (1980b) dismantles this paradox fairly convincingly by pointing out that we also have to take account of one more measure of infant vision. *Depth of focus* is defined as the range over which a stimulus can be moved without loss of visual resolution, assuming that accommodation is fixed. 'Instamatic' type cameras have a relatively large depth of focus, so that they take reasonably sharp photographs over a wide range of object distances, despite having a fixed focus lens. Banks argues that we can explain the lack of relationship between acuity and stimulus distance through the fact that the young infant's depth of focus is greater than the adult's. This large depth of focus arises in large part due to the infant's poor acuity; the retinal image need only be sharp enough to provide the level of detail that the retinal and neural system can resolve, and so focusing errors can be quite large without affecting resolution. So rather than poor acuity being the result of lack of accommodation, lack of accommodation may result from poor acuity. Infants may be physically capable of accommodation but may only accommodate sufficiently to produce an image that matches up to the resolution of the neural part of the system. Consequently, as Banks (1980b) puts it, 'instead of stating that young infants see relatively clearly at one distance and not others, it is more accurate to say that they see equally unclearly across a wide range of distances' (p. 663).

Vergence eye movements When we shift fixation from a far to a near object, our eyes converge, and of course the opposite (divergence) happens when we shift fixation from a near to a far object. These movements are necessary to ensure that the image from the object falls on the fovea of both eyes (bifoveal fixation), and failure to make convergent or divergent eye movements results in a double image.

At one time it was thought that newborns were poor at performing these vergence movements, with relative eye position generally being more divergent than would be needed for bifoveal fixation (Wickelgren, 1967). However, Slater and Findlay (1972) suggested that this was a measurement artefact arising from the fact that the optical arrangement in the neonate eye differed from that of older infants and adults. In this sort of study, measurements of eye position are obtained by corneal reflection, which yields an estimate of the alignment of the optic axis of the eye. However, even in adults, the optic axis differs by about 5 degrees from the visual axis (the line between the midpoint of the lens and the fovea), and in young infants the difference is about 10 degrees. Add to this the fact that this difference is in the direction of greater divergence of the optical axes than the visual axes, and we have a possible explanation of the data that does not involve assuming that young infants do not achieve bifoveal fixation.

Even taking this into account, however, it would appear that newborn infants' vergence movements are not perfect. Slater and Findlay (1975) observed appropriate vergence movements for targets at various intermediate distances, but not for targets that were very close (5 inches). Also, Aslin (1977) found that while one-month-olds made appropriate convergence and divergence movements to new target distances, these movements were not sufficiently accurate to lead to bifoveal fixation. However, this seems to be a temporary problem, since two-month-olds' vergence movements were much more accurate.

Saccadic eye movements A *saccade* is a rapid eye movement which, in adults at least, is planned prior to execution and is not modified during its short execution time. This sort of eye movement is used to fixate a target that lies outside foveal vision. Harris and Macfarlane (1974) showed that newborn infants would execute saccadic movements in response to presentation of peripheral stimuli as long as they lay no further than 25 degrees from central vision. Interestingly, they found that saccades to peripheral targets occurred even if there was a stimulus present in central vision, although in this case the peripheral stimulus had to be within 15 degrees of central vision. They take this ability to leave a central target in favour of a peripheral one as evidence that newborns have control over their own fixations of figures, and are not passively 'captured' by stimulus features as many workers had suggested. However, as we shall see at the end of the section on pattern perception (p. 67), there may be reason to suspect that for young infants peripheral stimuli are more effective 'attention-getters' than central ones, so the notion of passive capture is not dead.

Aslin and Salapatek (1975) obtained more detailed data on saccadic movements in one- to two-month-old infants. First, they noted that the time between stimulus presentation and movement onset was relatively long, five times as long as adults would take. Secondly, they noted that target localization was achieved through a series of serious undershoots in the direction of the target, rather than through a single movement. This could occur because young infants compute the target distance inaccurately; alternatively, it might be that they execute a saccade that would be appropriate in coordination with a head movement. Banks and Salapatek (1983) argue that the latter explanation is unlikely, since even when care is taken to allow head movements (Regal and Salapatek, 1982) a similar undershoot pattern is obtained. However, precise control over head movements is a relatively late development, so simply permitting head movement does not mean that appropriate movements will be executed. It is therefore still possible that the infant executes an appropriate eye movement but fails on the head movement, with the result that further eye movements are needed.

Smooth pursuit eye movements   Smooth pursuit movements are normally executed in order to keep a moving target in central vision. Early work suggested that young infants were incapable of smooth pursuit, but more recent work has shown this to be only partially correct; young infants do execute pursuit movements, but they are far from smooth. Dayton and Jones (1964) found that although newborns' eye movements were generally in the appropriate direction, they consisted of a series of saccades rather than a smooth movement. It could be that this phenomenon was due to inability to keep up with the target, but Aslin (1981) found saccadic tracking even with low target velocities. Smooth tracking only began to emerge at about eight weeks, and then only in the case of low target velocities. So although newborns show ability to track objects, the form of their tracking attempts precludes continuous central fixation of the moving target.

Summary   Current evidence suggests that although the young infant's visual system is certainly functional at all levels, neonates experience a quality of vision a good deal poorer than that of adults. The main constraint on pattern vision appears to be limited acuity, probably primarily due to retinal immaturity. Contrary to previous beliefs, accommodative errors do not seem to be a major limiting factor, and the notion that young infants only see clearly at one distance seems to be false. All forms of eye movement are present early in life, although again these are inaccurate compared with adult movements. There is likely to be a link with acuity here. For instance, if vergence eye movements depend upon visual feedback, their accuracy will depend upon the quality of vision. At another level, if central vision is not initially a high acuity region relative to peripheral vision, there is not the same advantage in bringing peripheral stimuli to central vision by accurate saccades. This is an issue I shall return to later. But despite these early limitations, visual capacities of all sorts improve rapidly, so that in a matter of months infants' vision is in many ways reasonably comparable to that of adults.

Pattern preferences in early infancy

Through our knowledge of infant visual acuity we already have a starting point on the issue of pattern perception, if only to the extent that we know a good deal about the level of stimulus detail that the infant should be able to detect. And as has already been mentioned, we know that very young infants can discriminate between patterned and plain stimuli. But what of their ability to discriminate between two different patterned stimuli? Consideration of the young infant's poor acuity might lead us to think that pattern discrimination would be relatively undeveloped in the early months, but this would be a mistake. Acuity only sets limits on the fineness of the detail that can be detected, and as long as we make our stimuli large enough, we should be able to avoid the constraints it sets.

The best known work on pattern perception was done in the 1960s by Robert Fantz and his colleagues. It was here in particular that his *spontaneous visual preference* technique came into its own. The basic technique is as I described it in chapter 1. Infants are repeatedly presented with two stimuli, side by side, with stimulus positions reversed over trials to prevent a position preference from being confused with pattern preference, and the time the infants spend fixating each stimulus is summed over the period of the session. Under these conditions, looking at one stimulus significantly more than the other denotes a preference, and the rationale is that to show a preference, infants must discriminate between the stimuli.

The drawback of this technique is, of course, that an infant might discriminate between two stimuli but show no looking preference for one over the other. Hence, the method is liable to produce conservative estimates of perception. However, its major advantage is that, in measuring preference, it goes beyond perception and gives us information about what sorts of stimuli are important to infants at different ages. It would be strange if there were no reasons behind the preferences obtained, and a number of workers have attempted to identify the adaptive significance of early visual preferences (Banks and Ginsburg, 1985; Fantz, Fagan and Miranda, 1975). I shall return to one of these accounts later on.

A preference for facial patterns? With the issue of adaptive significance in mind, an obvious question is whether the young infant recognizes and prefers to look at the pattern of the human face, since it can be argued that there is adaptive value in looking at parents' faces and learning their characteristics. One of the early studies by Fantz (1961) tackled this question by showing infants pairings of the three stimuli shown in figure 3.2. These were two-dimensional stimuli, pattern A containing the major facial features in their usual configuration, pattern B containing the same features randomly arranged, and pattern C being a control stimulus containing the same amount of light and dark shading as the other two. As figure 3.1 shows, infants of all ages looked very much less at the control stimulus than at the other two. But also there was a fairly general preference for the facial configuration over the set of jumbled features, and although this difference was small, Fantz noted that it was consistent across infants. His conclusion was that 'there is an unlearned, primitive meaning in the form

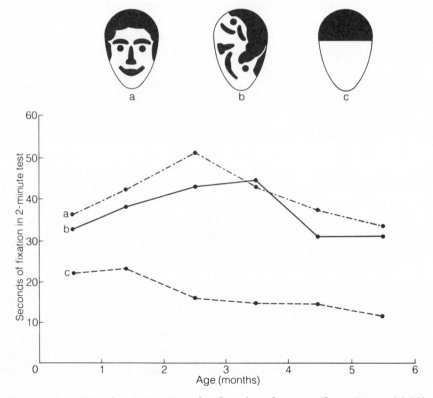

Figure 3.2 Stimulus patterns and infants' preferences (from Fantz, 1961).

perception of infants' (1961). Since his youngest infants were only four days old, there appeared to be little scope for learning.

This early study has a number of flaws, however, and current accounts of face recognition tell a more complicated story, with only rather tenuous evidence that newborns show a preference for face-like characteristics in two-dimensional stimuli. Indeed, Fantz (1966) recognized these problems and subsequently set the emergence of face recognition at nearer three months. However, I shall set this material aside until the section on perception of social stimuli in chapter 5. Here I shall concentrate on the alternative interpretations of Fantz's findings as starting points for a number of recent lines of investigation of pattern perception.

Looking again at figure 3.1, it is possible to identify differences between the stimuli other than the degree to which they approximate to the human face. First of all, there are far more elements in A and B than in C. For that reason, we could say that A and B are more complex than C, and this raises the possibility that the largest difference in figure 3.1 could be put down to a preference for greater stimulus complexity. This, however, would not explain the small preference for A over B, but here again an alternative to Fantz's interpretation can be found. Stimulus A is symmetrical whereas stimulus B is not, so could we be dealing with a preference for symmetry here? Later we shall encounter a less obvious distinction between these two stimuli, but I shall start by concentrating on complexity and symmetry. One of the great attractions of the experimental method is that having identified alternatives we can often isolate them and study them individually.

Complexity preferences A number of workers have investigated stimulus complexity preferences by presenting infants with checkerboard patterns that differ in the number of elements. For instance, Brennan, Ames and Moore (1966) used checkerboards with 2×2, 8×8 and 24×24 elements. They found that one-month-olds preferred the 2×2 stimulus, two-month-olds the 8×8 stimulus and three-month-olds the 24×24 stimulus. In other words, there was an optimum level of stimulus complexity that increased with age. We could explain younger infants' preferring less complex stimuli in terms of acuity deficits, since in this study the more complex stimuli had smaller as well as more elements. However, this would not explain why older infants preferred the more complex stimuli over the simpler ones, so there is more to this than limits set by acuity.

Unfortunately, stimulus complexity is rather a vague term and has been defined in a number of ways. Brennan's group (1966) defined it as I have here, in terms of number of stimulus elements. Munsinger and Weir (1967) defined it in terms of the number of angles in the pattern. And Karmel and Maisel (1975) argued that the relevant stimulus property was contour density (the summed length of light–dark contour per unit area).

Probably the reason for the lack of consensus here was the fact that few of these workers seemed to be considering *why* infants should prefer one type of stimulus over another. As Banks and Salapatek (1983) point out, we should really be trying to identify the functional significance of infant behaviour in general, and we may be better able to explain the preference literature if we can identify what the infant stands to gain by looking at some stimuli more than others. Banks and Salapatek's notion is that the preferred stimuli will be those that present maximum detail to the infant's visual system, taking account of the system's acuity limits, and they incorporate this assumption within their *linear systems analysis* of visual preferences (Banks and Ginsburg, 1985; Banks and Salapatek, 1981), a model that aims both to account for preferences and explain them. Since they claim that this model accounts for a whole range of other early preferences as well as complexity, I will defer further discussion of it for a few pages.

Symmetry preferences We know that children (Boswell, 1976) and adults (Pomerantz, 1977) are sensitive to pattern symmetry. Later studies of face preference were more carefully designed to control a number of factors including stimulus symmetry (see Maurer, 1985 for a review), and under these conditions, many studies find no reliable preference for a facial con-figuration until around four months (although see chapter 5 for exceptions). If symmetry is at the root of this preference, it should be possible to demon-strate preference for symmetrical patterns that have no resemblance to the human face. However, although four-month-old infants do detect stimulus symmetry, habituating more rapidly to symmetrical stimuli (Humphrey et al. 1986) and discriminating symmetrical from asymmetrical patterns (Bornstein, Ferdinandsen and Gross, 1981; Bornstein and Krinsky, 1985), a preference for symmetry has not been measured until infants are well over four months old (Bornstein, Ferdinandsen and Gross, 1981). It seems, then, that although symmetry may well be a principle that older infants use to discriminate between stimuli, current evidence does not make it a likely explanation of Fantz's early data on face preferences.

The salience of external contour In his later work (Fantz and Miranda, 1975), Fantz identified stimulus curvature as a major factor determining preference. Infants under seven days old showed consistent preference for curvilinear over rectilinear stimuli (see figure 3.3). However, this pref-erence was eliminated if the same figures were embedded in a standard surround, as shown at the left of figure 3.3. Fantz and Miranda concluded that newborn preferences were limited to pattern differences in the outer contours of figures. As we shall see a little later in this chapter, this find-ing is in keeping with the fact that younger infants generally fixate on peripheral features of a pattern, and seem to have a general difficulty in discriminating internal features. Taking account of these findings, it seems likely that in Fantz's early work the face pattern was preferred over the scrambled pattern because of differences between the two external contours;

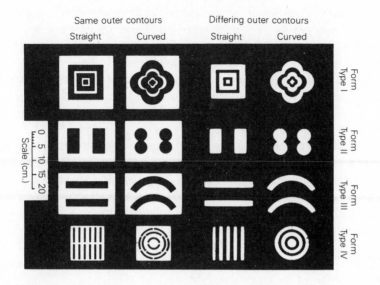

Figure 3.3 Stimulus patterns used by Fantz and Miranda (1975). Newborns showed a preference for curvilinear stimuli over linear stimuli.

in the face stimulus the peripheral features are arranged in such a way that there is a more or less continuous curvilinear contour around the top edge of the figure.

Explaining early preferences   While we could explain a preference for faces as an adaptive predisposition to learn about people, it is not so easy to come up with a simple explanation of the *function* of the early preferences that stands up to more rigorous testing than the early work on face perception. Why, for example, should infants look more at complex stimuli? This is where we need to return to Banks and Ginsburg's (1985) *linear systems analysis* model, since they claim that it can account for a wide range of visual preferences in terms of the relevance of these stimuli for early visual development. The model involves *Fourier analysis* of visual patterns and matching to the resolution of the infant's visual system. Its main principle is that the infant shows a looking preference towards those stimuli that provide greatest stimulation for, and are most readily detected by the visual system. From this it might appear that the most complex or detailed stimuli would always be preferred, however the model takes account of the limits on resolvable pattern detail set by the acuity of the visual system. Hence the optimum pattern complexity is that which provides maximum detail at a level that still passes the 'acuity filter' of the visual system.

Given the discussion of the way that the nervous system may develop through use (see chapter 2), we need go only one step further to build a functional interpretation of preferences. Blakemore and Cooper (1970) showed that rearing kittens in an environment of vertical stripes led to their being far better at detecting vertical contours than horizontals, so we know that visual input can affect the development of the visual system. It seems quite plausible then that early visual preferences reflect an adaptive tendency to attend to stimuli that provide maximum stimulation to the developing system. We do not know how much visual development depends upon such stimulation, but as the system develops, so the optimum stimulus should become more detailed, explaining the shift in preference towards more complex stimuli. So according to Banks and Ginsburg, the function of early looking preferences is the provision of adequate stimulation for the developing visual system. However, it does not look as if we can explain all preferences through such a mechanism. Banks and Salapatek (1983) note that simple models of this sort may only account for the visual preferences of infants in the first three months, and thereafter different models are needed to account for phenomena such as face preferences, and preferences for one face over another.

Habituation as a measure of visual learning and memory

If we present infants with a patterned visual stimulus they will spend at least a proportion of time looking at it, and as the previous section has shown, infants will look more at some stimuli than others. These measures do not tell us, however, whether infants are extracting information from the stimulus in the process, or whether they are capable of retaining this information over time. But, as we saw in chapter 1, if a stimulus is presented repeatedly over an extended period, infants *habituate*, that is, they progressively spend less time looking at it. On the face of it, this appears rather a commonplace finding; parents would simply say that their infant has become bored. So why do psychologists accord so much significance to the phenomenon? The answer becomes evident when we analyse what must be happening for habituation to take place. If infants look less at a stimulus over time, this indicates that they are becoming familiar with it, and familiarization involves the intake and storage of information. So if infants habituate to a stimulus, we must assume that they have encoded some of its properties and that these properties are retained in memory at least for the duration over which habituation occurs.

Of course, we have to be careful in our methods here, since without the proper controls, an observed reduction in looking might be due to some other factor. For instance, infants might be undergoing a change of state leading to reduced visual activity, resulting in less time spent looking at the stimulus. To check on this, after habituation had occurred we could replace the stimulus with a new one. If the reduction in looking had been quite unrelated to stimulus familiarization, presentation of a new stimulus should have no effect. However, if infants had really habituated to the stimulus before them, they should *dishabituate* when the new stimulus is presented. When such checks are made it does indeed turn out that infants actually are habituating to the specific stimulus before them.

The precaution I have suggested here carries with it a considerable added bonus for those interested in infant perception, since this habituation–dishabituation method can also be used to measure visual discrimination (see chapter 1). If infants could not detect a difference between habituated and novel stimuli we would not expect dishabituation, whereas if they did, we would. As we shall see in the next section, variants on this habituation–dishabituation method have proved invaluable as measures of infant visual discrimination. Here, however, I am primarily interested in the habituation method for what it indicates about infant memory.

Many habituation studies have shown that by the age of three months infants can encode in memory the properties of a variety of stimuli. For instance, Milewski (1979) showed learning with two-dimensional shapes, Cook, Field and Griffiths (1978) learning with solid objects, and Barrera and Maurer (1981) learning of social stimuli such as facial expressions. Even at this early age, habituation periods of one or two minutes are quite adequate for learning to occur, and even periods of 20 seconds or less have in some cases proved to be adequate (Rose and Slater, 1983).

Another important consideration is the duration of the resulting memory. A number of studies have shown that certainly by five or six months the effects of habituation persist beyond the duration of the experiment. Martin (1975) found continuing effects after 24 hours, and Fagan (1973), using photographs of faces, found that significant novelty preferences were still present two weeks later. However, we should be a little wary of concluding that results with face stimuli give an indication of the infant's general memory capacity, since there is evidence from adult literature that faces are processed by a specialized system (Ellis and Young, 1988), a system that might also be possessed by infants. But Fagan found that recognition memory for patterned stimuli lasted at least two days (the longest period used for these stimuli) so, taking this along with Martin's result, there is reasonable indication that infant recognition memory for stimuli other than faces lasts at least for a day or two. Recently, similar evidence has been obtained with infants as young as five weeks. Bushnell and co-workers (1984) found recognition memory for colour and form 24 hours after familiarization. Studies of infant memory based on classical and operant conditioning techniques indicate retention over days and even weeks (for a review, see Rovee-Collier, 1987), so it is clear that young infants have well established memory capacities. However, it appears that early infant memory is strongly context dependent, since it is reduced or even obliterated if retention testing takes place in a novel setting (Boller and Rovee-Collier, 1992; Borovsky and Rovee-Collier, 1990). Borovsky and Rovee-Collier suggest that this contextual dependency arises from the fact that, prior to independent locomotion, infants tend to engage in specific activities in specific spatial settings, and so associate new information with the setting in which it is encountered. This is an interesting point which, as we shall see in chapter 4, resonates with certain claims being made in the literature on infant spatial awareness.

When it comes to newborns, evidence of habituation has been harder to come by, although this may well be due to the added difficulties of working with very young subjects. Friedman (1972) demonstrated that newborns habituated to black and white checkerboards, but only a little over half of his subjects completed the test session and of those only 75 per cent showed habituation. However, Slater, Morison and Rose (1982) produced quite convincing evidence of habituation in newborns, without suffering the levels of subject loss experienced by Friedman. Currently, we do not know how lasting these newborn habituation effects are, so although there is now clear evidence that newborns can encode stimulus information, we do not know whether they retain this information beyond the duration of the experiment. However, research using conditioning techniques with newborns indicates retention over a period of hours (Panneton and DeCasper, 1982) and even days (DeCasper and Spence, 1986; Papousek, 1977). It should be noted that these studies measured capacities such as auditory recognition memory or memory for an association between events, rather than visual recognition memory, which has been the primary focus of the habituation studies mentioned here. It may thus be only be a matter of time before long-term effects of habituation are obtained from newborns, although the question remains open of whether only some types of memory have long-term persistence at birth.

Some workers have argued that we can gain quite a detailed picture of the learning process from habituation studies. For instance, Sokolov (1963) argues that there is an inverse relationship between the infant's level of fixation and the degree to which the stimulus has been encoded in memory. If this is the case it should be possible to plot a learning curve as the inverse of the habituation curve (the decrement in visual fixation over time). There is some evidence in support of this supposition. For instance, habituation takes longer for complex stimuli than for simpler ones, just what we would predict from the assumption that more complex stimuli should take longer to commit to memory.

However, there is a need to be cautious about inferring a precise relationship between habituation and learning curves. A number of studies using the *habituation–novelty* technique have shown evidence of learning over periods too short for a decrement in looking to show up at all. As noted in chapter 2, this method involves habituation followed by paired presentation of habituated and novel stimuli, and learning is measured independently of habituation by observing whether infants look more at the novel stimulus than the familiarized one. Using this technique, Rose and Slater (1983) found that a 10 or 20 second presentation of the habituation stimulus was as effective as a longer exposure in producing novelty effects.

In both cases three- to five-month-old infants looked reliably more at the novel stimulus after the habituation period. Rose and Slater conclude that memory may be formed before the habituation curve begins to dip, but they note that this memory may be very fragile, since a 30 second delay between initial exposure and novel–familiar pairing was enough to remove the novelty effect entirely. Their suggestion is that only parts of a stimulus are encoded in fairly fragile form during these brief exposures. Maybe it is only once the stimulus has been relatively well encoded that looking begins to decline. This would make intuitive sense, since it seems reasonable that decline in looking should only take place once the infant has encoded all the important features of the stimulus.

It should be said that habituation techniques are only one approach to the study of infant memory and, rather than producing a comprehensive review of research in the field, the aim of this section has been to outline an important application of habituation techniques. Rovee-Collier (1987) claims that habituation approaches give only a limited indication of infant memory, since they effectively measure short-term and not long-term memory. The fact that some habituation studies have obtained retention over periods that are clearly within the realms of long-term memory suggests that this is not entirely correct. However, conditioning techniques tend to obtain memory durations greater than habituation studies, so a fuller picture of infant memory is likely to be obtained from comparison of results obtained using different techniques.

Habituation rate and prediction of later achievement

The habituation phenomenon has been given further emphasis by recent attempts to link early recognition memory with later intelligence. There are noticeable individual differences in habituation rate even in newborns (Slater, Morison and Rose, 1982), and there is growing indication that at least from three months these differences are moderately stable over time (Colombo, Mitchell, O'Brien and Horowitz, 1987) and relate to differences in intellectual ability in later life. On the basis of a number of strands of evidence, Fagan and Singer (1983) argue that immediate recognition memory is a good predictor of later intelligence. Several studies have shown that recognition memory is poorer in infants from populations likely to be of lower intelligence later in life. For instance, Miranda and Fantz (1974) obtained novelty preferences at 13 weeks in normal infants but not until 24 weeks in Down's syndrome infants. Also, Sigman and Parmelee (1974) obtained poorer recognition memory in infants born pre-term, a group likely to score lower in intelligence tests later in life. Working on these indicators, Fagan and McGrath (1981) carried out a longitudinal investigation which indicated quite substantial correlations between early habituation-based recognition memory and later intelligence assessed by conventional psychometric tests. They conclude that, despite the failure of conventional sensori-motor tests of infant intelligence to predict later achievement, there is a factor tapped by habituation–novelty techniques that has continuity through into later childhood. One study (Madison, Madison and Adubato, 1986) has even found a relationship between fetal habituation rate (measured in terms of decline in rate of movement on presentation of a vibration stimulus) and scores on the Brazelton neonatal scale at 48 hours and the Bayley infant development scale (1969) at four months. There is now a sizeable literature reporting correlations between early habituation rate and later scores on cognitive tests. Analysing this literature, McCall and Carriger (1993) conclude that habituation rate within the first year predicts performance on IQ tests as much later as eight years. What is more, this measure predicts IQ better than other standard infant cognitive tests.

Why should habituation rate be such a good predictor of cognitive ability? Bornstein and Sigman (1986) identify encoding efficiency as the key factor here, claiming that those infants who encode stimuli more rapidly (as indicated by more rapid habituation) and show stronger preferences for novelty are likely to perform better in childhood tests of intelligence and language. They also point out that fast habituators tend to prefer greater stimulus complexity and among other things engage in more rapid environmental exploration. An alternative is that rapid habituators only process single features of stimuli, in other words, that they process more economically rather than more rapidly. However, Colombo, Mitchell, Coldren and Freeseman (1991) obtained little evidence in support of this possibility. A further possibility is that what characterizes rapid habituators is superior maintenance of attention rather than rapid processing (Lécuyer, 1989; Pêcheux and Lécuyer, 1989); those infants that maintain attention on the stimulus will as a result process it and hence habituate to it more rapidly. However, another piece of evidence suggests that effective control of attention rather than simple attention maintenance may be the key factor. Bronson (1991) found that slow habituators scan stimuli less extensively and spend more time on continuous inspection of a single part of the figure. But once one begins to consider the attentional process as one of effective direction of attention it becomes less clear that we are dealing with a process that is meaningfully separable from encoding processes, since it may be argued that a key component of rapid stimulus processing is effective direction of attention.

The roots of these differences are not easy to identify. It might be tempting to conclude that differences that are apparent in early infancy must be innate. However, Bornstein and Sigman point out that there is a likely link with parental style, since mothers of fast habituators tend to encourage more attention to properties of objects and the surrounding environment. Tamis-LeMonda and Bornstein (1989) showed, however, that even when effects of maternal stimulation were statistically isolated, there remained a relationship between early habituation and later cognitive

ability. Thus, although they found positive effects of maternal stimul
tion, it appears clear that there is a direct link between habituation ra
and later ability. Nevertheless, this does not rule out the possibility that
infant characteristics determine how the mother responds: an effective
strategy to keep a rapid habituator happy would be to work hard to direct
attention to new stimuli. Thus, rapid habituators may have a double
advantage. In addition to being more effective information processors,
their propensity to 'lose interest' in objects rapidly may ensure that they
receive extra social stimulation which further aids their development and
learning. As we shall see in chapter 5, possibilities of this sort are central
to any work that treats parent–infant interaction as part of the developmental process.

Habituation–dishabituation as a measure of visual discrimination

As we saw, the main drawback of the visual preference technique is that
we cannot conclude that absence of preference between two stimuli means
that the infant cannot discriminate them. Remember, however, that use of
habituation methods surmounts this problem, since even if no spontaneous
preference exists, we can impose a sort of negative preference effect by
habituating the infant to one stimulus. After habituation, infants should
dishabituate if a novel stimulus is presented, alternatively, if a novel and
habituated stimulus are presented together (the habituation–novelty
method), they should show a preference for the novel one (see chapter 1).
But these effects will only occur if the infants can discriminate between the
two stimuli. If they detect no difference, then the novel stimulus should be
treated in just the same way as the habituated one; there should be no
dishabituation and they should look at both equally if they are presented
together.

The habituation technique was developed in the early 1960s by Fantz as
an extension of the visual preference technique, and since then it has
served as a valuable supplement to it. Many studies using habituation
techniques have obtained data very much in keeping with the findings of
visual preference studies. For instance, Milewski (1976) obtained the same
sort of external contour effects as were found in preference studies. His
study is shown schematically in figure 3.4. Infants were habituated to the
left hand figure, and were tested for dishabituation on one of the four right
hand figures. Four-month-olds dishabituated in all groups other than Group
NS, but one-month-olds only dishabituated to the figures that differed from the
habituation stimulus in their external elements. The conclusion was that
young infants only attend to the external elements of a compound figure.

Subsequent work would appear to indicate that it is element salience that
determines attention, since young infants were shown to discriminate in
terms of internal detail if that detail flickered or moved within the bounds
of the external pattern (Bushnell, 1979). So although external detail may

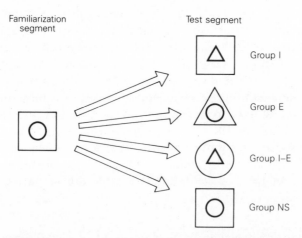

Figure 3.4 Experimental technique used by Milewski (1976). Infants were familiarized to the left hand figure, and different groups were tested for dishabituation on the right hand figures.

in general be more salient than internal detail, there may be all sorts of other determinants of stimulus salience that affect young infants' attention and hence their discrimination. The fact remains, though, that younger infants seem to concentrate on fewer aspects of a figure, a finding very much in keeping with the data on eye movements discussed in the next section.

Investigation of form perception through habituation methods

So far we have been looking at infants' capacity for discriminating two-dimensional patterns. There is, however, an important distinction to be drawn between pattern perception and form perception. Take, for example, a triangle. Adults would extract the triangle form from a wide variety of figures varying in size, line thickness, angular relation, orientation and so on. Form perception, then, involves the extraction of the higher order properties of a pattern that are unchanged by alterations in lower order properties such as size and line thickness. If we found that infants discriminated between a triangle and another figure such as a cross, the question would become whether they are making a discrimination between two general forms or between two specific patterns.

To show that infants are capable of form perception, it is necessary to eliminate the possibility that they are making the discrimination at a more basic level. It is relatively simple to equate variables such as brightness between stimuli. However, things become more difficult when it comes to equating contour density, for example; figures generally differ in contour density as well as in form. Considering the age of the infants being studied, this seems a daunting problem, but the issue has been tackled in a number of ingenious ways.

One way of avoiding the contour density problem is to use discontinuous figures made up of elements grouped so as to make forms. In this case the same number of elements are used in each figure, so contour density can be held constant. Dineen and Meyer (1980) habituated six-month-olds to a cross (+) made up of five circles, and tested for dishabituation on five circles arranged like the five on dice (×), or on the original cross form made up of five squares. They found that six-month-olds dishabituated to both stimuli, and concluded that infants extracted information about both the form and the elements within a form. However, Banks and Salapatek (1983) point out that the discrimination between the + and × forms might have been based on the positioning of a single element rather than on the whole form, so these results were inconclusive.

A study by Milewski (1979) appears to be closer to tackling form perception itself. Three-month-old infants were habituated either to a linear or a triangular array of three circles, and were then tested for dishabituation on either the same or the other array. The extra twist in this study was that the size and position of the stimulus were varied during habituation, which meant that dishabituation could not be based on the presence or absence of a single feature in a particular place in the field. The result was that dishabituation occurred in the presence of a different form but not in the case of the same form differing in size or position, so this looks like good evidence of form discrimination at three months.

In addition, Milewski's finding indicates a capability for organizing elements into a larger whole. Investigating Gestalt organization specifically, Quinn, Burke and Rush (1993) concluded that three-month-olds were capable of grouping stimulus elements in terms of brightness similarity. Figure 3.5 shows how they established this. Infants were habituated to one of two stimuli in which the similar brightness elements were either vertically or horizontally arranged. They were then tested for novelty preference between horizontal and vertical solid bars, whereupon they showed a preference for the orientation of stimulus not used during habituation. The argument is that in order to do this, they must extract the orientation implied by the organization of elements in the habituation stimulus. There are, however, some difficulties of interpretation here. For instance, it is possible that the dark pattern elements are just much more detectable, to the extent that the infant visual system effectively filters out the unfilled elements. If this were happening, we would really be dealing with a phenomenon based on relative proximity of the dark elements in one dimension versus the other. But Quinn and his colleagues went on to show that infants did register the form of individual stimulus elements independent of brightness differences, so it may well be that infants of this age have a general ability to group elements in terms of similarity. However, brightness similarity is the simplest basis of such grouping, and also the one

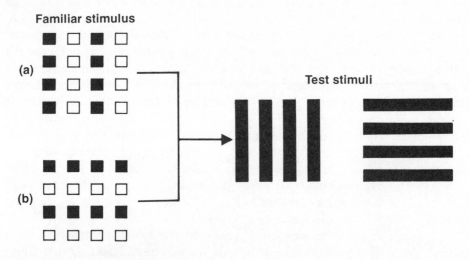

Figure 3.5 The stimuli used by Quinn, Burke and Rush (1993) to investigate brightness similarity in infant perception. Infants were familiarized with one of the stimuli on the left and tested for novelty preference on the pairing on the right.

most subject to alternative interpretation. Thus we need further work in this area looking specifically at grouping in terms of shape similarity before clear conclusions will emerge.

If we consider everyday object perception, it is clearly important that the constant form of an object be extracted despite changes in its position in the visual field and changes in retinal image size. So, while Milewski's study focused on perception of two-dimensional forms, it indicated abilities that should stand infants in good stead in object perception. We shall come on to studies of object perception later in this chapter, but it is worth pointing to one factor that has to be taken account of in object perception. As the viewing position changes or an object is moved, its orientation relative to the viewer changes, hence its constant shape has to be be perceived despite changes in orientation. When we are dealing with perception in three dimensions, this is known as shape constancy, but it has an obvious analogue in two-dimensional form perception, where the issue is whether infants can extract a constant form despite changes in its orientation.

Bornstein, Krinsky and Benasich (1986) showed that, depending on the task structure, four-month-olds would either discriminate between identical forms in different orientations, or would extract a constant form despite changes in orientation. In one condition, infants were habituated to one orientation of a particular form, and tested for dishabituation to it in a different orientation. In this condition, infants dishabituated, despite the fact that the orientation change was only ten degrees. In a second condition, infants were habituated to one form presented in several orientations, and were then tested for dishabituation on familiar and novel orientations of the original form, and on a new form entirely. Habituation took longer in this condition, indicating sensitivity to orientation, but once established, infants did not dishabituate to familiar or novel orientations of the habituated form, but did when presented with the new form. Taken together, these results indicate that infants can extract a constant form despite changes in orientation, changes that they would otherwise be sensitive to. This is a good indication of the way the habituation method can be adapted to become a very powerful tool for detecting perception of higher level perceptual features.

Figure 3.6 Stimulus patterns used by Slater, Morison and Rose (1983). Infants were either habituated to a random selection of crosses that differed in angular relationship and line thickness (rows 1 and 2) or to triangles that differed in angular relationship (row 3), and were then tested for novelty preference using the stimuli in row 4.

The next question is whether form perception can be shown in younger infants. Work by Slater, Morison and Rose (1983) suggests that it can. Using the habituation–novelty method, they showed first of all that newborn infants (about two days old) could discriminate between circle, cross, triangle and square. Striking though this finding was, these discriminations could have been based on differences in contour density, or differences in local angular relationship. Thus Slater's group performed a second study in which infants were tested for discrimination between a cross and a triangle under rather different conditions. In this case, the habituation stimulus (say a cross) was varied in terms of the angular relationship and thickness of the elements (see figure 3.6). Also, the stimuli presented on dishabituation trials (cross and triangle) were identical in countour density, but both differed from the habituated stimuli in terms of angular relationship. In other words, both were novel patterns, but one had a familiar form. In this experiment, newborns showed a clear preference for the novel form, and the logic of the experiment indicates that this discrimination must be based on the difference in forms rather than on differences in contour density or in local angular relation.

There is still a problem, however, in accepting this as unequivocal evidence of form perception. Although element thickness and precise angular relationship were varied in the habituation stimuli and contour density was held constant in the test stimuli, it is still the case that every example of a triangle has a more or less horizontal line at the bottom of the stimulus whereas no cross has such a feature. As Slater (1989) points out, it is impossible to equate two shapes for all lower order variables, and so it is very hard to pin down the level at which a discrimination is being made. Another approach to assessing form perception in newborns is to start from the lower order variables and work upwards. One relatively simple basis on which cross and triangle differ is in terms of the gross orientation of the stimulus elements. Initially, it was thought that newborns were incapable of discriminating different orientations (Braddick, Wattam-Bell and Atkinson, 1986), however, later studies revealed clear evidence of orientation discrimination at birth (Atkinson, Hood, Wattam-Bell, Anker and Tricklebank, 1988; Slater, Morison and Somers, 1988).

The next question is whether infants are sensitive to differences in angular configuration. Cohen and Younger (1984) investigated this in infants between six and fourteen weeks through the habituation–dishabituation procedure shown in figure 3.7. Infants were habituated to either the

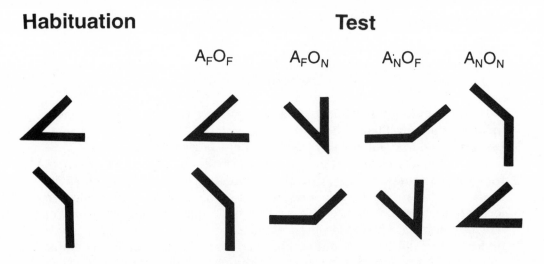

Figure 3.7 Stimuli used by Cohen and Younger (1984) to investigate perception of angular relations in infancy.

acute or the obtuse angle and were then tested for dishabituation on the stimuli shown to the right of the figure. Note that these were such that infants responding in terms of line orientation would treat both stimulus A_FO_F and A_NO_F as familiar whereas infants responding in terms of angular relationship would treat stimulus A_FO_F and A_FO_N as familiar. They found that six-week-olds showed the first pattern, dishabituating to A_FO_N and A_NO_N whereas the fourteen-week-olds showed the second pattern, dishabituation to A_NO_F and A_NO_N. This suggest that only the older infants were sensitive to angular configuration, the younger ones being limited to responding in terms of line orientation. However, it is possible that the younger infants were capable of detecting angular relationships, but simply habituated to the lowest order stimulus variable, the orientation of the lines. After all, in this procedure we cannot tell infants which is the relevant stimulus variable. Slater, Mattock, Brown and Bremner (1991) tackled this problem by varying the orientation of the stimulus during habituation (see figure 3.8): infants were presented with either the acute or the obtuse angle habituation set and were then tested for novelty preference on a pairing of the acute and obtuse stimuli in which line orientation was held constant. In addition to stimulus orientation varying during habituation, the test stimuli were presented in an orientation not encountered during habituation. Under these test conditions, newborns showed a clear novelty preference for the angular relationship not presented

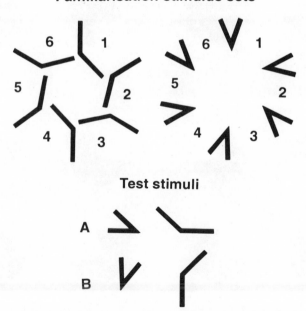

Figure 3.8 Stimuli used by Slater et al., (1991) to investigate perception of angular relations by newborns.

during habituation. This variant of the habituation–novelty technique in which stimulus variables other than those under test are varied during habituation is referred to as the *familiarization–novelty* technique and, as we shall see further on in this chapter, has proved particularly useful in a number of areas of investigation.

If infants are capable of perceiving angular relationships a further question is whether they are capable of integrating the separate angular features that make up a form such as a triangle or square. A good example of the operation of such a process in adults is the phenomenon known as perception of subjective contours, illustrated in figure 3.9. Although the figure consists only of four circles with missing segments, their arrangement strongly suggests a square. The assumption is that this occurs because we integrate information about the four right angles and their layout to perceive a square. Applying the habituation–dishabituation technique to stimuli of this sort, Bertenthal, Campos and Haith (1980) obtained evidence for perception of subjective contours by seven-month-olds and,

Figure 3.9 Stimuli used by Ghim (1990) to investigate infant perception of subjective contours. Only the top left stimulus produces subjective contours specifying a square.

using the more sensitive habituation–novelty technique, Ghim (1990) detected the phenomenon as early as three months.

This section has focused on form perception in young infants, appropriately enough, since that is the age group with which the bulk of the work has been done. However, it is appropriate to end with an example of an impressive ability which so far has not been detected in infants under 12 months. If a shape is traced out on a surface with a finger or some other nonmarking implement, adults have no problem in integrating this sequence of movement to arrive at a percept of the shape. It appears that 12-month-old infants can do the same, since Rose (1988) showed that if infants were familiarized with a light point tracing of a shape, then shown a three dimensional example of that shape paired with a novel shape, they showed a looking preference for the novel shape. Skouteris, McKenzie and Day (1992) replicated this result, although they found that the effect was stronger for rectilinear than curvilinear figures, and that it was eliminated altogether if the post-familiarization stimuli were two- rather than three-dimensional. This last finding is intriguing, since if anything one might expect the translation from a light point tracing to a 2D form to be more direct, since both are two-dimensional.

Visual scanning patterns

The visual preference and habituation techniques involve a fairly rough and ready measure of visual fixation; it is enough in these cases to know just whether or not an infant is looking at a stimulus. The corneal reflection technique, however, allows a much more accurate estimate of locus of fixation. The technique is based on an everyday phenomenon; if someone looks at a light source, an observer behind the source will see a reflection of the light near the pupil. If the person then shifts fixation the reflection will appear offset relative to the pupil. The corneal reflection technique involves the systematic harnessing of this phenomenon. Reference lights (often infrared to make them invisible to the subject) are shone in front of the eye, and their corneal reflection is picked up by a video camera. Once on videotape, the position of these reflections relative to a reference point on the eye (often the pupil) can be measured and a fairly accurate estimate of the direction of fixation made.

This method has the advantage of yielding precise information about which part of a stimulus an infant is fixating at any particular time. It also allows measurement of scanning patterns over time, and hence indicates the sequence in which elements are fixated. For some theories, this sort of information is of central importance. Hebb (1949), for example, argued that shape perception is gradually built up through scanning key elements. The overall shape is encoded through integration of separate fixations of elements with specific eye movements to the next feature. There are problems with this notion, however, since there seems to be little relationship between eye movements and shape perception even in adults. Consequently

Perceptual development

we should be on the lookout for other explanations of scanning patterns, particularly those of infants.

Salapatek and Kessen (1966) measured the fixation patterns of newborns presented with a triangle, and found that fixations tended to cluster around one of the vertices of the triangle (see figure 3.10). In contrast, older infants show more extensive scanning of stimuli (Leahy, 1976). The finding with newborns fitted the notion, popular at the time, that young infants were visually captured by stimuli. However, as already noted, there are arguments against this theory (Harris and MacFarlane, 1974). Also, other evidence showed that if infants were given longer to look at the stimulus, even the youngest ones showed some signs of shifting fixation to other

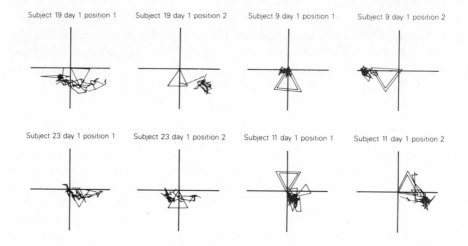

Figure 3.10 Scanning patterns of newborns obtained by Salapatek and Kessen (1966). Figures on the left show patterns in the absence of a stimulus, figures on the right show patterns in the presence of a solid black triangle.

features (Salapatek and Kessen, 1973). But these studies were done at a time when measurement of scanning was fairly crude. A more recent study incorporating more sophisticated measurement techniques (Bronson, 1990) replicated the previous finding of increasingly wide scanning with age, but found that at one month some infants showed no signs of relating their fixations to the stimulus in any way. Thus, for once, early studies may have overestimated young infants' ability.

Jeffrey (1968) explains scanning patterns in terms of serial habituation. Infants fixate a pattern element until habituated to it, when they shift fixation to another element. Because young infants generally habituate more slowly than older ones, their scanning is slower. This sounds a plausible account. However, it is based on the notion that the feature fixated is the feature attended to, a very plausible idea from the adult's point of view, but possibly suspect in the case of the infant. For adults, the advantage of fixating an element centrally is that it is brought into the region of high acuity vision, but young infants have not yet developed this region, so the obvious advantage of foveation is absent. As we shall see in the next section, Bronson (1974) has carried this sort of argument much further, arguing that fixation patterns tell us nothing about pattern perception.

Mechanisms underlying infant visual perception

Most attempts to explain early visual perception are based on what we know or can guess about the neurophysiology of the infant's visual system. Often neurophysiological evidence is used simply to back up theories based purely on behavioural evidence, but Bronson (1974) gives a quite radical account based on speculation about the development of the brain, which, if correct, would mean that we should completely rethink what is happening in early infant perception. He bases his account on a distinction between the functions of the cortical and midbrain visual systems. The former is specialized for pattern detection in the central regions of the retina, whereas the latter operates to locate more peripheral stimuli and direct fixation to them so that the cortical mechanism can be used to identify them. Bronson claims that the visual cortex is immature at birth, whereas the midbrain is mature. The outcome is that the midbrain locates stimuli and directs them to a cortical system that is not yet mature enough to do anything with them. So preferred stimuli are those that trigger the midbrain attentional mechanism, and once in central vision, little is made of them. Object scanning patterns reflect the salience of particular features as triggers of this mechanism and indicate nothing about pattern perception. In addition, Bronson claims the inaccurate tracking of moving objects is due to the fact that the infant is relying on crude midbrain localization mechanisms in the absence of a precise cortical system for locking on to moving targets. He also reinterprets habituation phenomena, claiming that it is the midbrain attentional mechanism that is becoming habituated during successive exposures. And since the cortical pattern system is inoperative, habituation should not be taken as an indication of pattern encoding.

Bronson's model has come in for criticism, mainly because he appears to have underestimated the maturity of the cortical visual system and overestimated the maturity of the midbrain system. Current opinion seems to be that there is a fair degree of cortical function at birth, although it would seem that a good deal of organization has still to occur in this region. Also, the fact that newborns discriminate different orientations (Atkinson, et al., 1988; Slater, et al., 1988) suggests a functional cortex, since orientation selective cells are found only in the visual cortex. On the other hand, the fact that the visual cortex is partially functional at birth does not indicate that it is the centre of visual control from birth. Atkinson, Hood, Wattam-Bell and Braddick (1992) have shown that one-month-olds are far less able to switch visual attention than three-month-olds, and they put this down to the fact that younger infants' attention is controlled by a relatively simple 'stimulus driven' midbrain system.

It may well be productive to put Bronson's account together with the explanation of preferences put forward by Banks and Ginsburg (1985). Maybe the early role of the midbrain is to detect the sort of stimuli that provide optimum stimulation for the cortical system and bring them to central vision. So it might still be true that preferences are determined by what best triggers the midbrain system, a system that is tuned to detect optimal patterns for cortical stimulation. Thus, instead of acting in vain, as would appear from Bronson's analysis, the midbrain might perform a vital function in early perceptual development.

However, even an amalgamation of different neurally based accounts only serves to explain the more basic phenomena. As Banks and Ginsburg note, their model does not account for visual preferences found later in infancy. Also, even the modified Bronson model does not account for higher level perceptual abilities that appear from the time of birth. If it is the midbrain attentional mechanism that is habituating to a cross and dishabituating to a triangle, it must contain mechanisms for form perception not generally attributed to it. It seems much more likely that these findings tell us about the relatively sophisticated functional state of the cortical visual system, and when it comes even to this relatively simple level of perception, the account has to be driven once more by the behavioural data, since we know little enough about the neural mechanisms of form perception in adults let alone in infants.

Colour perception

Early preference studies (Fantz, 1961; 1963) indicated that infants preferred certain patterned stimuli over brightly coloured ones, a finding that could either mean that infants do not perceive colour, or that colour is less salient than pattern. Although it was claimed that infants as young as a month old discriminate between colours (Milewski and Siqueland, 1975), colour perception is a notoriously difficult thing to study. The basic problem is that the hue and brightness of a stimulus are generally confounded. Because the visual system is not equally sensitive to all wavelengths of light, two different frequencies of light will differ both in hue and in perceived brightness, despite having the same physical intensity. In the case of adult studies, we can control these brightness differences, because we know the relationship between frequency and visual sensitivity (what is called the 'spectral sensitivity curve'). However, we cannot assume at the outset that the young infant's sensitivity function is the same.

There are two ways around this problem. First, we could measure the infant's spectral sensitivity curve and use this in controlling for brightness differences. This information is gained from adults by asking them to report when they first see a light that is gradually increased in luminance, a process that is repeated over the range of the visual spectrum to give rise to the sensitivity curve. Of course, we cannot ask infants to report these thresholds, but we can use the *visual evoked potential* technique to obtain similar data. In this case the sensitivity curve is derived from the minimum luminance at different frequencies that gives rise to an evoked response in the visual cortex. Using this method with two-month-old infants, Dobson (1976) concluded that infants' spectral sensitivity was reasonably similar to that of adults.

Secondly, while testing for colour discrimination, we could vary stimulus luminance over a reasonably wide range. For instance, in a visual preference study we could make repeated presentations of two stimuli, say a red and a green one, in which for some presentations the red one had higher luminance while in others the green one had higher luminance. A consistent preference for one colour under these conditions could not be put down to discrimination on the basis of brightness.

In practice, most workers use more complex methods of measuring colour discrimination. For instance, Peeples and Teller (1975) used a technique that relied on infants' preference for patterned over plain stimuli. A plain field was paired with a similar field containing a red stripe. The rationale here is that if the brightness of background and stripe are the same, infants will only be able to see the stripe if they have colour vision. The catch as usual is how to equate brightness between stripe and background, and Peeples and Teller's method was to vary the luminance of the red stripe over a range in keeping with the spectral sensitivity function, so that in some cases at any rate, detection of the stripe could not occur on the basis of brightness differences. Despite this precaution, two-month-olds were able to discriminate the red bar from the uniform field under all presentation conditions, so it was concluded that two-month-olds had at least a basic ability to perceive colour. Subsequent work (Teller, Peeples and Sekel, 1978) suggested that infants of this age have well-developed colour discrimination, but that they have a deficit when it comes to blues.

Until recently, there was no evidence at all on newborn infants' colour perception. However, Adams, Maurer and Davis (1986), using a variant on Peeples and Teller's method, found that newborn infants differentiated red, green and yellow from a non-chromatic stimulus. They did not, however, discriminate blue, a finding that fitted previous results with two-month-olds. However, Maurer and Adams (1987) found that by one month of age, infants had developed some ability to make such a discrimination in the case of blue, so although the deficit in the blue range seems to be complete at birth, there is rapid improvement within the first month.

Bornstein (1975) took a new line of approach, asking whether infants' colour *preferences* matched those of adults. Testing four-month-olds, he found a remarkable agreement between adult ratings of pleasantness and infants' looking times, which suggests first that there is a degree of similarity between colour perception at four months and in adulthood, and secondly that adult colour preferences are not, as is often assumed, culturally determined. Bornstein, Kessen and Weiskopf (1976) went on to see whether infants categorized colours in the same way as adults. Although light wavelength is a continuous variable, adults categorize light into the discrete hues, blue, green, yellow and red (Boynton, 1979), and Bornstein's group wanted to see whether the same was true of infants. Their technique was to habituate an infant to a colour stimulus that lay near to an adult category boundary (say a blue near to the blue–green boundary), and then to test for dishabituation with stimuli that were equally distant in wavelength from the habituated one, but some of which were within the same colour category (blue) as the original, whereas others were in the adjacent category (green). They found that four-month-olds only dishabituated to stimuli lying in a different colour category from the habituated stimulus, and concluded that infants, like adults, show categorical perception of colour. Bornstein goes on to argue against the conventional notion that colour categories are culturally and linguistically derived, claiming instead that these categories are determined by the structure of the visual system. It is worth noting, however, that not all workers accept Bornstein's evidence. For example, Banks and Salapatek (1983) have argued that his categorical effects may be complex artefacts arising from infants' pre-existing colour preferences.

Another important property of colour vision is colour constancy. That is to say, as illumination levels change in the course of the day, the spectral characteristics of light reflected from a given object change markedly, and yet, within a wide range of illumination levels, that object is perceived by adults as maintaining the same colour. So far, it appears that colour constancy is a relatively late development, the evidence suggesting that it is only partially developed at four to five months (Dannemiller, 1989; Dannemiller and Hanko, 1987) and completely absent at two months.

In summary, there is evidence for colour perception right from birth. However, we do not yet possess a detailed knowledge of infant colour vision, largely because of the significant methodological problems that arise in this sort of investigation.

Visual perception in three dimensions

So far I have covered research devoted solely to the infant's perception of two-dimensional patterns. Using two-dimensional stimuli has many methodological advantages, particularly when the investigator is bent upon measuring capacities that require very tight experimental control. Use of three-dimensional stimuli brings in a new set of variables that can lead to spurious results. It is, for example, much more difficult to control brightness or contour density between two real objects than it is to do so between two patterns. However, there are many questions about infant perception that can only be tackled by using real objects. For instance, we might want to know whether infants perceive the properties that distinguish an object from an equivalent two-dimensional shape. Also, questions regarding space perception can only be answered by varying the distance between the infant and the stimuli. Both these questions are linked, since both are to do with the infant's perception of extension in the third dimension. In the case of object perception the issue is whether they perceive the three dimensionality of the object. In the case of space perception the major issue is whether they perceive the third dimension in their surroundings.

Depth perception

Visual cliff studies I shall start with a classic study of depth perception. Gibson and Walk (1960) were concerned with the basic question of whether infants are capable of perceiving depth, a simple enough question, but one that has exercised the ingenuity of many workers since. Gibson and Walk narrowed down the question by focusing on the infant's perception of vertical drops, noting that once babies begin to crawl they become prone to falls over vertical drops of varying heights. Their question was whether infants learned about drops from hard experience or whether this perception was innate.

They tackled the problem with great ingenuity, using the method illustrated in figure 3.11. The *visual cliff*, as it has become known, consists of a central platform with a shallow drop on one side and a deep drop on

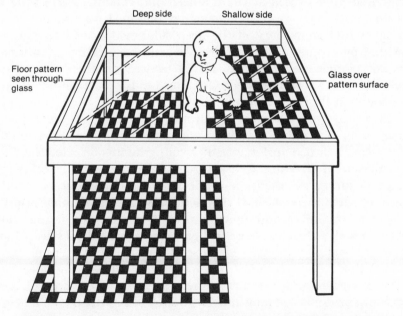

Figure 3.11 Gibson and Walk's (1960) visual cliff apparatus.

the other. On the deep side there is a strong sheet of glass at the same height as the shallow drop, both to safeguard the infant and to make both sides identical to the sense of touch. Infants ranging in age from six to 14 months were placed on the central platform and attempts were made to entice them across both the shallow and 'deep' drops successively. Of 27 infants tested, only three ventured on to the side with the apparent deep drop, whereas all crawled across the shallow side.

Two main issues arise from this study. First, what sort of depth cues are infants using to detect the vertical drop? This is an issue to which we shall return later in this section. Secondly, what can we say about the origins of depth perception? Gibson and Walk take their results as support for the notion that depth perception is innate. But the visual cliff technique requires that infants are able to crawl and even Gibson and Walk's youngest subjects were six months old when they were tested. This raises the possibility that depth perception was learned during the months prior to crawling, and Gibson and Walk rely on comparative evidence to back their conclusion that we are dealing with an innate ability. Day-old chicks all avoided the deep side of the cliff, a response that could hardly have been learned in their case. But although depth perception may be innate in chicks, it is a risky assumption that the same is true of human infants, particularly when we bear in mind that depth perception is more likely to be innate in species that locomote immediately after birth.

The major limitation of the visual cliff technique is the requirement that subjects be old enough to crawl. One rather bizarre way around this problem was devised by Scarr and Salapatek (1970). They placed infants in a trolley and pulled them across the deep and shallow sides of the visual cliff. Using this 'crawligator' method, they obtained no evidence that pre-crawling infants were wary of the deep side, evidence in support of the notion that perception of vertical drops was learned rather than innate.

Campos, Langer and Krowitz (1970) devised another way of testing younger infants. They measured two-month-olds' heart rate as they were placed successively on the deep and shallow sides of the visual cliff, and found that heart rate *decreased* significantly when infants were placed on the deep side, but did not change when they were lowered on to the shallow side. Their conclusion was that young infants detected the drop but were unafraid of it, since a heart rate drop is generally taken as an indicator of increased attention, while fear should produce a heart rate increase. Further work clarified the picture. Schwartz, Campos and Baisel, (1973) compared five- and nine-month-old infants and found that the younger ones showed a decrease in heart rate on the deep side of the cliff, whereas the older ones showed a heart rate increase. From this they concluded that although depth perception is a fairly early development, wariness of vertical drops (indicated here by heart rate increase) does not emerge until around nine months. As we shall see in the next chapter, they relate this second development to the onset of active locomotion.

There is one snag about this sort of technique, however. If we conclude that young infants show greater attention to the deep side, can we assume that this is because they perceive the drop, or could they be responding to some other variable? Thinking back to the previous sections, we have to impose very careful controls before we can be sure that young infants are responding to depth itself and not to changes in some lower order variable like brightness or contour density. Banks and Salapatek (1983) claim that insufficient control was exercised over these sorts of variable in the studies by Campos and his colleagues, so increased attention by young infants on the visual cliff may not indicate that they perceive depth as such.

Reaching and depth perception   One solution to the interpretative problems mentioned above is to go back to measuring the infant's overt behaviour. Although studies using indirect measures of attention often yield evidence about perceptual capacities, they do not tell us much about infants' ability to use their potential. As Bower (1982) points out, we would be more convinced of infants' perceptual competence if we could observe them acting appropriately in response to particular perceptual events. Gibson and Walk did this, but in so doing restricted the scope of their study to infants who had begun to crawl. Another method relying on measurement of 'depth appropriate behaviour' was adopted long ago by Cruikshank (1941). The rationale here was that if infants had good depth perception they should reach for objects that are within reach but not for those out of reach. Cruikshank observed the reaches of three- to 12-month-old infants under three object presentation conditions; (1) a small object within reach of the infant; (2) a small object out of reach; (3) a large object out of reach. Conditions (1) and (3) were arranged so that the retinal image was similar, that is, the object in condition (3) was larger in proportion to its additional distance from the infant. Even at the earliest ages, infants reached more in condition (1), although prior to five months there was some evidence that some infants were responding to retinal size rather than distance, as evidenced by more reaching in condition (3) than (2). Cruikshank concluded that at least by six months infants had developed quite sophisticated depth perception.

A more recent study involving much the same technique confirms this conclusion. Field (1976) measured the reaching behaviour of two- and five-month-old infants when the target object was either within reach, just out of reach, or well out of reach. In one condition the same object was used for each distance, whereas in another its size was varied with distance so that retinal image size remained constant. Although two-month-olds showed little evidence of being selective, reaching by five-month-olds declined as object distance increased, even in the condition in which the retinal image remained constant. So here we have the suggestion that at least by five months infants have sufficient depth perception to know when an object is out of reach.

Despite these positive findings with older infants, the important issue is whether the less convincing performance by younger infants really indicates a lack of depth perception. Bower (1982) argues otherwise, suggesting that the 'reaches' for out-of-reach objects produced by Cruikshank's younger infants might have been social appeals to adults rather than true reaches. Hence, despite its simple rationale, this method has potential limitations. Also, it will only work if infants can reach for objects, and as we saw in chapter 2 there is considerable disagreement over the earliest point at which visually guided reaching can be detected, with estimates ranging from birth to around four months. This highlights one of the major difficulties encountered in infant work. Potentially we stand to learn most about infants' abilities through observing their purposeful acts, but the motor skills of young infants are such that unambiguous evidence of this sort is hard to come by.

This is where Bower has probably done most to revolutionize infant work, since he takes a far less pessimistic view of the existence of intentional acts in early infancy. As we saw in chapter 2, Bower departs from the conventional story on visually guided reaching, claiming that it can be elicited in newborns. So in his view, one good measure of depth perception, even in early infancy, would be the accuracy of reaches to objects at different distances; in fact he has used this method within the first two weeks from birth (Bower, 1972). Infants were presented with two objects in succession, one of them just out of reach and the other double the size and twice as far away, and their reaching was measured in each case. Bower found that infants reached twice as often for the near object as for the far one despite the fact that the retinal image size was the same for both. He concludes that newborns have sufficient depth perception to know when an object is in or out of reach, and although he concedes that their reaching is far from accurate, he puts this down in large part to problems of calibrating the developing motor system with perceptual input.

Reactions to approaching objects   Another way of investigating depth perception is to see whether infants show any defensive reaction to approaching objects. If they do, the argument is that they must interpret the optical expansion as the movement of an object in depth. White (1971) observed infants' reactions as a disk fell down a tube towards them, and found the first evidence for a clear defensive response at nine weeks. At this age infants consistently blinked in response to the event, and although blinking was observed around two weeks it was inconsistent and may not have been connected with the event. White concluded that by nine weeks infants' depth perception was sufficiently good to interpret the event as an object approach.

Bower suggests that this method underestimated younger infants' ability, since testing was carried out with the infant supine, a posture in which they are often in a drowsy state. It seems unlikely that this is the full explanation, however, since White's results have been replicated with infants in an upright posture. Pettersen, Yonas and Fisch (1980) obtained a clear increase in blinking between six and ten weeks when an object approached seated infants along a horizontal path. Nevertheless, we should remember that many neonatal responses go through a decline, only to re-emerge later. Could defensive responses to approaching objects be yet another case in point? Work carried out with very young infants suggests that it might be. Bower, Broughton and Moore (1970) presented very young infants with a three-dimensional cube that moved towards them as they sat facing it. In this study, infants less than two weeks old showed defensive reactions consisting of head raising and arm raising. Moreover, this reaction occurred in the case of a small object approaching to within a few inches of the infant, but not in the case of a larger object approaching at a greater distance (same retinal image). Also, they found that a similar (although reduced) reaction occurred if object approach was simulated by an optical expansion pattern. Bower (1982) concludes that 'one-week-old infants do perceive distance and change in distance as specified by, at least, the optical expansion pattern.' (p. 86).

Ball and Tronick (1971) replicated these findings, and also found that infants did not show defensive reactions if the object approached on a 'miss path'. This suggests quite amazing perceptual sophistication on the part of infants, since it would appear that they not only perceive approach but know when an object is likely to hit them and when it is not. But not all workers are convinced that a defensive response is being measured. A group of workers led by Yonas performed a series of studies that suggested an alternative interpretation of the findings (Yonas et al., 1977). First, they found that head raising occurred on presentation of a number of dynamic stimuli, including rising contours that did not specify an approaching object. Secondly, arm raising occurred roughly equally for all stimuli until eight months, when it became limited to patterns of expansion specifying approach. They conclude that head raising by young infants occurs due to infants' tendency to track rising contours in the visual field. According to them, therefore it is not a defensive response at all. To press home this point they did a further study with one- to two-month-olds in which expansion patterns specifying a hit or miss approach were presented in such a way that there was no rising top contour. In this case, no head rotation or withdrawal was measured.

Bower (1977a) criticizes this study, claiming that infants were not supported in the way necessary to allow them to make defensive responses, and he also cites evidence of defensive head withdrawal in the face of a stimulus whose upper contour drops during approach. So the controversy over this issue is not settled and, on balance, there is sufficient disagreement for us to suspend judgment on whether this technique yields an accurate measure of the young infant's depth perception.

Object perception

Many years ago, Fantz investigated infants' sensitivity to three-dimensional forms by presenting a sphere paired with a two-dimensional disc of the same dimensions. He found that one-month-olds showed a clear preference for the real object, and concluded that they were capable of picking up information that specified its three-dimensionality (Fantz, 1961). However, this study does not tell us which cues infants were using; indeed, since the two stimuli were discriminably different in terms of texture and shading, we cannot be sure that the preference was based on detection of three-dimensionality at all. Nevertheless, in a more recent study that controlled these variables, Slater, Rose and Morison (1984) found that newborns showed a clear preference for a three-dimensional object, so there is an indication that at least a crude method of detecting three-dimensionality is present at birth (we shall return to this study in the next section since it also tested for the sort of depth cues used by infants).

Another method of investigating object perception is to measure infants' manual responses to objects. As already noted, Bower found that young infants attempted to grasp a virtual object whose three-dimensionality is simulated. For him this was evidence that they perceive a three-dimensional object. In addition, Bruner and Koslowski (1972) found that infants of two months and older were more likely to make arm movements to the midline in the presence of an object of graspable size than when they were faced with one too large to grasp. So at least by this age they perceive something of this property of objects.

A third method of investigation is to see whether infants are sensitive to the constancies that govern object perception in adults.

Size and shape constancy   When we see two people of equal height, one close to us and the other far away, we do not conclude that the far person is smaller than the near one, despite the fact that the retinal image is very much smaller. This automatic correction made by the perceptual system is known as *size constancy*. The conventional view about infants, however, is that they are initially limited to processing retinal images. Later they begin to perceive depth and can then go on to use distance information to compute the true size of an object from its retinal image. However, many workers would now want to depart at least in part from this account. We already have some arguing that very young infants perceive depth, and Bower goes further to argue that size constancy is either innate or a very early acquisition.

Bower used an *operant conditioning* technique to test for size constancy (1964, 1966). The rationale behind operant conditioning is that any behaviour that is reinforced is likely to be repeated, and infants can be trained to make repetitive responses such as head movements in order to gain the reinforcement of social stimulation. In Bower's study, head turning was measured by a pressure sensor, and after a set number of responses the infant was reinforced by the sudden stimulating appearance of his or her mother. This technique was applied in such a way that infants only received reinforcement for head turns when a 30 cm cube was present one metre in front of them (see figure 3.12), a selective reinforcement that results in the infants' responding only when the cube is present.

Once infants were responding consistently when and only when the cube was present, they were presented with various cubes at various distances, and a measure was taken of the degree to which the head turning response generalized from the original training situation, the argument being that significant generalization indicated that the infant had noted a similarity between the training and test stimuli. The test cubes used are shown in figure 3.12. In condition 1 the cube was the same as the original but was presented at three times the distance. In conditions 2 and 3 the cube was three times the size of the original, and in condition 2 it was presented at the same distance, whereas in condition 3 it was presented at three times the distance. These conditions were picked carefully in order to distinguish between two possible bases for infant perception. If infants were operating at the level of retinal images, they would be expected to generalize most in condition 3, as an object three times the size at three times the distance projects the same retinal image. However, if they were operating at the level of real objects, most generalization would be expected in condition 1, in which the cube has the same true size as the original. To provide a standard for comparison, Bower also measured generalization to the original stimulus at the original distance.

Infants under two months old responded most in condition 1, so they seemed to generalize to the same object even when it was presented at a different distance. However, they responded almost as much in condition 2, when only the distance of the object remained the same. They generalized least in condition 3, in which the retinal image was the same as during training, so there is little evidence that infants were responding in terms of the projected image. In general the results fitted the idea that even very young infants perceive true objects rather than retinal images. The high generalization in condition 2 complicates the issue a little though, and Bower concludes that infants respond in terms of object distance *and* in terms of the true size of the object, and certainly not in terms of retinal image size. So they both perceive the third dimension and make the appropriate correction in order to maintain size constancy of the object over a range of distances.

Some workers have found it hard to detect size constancy in very young infants. McKenzie and Day (1972) used a habituation task incorporating the same logic as Bower's conditioning study. Infants were habituated to one object at a set distance and tested for dishabituation to the same or different objects at the same and different distances. It was found that

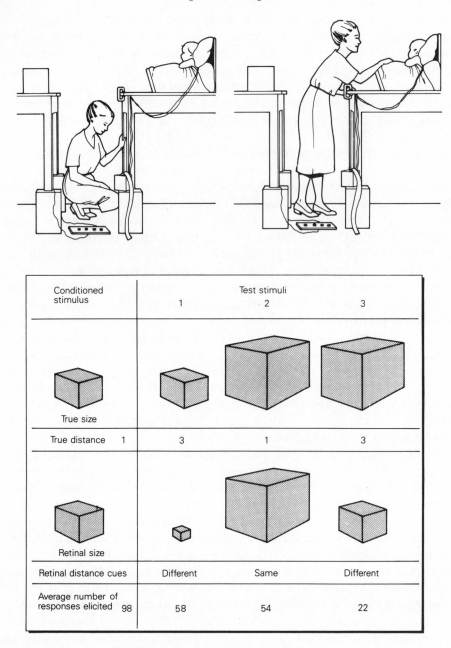

Figure 3.12 (a) Apparatus used by Bower (1964, 1966) to test for depth perception and size constancy. (b) Test stimuli showing true sizes, distances and corresponding retinal image sizes.

infants between 6 and 20 weeks only dishabituated to a change in stimulus distance, an object at a new distance led to dishabituation whether it was the same true size or projected the same retinal image size. There was certainly evidence for distance discrimination here. In fact McKenzie and Day (1972) found that stimulus distance was a strong determinant of spontaneous attention, looking declining steadily as stimulus distance was increased, even if retinal image size was held constant by increasing stimulus size. But in this study and in a follow-up (McKenzie and Day, 1976) there was no evidence of size constancy. Reviewing the evidence, Day and McKenzie (1977) concluded that 'size constancy in infancy has not yet been convincingly demonstrated' (p. 307).

This is not the final story, however. In a later study, McKenzie, Tootell and Day (1980) obtained evidence for size constancy at six months. These infants dishabituated to an object that differed in true size from the habituated stimulus, but did not dishabituate when the stimulus was the same size but at a different distance. The researches also obtained weak evidence for size constancy in four-month-olds, a finding subsequently confirmed by Day and McKenzie (1981). For some time this appeared to be the earliest age at which reliable evidence of size constancy could be obtained. However, there was a potential problem with all these studies. If, as McKenzie and Day concluded, stimulus distance is highly salient, it is possible that younger infants possessed size constancy, but habituated to stimulus distance rather than stimulus true size (remember the same problem arose in the case of perception of angular relationships versus orientation, in which younger infants appeared to respond to the lower order variable – see page 77). In order to correct for this problem, Slater, Mattock and Brown (1990) tested newborns for size constancy using a procedure in which the habituation stimulus was presented at various distances. With object distance no longer a constant during habituation, infants habituated to the true size of the object, showing a novelty preference for a different size of object. Thus it appears that when a sufficiently sensitive technique is used size constancy can be detected at birth.

Shape constancy is the perceptual correction that leads us to see an object's shape as the same despite changes in its orientation. The reader probably sees a link here with two-dimensional form perception. The issue in that case was whether infants could extract the general form from different orientations of the same figure, but since these figures are presented perpendicular to the line of sight, rotation of a particular form leads to projection on the retina of a rotated version of an unchanged form. As figure 3.13 indicates, the problem is more complex in the three-dimensional case since a real object can be reoriented in any plane, and most rotations result in a change in the form as well as the orientation of the retinal image. The general technique in studies of shape perception has been to concentrate on those rotations of the stimulus that lead to a maximum change in the form projected on the retina.

Bower (1966) used the same operant conditioning method to study shape constancy. He trained two-month-old infants to make head movements in the presence of a flat rectangle at an angle of 45 degrees to their line of

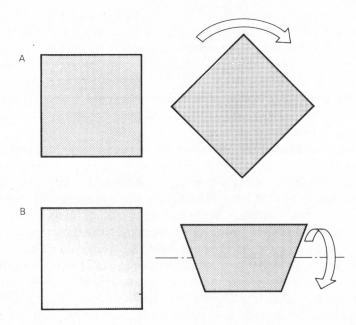

Figure 3.13 Diagram illustrating how the retinal image is affected by stimulus rotation in the plane perpendicular to the line of sight and by rotation in the plane parallel to the line of sight. The former yields a rotated version of the same retinal form (A) whereas the latter yields a different retinal form (B).

sight. Once the response only occurred when this stimulus was present, he tested their response generalization to the original stimulus and three other stimuli: (1) the same rectangle presented at right angles to the infant's line of sight; (2) a trapezoid at right angles to the line of sight such that the retinal image was the same as that produced by the training stimulus; and (3) the trapezoid at 45 degrees to the line of sight. Again, the argument is similar to that in the size constancy study. Maximum generalization is expected to the original stimulus, but different predictions arise for the others depending upon the basis of infant perception. If infants are operating at the retinal image level, there should be as much generalization to the trapezoid perpendicular to the line of sight. However, if the infants are responding in terms of true shape, there should be as much generalization to the rectangle in its new orientation. Finally, they might be responding in terms of stimulus orientation, in which case the 45 degree trapezoid should produce high generalization. The outcome was that the two rectangles, the original and the reoriented version, produced about double the generalization seen with the two trapezoid stimuli, and Bower concluded that shape constancy was present at two months.

Other workers (Caron, Caron and Carlson, 1979; Day and McKenzie, 1973) also found evidence for shape constancy in early infancy. The technique used by Caron et al. (1979) involved habituating infants to one shape (a rectangle or a trapezoid) and then testing for dishabituation to the same shape at a different angle to the line of sight or to a different shape. The rationale was that if infants had shape constancy they would not dishabituate to the same shape tilted at a different angle. However, it is possible that infants have shape constancy but are also sensitive enough to stimulus orientation in depth to dishabituate to a new orientation of the stimulus. In order to reduce the likelihood of this happening, the same stimulus was presented tilted at various angles during habituation trials, in effect to habituate infants to orientation as well as shape. After this, three-month-olds dishabituated much more to a different shape than to the same shape in an orientation not used during habituation.

There seems clear evidence, then, that infants of two or three months have shape constancy, but can this be demonstrated earlier? Slater and Morison (1985) suggest that it can. Testing newborns, they first established that they could discriminate stimulus orientation in the depth plane. Infants showed consistent preferences for particular orientations of stimuli, even with retinal image held constant. In the light of this finding, they adopted the same sort of technique used by Caron et al. (1979) to desensitize infants to stimulus orientation. After habituation trials in which one shape was presented at various angles, newborns showed a strong preference for a novel shape over the original shape presented at an angle not previously encountered. Since the habituation stimulus was presented at a variety of angles, and since it appeared at a new angle during test trials, these results could not be due to habituation to a particular retinal image, and Slater and Morison concluded that newborns have shape constancy.

The evidence for shape constancy implies that young infants are processing information about objects rather than just the two-dimensional form of the retinal image, a conclusion that is further supported by Cook, Hine and Williamson (1982). They found that if a real cube was presented on successive trials, the habituation rate of three-month-olds was similar whether it was presented in a single orientation or in different orientations across trials. In contrast, if the same comparison was made using photographs of the cube, infants habituated more slowly in a condition in which several photographs were presented showing the cube from different angles. Their conclusion is that in the three-dimensional conditions infants were habituating to the solid form of the object, so that changes in orientation made no difference to habituation rate. In contrast, in the two-dimensional conditions, infants were presumably habituating on the basis of two-dimensional form, and since this changed with cube orientation, habituation was much slower.

In summary, it would appear that young infants perceive three-dimensional forms and not two-dimensional projected images as earlier theories suggested. In addition, both shape and size constancy appear to be present at birth. However, this is not to say that young infants perceive objects with the same efficiency as you or I. Kestenbaum, Termine and Spelke (1987) showed that three-month-olds were unable to treat two objects in contact as separate entities. They appear unable to perceive boundaries involving contact, although they do perceive separate objects as distinct, even if one partially occludes the other. It seems likely that in the latter case they use depth information to identify the separation between the objects, but when objects are in contact they are treated as a single unit. It remains to be seen whether this is due to high level problems in object perception or simply due to the relatively poor visual acuity of the young infant.

Finally, there is another respect in which newborn object perception appears to be limited compared with perception a few months later. Take the diagram in the upper part of figure 3.14. This appears as a block with a continuous rod behind it, due to the fact that our perceptual system 'fills in' the hidden part of the rod. Of course, there is no way of knowing that the rod is continuous, but the alignment of linear elements suggests that it is, and if we add common motion of the two visible elements, the effect becomes even more persuasive. Kellman and Spelke (1983) habituated four-month-olds to this display, with the rod in motion behind the block, and then gave them trials consisting of single presentations of the two test stimuli shown in the bottom part of the figure. On these trials, infants generalized habituation to the continuous stimulus but dishabituated to the discontinuous stimulus. Kellman and Spelke concluded that during habituation infants had perceived the rod as continuous and so treated the discontinuous stimulus as novel, despite the fact that it coincided with what had actually been visible. Slater and his colleagues replicated this effect with four-month-olds but obtained the opposite result with newborns, a looking preference for the continuous stimulus (Slater et al., 1990). It seems that newborns habituated to what was literally visible, thus it appears that the ability to fill in invisible parts of objects is absent at birth but develops by the third month.

What depth cues do infants use?

Texts on perception generally divide depth cues into two categories, binocular and monocular. Binocular depth perception can be derived from two principle cues, *convergence* and *retinal disparity*. The degree of convergence required to produce bifoveal fixation depends on the distance of the object – the closer the object the greater the convergence. So convergence angle correlates with object distance and is hence a potential cue for it. Nevertheless, retinal disparity seems to be a more important depth cue. When both eyes are oriented towards the same object, each picks up a slightly different image due to the fact that the viewing angle for each eye is different. Also, objects nearer and further from the point of fixation fall on different parts of each retina, so the whole scene is projected slightly differently to the two eyes. The closer the object the greater the convergence

Habituation display

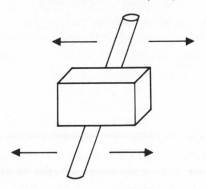

Test displays

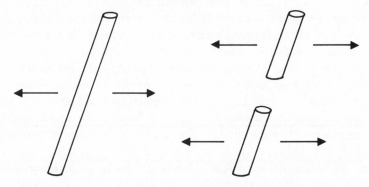

Figure 3.14 Stimuli used by Kellman and Spelke (1983) to investigate object perception in young infants. © American Psychological Society.

needed for bifoveal fixation, and also the greater the disparity between the images. In adults, very small disparities of this sort result in stereopsis, the perception of three-dimensionality in the object, and the illusion of solidity can be obtained by projecting two disparate but two-dimensional images to the two eyes.

Monocular depth cues are those that would be effective if we had only one eye, and can be either static or dynamic. The static category consists of *pictorial cues*, so called because artists employ them to indicate depth in pictures. These are cues like texture gradient in which texture becomes finer with increasing distance, pictorial interposition (partial occlusion of far objects by near ones), linear perspective, and so on. The principle dynamic monocular depth cue is *motion parallax*. A sideways movement of the head produces apparent movement of the whole visual field in the opposite direction. However, within the visual field, this motion is greater for near than for far objects in a way that yields systematic information

about the relative positions of objects in space. Also, if we move forwards
we experience an optical expansion, which is greater for near objects than
for far ones. Both motion parallax and optical expansion are dynamic cues,
and it is worth comparing the latter with the localized optical expansion
that arises as an object moves towards us (see 'Reactions to approaching
objects' p. 88).

One method of testing for binocular depth detection is to present different
information to each eye, as in a stereoscope, so that the illusion of the
three-dimensional object is created for adults. As noted in chapter 2,
Bower, Broughton and Moore (1970a) claim that infants as young as one
week old reach out to try to grasp such a stereoscopically projected object,
which would suggest that they have fairly precise depth perception based
on retinal disparity. However, we must remember that some workers have
failed to measure reaching that is clearly distance related at this age (see
chapter 2). Also, since young infants show large convergence errors (Slater
and Findlay, 1975), there is some doubt whether these young subjects
achieve the precision of bifoveal fixation required for the detection of retinal
disparity. On the other hand, Granrud (1986) found that four- and five-
month-old infants showed more accurate judgement of distance under
binocular viewing conditions. In addition, Yonas, Arterberry and Granrud
(1987) found that four-month-olds were capable of using binocular disparity information to extract the three-dimensional shape of an object. So
it would appear that at least by this age infants use binocular depth cues.

Earliest estimates of sensitivity to monocular cues depends very much on
whether they are static or dynamic. Responsiveness to static cues appears
to be relatively late, with evidence for response to pictorial interposition
appearing at around six months (Granrud and Yonas, 1984) and response
to texture gradient and linear perspective at around seven months (Arterberry, Bensen and Yonas, 1991; Yonas, Granrud, Arterberry and Hanson,
1986). On the other hand, dynamic cues have long been suspected to be
the earliest detected by infants. Gibson and Walk (1960) concluded that the
probable depth cue used in visual cliff studies was motion parallax.
However, they came to this conclusion largely on the basis of excluding
unlikely alternatives. Walk (1968) subsequently showed that binocular
vision was not needed for visual cliff avoidance; infants wearing an eye
patch showed the same level of deep side avoidance as those who did not.
However, while this shows that infants are capable of using monocular
cues, it does not identify motion parallax as the one used. Motion parallax
is difficult to isolate since it depends on movement by the infant, and the
case is similar for optical expansion resulting from forward motion. However, as we shall discuss in the next section, optical expansion is used by
quite young infants to control posture (Butterworth and Hicks, 1977). In
addition, Hofsten, Kellman and Putaansuu (1992) used a nice technique to
show that three-month-old infants were sensitive to motion parallax. While
seated in a chair that moved from side to side, infants were habituated to

a display of three rods. Although all three rods were at the same distance, the middle rod moved in synchrony with the infant's movement so as to create a motion parallax effect indicating that it was behind the other rods. After this phase, under static viewing conditions infants were tested for dishabituation to two static displays, the original display with all rods at the same distance and a new display in which the middle rod was further away than the other two to the same extent as had been specified by the motion parallax information during habituation. Infants failed to dishabituate to this display, but dishabituated to the equidistant display, indicating that they had processed motion parallax information during habituation and had thus perceived the middle rod as further away than the other two.

Bower (1975) notes that progressive occlusion is one common cue in all these cases involving movement. When we move our head from side to side, near objects progressively occlude (and expose) far objects, and similarly when we move through space. When an object moves across the field or towards us, it progressively occludes the background. Bower goes on to argue that infants pick up this constant factor to perceive depth relations in all these cases. This sort of thinking derives largely from Gibson's theory of direct perception (1966, 1979), an alternative conceptualization of space perception that will be discussed later on in this chapter and in chapter 4, since it has important implications for perceptual and cognitive abilities. Craton and Yonas (1988) tested sensitivity to boundary flow information of this sort by presenting infants with a computer generated 2D display indicating flow between an object and a background. Despite the fact that all points of the display were equidistant, five-month-old infants reached more for the apparently near surface, indicating that they were capable of interpreting boundary flow information as a depth cue.

In summary, there is evidence that by the age of seven months infants are capable of using a wide range of depth cues. It appears, however, that dynamic cues are the first to be used. Commenting on a range of research, Yonas and Granrud (1985) concluded that infants begin by using dynamic depth cues, maybe as early as four weeks, then become sensitive to binocular cues at around four months, and finally begin to detect static monocular cues at around six months. While more recent research has extended our knowledge considerably, this sequence appears to be confirmed. However, we should note that these are the earliest ages at which use of particular cues has been convincingly shown. If newborns have shape and size constancy, they must be able to perceive relative distance within the stimulus, so some depth cue or cues must be detected at birth. This conclusion is supported by the finding that newborns show a marked preference for a solid stimulus over a two-dimensional version equated for shadows, light and shade (Slater, Rose and Morison, 1984: see previous section), and the fact that this preference remained even under monocular viewing conditions makes it more than likely that motion parallax was the cue in use.

Visual control of posture and locomotion

The conventional view on postural control is that information about posture is derived from information about relative position, orientation and movement of the body and its parts, deriving from the muscles and joints and from the vestibular system in the inner ear. The muscles responsible for posture and balance act to compensate for any postural changes signalled by these internal proprioceptive cues. However, Gibson (1979) and others (e.g. Lishman and Lee, 1973) have argued that there is an important visual component to proprioception, and Lee and Lishman (1975) showed the importance of this in what is now a classic study. Adults were put in a 'swinging room' in which the floor was stable but the walls could be made to move. When the walls moved, subjects reported feeling that it was they who were moving rather than the walls, and if asked to balance on a bar, they often fell off. This was a clever demonstration of the importance of visual input in the maintenance of posture.

Lee and Aronson (1974) detected the same phenomenon in infants who had just learned to stand upright. When placed in the swinging room, these infants fell over when the walls moved, despite the fact that the floor on which they stood was rock solid. Butterworth and Hicks (1977) went on to show the same phenomenon in nine- and 18-month-old infants in a sitting posture. Again, infants at both ages compensated their posture in accordance with the visual information. Butterworth (1983) also quotes an unpublished study from 1981 by Pope in which even at two months (the youngest age tested) infants showed compensatory movements of the head when the room moved. So at each age, if we pick the highest level of postural control achieved by the infant, we can see that it is strongly influenced by visual input. Butterworth and Cicchetti (1978) noted that the degree of postural adjustment in response to visual information declined as the infant gained more experience of sitting or standing. This might indicate that visual input has less effect on posture over time, or it could just be due to the improvement in muscular control. If you have only just developed the muscular control to stand, you are more likely to fall over as a result of a slight disturbance than if you have developed full control. However, in addition to confirming that the effects of visual flow were greatest just when infants had begun to walk, Delorme, Frigon and Lagacé (1989) found that the best synchronization between visual flow and body sway occurred in this early phase. This suggests domination by visual information rather than poor control of standing. Whatever the final conclusion, however, the main point to emerge here is that at least from the age of two months, visual proprioceptive cues are important, and Butterworth (1983) concludes that it is unlikely that visual proprioception is learned from experience in the world.

This does not mean, however, that infants are totally dependent on visual information for postural stability. If that were the case, they would

presumably fall over in the dark. However, it has been shown that twelve-
to fourteen-month-old infants show no less postural stability in the dark
than in the light (Ashmead and McCarty, 1991). This contrasts with the
adult case, in which stability declines in the dark, and Ashmead et al.
(1991) suggest that infants are quite flexible in their use of visual versus
body sense information for postural stability.

Visual flow information also appears to very important in control of
locomotion. Stoffregen, Schmuckler and Gibson (1987) showed that imposed
optical flow affected both bodily stability and direction during locomotion.
They also found that flow occurring in the periphery had a greater effect
than central flow, a result in keeping with the findings of Bertenthal and
Bai (1989) who found that peripheral flow had a greater effect on posture
in sitting and standing infants. Additionally, Schmuckler and Gibson
(1989) found that the disrupting effects of imposed optical flow were
greater when the infants had to locomote in a cluttered environment where
objects had to be negotiated. So increasing the complexity of the task
appears to augment the disruptive effects of misleading visual flow.

Summary

The extent of this discussion on visual perception reflects the range of levels
of analysis of infant perception and the diversity of methods used to study
them. We probably now know most about the very basic level of analysis
concerning visual acuity and accommodation, but this has probably come
about because these properties of the system are open to more precise
measurement rather than from want of effort in other areas. As we proceed
to higher order perceptual functions, the data become progressively more
open to confounding with lower order variables. For instance, as soon as
we start asking questions about pattern or shape perception it becomes
important to control the overall brightness of the stimuli, and while this is
relatively easily achieved with two-dimensional stimuli, it becomes more
difficult when we go on to use three-dimensional stimuli to study object
perception.

One of the main quandaries that the infant investigator faces has to do
with choice of response measure. A well-adjusted intentional act directed
to a stimulus is a very good indicator of an infant's awareness of its spatial
properties. However, such acts are hard to measure in young infants, and
we are often forced back on less direct measures such as heart rate change,
habituation, visual preference and so on. And because these measures have
a less obvious functional link with the stimulus, it is particularly in these
cases that questions arise about the level at which infants are discriminating
between stimuli. If an infant reached out accurately and successfully
grasped a near object, we would have strong evidence about his or her
depth perception, whereas if we found that an infant preferred to look at the
nearer of two objects, we would have to rule out many stimulus variables

such as brightness, size and contour density before we could conclude that the preference was based on depth perception itself.

Despite these difficulties, ingenious technical and experimental innovation has led to very significant advances in our understanding of early perception. Probably the main constraint on early perception is the infant's limited visual acuity, but this may only be a severe limiting factor as far as resolution of fine pattern detail is concerned. There is growing evidence that even neonates can detect quite high order perceptual variables such as true object shape, so whatever the lower order constraints, it seems that the infant can surmount them.

Finally, given the way in which the emergence of particular abilities has been successively pushed back closer to birth as new evidence has been obtained, there is no reason to take the current view of perceptual development as final. As research proceeds there is no doubt that some of the abilities currently judged to emerge after a few months will be shown to exist in neonates.

Auditory perception

Discussion of auditory perception will be brief in comparison with that of visual perception, largely because there is a good deal less work on infant hearing than on vision. One reason for this was mentioned at the beginning of the chapter – vision is generally treated as the primary sense. Nevertheless, there are many ways in which studies of auditory perception are likely to yield vital information about the infant's early world. For instance, an understanding of the infant's ability to perceive speech sounds and to discriminate between different speakers must have implications for our understanding of early social perception, and could have important implications for our understanding of the development of language and attachment.

Another reason for the paucity of studies of hearing is that auditory abilities are difficult to measure. This is because there is generally no external measure of auditory attention. We can tell when infants have a visual preference from the direction of their gaze, but we generally lose this source of information in the case of hearing, since the infant does not have to orient to a sound as part of the attentional process. For this reason, workers investigating auditory discrimination have often had to use less direct measures than are available to those studying vision. For instance, where visual studies can take decrement in looking time as the measure of habituation, those working on auditory discrimination have had to rely on other measures such as change in heart rate or sucking rate. True enough, infants sometimes orient spontaneously to a sound presented away from the midline, a response that gives us vital information about auditory localization, but for the reason already given, we cannot assume that no orientation indicates failure to detect a sound. Nevertheless this response can be trained to a level at which it is a more reliable indicator of auditory function. The visually reinforced head turning procedure achieves this through presenting a visual event (reinforcer) following a head turn towards an auditory stimulus, and this method has been used to good effect. For instance, because the trained response is contingent on detection of an auditory stimulus we can obtain an estimate of auditory thresholds by finding the lowest intensity of stimulation that produces the response.

Partly for the reasons discussed above, infant auditory perception was left fairly well alone until around the beginning of the 1970s. From then on, however, research in this areas has grown fast and we now have a reasonably good understanding of the infant's ability. I shall focus briefly on three areas: auditory thresholds and discrimination; speech perception; and auditory localization.

Auditory thresholds and discrimination

Can newborn babies hear, and if so, how well can they hear? Early work (Pratt, 1946) gave a positive answer to the first part of this question, but indicated very little about the second. Further work suggested that the newborn threshold (the intensity at which a stimulus becomes audible) is 10 to 20 dB higher than the adult threshold. More recent evidence suggests, however, that very young infants' thresholds for relatively low frequencies are really quite close to adult thresholds, but that, on the other hand, thresholds for higher frequencies are poorer and go through considerable development in the early months (Werner and Gillenwater, 1990). These conclusions are extremely tentative, however, since it is never clear with young infants whether they do not hear a sound or simply do not respond to it. This leaves open the possibility that young infants find high frequencies less salient, and it is worth noting that work with older infants actually indicates that high frequency sensitivity is closer to adult levels than low frequency sensitivity (Trehub, Schneider and Endman, 1980). It thus seems entirely possible that as new techniques are developed, young infants' auditory sensitivity will be shown to be fairly well developed across the full frequency range.

One of the fascinating things about auditory perception is that we can potentially study it before birth. The fetus exists in an auditory environment to the extent that auditory stimuli reach the womb from the outside world, and although we would expect the auditory environment to be very different in utero, Querleu and Renard (1981) have shown that stimuli below 1,000 Hz are transmitted very well. Bernard and Sontag (1947) obtained fetal heart rate acceleration in response to external auditory stimuli, apparently evidence for responsiveness to sounds; but could this response have been a reaction to the mother's response to the stimulus? It seems not, since Grimwade and co-workers (1971) replicated this finding and also employed the necessary controls to allow them to rule out the

possibility of this sort of maternal mediation. Both these studies looked at
fetuses one month before birth. However, as indicated in chapter 2, we
know that the fetus is responsive to vibroacoustic stimulation from 26
weeks gestation (Kisilevsky, et al., 1992), with some evidence of auditory
responsiveness even at 12 weeks (Hepper, 1992). We should, however,
bear in mind that these studies measure only a very general indicator
of auditory function, giving no information about thresholds, let alone about
auditory discrimination.

There is a range of evidence for auditory discrimination in early infancy.
Using a heart rate habituation method, Moffitt (1973) showed that six-
month-olds could discriminate tones that differed by 10 dB in intensity.
Since this was the smallest intensity difference used in the study, it could
not be taken as the smallest detectable difference, and Schneider and
Trehub (1985) indicate that this may be nearer 1 dB. A number of studies
have shown that infants around this age can also discriminate different
frequencies with considerable accuracy. Olsho (1984) showed that five- to
eight-month-olds discriminated high frequencies that differed by only 1 per
cent, the same as the adult level, whereas for low frequencies their discriminative ability fell to about half the adult level. In addition, Weiss, Zelazo and
Swain (1988) showed that newborns were capable of discriminating
frequencies, provided the difference was greater than 7%. This study used
only low frequencies, however, so it does not provide an estimate of high
frequency discrimination at birth, which may be considerably better.

In summary, there is evidence for sensitivity to auditory stimulation from
as early as the twelfth week of gestation. In addition, infants discriminate
different intensities and frequencies at birth. There is a fairly complex
relationship between these thresholds and the frequency of the sounds
concerned, both at birth and later in infancy. At present, it is not entirely
clear whether there are marked deficits in certain frequency ranges or
whether certain frequencies are less salient to young infants. However, it
would appear that there are real improvements in thresholds during the first
year. What is striking however, is the extent to which the auditory system
appears to be developed at birth: in comparison with the fairly poor visual
acuity of the newborn, auditory resolution appears in a favourable light. On
the basis of these indicators, one might expect to find quite sophisticated
auditory abilities even in early infancy. Indeed, a number of workers have
gone beyond basic discriminations to study infants' auditory pattern perception, and it turns out that well within the first year infants are capable of
discriminations between different intensity patterns and rhythms, and even
discriminate between simple melodies (for a review, see Morrongiello, 1988).

Speech perception

Speech is an extremely complex auditory pattern, both in terms of the mix
of frequencies within a sound, and in terms of the temporal patterning of

components. The full complexity becomes evident when we discover how many different factors such as shape of the vocal tract, place of articulation, and timing of articulatory elements, contribute to the distinctions between speech sounds. Despite this, it has been shown that two-months-olds (Jusczyk and Derrah, 1987) and even newborns (Moon, Bever and Fifer, 1992; Moon and Fifer, 1990) distinguish between certain speech syllables. Additionally, infants from two months of age showed what might be called 'vowel constancy', that is, they identified a vowel as constant even if the speaker changed, responding to vowel changes but not speaker changes (Marean, Werner and Kuhl, 1992).

Speech perception is another area in which there is evidence that adults perceive categorically. Remember how, despite the fact that light frequency is a continuous variable, adults categorize colour into distinct hues, discriminating well between hues but badly within them, even when the frequency difference is held constant (see 'Colour perception', pp. 82–4). The same is true in the case of speech perception, that is, adults are good at discriminating sound differences that cross category boundaries, and poor with those that do not (Liberman et al., 1957). In this case, the categories consist of the different phonemes used in the native language such as [p] and [b], and adults are relatively poor at discriminating some distinctions used in other languages but not in their own (Abramson and Lisker, 1970).

It turns out that infants show categorical speech perception before they produce recognizable speech sounds, and before they have had very much exposure to spoken language, postnatally at any rate. A number of studies have shown categorical perception of a range of speech sound distinctions in infants as young as one month. I shall focus on just two of the distinctions here. First, *voice onset time* (VOT) is a complex measure of relative timing of articulatory components which distinguishes sounds such as [b] and [p] or [d] and [t]. It is a continuous variable, but adults only make VOT discriminations when they cross phoneme boundaries; that is, when a difference in VOT leads to a different language sound, they discriminate the difference, but if a difference of similar magnitude yields a sound that does not cross a phoneme boundary, they do not discriminate the difference. Looking at the [b]–[p] distinction, Eimas and colleagues (1971) found that the same thing applied in the case of month-old babies, and a further study (Eimas, 1975) indicated that they also showed categorical perception of the [d]–[t] distinction.

Secondly, some distinctions between speech sounds concern the place in the vocal tract at which articulation occurs. For instance, the sounds [b], [d] and [g] are articulated successively further back in the vocal tract. Again, the results of a number of studies (reviewed by Aslin, Pisoni and Jusczyk, 1983) indicate that these distinctions are categorically perceived at least as early as the second month.

These findings are complemented by evidence of categorical perception of other speech distinctions such as between medial stop consonants (Cohen,

Diehl, Oakes and Loehlin, 1992), and lead to a set of important questions. Are these categorical distinctions innate, or have they been learned in the brief period from birth (or maybe before birth)? If they are innate, are there other distinctions not used in the native language that are distinguished categorically? Surely we would predict this, since it seems far-fetched to suggest that infants are innately sensitive to their native language alone. Current evidence suggests that infants distinguish categorically between distinctions used in other languages as well as those in their own (e.g. Trehub, 1976; Eilers, Gavin and Oller, 1982). From this it is tempting to surmise that infants are born linguistically pretuned to distinguish between all the sounds in all languages, and that they subsequently focus in on the distinctions used only in their own language (Eimas et al., 1971). However, if we were dealing with a specific linguistic capacity, we would expect non-speech sounds to be perceived on a different basis, and we would also not expect to find this sort of perception in animals. But we discover that categorical perception is also applied to synthesized non-speech sounds differing on the same characteristics as speech sounds (Jusczyk et al., 1977), and similar categorical distinctions are made by chinchillas (Kuhl and Miller, 1978) and monkeys (Kuhl and Padden, 1982). These findings suggest that categorical auditory perception found early in life is related to general properties of the auditory system rather than to some specific linguistic mechanism. This, however, does not rule out the possibility that linguistic input has a modifying effect during development, maybe by making some sound distinctions more salient than others, and Werker and Tees (1984) present evidence that infants gradually lose the ability to make distinctions not contained in their language as they grow older.

As should be evident, the whole topic of speech perception is complex, and quite sophisticated methods of controlled stimulus presentation are required to study it in some cases. While important advances have been made, there are still a number of major issues to be tackled. For instance, Eimas (1985) points out that we still understand little about the processes underlying categorical perception, or about the developmental mechanisms through which linguistic input leads to further tuning of auditory perception. Clearly we are only at the beginning on these issues.

But there is a much more modest question about speech perception that must have important implications for the infant's development, particularly in the social domain. One of the central notions in the literature on parent–infant attachment is that before infants can become attached, they must discriminate between their attachment figure and other people. Hence, with the usual bias towards vision, the infant's ability to discriminate faces is often considered in attempts to identify the age of onset of attachment. However, person discrimination could equally well be based on auditory information, and consequently we need to know how early and how well infants can discriminate between different voices. Since this issue is of central importance in social development, the relevant work will be discussed in chapter 5.

Auditory localization

The main cues for auditory localization are binaural. For instance, the relative intensity of sound reaching the ears gives a crude measure of stimulus direction; the sound will be louder in the ear closer to the source. More sophisticated measures of direction involve detection of disparity of sound onset and phase disparities between the two ears. Since sound from a lateral source takes longer to reach one ear than the other, it will be picked up first by the near ear, and there will be a continuous phase difference in the auditory patterns reaching the two ears.

Butterworth and Castillo (1976) attempted to detect auditory localization in newborns by presenting lateral stimuli and looking for visual shifts towards the source. They obtained no evidence that newborns were capable of making appropriate eye movements, in fact they showed a marked tendency to look in the wrong direction. In a subsequent study, however, Castillo and Butterworth (1981) found that newborn infants could orient appropriately if there was a visual pattern at the source of the sound, a more positive finding that would also seem to have implications for inter-modal perception (see the following section). In addition, Crassini and Broerse (1980) found that increasing the duration of the stimulus led to significant but rather inconsistent visual orientation to sound by neonates.

Using a different measure of orientation yields a clearer picture. Muir and Field (1979) found that newborn infants will make consistent head turns towards a sound source even when there is no visible stimulus at the sound locus, and Field and co-workers (1980) went on to show that this ability went through a decline around two months, to re-emerge at around four months. Apart from the relatively short period of absence, this is reminis-cent of Bower's claims about the developmental history of visually guided reaching. Is early orientation to sound a 'reflex' controlled by the midbrain? If so, its disappearance might be explained by cortical inhibition, and we would expect the re-emerging ability to be more sophisticated (see chapter 2). There is some evidence in keeping with this interpretation. Clifton and colleagues tested newborns (1981a) and two- and five-month-olds (1981b) for orientation to an auditory stimulus under two conditions. In one, there was a single lateral sound source, and this presentation produced accurate head turns at birth and five months. In the second condition, a sound location to one side was simulated by presenting sounds to both ears but with a slight difference in onset time. Thus, this was a simulated binaural cue to direction. Under this condition, only the five-month-olds showed reliable orientation. Clifton et al. (1981a) suggest that newborn orientation is a midbrain mediated reflex stimulated by crude binaural cues such as intensity difference, whereas processing of the more subtle cue of stimulus onset difference is more complex and can only be performed once the auditory cortex is sufficiently developed.

Recent work has added detail to the picture, indicating that infants' ability to discriminate the location of a sound increases considerably between two and eighteen months. Various techniques are used, but most are based on looking for changes in direction of looking or other attentional changes when a sound source is moved. In comparison to the adult capability of discriminating sound locations that differ by only one or two degrees of auditory angle, two-month-olds only detect shifts of 27 degrees or more (Morrongiello, Fenwick and Chance, 1990), while six- to seven-month-olds detect shifts of 19 degrees (Ashmead, Clifton and Perris, 1987), and 20-month-olds detect 5 degree shifts (Morrongiello, 1988). In addition, there are now some data on the type of binaural cue infants use to locate a sound. At four months, infants interpret inter-aural intensity difference as specifying a laterally offset sound source and interpret lack of an intensity difference as indicating a source straight ahead (Hillier, Hewitt and Morrongiello, 1992). Additionally, the same age group are capable of using inter-aural time differences to specify the direction of a source (Ashmead, Davis, Whalen and Odom, 1991).

While auditory localization in the horizontal plane is generally assumed to be based on binaural cues, localization in the vertical plane has to be achieved monaurally through complex spectral effects that vary depending on the direction in which the sound enters the outer ear. Consequently, one might expect this type of localization to be a later development. However, it appears that between six and eighteen months localization in the vertical plane is comparable to that within the horizontal plane (Morrongiello and Rocca, 1987).

Finally, there is the issue of localization of sounds in the distal plane. It appears that by at least seven months, infants are capable of deciding whether a sound source is in or out of reach (Clifton, Perris and Bullinger, 1991), and by six months they are capable of distinguishing changes in the distance of a sound source as specified through intensity changes (Morrongiello, Hewitt and Gotowiec, 1991).

In summary, there is considerable evidence for auditory localization at birth, and there is also some evidence that this behaviour disappears for about two months, to re-emerge in more sophisticated form. There is also plenty of evidence for improvement in auditory localization over the first two years. Additionally, at least by six months infants are capable of localizing stimuli in the distal plane as well as the vertical and horizontal. What is striking is the fact that much of this evidence is derived from direction of orientation, despite the fact that looking at a stimulus need not make it any more audible. This raises the possibility that, right from the start, infants are actually turning in order to see the source of the sound (Castillo and Butterworth). If this is the case, the data on orientation to auditory stimuli may tell us as much about intersensory coordination as they do about auditory localization.

Intersensory coordination

The empiricist view in philosophy (e.g. Berkeley, 1709/1963) would have us believe that there is no relationship between different senses at birth. Instead, any coordination must take place as a result of experience in the world. From this point of view there can be no question of coordination between the senses at birth; an object touched cannot be identified with an object seen, nor can a sound be associated with a visual sensation. Piaget is widely interpreted as holding this view, although as we shall see in chapter 4, his arguments were more to do with the separateness of the sensori-motor action schemes for seeing, hearing and touching, than with the separateness of the senses themselves.

A radical alternative, more in keeping with nativist theories, is that the senses are coordinated at birth. This springs much from the work of Werner (1948), who believed that early perception was *synthetic*, that is, that there is an equivalence between seeing something, hearing something and touching it. There is now growing empirical support for this second view, a view which, some one hundred years earlier, was summed up well by Cardinal Newman in his poem of 1866, 'The Dream of Gerontius',

> ...I hear a singing: yet in sooth
> I cannot of that music rightly say
> Whether I hear, or touch, or taste the tones.

Newman was almost certainly not thinking of infancy when he wrote these lines, indeed Gerontius was in transition between this world and the next when he had this experience. However, the description parallels a current argument about the nature of infant perception. According to Bower (1989), young infants pick up the very general properties of stimulation, so general that they cannot distinguish the perceptual channel through which they arise.

Auditory-visual coordination

As we saw in the previous section, under the proper conditions newborns make head or eye movements towards the source of a sound. This response is not always easy to elicit, but its occurrence under some stimulus conditions indicates at least a limited ability to locate a sound in space. However, could it indicate more? Harris (1983) interprets orientation towards a sound as evidence of cross-modal integration, at least in terms of a reflex link-up between sensory systems. At this level, a sound triggers the visual orienting mechanism, and it is not necessary to assume that the infant expects to see something as a result. Of course, it is possible that a higher level of coordination is involved, in which the infant actually turns in order to locate the object that made the sound. But Harris argues that there is little indication that infants are operating at this higher level, giving as evidence the fact that eye movements to sound can be obtained in darkness (Mendelson and Haith, 1976) and even when the baby's eyes are closed (Turkewitz et al., 1966). In these cases, there is no chance of the infant's seeing anything, and certainly an absence of orienting movements in the dark would have been stronger evidence for the notion that the movement was a real attempt to locate an audiovisual stimulus. However, it is still possible to argue that we are seeing the persistence under dark conditions of a response that is normally geared to stimulus detection.

In contrast to Harris, Butterworth (1983) takes the view that there is a fundamental unity of senses at birth. He claims 'the innate relation between eye and ear is not simply a reflexive motor coordination . . . vision and audition interact right from birth'. He bases this claim on the results of the study by Castillo and Butterworth (1981) mentioned briefly in the previous section. They found no evidence for orientation to a sound when there were no stimuli in the visual field, but found significant orientation to the sound when there was a visible pattern (two red dots) at the locus of the sound. This could simply have been a matter of infants fixating the only stimulus in the field, since if the visual stimulus was presented to the opposite side from the sound, infants turned to the visual stimulus rather than to the sound. However, Castillo and Butterworth performed a second experiment in which there were two visual stimuli to left and right of the infant, with the sound coming from only one. In this case, infants oriented predominantly to the stimulus from whence the sound came, clearer evidence that the sound guided their looking.

In summary, the results in this area are not clear cut. Visual orientation to a sound can happen in some cases even if there is no visual pattern at the locus of the sound. Under other conditions of testing, orientation only takes place when there is something to be seen at the locus. One possibility is that there is additivity between visual and auditory cues. An auditory cue presented alone may be a fairly weak stimulus for orienting, whereas if both an auditory and a visual cue are presented, they may add together to provide a strong stimulus. If there is intersensory coordination, then cue additivity of this sort is possible.

Another method of investigating cross-modal integration is to see whether infants note a spatial disparity between auditory and visual stimuli that in real life come from the same source. Aronson and Rosenbloom (1971) did this by using the infant's mother as the visual stimulus, and her voice as the auditory stimulus. Month-old infants viewed mothers through a window in front of them, and in the first condition they heard her voice through two speakers to left and right. This arrangement was intended to result in infants hearing the sound as if it came from in front. In the second condition, the voice came from only one speaker, and so there was a mismatch between the locations of visual and auditory events. Aronson and

Rosenbloom found that infants showed increased mouthing of the tongue in this second condition, taking this as indication of distress at the dislocation between the mother's face and voice.

Unfortunately, however, this study is flawed in a number of ways. As McGurk and Lewis (1974) point out, the major problem is that the *dislocation* condition always occurred second, so it is possible that the increased distress was simply due to fatigue or a gradual build up of anxiety about the test setting. But this apart, it can be questioned whether mouthing can safely be taken as an index of distress in the first place. McGurk and Lewis controlled for these and other problems and, testing one-, four- and seven-month-olds, found no evidence for increased distress in the *dislocation* condition. Four- and seven-month-olds did show significant turning towards the auditory stimulus in this condition, but this could simply have been an auditory orientation response of the sort discussed earlier. Condry, Haltom and Neisser (1977) also failed to find distress at audiovisual discrepancy in one- and four-month-olds.

Of course, it is possible that infants note the spatial discrepancy, but are not distressed by it. This means that we really have to look for other measures of cross-modal integration. When a person talks, apart from expecting the sound to come from the person, we expect there to be synchrony between facial movements and voice. You only have to watch a film in which the sound is out of synchrony to appreciate that adults are quite sensitive to this match. We also expect the voice to be that of the person in front of us rather than someone else's. These two types of audiovisual match are rather different. In the former case, there is a necessary relationship between auditory and visual patterns; without previous experience one is predictable from the other. In the latter case, however, we cannot predict the voice of a stranger from their visual appearance, except to the extent that we expect a male voice from a male person. So within quite wide limits a voice could vary without us perceiving a mismatch. If intersensory coordination is present at birth, we would expect the first type of mismatch to be detected very early. However, our prediction about the second would depend very much on the amount of experience needed to build up a learned audiovisual association.

Spelke (1976, 1979, 1981) performed a series of studies, mainly using inanimate stimuli, to investigate infants' sensitivity to audiovisual synchrony. One of her techniques was to present simultaneously two films of different rhythmic movements and to play a sound-track in synchrony with one but not the other. Her general finding was that four-month-olds looked more at the film that was in synchrony with the sound-track, suggesting that by at least four months, infants are very sensitive to this sort of audiovisual match. Additionally, Bahrick (1988) found similar effects with three-month-olds, provided they were given sufficient prior experience with the events. Positive evidence of this sort has not appeared in all studies, however. For instance, Lewkowicz (1985) presented four-month-olds with two stimuli flashing at different rates and a sound that co-occurred with one, but found no evidence of preference for the co-occurring visual stimulus. Lewkowicz (1992) did, however, obtain positive results when infants were presented with a sound in synchrony with one of two moving stimuli that moved at the same rate but were out of phase. These results suggest that four-month-olds only respond to audiovisual synchrony when only synchrony and not other features such as rate differentiate the visual choice stimuli. However, we must always be cautious about the generality of findings arising from studies in which relatively arbitrary correspondences are established between stimuli such as the infant is unlikely to encounter in everyday life. It may well be that audiovisual correspondence effects can be shown to occur with complex stimuli provided the correspondence is not arbitrary and occurs in real life. In support of this supposition, Bahrick (1992) found that while three-month-olds responded to natural auditory-visual synchrony (such as the case of the sound arising from a ball bouncing) they did not respond to arbitrary auditory-visual relationships.

One obvious case of natural auditory-visual matching is face–voice synchrony. In this case, both the auditory and visual stimulus are extremely complex. However, Dodd (1979) found that infants looked more at a face in front of them when a sound-track was in synchrony with facial movements than when it was out of synchrony. This effect appeared in infants as young as ten weeks. Also, Spelke and Cortelyou (1981) found that when four-month-olds were presented with a pair of speaking faces, they looked more at the one that moved in time to the sound track.

These last two studies do not show what it is that infants are using as the basis of their audiovisual match, although it seems quite likely that they are matching the rhythms in the way they do with inanimate stimuli. However, Kuhl and Meltzoff (1982) have shown that five-month-olds are capable of making an audiovisual match at the level of specific speech sounds. Infants presented with two silent faces forming different vowel sounds looked more at the face that matched the sound that they heard over a loudspeaker. This suggests a very high level of sophistication in intermodal perception. Furthermore, Legerstee (1990) has shown that three- and four-month-olds function at this level of matching in their imitative behaviour. Infants were exposed to one of two vowel sounds, /a/ or /o/, while seeing an adult produce either the matching or the other sound. Evidence of vocal imitation of these sounds was shown only by infants who had been exposed to matching auditory and visual information.

As noted already, we might expect the association of a particular voice with a particular person to be a later acquisition, since it depends on some experience of the person in question. But, given what we know about auditory input before birth, it is possible that the infant might learn his or her mother's voice even before birth. Cohen (1974) suggests, however, that this ability does emerge relatively late. She had the mother and a female stranger sit side by side in front of the infant, and one or other of the mime to a sound-track, either of their own voice (match condition) or the other's voice (mismatch condition). Five-month-old infants did not respond differently in the two conditions, whereas eight-month-olds did, showing shorter initial fixations and also tending to look away from the sound source in the mismatch condition. In contrast, Spelke and Owsley (1979) provided evidence that younger infants had some ability of this sort. Infants of three, five and seven months faced mother and father side by side and heard the voice of one or other presented centrally. Even the youngest infants looked earlier and longer at the person whose voice was presented at the time. But this finding did not emerge when the mother was paired with an unfamiliar female. It is possible that the large visual and auditory differences intro-duced by using a male and female pairing may have made a matching simpler in this case, and that more detailed matches allowing detection of face–voice disparity within the same sex may take longer to develop.

In summary, there is evidence for several types of audiovisual matching in infancy. Some form of matching in terms of stimulus location appears to take place very early, probably at birth. Matching in terms of temporal patterning appears at four months in the case of inanimate objects, and would appear to occur even earlier in the case of face–voice matching. At this age infants also appear to be able to make audiovisual matches at the level of specific speech sounds. Finally, learned person–voice associations seem to appear at about eight months, and may appear a good deal earlier although maybe in less precise form.

Coordination of vision and touch

One finding with apparent implications for coordination of touch and vision was mentioned briefly in chapter 2. Bower, Broughton and Moore (1970) found that newborn babies were upset when they failed to make tactual contact with something that looked like an object, but which was in fact a binocularly presented image that created the illusion of three dimensions. As well as telling us something about visually guided reaching and object perception, this result appears to indicate that infants expect a seen object to be tangible, a basic form of intermodal perception. However, as already noted, this finding has not been easy to replicate with young infants. While Field (1977) replicated Bower's result with seven-month-olds, he found no evidence that infants of three or five months detected an anomaly in failing to contact a virtual object. It is hard to reach a clear conclusion about the age of onset of this response, particularly when we remember the tempor-ary suppression of reaching that occurs between four and twenty weeks. So much depends upon whether others replicate Bower's result in the future.

Bryant and co-workers (1972) adopted a more direct approach. They were interested in whether infants could make a match between the tactual and visual features of an object, the rationale being that if infants were

capable of cross-modal matching, they should continue to show a preference for an object presented to vision that they had hitherto only touched.
They endeavoured to ensure a preference for the initial object by having it
emit a sound. While it was sounding, infants were allowed to explore it
tactually, but were not permitted to see it. Then the tactually familiarized
object was presented paired with an object of different shape, and they
measured which the infant picked up. The infants in this study were
between six and 12 months old, and Bryant et al. (1972) found that from
eight months onwards, infants consistently chose the tactually familiarized
object.

Rose, Gottfried and Bridger (1983) confirmed this result using the
habituation–novelty method with 12-month-olds. The key condition was
one in which infants were habituated to one object tactually and were then
tested for preferential looking on visual presentation of the habituated
object and a novel one. Infants showed significant novelty preferences,
despite the fact that they had seen neither object before, good evidence for
cross-modal transfer. In addition, Rose's team (1983) showed that if the
tactual habituation period was extended, infants even showed visual novelty
preferences when presented with pictures or line drawings of the habituated and novel object. This extended finding indicates how crucial it is to get
the methodology right. It may be particularly important to give extended
tactual familiarization if we are to see the full extent of cross-modal
transfer, particularly since tactual habituation appears to be a slower
process than visual habituation (Streri and Pecheux, 1986).

Refinements in technique have led to evidence of tactuo–visual transfer
in quite young infants. For instance, Streri (1987) obtained evidence of
transfer by two- to three-month-old infants. However, it turned out that this
only worked in one direction; infants showed transfer from touch to vision
but not vice versa. In addition, recent research has obtained evidence of
transfer of relatively high level perceptual information. Pineau and Streri
(1990) showed that four- to five-month-olds were capable of discriminating
tactually between objects that differed only in terms of the spatial arrangement of three features and also that they transferred this spatial arrangement
information from touch to vision. It also appears that infants are capable
of transferring from touch to vision information about the physical properties an object. Gibson and Walker (1984) tactually familiarized 12-month-
old infants with either a hard or a soft object and found that they showed
a looking preference for the object familiarized when presented visually.
Note here that the looking preference is the opposite of the normal
preference for the novel object. This sort of reverse preference effect is
common in cross-modal transfer studies, and Walker-Andrews and Gibson
(1986) suggest it arises because infants recognize the object as the same
but at the same time different in terms of the sensory medium. Thus,
preference for the familiar object is due to an interest in this similar yet
different percept.

These techniques work well with infants as soon as they are old enc
to manipulate objects. However, although Rochat (1987) found evid
that newborns applied different types of pressure to soft versus hard objects
(see chapter 2), there is less likelihood that newborns will be able to extract
shape·detail through touch. But we know that from birth infants transfer
objects to the mouth. This led Meltzoff and Borton (1979) to present objects
orally. They constructed two dummies of markedly different shape (see
figure 3.15), and two larger scale replicas for visual presentation. Infants
were familiarized with one of the shapes by being allowed to suck it, and
then were presented visually with the large scale replicas of both stimuli.
Infants only one month old showed clear preferential looking towards
the object that they had just explored orally, and Meltzoff and Borton
conclude that intermodal matching is well established at this age, favouring
the notion that there is an innate unity of the senses.

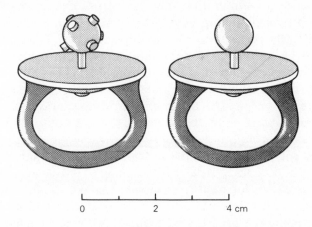

Figure 3.15 Stimuli used by Meltzoff and Borton (1979). Newborns were tactually
familiarized with one of the shapes in dummy form, and were tested for preferential
looking with larger versions of both stimuli. Reprinted by permission from *Nature*,
282, 403–4, Copyright © 1979 Macmillan Magazines Limited.

This is a fascinating result. However it has turned out to be somewhat
contentious. While some workers (Pêcheux, Lepecq and Salzarulo, 1988;
Walker-Andrews and Gibson, 1986) have replicated the general effect,
others (for instance, Brown and Gottfried, 1986) have not. It is, however,
notoriously easy to obtain negative results from very young infants, so it
seems reasonable at this stage to accept that cross-modal transfer occurs at
least as early as one month.

Summary

There is a body of evidence suggesting that both audiovisual and tactuo–
visual coordination are present early, certainly by the middle of the first

year. In addition, some studies suggest that this coordination is present very much earlier, probably from birth. But because of the difficulties involved in studying such abilities in newborns, there is a scarcity of data at that age, and such as there is has not always proved easy to replicate. However, intermodal perception is a key issue with implications in a number of areas of infancy. Apart from its general importance within some theories of perceptual development (discussed in the following section), recent accounts have linked it intimately with imitation (Meltzoff and Moore, 1985), and with language acquisition (Sullivan and Horowitz, 1983). As a result, the topic will re-emerge in chapters 4 and 5.

Before leaving this section it is worth returning to Bower's view of the nature of early perception. His claim, outlined at the beginning of the section, is that newborns do not initially distinguish between information in terms of the modality in which it is delivered, responding instead to abstract properties of stimulation that cut across modalities. For example, infants pick up information specifying the positions of events in the world, but do not identify these events as auditory or visual. According to this view, if we devised a means of providing an auditory equivalent of visual perception, the prediction is that infants would be able to use this information in much the same way as visual information. In other words, they would be able to 'see' in the dark, or more importantly, a form of sight would be given to blind children. Bower (1977b; Aitken and Bower, 1982) has achieved this through a device based on the sonar principle. This *sonic guide* analyses spatial information and transforms it into auditory patterns, and the claim is that congenitally blind children provided with the guide show impressive developmental progress. Instead of finding the usual caution in exploring the world and lags in cognitive and language skills, these infants apparently progress normally, if not precociously. It is particularly gratifying when a theory throws up such an important application (only too rare an event), and although the sonic guide work does not give direct evidence for intersensory coordination, it is hard to see how infants could learn to perceive the world through a new sense unless their perceptual system was at least extremely flexible about the modality through which information arrives.

Mechanisms underlying early perception

This chapter started at the level of basic visual capacities such as acuity and has worked progressively towards more complex perceptual capacities such as perception of the third dimension and cross-modal perception. The existence of all these different levels of inquiry makes it quite difficult to obtain an overall view of what is happening in perceptual development, or to provide a single theoretical framework that ties everything together. However, in this section I shall give a brief resumé of some pieces of theorizing that may be useful in putting together a picture of the mechanisms underlying early perception and its development.

Low level measures of perception such as acuity and accommodation are quite well explained in neurophysiological terms. For instance, the poor acuity of early infant vision seems most simply explained by the low density of receptors (cones) in the foveal (central) region of the retina (Banks and Salapatek, 1983). Again, when we reach the level of pattern preferences, particularly in early infancy, neurally based theories may be appropriate. As we have seen, one particularly promising argument is that preferential looking is a matter of the infant attending to pattern detail that provides the best ·stimulation for the visual system. As Banks and Ginsburg (1985) put it, 'young infants' looking behavior reflects a fixation strategy that tends to expose the central retina to quite visible pattern information in order to provide the stimulation required for normal cortical development'. These authors claim that if we take account of the resolving power of the infant's visual system we can predict both the type of figure preferred at different ages and the tendency for infants to fixate the edges of patterns. We also saw how this account could be employed as a useful modification of Bronson's (1974) neurophysiologically based model of early perception. Bronson's argument is that infants' looking patterns are determined by a mature midbrain visual system that directs central vision to stimuli which the immature visual cortex can make little of. This argument relies upon the assumption that the cortex is markedly less mature than the midbrain at birth, an assumption that appears to be false. But if we put together Bronson's and Banks and Ginsburg's accounts, a useful picture may still be gained. Although the visual cortex is functional at birth, it appears to be not very well turned for precise perception, and the role of the midbrain may be to detect the sort of stimuli that provide optimum stimulation for the cortical system and bring them to central vision.

As we progressed to more complex findings and issues, however, these models lost their explanatory power. Neither, for instance, accounts for the form perception found even in neonates. The problem is that our current knowledge of developmental neurophysiology is too scant to provide hard evidence on more complex perceptual issues. In particular, when it came to perception of the third dimension and cross-modal integration, two main theoretical issues emerged that derive largely from behavioural data and theoretical speculation rather than from known neurophysiology. First there is the issue of whether infants are born perceiving retinal images or real objects. Secondly, there is the issue of whether infants initially perceive in entirely separate modalities which they proceed to integrate, or whether they are born with a system that is so integrated that development involves differentiating between separate modalities of input. In these instances, interpretation of behavioural data may feed speculation about developing brain function, but it may be some time before neurophysiological knowledge advances far enough to provide a hard explanatory basis for the experimental findings.

These last two issues come together within J. J. Gibson's theory of direct perception, a theory that, while not directed specifically to developmental issues, has important implications for infant perception. Gibson's basic claim (1979) is that perception is not a matter of constructing a three-dimensional reality from the retinal image, either in development or in the perceptual acts of adults. The structure of the environment is 'out there' to be picked up, and perception is a matter of picking up invariant properties of space and objects. Bower (1982) has done much to put this theory to work on issues in infant perception, and there appear to be two implications here for development. First, since there is no need to construct space or objects from images, the infant perceives a three-dimensional world from birth. Secondly, the invariants that are picked up are 'amodal', that is, they are so general that they cross boundaries between modalities. Hence, intermodal integration is assumed from birth, or as it is probably better to think of it, there is a lack of differentiation between modalities at birth. From this viewpoint, newborns perceive very general abstract properties of the world, and development is a matter of proceeding from the general to the specific, both in terms of differentiation between modalities and differentiation of lower level distinctions within modalities.

All this seems a world removed from explanations based on neural mechanisms. Indeed, Gibson saw no point in considering the neural mechanisms underlying perception. However, there may still be links to be made. First, it may be that the poor acuity of the infant's visual system actually makes it easier to extract the general abstract properties of space through filtering out fine pattern distinctions that are so evident to the adult. However, this sort of notion needs to be tied down much more tightly before it can be assessed. For instance, we need to know more about the structure of these abstract properties of space to which Bower refers.

A second link may be made through another suggestion that has been raised about the midbrain visual system. It appears that in the deeper layers of the superior colliculus there are cells that respond not only to visual stimulation, but to auditory and tactual information as well (Gordon, 1972). Furthermore, there appears to be accurate intersensory mapping involved. A cell that responds only to stimulation from one locus in the visual field also responds only to auditory stimulation in the same region of auditory space, and the same can be shown between touch and vision. This at least raises the possibility that a neural mechanism exists at midbrain level which could support an amodal perceptual system. If development is more a matter of differentiation than integration, this differentiation may be part of the process occurring as the cortical sensory areas develop, not just through maturation, but through the stimulation arising from perceptual input. Again, however, this issue is currently a matter of speculation, since we know relatively little about the processes involved in cortical 'take-over'.

One final point needs to be made about the developmental process. Bower notes how infants seem to progress towards an excessive separation of experience into different modalities, and if vision were to become entirely differentiated from hearing and touch, there would then be a need for a positive reintegration, otherwise cross-modal perception would not be possible. Future research may clarify whether this indeed happens and give us information about the processes involved, maybe even providing links with neural mechanisms, but currently we are largely in the dark on this issue. Nevertheless, this is an appropriate point on which to end this chapter, since it provides a bridge to the next. Theories of cognitive development in infancy are heavily influenced by Piaget and, as we shall see, for him differentiation and integration were also crucial processes in the development of intelligence.

4

Cognitive development: Piaget and infancy

As I indicated at the beginning of chapter 3, the term *cognition* is generally used to denote psychological functions that in one way or another go beyond perception. Conventionally, there are two important respects in which this is true. First, there is the notion that perceptual information has to be interpreted in order to make sense. Take, for instance, the visual cliff studies discussed in chapter 3. The conclusion there was that quite young infants discriminated between the deep and shallow sides of the apparatus, but that only the older ones appeared to understand the danger of a large vertical drop. In this case, we can ask whether this understanding comes as a result of better tuned perceptual processes, or with the development of mental structures that *interpret* the perceptual information. In other words, is it the product of perceptual development or of cognitive development? The conventional view would favour the latter alternative; perception may provide the basis for discrimination along dimensions such as stimulus distance, but it is a discrimination that remains meaningless before the development of appropriate interpreting structures.

Secondly, there is the claim that cognition involves processes of *mental representation* that can operate in the absence of relevant perceptual input. Conventionally, perception is supposed to deal only with the here and now, so any activity involving objects or events that are absent to the senses must involve some form of mental representation. So, in addition to identifying a role for cognitive structures in the interpretation of perceptual input, cognitive representational structures are also seen as a necessary basis for activities not directly linked to what can be perceived at the time.

The field of infant cognitive development is still heavily influenced in one way or another by the findings and theorizing of Jean Piaget. Some time after publication of English translations of his work on sensori-motor intelligence (Piaget, 1952, 1954), there followed a substantial body of research aimed at testing some of the phenomena he noted, or extending various aspects of his theory, with most emphasis on his claims about the development of object permanence. But saying that Piaget's work is influential is not to say that his theory is generally accepted. Although many of the basic phenomena on which he based his arguments have been confirmed in subsequent experimental tests, there are many workers who interpret these findings in other ways, fitting them into quite different models of cognitive development. Part of the continuing strength of Piaget's theory, however, is its grand scale. Although other workers have produced alternative theories to explain the development of specific knowledge, such as object permanence, none has yet produced an account that spans such a range of infant ability, and such a range of age. A second reason for the durability of Piagetian work is the richness of his observations of infant behaviour. A number of the phenomena that he noted are still the focus of investigation today.

Interpretation and representation are both central aspects of Piaget's theory. His aim is to account for the development of *knowledge* of the world in infancy, and so the theory is about the processes by which infants *interpret* perception rather than about perception itself. The infant is seen as constructing progressively more complex cognitive action-based structures through operating on the world, and the end point of this construction process is marked by the emergence of mental activity divorced from action, in other words, representational activity. By the end of the sensorimotor stage the infant is capable of interpreting perception so as to reach an objective view of the world, and can go beyond perception to represent the world mentally.

In short, the theory describes the development of knowledge structures that become progressively less tied to the infant's actions and percepts. In this sense, Piaget's aims were very different from those of workers studying infant perception. However, as we have already seen in chapter 3, some contemporary theorists, notably J. J. Gibson (1979), have argued that there is no need to look for the development of cognitive structures to interpret perception, since perception itself provides objective information about the world. There is an obvious tension here between these opposing accounts; it is a fundamental disagreement that will surface repeatedly in this chapter.

Being largely an evaluation and extension of Piaget's thinking on infancy, this chapter is more focused and specialized than earlier ones. As a result, rather fewer studies will be discussed, but these will be covered in more detail. This strategy is partly dictated by the focused nature of research in cognitive development, and partly by the importance of rigorous interpretation of data in this area. While many of the advances in understanding of infant perception have arisen through sheer accumulation of evidence about infants' abilities, progress in understanding cognitive development has arisen more through testing the alternative interpretations that almost always arise from any one phenomenon. This is not surprising given that there is a greater interpretative component involved in explaining behaviours than in establishing whether or not they exist.

Piaget's sensori-motor theory

The middle-ground position of Piaget's theory with respect to the nature–nurture issue was outlined in chapter 1. On this view the infant is born with no intellectual structure as such, but is capable of acting on the world in quite specific ways, which in Piaget's view, ensure progressive adaptation to the world. The infant's acts are initially limited to a set of reflexes, but an *adaptation* process ensures that through their use these are gradually altered and then combined to form more complex acquired activities. But the account is far from being a simple theory of motor development; the sensori-motor structures that are constructed in this way are the basis for intelligence, ultimately becoming divorced from action in the form of mental representations.

First, we need to define our terms. There are two components of adaptation, *assimilation* and *accommodation*. These are universal modes of functioning that operate to modify sensori-motor structures, which Piaget calls *schemes*.* Initially, these schemes are no more than innate reflexes, but through the processes of assimilation and accommodation, they are modified and later inter-coordinated to provide underlying patterns for action more adapted to the world.

The processes of assimilation and accommodation are best explained through an example. Take an infant a few months old who is used to reaching for certain objects. This infant has developed a sensori-motor scheme for reaching out and grasping which he or she will attempt to exercise in as many circumstances as possible. Hence, if we present a new object within reach it is likely that the infant will reach out and attempt to grasp it. This attempt to generalize an action to a new object is *assimilation*; the infant is attempting to assimilate the new object to the grasping scheme. However, let us say that the object is much larger than objects previously acted on in this way. If the fingers are not opened wide enough, the grasp attempt will be unsuccessful. Hence, every new object presents a degree of resistance to straightforward assimilation, and it is necessary to alter the act to meet this resistance. If this alteration leads to successful grasping two things will have happened. The new object will have been assimilated to the scheme, and the scheme will also have been altered through the addition of the variation applicable to that particular object. This alteration is *accommodation*. As more and more objects are encountered the scheme becomes progressively generalized in its application. But in the process, it becomes progressively more complex through incorporation of

*In translations of the infancy work *scheme* appears as *schema* (plural *schemata*). However, in his later work Piaget distinguished between sensori-motor schemes and figurative schemata of the later period of concrete operations, so *scheme* is now more commonly used with reference to infancy.

the variations required to meet the properties of different objects. Thus, assimilation and accommodation are complementary processes that occur hand-in-hand. Assimilation is the incorporation of a new object or event within an existing scheme, and accommodation is the modification of the scheme that is required if assimilation is to result.

The important thing to keep in sight is that the scheme is the basis of sensori-motor intelligence. When an object or event is assimilated to a scheme it acquires meaning in relation to the infant's actions. Going back to the example above, the infant is progressively constructing a sensori-motor category or concept of 'graspable objects', incorporating both their similarity (graspability) and the differences between them (e.g. size) that demand alterations to the act. Furthermore, Piaget states that we can see both these processes of generalization and discrimination in the infant's use of the same scheme at different times. For instance, when an infant is content and recently fed she will suck as many objects as come in contact with her face or mouth, the process of generalization in operation. However, when she is hungry, she will suck only from the bottle or breast, discriminating between those and other suckable but unrewarding objects.

According to Piaget, it is through these processes that infants construct increasingly elaborate structures for interpreting sensory input. However, as we shall see, these interpretations are initially in terms of the meanings of particular sensations within the context of the infant's actions. It is only very gradually that infants come to interpret sensations as arising from external objects independent of their own activities.

It is worth noting here why it is difficult to categorize Piaget's view on the nature of early perception (see chapter 3). Many assign to him the view that the senses are initially separate and become progressively integrated during infancy. However, for Piaget it is the sensori-motor schemes that are initially separated rather than the senses themselves. So schemes for looking, grasping and hearing are separate and require integration during development if the infant is to understand the world as we do. However, Piaget says little about the nature of the perceptual input on which the infant operates, since this is not what he is primarily concerned with. The hints that he does give, however, suggest a degree of intersensory co-ordination, since he points to the case of a young infant turning as if to see a sound, giving this as an example of how schemes are extended to incorporate as many events as possible. As he says, 'the child tries to see what he hears because each schema of assimilation seeks to encompass the whole universe' (1954, p. 8). The newborn infant encounters a chaotic series of sensory impressions, in which internal and external sources are not differentiated, let alone segregated into different modalities. Sensori-motor intelligence initially develops in the form of separate schemes that may relate primarily to input from particular senses, but the separation is in the structures that the infant builds to interpret the sensory information rather than in the sensory information itself.

Cognitive development

Piaget (1952) describes six stages in the development of sensori-motor intelligence (see table 4.1), starting with an initial stage of physical reflex activity, and ending with the onset of purely mental activities at about 18 months. He devotes a whole book to this task, and the general theory that emerges is complex and not particularly attractive to the casual reader. He creates the richest images of infancy when he applies this stage theory to explain the course of development of knowledge within specific domains (Piaget, 1954).

Table 4.1 Piaget's stages of sensori-motor development

Stage	Approximate age (months)	Level of scheme	Knowledge of the world
I	0–1	Reflexes	None
II	1–4	Primary circular reactions	Objects are images linked to infant's actions
III	4–8	Secondary circular reactions	Beginning of means–ends separation – search for partially hidden objects
IV	8–12	Coordination of schemes	Search for fully hidden objects indicates partial understanding of object as a separate entity
V	12–18	Tertiary circular reactions	Objective understanding of spatial relations but not of the invisible displacements of objects
VI	18–24	Mental representation	Ability to represent the positions and displacements of objects. Fully objective knowledge of world

The construction of space and object concepts

One of the fundamental assumptions of Piaget's theory is that babies are born in a state of extreme *solipsism*; initially they draw no distinction whatsoever between self and external world. Objects are no more than sensory impressions that are tangled up in the act of seeing them. Furthermore, the infant has no better understanding of self, 'the subject does not know himself and is absorbed into things' (1954, p. 105). From this initial state, infants gradually construct an external world separate from themselves and then finally integrate themselves within this world.

Piaget describes six stages in the development of an infant's understanding of the physical world, approaching the topic from four different angles, namely, understanding of objects, space, causality and time. These should not be thought of as separate topics, but as different ways of looking at the same developmental process. For instance, from Piaget's perspective, knowledge of space and knowledge of objects cannot be separated since, 'Space . . . is not at all perceived as a container but rather as that which it contains, that is, objects themselves . . .' (1954, p. 98). Also, initially objects are simply detected as sensations accompanying and inseperable from the infant's actions, and until a separation between object and action is drawn, there is no question of understanding causality. Finally, since causality presupposes a temporal relationship between cause and effect, understanding of time and causality are interlinked.

Here I shall describe the stage sequence mainly as it pertains to understanding of objects and space, since these are the topics that have generated most research interest. Two major but complementary issues arise in Piaget's account. With regard to object knowledge, he is concerned to trace the emergence of activity towards hidden objects as an indicator that the infant is beginning to understand the permanence of objects. With regard to spatial understanding, he is looking for evidence in infants' behaviour to indicate that they are constructing a separation between self and surrounding space, and between their own actions and object displacements. Tied up in both these issues is the concept of infantile *egocentrism*, the lack of a distinction between personal action and external events, and whichever part of Piaget's account we look at, progress in sensori-motor intelligence involves a reduction in this egocentrism through construction of an objective concept of the world.

Stages I and II

In stage I the infant's activities are limited to a number of innate reflexes such as sucking, rooting and grasping, while during stage II (one to four months) these reflexes are progressively modified through the processes of assimilation and accommodation, leading to the emergence of new behaviour patterns that were not there at birth. These behaviour patterns Piaget calls *primary circular reactions*, and although they may appear quite sophisticated, such as grasping objects and bringing them to the mouth, he argues that they are exercised for their own sake. The satisfaction is in the act rather than in the object that it may capture, and although to the observer it may be evident that the object supplies the satisfaction, the infant, unable to separate object from act, is unaware of this. During these stages, Piaget claims that infants have no concept of an external world of tangible objects. Instead, the object is just a sensation inextricably linked with the act of grasping it or seeing it. Similarly, action is seen as creating space rather than being situated in it, and the displacement of an object is confused with the act that displaced it.

On the understanding of depth, Piaget says, 'the child certainly perceives at various depths, but there is no indication that he is conscious of these depths . . .' (1954, p. 111). This makes it clear that Piaget saw understanding as something different from perception. His view was that perception is not sufficient in itself to supply objective information about the world, and his interest was in seeing how infants construct intellectual structures that transform subjective perception into objective reality.

Stage III

The major step forward in stage III is that infants begin to observe themselves acting on objects. Through this, they begin to realize that their actions produce interesting sights, and henceforth actions are repeated not just for their own sake, but for the sights they produce. In other words, with the development of these *secondary circular reactions* there is the beginning of separation between means (the action) and end (the interesting sight) and so the beginnings of understanding of casuality. Also, the correspondence recognized between manual action and visual events leads to the realization that both occur in a common external space. However, the positions and movements of objects in space are not yet interpreted other than in relation to the infant's actions, and so the separation between self and environment is only beginning.

An indication of this is the fact that stage III infants will not search for a hidden object. This is a striking phenomenon and is easily observed in infants of about six months. At this age they manipulate objects competently and will go to great lengths to obtain objects that interest them, but if a desirable object is put within their reach and covered with a cloth, they will show no attempt to find it, not even reaching out. To Piaget, this indicates that infants still have no notion of the permanence of an object. Its location in space relates to the infant's acts rather than to other objects in space. Hence, when the object is covered, the infant does not comprehend the spatial relationship between cover and object and so fails to search.

The externalization of space that results from observing actions is also limited in its extent to the realm of near space in which action takes place. Remember that infants in this stage are not generally able to crawl, so near space only extends to the length of the infant's reach. Within this region depth is coded in terms of differences in extent of reaches; beyond it there is no understanding of differences in depth. The picture emerging here is much like the naive concept of astronomical space of past history, in which the stars were thought of as if arranged on the inside of a hemisphere at a fixed distance from the earth. In the infant's case, it is as if everything beyond reach is fixed at the same distance on the outer boundary of near space. Despite this limitation, however, there is clear progress over the previous stages. Now near space is definitely external, and even far space is external by virtue of being beyond near space.

Stage IV

In stage III the infant discovered that a manual act produced an interesting visual sensation and as a result discovered by chance the relation between means and ends. In stage IV, however, means and ends are differentiated even before the act is executed. Infants in this stage begin to put together schemes that previously they had only used separately, and these coordinations are constructed in order to obtain objects that would not be obtained by one or other of the schemes on its own. Piaget argues that to form these novel coordinations the infant must have had the goal in sight from the outset; these are not random coordinations but acts combined to reach a goal. An example of such a coordination can be seen in an infant's solution of the problem of an object placed out of reach on a cloth, part of which is within reach. The stage IV infant solves this problem by first pulling the cloth so that the object is brought within reach, and then reaching out and grasping it. A second example is the fact that the infant will now search for hidden objects, by first lifting the cover and then grasping the object.

This clear differentiation of means and ends brings with it a much better understanding of the causal nature of acts. Also, the systematic temporal ordering of separate acts indicates an improved understanding of temporal sequence. But most important, searching for hidden objects indicates vital progress in the infant's understanding of objects and spatial relations. According to Piaget, the coordination of cover removal and grasping carries with it understanding of the spatial relationship between cover and object. So, whereas the stage III infant only coded object positions in relation to self (through actions), the stage IV infant has begun to relate objects to each other. From the point of view of object permanence, understanding of this relationship brings with it the knowledge that the object continues to exist even when out of sight. As Piaget puts it, 'Things are not only in front or in back, but they are in front of or behind such and such a landmark, and they continue to exist even when actual screens mask them' (1954, p. 170).

On this basis we might conclude that infants now have a mature understanding of objects and spatial relations. However, Piaget introduces a simple complication of the search task which indicates that their understanding is still only partial (see figure 4.1). Suppose we face an infant with two hiding locations side by side. In this case the infant will search successfully for the object as long as it is hidden at one place (A), but if we then take the object and, in full view of the infant, hide it in the second location (B), a surprising thing happens. The infant watches attentively as the object disappears at place B, but then searches at place A.

Piaget interprets this error as an indication that infants only understand the relationship between object and cover in relation to their action at a particular place. Through searching at the first place with two coordinated actions, they discovered the objective relationship between object and

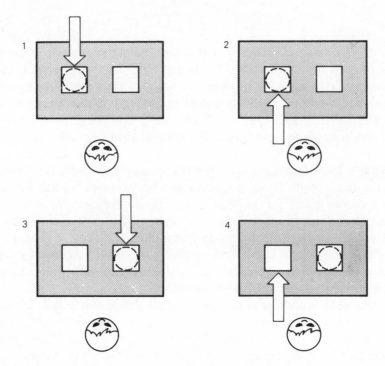

Figure 4.1 The stage IV search task. The experimenter hides the object in the first place (1) whereupon the infant searches successfully (2). But when the experimenter hides the object at the second place (3) the infant searches again at the original location (4).

cover, but this relationship is not immediately identified when it is created elsewhere. So when a new location is used, infants fall back on repeating the act that was successful before, a phenomenon that shows that the link between action and object is not yet completely broken. Again, they rely on action at the old place as if it is the only place in which the object can be conceived to exist, and for Piaget, this is clear indication that infants' concept of the surrounding world is still partly egocentric.

The first hint of mental representation can be seen in this stage, since infants now understand (represent) the object's continued existence behind the cover. Yet for Piaget this is not true representation, since it is still tied up with their activity at a particular place.

Understanding of depth also develops further in this stage, although in a fairly minor way. Due to better bodily control, infants can reach out further, and hence the zone of tactuovisual near space is progressively pushed out into regions that were hitherto far-space sampled through vision alone. But oddly enough, Piaget does not mention the onset of crawling as a factor likely to extend this process, despite the fact that most infants begin to crawl around this time.

Stage V

In all the preceding stages development has occurred as a result of assimilation of new information to existing schemes, and accommodation has taken place in these schemes to the extent that the environment forced it. In other words, the infant has been essentially conservative, attempting to fit new experiences into existing structures. From this stage on, however, infants become interested in novelty itself and engage in active experimentation as a means of developing new solutions to problems. In a way, they have taken a step 'outside' activity to see how activities work and to develop new activities that will have desired outcomes. Piaget calls these forms of experimentation *tertiary circular reactions*.

This interest in novelty means that when faced with new events infants will not simply attempt the old solution. Instead, when faced with the two-position object search task, they change their solution when the object is moved, now searching accurately wherever the object is hidden. This indicates that the object concept is now almost fully formed; infants understand the continued existence of objects wherever they are hidden. Looking at this from the spatial point of view, the implication is that infants now view space in an objective manner. The positions of objects relative to each other can be represented, as well as perceived, independently of infants' activities.

But they are not home and dry yet. First, Piaget claims that infants still do not understand their own equivalent status as objects in space. They have constructed an objective space, but have not yet distanced themselves from their own view of it to see themselves as objects like any other. Secondly, with his usual ingenuity, Piaget devised a more complex search task to test the infant further (figure 4.2). This time, the infant is shown an object which is then put in a container. The container is then moved to a new location and put under a cloth, under cover of which the object is tipped out, and the container re-emerges empty. From the adult's view-point, the object might still be in the container, or it might be under the cover, but infants at the beginning of this stage only search where they saw the object disappear, that is, in the container. Failure there does not lead them to try the cover until later on in this stage, and Piaget argues that, even then, this solution is acquired through trial and error rather than through insight. His evidence for this is that if the same procedure is followed using a second cover, infants search at the original cover. In other words, the stage IV error re-emerges when the task is complicated by the addition of an invisible displacement. He concludes that although infants are capable of understanding the spatial relations between objects to the extent that they can represent invisible relationships, they can only do this in the case of static relationships, being unable to represent the movements of an object if these are not visible.

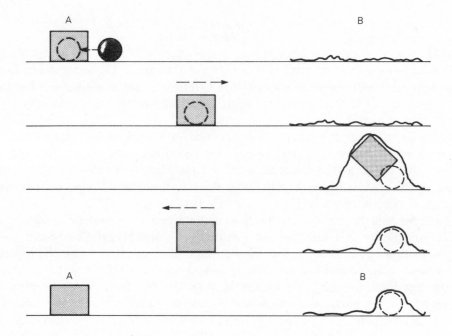

Figure 4.2 The stage V invisible displacement task. The object is hidden in a container. The container is moved under a cover and the object is tipped out there. Then the empty container is moved back to its original location.

Stage VI

This stage marks the onset of mental processes that are completely independent of overt action. The infant no longer has to actually try out new methods, but can predict the outcome of particular actions in advance. An example of this can be seen in spatial problem-solving. Piaget observed infants of this age making quite elaborate detours to reach objects, and he claims that these detours are not established by trial and error, but are worked out mentally in advance of action. In so doing, the infant is imagining his own displacements 'as if he saw them from outside' (1954, p. 204), and thus finally becomes capable of escaping the last vestiges of egocentrism to locate himself in space like any other object.

Stage VI infants also have the ability to form mental representations of the invisible movements of objects, solving the tasks at which stage V infants failed. And although the beginnings of representation can be traced back to stage IV, Piaget only really accepts this final form as true representation. Going back to the example of search at stage IV, he points out that the infant sees the relation between object and occluder being created as the object goes out of sight, and that once it is out of sight, the cover can act as a 'sign for the actual presence of the object' (1954, p. 85). In contrast, in the case of invisible displacements there is no such direct sign to the presence of the object after its displacement. So, although Piaget accepts that the stage IV infant understands the continued existence of objects, this understanding is limited to a particular context, and is bolstered by the presence of the cover as a sign for the object. In contrast, the fully developed representational ability of stage VI allows imagination of the absent object even when nothing directly cues its presence.

Key issues and some question marks

Piaget's theory is lengthy and complex, but several key issues can be extracted. First of all, there is his assertion that representation is a mental activity that grows out of sensori-motor activity, as a result of the exercise of that activity itself. Secondly, there is the notion of infant egocentrism, at birth taking the form of a complete failure to distinguish between self and world, and later appearing in the way infants relate objects to their own actions rather than to other objects in space. Piaget puts this another way in saying that there is a gradual shift from subjective understanding to objective understanding, the final step involving infants getting sufficiently outside self to place themselves within a common space along with other objects.

In addition, implicit in all these points is the very strong link between action on the world and awareness of the world, Piaget's claim being that these are really one and the same thing in early infancy. The reader may be rightly wary of such a claim, given the evidence on young infants' perception of objective properties of the world, reviewed in chapter 3. With this evidence in mind, we should entertain the possibility that Piaget's observations tell us more about infants' developing ability to act on the world than their developing awareness or perception of it. Young infants may perceive the world in an objective manner without having learned to act appropriately on the basis of this perception, a view that we shall be returning to later in this chapter.

Here it is worth contrasting Piaget's account with Bruner's view of the developmental process (1973). According to Bruner, infants are born with considerably more perceptual and motor preadapation than Piaget would allow, a state of affairs that is not immediately evident because the infant has yet to fit together the preadapted components of action so that they are effective. For example, although young infants will make grasping movements adapted to the size of an object, these do not result in capture of the object, since they are not coordinated with reaching (Bruner and Koslowski, 1972). Only once behavioural components are fitted together in the correct serial order do these preadaptations become effective. While Bruner agrees with Piaget in identifying the roots of representation in activity, he appears to assign more of the young infant's limitations to a lack of coordinated skill than a lack of awareness of the world.

Much recent work has been aimed at specific Piagetian phenomena rather than at the general principles of his theory. Of all Piaget's observations, it is probably the object search examples that he uses most to make his case. Piaget saw the onset of search for objects as crucially important since it marked the beginning of intelligent activity proper, and the beginnings of a properly objective understanding of the world. Consequently, it is maybe not surprising that the bulk of work stimulated by his writings has concentrated on investigating the development of object permanence.

Recent studies of infants' knowledge of objects

Studies of object permanence can be divided into two broad groups. Some workers have identified alternative interpretations of some of Piaget's observations, and this has led to further experimental analysis of basic Piagetian phenomena, in particular the stage IV search error. Other workers, through their radical disagreement with Piagetian theory, have been motivated to develop new experimental methods for testing the infant's understanding of objects and events. As long as we accept the notion that knowledge is constructed through action, then Piaget's methods of testing for understanding of object knowledge are reasonable. However, as soon as we begin to entertain the possibility that knowledge of permanence is either innate or develops independently of action, Piaget's methods begin to appear less adequate, since they are not particularly well adapted to the young infant's limited manipulative skills. To test for understanding of permanence in young infants, we need measures of object knowledge that do not rely on coordinated manual action by the infant.

In the following sections recent data on object knowledge are reviewed, starting with innovative work with young infants pioneered by Bower and his colleagues, then moving on to look at some more recent work that bears similarities to Bower's approach, and finally returning to the basic object search phenomena to see how current evidence has modified our interpretation there.

Bower's research: violation of expectancy and object tracking as measures of object knowledge

If young infants have knowledge of object permanence we would expect them to be surprised if objects disappeared in a mysterious manner. In contrast, if Piaget is correct and young infants see the object as 'a mere image which re-enters the void as soon as it vanishes, and emerges from it for no objective reason' (1954, p. 11), mysterious disappearance and reappearance is the rule and should not provoke surprise.

Bower (1982) reports a study that tackles this issue. Infants as young as 20 days were shown an object, which was then gradually occluded by a screen moving in front of it. After a variable delay, the screen was moved aside again, in one condition revealing the object again, and in another

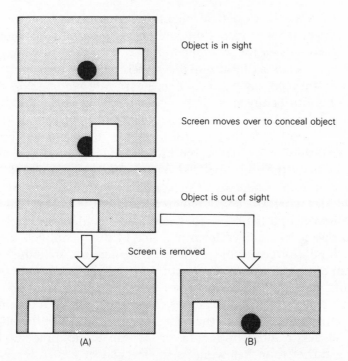

Object is in sight

Screen moves over to conceal object

Object is out of sight

Screen is removed

(A)   (B)

Figure 4.3 Bower's test (1966) for object performance in young infants. An object is hidden by a screen. After a delay it is moved back either to reveal the object (B) or to reveal an empty space where the object once was (A). From *Development in Infancy*, 2nd edn., by T. G. R. Bower. Copyright 1974, 1982 W. H. Freeman and Company. Used by permission.

revealing an empty space where the object had been (figure 4.3). Even the youngest infants showed surprise (indicated by heart rate change) in the second condition, the one qualification being that this reaction only occurred with very young infants if the occlusion period was quite short. Can we explain this result in any other way than by concluding a knowledge of permanence in young infants? Could it be that we only need to posit a perceptual mechanism that detects the presence of an object in a particular place and notes a violation of normal rules if the object disappears without having been seen to move away. But note that the object disappears when the screen moves in front of it, but the surprise comes when the screen is drawn back. If we are dealing with a perceptual mechanism, it is a fairly sophisticated one that distinguishes between lawful disappearances (occlusions) and unlawful ones. This comes very close to perception of permanence.

In fact, Bower argues much along these lines, and produces further evidence from infants' reactions to different types of disappearance in support of a perceptual basis for object permanence (Bower, 1967). Infants under two months were shown an object disappearing in a variety of manners. In some cases optical means were used to contrive apparently magical disappearances into thin air, either gradually or suddenly, and reactions to these cases were compared to a condition in which the object was gradually occluded by a moving screen. On the basis of a number of measures of anticipation (for instance, heart rate suppression after disappearance) infants behaved as if the object still existed after the gradual occlusion, whereas in the other cases 'out of sight' did appear to be 'out of mind'. The argument is that infants perceive this event for what it is, a gradual occlusion of a further object by a nearer one, and that this is enough to specify the continued existence of the hidden object.

If young infants understand object disappearance, we might expect similar abilities when the object moves instead of the screen. This possibility prompted Bower and his colleagues to perform a different set of studies in which an object was moved from one side of the visual field to the other, passing behind a screen at the middle of its trajectory. If infants understand this movement sequence as the continuous movement of one object, they should anticipate the re-emergence of the object from the opposite side of the screen. Bower (1982) claims that two-month-old infants make anticipatory eye movements towards the point of re-emergence of the object, movements that occur either prior to or at the same time as the object re-emerges rather than following its re-emergence.

It is tempting to take this finding as further evidence that infants see the world more or less as we do, using knowledge of permanence to fill in the gaps in perception when the object goes out of sight. But Bower, Broughton and Moore (1971) went on to conduct a series of object tracking studies that revealed a number of ways in which young infants' perception of objects seemed peculiar. In one condition, they presented infants with a series of tracking trials, in some of which the object stopped in full view. Under these circumstances we would expect tracking to stop, but young infants continued to track as if the object was still in motion. It is just possible that such a result could have arisen because infants have poor control over their eye movements, not being able to halt a movement when the object stops. However, Bower's team tested infants tracking an object moving in a circular trajectory and found that when the object stopped, tracking continued in the same controlled circular trajectory. In addition, Bower and Paterson (1973) noted that there was actually a momentary disturbance in tracking when the object stopped. It was as if infants noted the change, but then continued tracking all the same.

Bower's interpretation of these findings is that young infants have difficulties making a link between stationary and moving objects. The notion is that they understand object permanence but not object dynamics. When an object begins to move it ceases to be the same object, instead it becomes a movement sensation unlinked with its stationary self. Thus when a moving object comes to rest, the infant notes the stationary object, but does not link it with the movement sensation he or she was pursuing.

More evidence for this interpretation comes from another tracking study in which the stimulus was a toy train that went through a sequence of movements and stops. Initially, the train moved periodically between a central position and a position to one side of the infant. On these trials infants tracked the object successfully between its successive locations. However, if the train then moved off from the central position in the opposite direction to take up a position to the opposite side, infants tracked in the wrong direction as if seeking it in the usual place. Bower concludes that infants do not make a link between the stationary object and the same object in motion, so they do not realize the implications of a new movement for the future position of the object when it becomes stationary. Since there is no dynamic link between the successive locations of an object, there is no way of recognizing its identity over a movement, so the young infant is in the peculiar position of perceiving the permanence of stationary objects occluded by screens, but not doing so when the object stops or starts in full view. An object's identity is defined by its place in space or its path of movement, and changes in either of these lead to loss of identity.

Pursuing this line of investigation further, Bower, Broughton and Moore (1971) set up a tracking task in which the object was periodically exchanged for a different one behind the screen, so that infants saw one object disappear but a different one reappear. They found that young infants showed no surprise at this change, and took this as evidence that young infants do not note the features of moving objects. On the other hand, infants over six months old did show considerable surprise and disruption of looking on object-change trials, and the researchers concluded that by this age they have begun to note the features of a moving object, something that leads them to discover the single identity of stationary and mobile object.

In summary, Bower and his colleagues tell a very different story from the Piagetian one. Very young infants understand the permanence of stationary objects, but have difficulty interpreting object movement, so that objects effectively cease to exist when they move, being replaced by movement sensations. By six months, however, well before Piaget would recognize the presence of objective awareness of space and objects, they claim that infants have overcome difficulties in linking moving and stationary objects, and perceive space very much as adults do.

This account poses several problems, however. First, can tracking data be taken as evidence of *understanding* of permanence or object movement? Simply noting the violation of a consistent event sequence does not indicate that the infant understands the events concerned at a conceptual level, and certainly Piaget would have set much more stringent tests of understanding. Secondly, if six-month-old infants have such a sophisticated understanding of objects, why do they not search for them when they are covered up? As we shall see, Bower has an answer to this, but first we need to look at a third problem. This is that many other workers have either reinterpreted Bower's results, or have failed to replicate them.

If Bower's account is correct, infants must be faced by a confusing world. On the one hand, they understand the permanence of stationary objects. On the other, they must encounter many unexplained object 'annihilations', since this happens whenever objects move. Thinking along these lines, Moore and Meltzoff (1978) argue that object identity is a necessary prerequisite for object permanence. They reject the notion that young infants understand permanence and reinterpret the data gathered by Bower and his colleagues in terms of the acquisition of three successively higher levels of object identity. The first level is a sort of 'steady state' identity; an object stays the same as long as it stays in the same place or follows the same trajectory. They claim that infants under six months old in Bower's studies were operating at this level. The second level extends identity across changes in position or trajectory, so that moving and stationary objects are treated as one. They claim that this level of identity is enough to permit six-month-olds to perform as they did in Bower's work. At both of these levels, the infant recognizes the identity of an object seen at successive times, and there is no need to assume that the infant understands the actual existence of the object while it is hidden from view. Only the third level involves representation, so that an object maintains its identity when it is out of sight, and it is only once this level is reached that infants can be said to understand permanence.

Moore, Borton and Darby (1978) obtained evidence that appears to support this progression. The key condition they used to detect the third level of identity involved two screens instead of one (see figure 4.4). On normal trials an object went behind the first screen, emerged, went behind the second screen and then emerged from it. On 'violation' trials the object moved on the same trajectory, but did not appear between the screens. Their argument was that since the object's features remained the same and it stayed on the same trajectory, infants working on the second level of object identity would not detect anything amiss in the 'violation' trial. But infants who actually represented the object's trajectory while it was behind the first screen would know that it must appear between the first and the second screen. They found that this condition led to tracking disruption in nine-month-olds but not in six-month-olds, and concluded that representational object identity (object permanence) did not emerge until around nine months.

There are alternatives to this account, however. Maybe younger infants do not note the violation in the twin screen condition because they are simply not very good at taking note of more complex event sequences. Indeed there is a real possibility that many of the basic tracking phenomena can be explained in terms of different levels of event prediction. Goldberg (1976) argues that since these studies typically involve a very large number of trials, infants have time to learn an event sequence, for instance, 'movement on the left is followed by movement on the right'. Hence, anticipation of emergence is really anticipation of a repetitive event

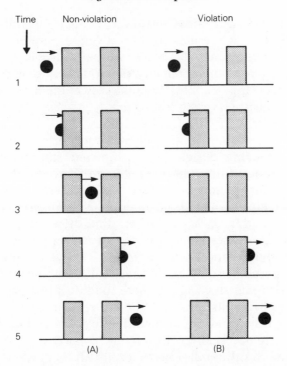

Figure 4.4 Tracking task used by Moore, Borton and Darby (1978) to test for level 3 object identity (permanence). On normal trials the object emerges between the screens as it should (A), but on violation trials it fails to emerge between the screens (B).

sequence, and there is no real indication that infants are tracking a continuous trajectory movement. Goldberg adds that by six months infants are sufficiently fussy about the type of events at the two sides of the screen to discriminate a new event (new object) on object change trials. So their surprise is not at the violation of object identity but at the violation of a consistent event sequence. There is a real worry about the degree to which infants' responses are learned at this level during the tracking trials, and this re-analysis shows that we should not be too confident about tracking performance as an indicator of permanence.

Several workers have failed to replicate a number of Bower's main findings. Muller and Aslin (1978) tested two-, four- and six-month-olds, and found that six-month-olds rarely showed tracking disruption if the object changed colour or shape behind the screen. But probably more important, they found that not even the youngest infants continued tracking when the object stopped in view. Meicler and Gratch (1980) tested five- and nine-month-olds on tracking, with test trials in which the object either stopped or changed behind the screen. They found that only the nine-month-olds anticipated emergence, and that infants seemed only mildly puzzled on 'stop' or 'change' trials. One reason for the difference between their results and those of Bower, Broughton and Moore (1971) may well be to do with the amount of tracking experience given; Bower's group typically gave around 80 trials, whereas Meicler and Gratch gave only 18. This increases the possibility that Goldberg's objection is a valid one. The more tracking 'training' infants receive, the better they should be adapted to the consistent event sequence.

In addition, evidence from visual discrimination studies casts doubt on Bower's claim that young infants do not recognize a link between the features of the moving object and itself when stationary. Hartlep and Forsyth (1977) showed that ten-week-olds transferred a visual discrimination from stationary to moving objects, and Slater, Morison, Town and Rose (1985) detected an ability of this sort even at birth. As Slater et al. (1985) point out, this does not mean that they recognize the unique identity of moving and stationary object, but it does show that Bower was wrong to claim that infants do not note the features of moving objects.

In summary, a number of workers have replicated Bower's basic findings, but have reinterpreted them along more modest lines, and some workers have failed to replicate his results. Although replication failure is always a worry, I do not think we should take the negative results as grounds for dismissing the original findings. In infancy in particular it is very easy to obtain a negative result, and positive results are often only achieved after painstaking adaptations of technique. The replication failures must, however, be borne in mind, and we badly need further work here to clarify the picture.

We would have a more convincing indication that tracking behaviour relates to object permanence if we could show a relation between it and some other measure of object permanence, and it appears that we have evidence of such a link in a study by Wishart (1979). She gave three-month-olds weekly sessions involving a number of tracking tasks in which an object entered into a number of different spatial relations with an occluder. For instance, it might pass behind a screen or through a tube in the middle of its trajectory. She then tested the infants on Piaget-style object search tasks as soon as they had begun to reach for objects. The striking finding was that these infants almost immediately succeeded in searching for a hidden object, and made few of the search errors characteristic of infants in Piaget's stage IV, all this at an age when they would not normally have started to search at all. In addition, they went on to solve search tasks involving invisible displacements much earlier than usual. This seems a convincing demonstration of a link between tracking tasks and manual search tasks, but unfortunately, in a comparable study, Simoneau and Decarie (1979) failed to find any relationship of this sort. So yet again the area is dogged by replication failures.

Summary of Bower's findings Bower and his colleagues obtained data indicating that very young infants understand the permanence of objects, but that they have difficulty linking moving and stationary objects, and further data suggested that by six months they have overcome this problem to understand object identity as well as permanence. Other workers, however, have either reinterpreted these data in ways that make more modest claims about the young infant's ability, or have failed to replicate the basic findings. Wishart has shown a relationship between tracking tasks and Piagetian object permanence tasks, but again there has been a failure to replicate this finding. It seems likely that there is some link between object tracking tasks and permanence, and the suggestion that young infants take in information about spatial relationships from these tasks to use it to good effect in object search at a later date raises the possibility that Piaget underestimated their ability to benefit from perceptual experience. But it remains to be seen whether tracking behaviour itself can be taken as a direct indicator of object permanence or even object identity of the lower levels suggested by Moore and Meltzoff.

Recent work on object knowledge in early infancy

Recent work, particularly by Baillargeon and her colleagues, indicates that although tracking data may be unreliable as measures of permanence in early infancy, there are other very effective ways of finding out about young infants' object knowledge. Baillargeon's basic technique has something in common with Bower's in the sense that a measure is taken of infants' responses to an event that violates physical reality in some way. It also has much in common with the habituation–dishabituation technique, since infants are presented with a series of trials involving lawful physical events, followed by new events which are either lawful or are not. Like the habituation technique, duration of looking is the dependent measure, but in this case, rather than indicating detection of stimulus novelty it is taken to indicate that the infant has detected that the event violates the rules of reality. Figure 4.5 illustrates one of the earlier studies using these principles (Baillargeon, Spelke and Wasserman, 1985). Five-month-old infants were familiarized with a repeated event in which a flap, initially flat on the table, rotated 180 degrees in front of the infant and then 180 degrees back to its original position. After these trials, a cube was placed in the path of the flap and two types of flap rotation followed. In the possible event, the flap rotated until it came to rest against the now hidden cube. In the impossible event, however, the flap rotated the full 180 degrees, just as in initial trials and thus moved through the space occupied by the cube, which disappeared in the process. Infants looked significantly longer at the impossible event, and Baillargeon et al. (1985) concluded that five-month-olds both understood the continued existence of the cube and realized that the flap could not move through the position occupied by another object.

In a later study, Baillargeon (1987a) replicated this result with younger infants, finding that 4.5-month-olds and even some 3.5-month-olds responded

A Possible event

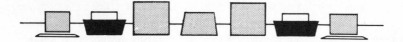

B Impossible event

Figure 4.5 The infant's view of the possible and impossible events in the study by Baillargeon et al. (1985).

in the same way as infants in the earlier study. Thus she concludes that even at 3.5 months infants understand object permanence and the rules by which objects move relative to each other. Using the same basic technique, she also found that by seven months infants' expectations were really quite specific in this task (Baillargeon, 1987b). For instance, they expected the screen to stop rotating sooner if the cube was larger or closer to the screen, but expected it to stop rotating later if the object was compressible rather than rigid.

Another technique used by Baillargeon is illustrated in figure 4.6. Infants were familiarized with an event in which a toy car ran down a ramp to pass behind a screen and re-emerge at the other side (the screen was first raised then lowered again so that the infant could see that there was nothing behind it). Following this two test events were presented. In the possible event, the screen was raised while a box was placed behind the car track and was lowered again, whereupon the car ran down the track as usual. In the impossible event, everything was the same except that the box was placed on the track, blocking the car's progress. Despite this, however, the car re-emerged as before. Baillargeon (1986) found that 6- and 8-month-olds looked longer at the impossible event, apparently noting that the box should have impeded the car's progress. More recently, Baillargeon and DeVos (1991) obtained similar results with infants as young as four months. What is particularly striking about this finding is that the box is hidden when the car makes its movement, and thus infants must be using memory of the relationship between box and track to reach the conclusion that the car's re-emergence is impossible.

Spelke and her colleagues have used a simplified version of this technique to test even younger infants (Spelke, et al., 1992). In the version they used

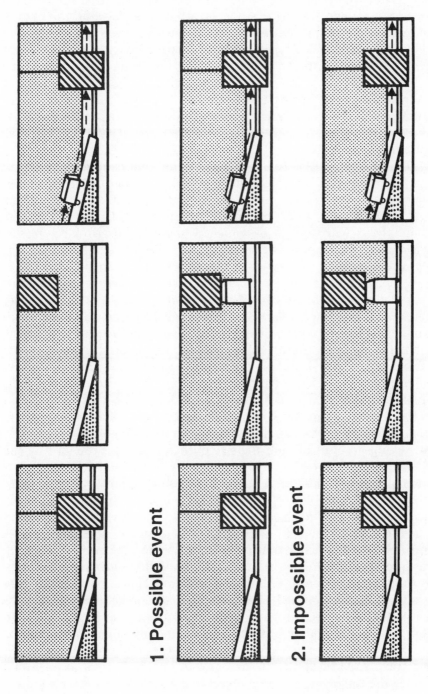

1. Possible event

2. Impossible event

Figure 4.6 The procedure used by Baillargeon (1986) to investigate young infants' object knowledge. The familiarization event is at the top and the two test events are below.

with 2.5-month-olds, during familiarization, infants watched a ball roll behind a screen whereupon the screen was lifted to show that the ball had come to rest at an end wall. On test trials, a box was placed in the path of the ball in such a position that when the screen was lowered, only the top of the box was visible. Two types of test trials were given, a possible event in which on removal of the screen the ball was revealed resting against the box in its path, and an impossible event in which the ball was revealed in its usual place, beyond the box and against the wall. Infants looked longer at the impossible event, evidence which is interpreted as indication that even these very young infants understand that one object cannot move through another in its path.

It has also proved possible to investigate young infants' understanding of how the dimensions of an object affect its visibility or invisibility under particular circumstances. The experimental arrangement used by Baillargeon and DeVos (1991) to investigate this is shown in figure 4.7. Infants were familiarized with events in which a small or large object moved behind a screen to re-emerge at the other side. On test trials the screen was replaced by one with a window cut in its upper half, such that the top of the larger object (but not the smaller object) would appear in the window while passing behind the screen. However, on test trials, neither object appeared at the window. This was appropriate in the case of the small object, but constituted an impossible event sequence in the case of the large object. Infants of only three and a half months looked longer at the large object test event, suggesting that they understood that the object should have appeared at the window on its path behind the screen. This result replicates that of an earlier study with 5.5-month-olds (Baillargeon and Graber, 1987) and makes it clear that quite young infants have a fairly good understanding of the conditions under which one object will occlude another, taking account of both the size of the object and the form of the screen.

In summary, these studies indicate that young infants have a fairly sophisticated understanding of the physical world, including object permanence, the rules by which one object can move relative to another, and the conditions under which one object will occlude another. This is supplemented by other work that portrays the young infant in a similarly positive light. For instance, Spelke (1985) presents evidence that three-month-old infants were surprised if an object 'came apart', part of it moving off with its background, and she takes this as indication that infants perceive objects as distinct units from the background, expecting them to maintain their boundaries when they move. Additionally, young infants appear to have a rudimentary understanding of the conditions under which one object will support another. The basic technique here is to push one object along the top of a supporting object to come to rest either adequately supported, inadequately supported, or in mid air completely clear of the supporting object. Initially, it seems to be enough that one object be in

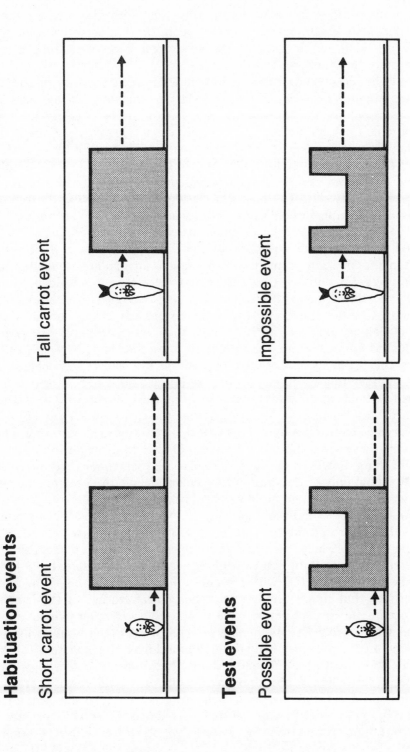

Figure 4.7 Investigation of infants' knowledge of how the dimensions of an object affect its visibility (Baillargeon and DeVos, 1991).

contact with another, but after six months infants acquire a better tuned understanding of conditions for support, realizing that some cases of contact are not sufficient to prevent the supported object from toppling off (Baillargeon, Needham and DeVos, 1992).

It would be incorrect to suggest that these studies reveal no limitations in young infants' knowledge of the world. For instance, Spelke and her colleagues conclude that four-month-olds do not appear to understand the rules by which objects move under the influence of gravity, seemingly not expecting that a falling object must continue to move until it hits a surface (Spelke, et al., 1992). Additionally, although young infants distinguish between an object and its background, they appear to be poorer at distinguishing between two objects in close proximity, apparently treating them as a single unit (Kestenbaum, Termine and Spelke, 1987; Prather and Spelke, 1982, see chapter 3). For once this corresponds to Piaget's (1954) account, and raises the question of how infants can have a primitive understanding of support while at the same time failing to distinguish between objects in contact. Could it be that three-month-olds do not have an understanding of support, but just treat any two objects in contact as a single unit? One the one hand, this seems an unlikely interpretation of the results of Baillargeon et al. (1992) since they showed infants one object being pushed along the top of another. On the other hand, Spelke (1985) suggests that even at six months, infants do not expect two objects in contact to move relative to each other, so one would expect all the events presented by Baillargeon et al. to be surprising, the non-support cases being more surprising because the 'deformation' of the single unit is perceptually more extreme. Thus, although great strides have been made through work of this sort, there are still quite a number of issues that remain unresolved. The main thing, however, is that we possess the tools to tackle these issues and so it should only be a matter of time before the picture becomes clearer.

This work on understanding of physical principles complements research by Leslie on understanding of causality in event sequences. In one study (Leslie, 1984a), seven-month-olds who were habituated to a sequence involving a human hand picking up an object, showed no dishabituation for different versions of the same event sequence, but did dishabituate if the hand failed to make contact with the object before both moved off together. Leslie argues that infants understand the crucial feature of this sort of causal event, the contact between hand and object. Similar evidence was obtained with events in which objects underwent billiard-ball collisions (Leslie, 1984a), so the effect is not limited to animate event sequences. This evidence runs counter to Piaget's claim that infants of this age only understand causality within their own acts. It would seem that they also understand causality both in frequently witnessed event sequences produced by others and in more abstract sequences. However, we should not overestimate young infants' knowledge of causality, since Leslie's (1984b) effects were quite small and Oakes and Cohen (1990) only obtained clear evidence of perception of causality at ten months. Additionally, Cohen and Oakes (1993) found that even at that age, perception of causality did not generalize across different objects, since causal events were no longer perceived as special when each trial involved a different object pair. Nevertheless, these studies indicate at least the beginnings of yet another infant ability, and this is another example of how techniques developed over the last ten years are powerful tools for detecting the young infant's awareness of the world, revealing a sophistication that goes far beyond the levels of knowledge that Piaget assumed.

Failure to search at six months

In the light of Bower's account, with its stress on the early understanding of object permanence, it seems puzzling that six-month-old infants should fail to search for an object hidden under a cover. And yet there is no problem in replicating Piaget's finding. Work on search failure at this age is surprisingly scarce, however; surprisingly so because of the importance that Piaget attributed to the onset of search at around eight months.

Before we could be confident that the beginning of search for objects could be taken as an indicator of progress in constructing an objective reality, we would want to rule out the possibility that younger infants fail to search simply because they lack the motor skill. But there is good evidence that this cannot be the whole problem. Bower and Wishart (1972) suggested that if infants simply had a problem organizing the response required to disentangle an object from an occluder, this difficulty should be just as marked if the object was visible under a transparent occluder. But in fact they found that most six-month-olds retrieved an object from a transparent cup, while none retrieved it from an opaque cup. This indicates that there is a real problem with invisible objects at this age. But Bower and Wishart obtained another important result. Infants took about twice as long to pick up a transparent cup when it covered an object as when it did not. It seems as if they were puzzled by the relationship between object and cup, even when it was visible.

One group of workers suggest that part of the problem does lie with inadequate motor skill. Rader, Spiro and Firestone (1979) found that infants searched for an object hidden under a small card, but failed to do so when it was hidden under a larger cloth, arguing from this that search failure is due to lack of manual dexterity. However, there is the danger that in simplifying the task they made it possible for the infant to reveal the object either fortuitously or through a non-specific 'swipe' at the location of disappearance, so there is no really clear evidence pointing towards a motor deficit account.

Why, then, should six-month-olds have difficulties with invisible objects if, as Bower found, one-month-olds understand the permanence of an object masked by a screen? In parallel with his earlier arguments, Bower claims that their problems are limited to certain types of disappearance. In support of this, Bower and Wishart (1972) found that six-month-olds who did not search under an occluder were nevertheless quite able to reach out and grasp in the dark for an object that they had seen dangled in front of them before the lights went out. Bower claims that this shows that 'out of sight' is certainly not 'out of mind'. However, there is one clear methodological flaw in this study. The object was presented at the infant's midline, and so contact could have been the fortuitous outcome of relatively random arm movements.

Hood and Willatts (1986) performed a revised study in which it is clear that infants were really reaching for the object. Five-months-olds were presented with an object to one side of the midline, and direction of reaching was measured once the lights were extinguished, with the object removed so that fortuitous contact could not direct the reaches that followed. Under these conditions, infants reached significantly towards the side at which the object had been presented, and this happened despite the fact that they had never had the opportunity to reach for it there when the lights were on. In addition, it seems unlikely that these results were due to immediate execution of an act preprogrammed before the lights went out, since infants typically first reacted non-specifically, as if in surprise at the sudden darkness, and returned to reach for the object afterwards.

This makes it fairly clear that the manner of disappearance is important in determining whether or not search occurs, and Bower initially identified hiding relationships involving *enclosure* as the sort likely to puzzle infants, since here the occluder appears to take up the position of the object. Brown (1973) obtained evidence that supports this conclusion, finding that infants who failed to search under a cover would search when the object was placed behind a vertical screen. In the latter case, we have a separate ordering of two objects in depth rather than an enclosure of one by the other.

Other evidence, however, indicates that we probably have to modify this conclusion. Dunst, Brooks and Doxsey (1982) tested infants between six and ten months on search for an object hidden in a variety of ways, and found that although search in boxes was more difficult than search behind a screen, search under a cover was actually easier than in both other cases. These findings are in keeping with the notion that some types of object–occluder relationship are difficult, but does not support the notion that difficulty is a function of whether or not the relationship involves enclosure. Other evidence suggests that the important factor is the degree of separation between object and occluder. Neilson (1977) found that six-month-olds would retrieve an object from behind a screen provided the separation in depth was considerable, but failed if the screen was placed immediately in front of the object. This would indicate that at least one of the factors determining whether or not search will take place is the degree of perceptual separation existing between object and occluder at the point of its disappearance. In fact, Neilson also found such an effect when the object was placed in view in front of the screen. This finding fits Bower's claim that infants have difficulty in separating objects conceptually when they are difficult to separate perceptually.

In summary, there is enough evidence to rule out a simple 'motor deficit' explanation of search failure at six months. But there is also sufficient conflicting evidence to prevent a clear identification of the factors that determine search. The fact that search occurs in some cases and not in others might seem to detract from Piaget's explanation in terms of a general lack of understanding of the continued existence of the object. However, we must remember that he set high criteria for understanding. Search for an object once the lights had been extinguished would not measure up to stage IV ability, since it does not involve putting two schemes together to obtain the object; the infant can use the same act that would have been used if the object were visible. In fact, Piaget gives examples of stage III infants reaching for objects that have left the visual field. All his examples, however, involve the infant repeating or extending an act previously used on the object, and it is not clear whether he would have predicted reaching in the dark for an object not previously grasped in that location. Nevertheless, we should remember that Piaget also stressed the importance of understanding the spatial relationship between object and occluder, since in his account this comes through coordinating schemes directed to each in turn, and carries with it the beginnings of understanding of the object's continued existence.

Some of the other findings showing the effects of different hiding relations may relate to differences in the complexity of the sequence of acts required for successful retrieval. However, it appears that perceptual factors are also important. Separation between object and occluder appears to affect search when the act required for retrieval is the same. So although Piaget's account comes out of recent research on this particular topic not too badly scarred, we must entertain the possibility that the infant's perception of spatial relations in itself may determine whether or not search takes place. This, taken together with Bower's and Spelke's work with young infants, suggests that Piaget's account at least needs considerable modification to take account of a level of perceptual functioning that he did not truly recognize. It seems that many of infants' successes and failures may relate primarily to perception rather than to constructed understanding of the Piagetian sort.

Finally, what if we throw off all the theories about object permanence and try to explain the phenomenon at a more 'common-sense' level? It is very tempting to interpret search failure as indication that infants simply forget very quickly, and fail to search because they have forgotten the object. It is a commonplace observation that adults often forget about the existence of an object tucked away in a drawer, to discover it with surprise at a later date, although in this case, we do not doubt the adult's belief in object permanence. But if there is to be anything in this analogy, the time scale has to be very different; infants would have to forget very rapidly. And what really makes a memory explanation weak are the very data that we have been discussing in this section. Why should infants 'forget about' an object that was placed close up behind a screen but not do so when it was placed fairly far behind it? Again, we are led back to the conclusion that the problem has to do with what the infant perceives of surrounding events rather than with whether or not he or she remembers them.

The stage IV search error

Bower (1982) claims that even when infants begin to search for objects, they do not understand the hiding relation, assuming that the object has been replaced by the cover. Instead, through experience, they have developed a rule, 'When one object replaces another, pick up the replacement object, and the original object will appear'. They make errors when the object is moved because they are using another rule for repeated search, of the form, 'When a desired object is not in sight, search for it where it has previously been found'. Bower bases his argument on extrapolation from younger infants' behaviour and has not tested his account through experiment. In contrast, many other workers have made the stage IV error their focus of experimentation. The main outcome of much of this work has been to rule out a number of explanations and to indicate a number of problems with Piaget's account. In addition, various alternative explanations have been developed, and even if none fully explains the stage IV error, a wealth of information about infant ability has been gathered in the process.

Manual activity and error   According to Piaget, the stage IV error indicates that infants are only capable of searching in the place where previous action has been successful, and although action does not have the same magic creative properties that it had in stage III, the object's existence, as far as it is understood at all, is understood only in relation to a place at which past search has succeeded. From this viewpoint, error should only occur if the infant has previously acted at the initial position. In addition to testing the Piagetian view, it is important to investigate the possibility that the error is a form of response perseveration, infants automatically repeating a response without really attending to what is happening.

Several workers (Butterworth, 1974; Evans, 1973; Landers, 1971) have investigated the role of manual activity by looking at what happens if infants are allowed to search at a new place (place B) for an object that they had only seen hidden and revealed at place A. On either of the counts outlined above, errors should be less after observational experience, but it turns out that when infants are allowed to search, the error of searching at place A occurs with much the same frequency as usual. These findings allow us to rule out the notion that the error is the result of some sort of mindless response repetition. But they also point out a weakness in Piaget's account, since there is no evidence that previous manual activity is a necessary condition for error.

Memory limitations and error   Another question is whether we can explain the error in terms of some sort of memory deficit. Although I argued that search failure at six months was unlikely to be due to forgetting that an object had been hidden, could the present phenomenon be a case of the infant forgetting *where* the object is? Certainly, it is tempting to draw the analogy with an absent-minded adult searching in the wrong place for an object only recently put somewhere else. In this case, the adult neither has problems representing the object nor remembering its existence, he or she simply cannot remember where it is. But, as Piaget points out, these examples arise when adults are distracted by other events, whereas infants err when they are fully attentive to events happening before them. Also, the time scale of adult forgetting is usually much longer than that involved in the stage IV task.

Despite these cautions, there is some evidence in keeping with a memory interpretation. Harris (1973) found that infants rarely made search errors if they were allowed to search immediately after the object was hidden at B. His interpretation of this was that there was interference in memory between information about present location and information about past location, such that the latter dominated infants' subsequent search. Allow them to search immediately, however, and this interference would not have time to take place. Following this further, Gratch and his colleagues found that a delay between hiding and search of as little as one second was enough to produce errors at the usual level (Gratch et al., 1974). However, they conclude that this is rather too short a timescale for memory interference to have an effect, and interpret successful immediate search in terms of the existence of a short-term motor set towards the correct location. When there is no delay between hiding and search, infants search correctly by carrying through a reach for the object that had been prepared while it was still visible, but a short delay is enough to break this set, whereupon they err in the usual way. This is certainly a plausible alternative, but unless it can be shown that memory interference could not occur within a second, this group's data are equally open to a memory interpretation.

Bjork and Cummings (1984) also favour a memory interpretation of the error. They put forward an account that differs slightly from Harris's, suggesting that infants make a rather vague coding of the object's position on hiding at B, so that they often make errors. This interpretation arises from the fact that when several search locations are present, infants do not make errors to the original location, but to positions close to the new location (Cummings and Bjork, 1983). Thus they are not confused over whether to search at the old or the new location, they simply have trouble identifying the new location. But Cummings and Bjork (1983) actually obtained relatively few errors in this multi-position task, so they do not appear to have tapped the usual phenomenon. (See the following section for discussion of a possible reason for reduced errors in this task.)

Despite a number of strongly argued cases, one finding creates a major problem for all memory explanations. Piaget (1954) noted search errors even when the object was in full view at its new location, and this finding has been replicated by a number of workers. Butterworth (1977) and Harris (1974) both obtained errors when transparent occluders were used, and Bremner and Knowles (1984) found that infants would search at A for an object totally visible and uncovered at B, provided place A was covered as it had been during A trials. It is not clear how memory explanations can account for these phenomena. Additionally, Baillargeon and Graber (1988) have shown that if the search component is removed from the stage IV task, infants expect to find the object where it was placed whether this be position A or B, and that they do this despite quite long delays. This both presents problems for memory based accounts and suggests that the error may be more to do with appropriate direction of manual action. We shall come across this issue again in a few pages (see the section *A neurophysiological account: interaction of memory and action*).

Spatial analyses of the error The notion underlying many of the studies attempting a spatial analysis of the stage IV task is that the error may be largely due to problems in differentiating between locations in space, or in keeping track of the movements of the object between locations. The major focus here has been on the way or ways in which infants code positions in space. When the object is moved from A to B, it goes from the left hand to the right hand container, or vice versa. In addition, its position relative to the infant changes. Infants might code the object's location in terms either of a direction from self (what is often called absolute coding) or as in the left or right hand container (relative coding), but since these two codes coincide in the standard task, we have no way of telling which coding infants use. However, figure 4.8 shows that by moving the two containers sideways after A trials, we can disambiguate these two codes. This manoeuvre means that the object can be hidden in the same position relative to the infant but in the opposite container, or can be hidden in the same container but in a different position relative to the infant. Harris (1973) and later Butterworth (1975) carried out such studies, and Butterworth, who performed the fullest study, found that either of these changes led to error at much the same level as when both changes took place together.

Again we have evidence that the error is not simply a tendency to repeat exactly the same response, since this would have led to success whenever the object's position relative to the infant stayed the same, a condition in which Butterworth obtained errors. In fact, we know that even at five months infants do not simply repeat an old response to regain an object if it is no longer in its customary place (Willatts, 1979), so even at this age there is no evidence of blind response repetition. We also know from Butterworth's result that infants do not code the object's position solely relative to self; they also take external cues into account. If infants are responsive to external features in this way, why are they not responsive to the crucial information, seeing the object hidden at B? A clear answer to

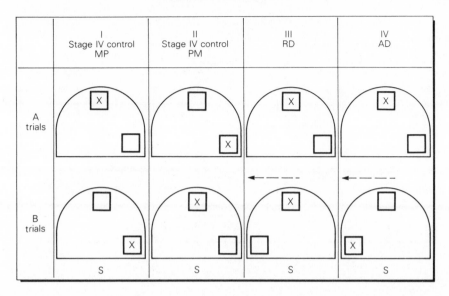

Figure 4.8 Tasks used by Butterworth (1975) to separate self-referent (absolute) position from position of one container relative to the other (relative). X = location of object; S = subject's midline; MP = midline to periphery; PM = periphery to midline; RD = relative location different on B trials; AD = absolute location different on B trials.

this question has proved singularly elusive, despite the volume of research on the problem.

There is another way that the task needs to be broken down. As long as the infants remain in the same place and orientation, we do not know whether they are searching at a fixed place relative to self or relative to an external frame of reference. Figure 4.9 shows how these two possibilities can be separated. Bremner and Bryant (1977) moved infants to the opposite side of the hiding places after they had completed trials at A. This meant that the same place in space was now the opposite place relative to the infant, and vice versa. In this study, the results were quite clear. If the object was hidden in the same place relative to the infant, and hence in a new place in space, infants searched successfully. But if the object was hidden in the same place in space, and hence in the opposite position relative to the infant, most infants made errors, and this happened even though the two places were on clearly different backgrounds. Such an outcome would be predicted whether the infant was coding position in relation to self, or in terms of left–right container relations, so there is no conflict here with Butterworth's results. The point is that both of these types of coding depend on the infant's position, and so need updating whenever he moves. If these results do not lead to an immediate explanation of the error, they do suggest that the infant's understanding of space may be limited through too much reliance on fixed self-referent coding of

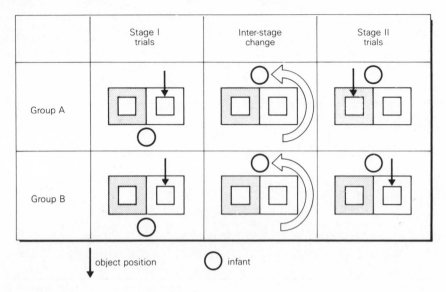

Figure 4.9 Task used by Bremner and Bryant (1977) to separate self-referent and external codings of position.

positions, an issue that will crop up again in the section on spatial orientation.

Although the hiding positions were on different backgrounds in Bremner and Bryant's study, there was no evidence that this helped infants to note the object's position on B trials. However, Bremner (1978a) introduced stronger position cues by using covers of different colours, and this produced a dramatic change in performance. Now, after movement, infants searched correctly wherever the object was hidden. This suggests that differentiating the two positions helps infants to note the new position of the object, and although these results are complicated by that fact that they arose in a non-standard version of the stage IV task, there is other evidence that making the two locations distinct helps the infant to avoid making errors. Butterworth, Jarrett and Hicks (1982) found that different covers on a uniform background led to fewer errors in a standard task. It also appears that increasing the separation between locations reduces error (Uzgiris and Lucas, 1978). This may explain why Cummings and Bjork (1983) obtained reduced errors when more than two hiding places are involved. Horobin and Acredolo (1986) obtained data suggesting that this reduction in error is due to the additional separation between A and B locations rather than to the number of locations as such.

These findings would suggest that the stage IV error is primarily due to difficulties in discriminating between locations. However, this would be an over-simplification, since infants have no difficulty in identifying the initial location of the object. The problem seems to be more to do with identifying its successive positions. If these are made distinct or well separated in space, errors are less likely than if they look the same and are relatively close together. It sounds very much as though we are tapping a spatial problem here, so does the error tell us anything about the infant's understanding of objects? According to Butterworth, Jarrett and Hicks (1982) the answer is yes. They claim that it is only through linking the successive positions of the object that infants perceive its identity over the move. If the visual field is not suitably structured, they will not have a perceptual framework in which to register the object's new position once it goes out of sight, and so they will fall back on searching at the old place.

A neurophysiological account: interaction of memory and action A recent approach to understanding of the stage IV error involves the suggestion that the error is due to incomplete development of frontal cortex (Diamond, 1988). This notion arises among other things from the finding that rhesus monkeys with lesions of frontal cortex perform poorly on the stage IV task (Diamond, 1990). On the basis of evidence from work with infant monkeys and with human infants, Diamond (1988) proposes that a primary function of frontal cortex is the integration of two capacities, the maintenance of an object representation in memory and the inhibition of an incorrect motor response. She claims that although infants can perform either function singly, coordination of the two functions is not possible until the frontal cortex has developed sufficiently to support this function.

In addition to evidence from studies of rhesus monkeys, there is more direct evidence supporting a link between development of the frontal cortex and human infants' success on the stage IV task. Bell and Fox (1992) found that infants who were capable of solving the stage IV task showed more developed EEG patterns in the frontal region. Thus, it seems more than likely that there is a significant link here. The question, however, is whether this takes us any closer to an explanation of the stage IV error. Diamond's account, like those couched in terms of memory deficits alone, has difficulty explaining the fact that infants still make the error when the object is in view. Under these circumstances, there is no need to hold the object in memory and hence no need to integrate memory representation and response inhibition, so Diamond's account would predict few or no errors with the object visible. Nor is it clear how Diamond's account would explain why errors are reduced if the two locations are made distinct. The problem is that we would be closer to an explanation of the error if we really understood in detail what functions frontal cortex supports in human infants. But unfortunately, understanding of this is far from complete. However, future research is likely to refine this account further so that it fits better with existing data. One strength of the account is that it identifies the error as due to problems in coordinating action systems with perceptual and representational systems, rather than with problems with a single system. I shall argue later that cognitive development in infancy is largely about the formation of coordinations between action and perception and that we can understand infants' search errors in this light.

Summary: the current status of the stage IV search error   Recent studies of the stage IV search error have clarified the conditions under which it occurs, and indicate that Piaget's explanation of the phenomenon was not entirely satisfactory. But they do not lead us to an obvious alternative explanation; we have to try to piece together the evidence to reach some conclusion. We already have Bower's suggestion that infants use simple rules to obtain objects that had disappeared mysteriously. Butterworth, Jarrett and Hicks (1982) suggest that infants have difficulties in updating an object's position (and hence its identity) when it moves to a new hiding location. Harris (1983) takes the identity argument further, to argue that infants generally assume that an object in a new location is a different object. Their world is inhabited by many identical versions of the same class of object, so when they see an object hidden at a new place they search for the old one in the old place.

The result that probably produces most problems for all these accounts is the fact that errors still occur even when the object is in plain view in the new location. With reference to Bower's account, it has not 'disappeared mysteriously', so why should the rule of searching at the old location be invoked? Butterworth's account needs modification to indicate why there should be problems with updating an object's position even when it is uncovered and clearly visible in the new location. And if Harris is correct in his suggestion that infants believe that there are objects to be obtained at both places, why do they return for the less accessible object at A instead of the visible one at B, and why in the standard task do they persist in searching unsuccessfully at A, sometimes over a lengthy series of trials? One would imagine that repeated failure would lead them to try for the 'other object'.

An alternative suggestion is that infants are trying to do more than trace the movements of the object. There are both objects and containers in these tasks, and infants may be as much preoccupied with attempting to understand the function of the containers in relation to action as they are with tracing the movements of the object (Bremner, 1985). Looked at this way, the error of searching at the old location may be a case of the infant trying out the hypothesis that this is the place where appropriate action will reveal objects. But this would not mean that search errors indicate nothing about the infant's understanding of objects. Spatial manipulations of the task reduce errors, and it is very likely that this occurs because infants are better able to keep track of the object's displacements in these cases. But we need to consider the possibility that the direction of search may be determined by the relative dominance of infants' notions about the object's movements and their notions about the properties of the container. When infants succeed it is because information about the movement of the object is so clear that it dominates the notions they have built up about the original location as a place where objects are found. When they fail it is because information about the object's movement is weaker, so that they are guided by their notions about the container. Errors with the object visible are still difficult to explain, but it is possible that although infants see the object at place B, they are still puzzled about how this information is to be reconciled with past evidence of its presence in the first container. In other words, they may be trying to work out the appropriate way to act in relation to the objects and events that are presented to them, and search at position A may be more a testing of a hypothesis than evidence that they do not know where the object now is.

There may be a basis for this in real life. Infants are adept at removing toys from toy boxes, but it is usually the parent who has to put them away, often after the infant has left the scene. Consequently, it would not be surprising if infants developed rather magical notions of containment that related to finding objects but not on seeing them hidden. Currently, there is little empirical research on infants' notions about containment. It appears that nine-month-olds are capable of perceiving convexity as an indicator of a container (Pieraut-Le Bonniec, 1985), and we know that infants have less problems in search tasks when both hiding places are familiar containers (Freeman, Lloyd and Sinha, 1980; Lloyd, Sinha and Freeman, 1981) or have open tops that suggest containment (Ulvund, 1983). However, we currently know little about how understanding of containment is first established, nor indeed about the general issue of how infants come to categorize objects in terms of their functions.

Spatial orientation in infancy

Spatial analyses of the stage IV search task may actually tell us more about spatial coding than about the error itself. For instance, we already have the suggestion that infants may rely on self-referent coding of the object's position. However, this sort of approach led on to more direct tests of spatial orientation ability. One key question was whether infants were capable of taking account of their own movements in space. Can they relocate an object or place after they have been moved to a new position? Some of the evidence presented in the previous section suggests that there may be circumstances under which they can (Bremner, 1978a), but in order to test this more directly, Bremner (1978b) used a new type of search task incorporating a movement of the infant while the object was out of sight. Infants saw an object hidden under one of the two covers, but were rotated to the opposite side of the table before being allowed to search. There was also a comparison condition in which the table was rotated instead of the infant; again the object was hidden under one of the covers, but infants were prevented from searching until the table had been rotated through 180 degrees (see figure 4.10).

Each of these conditions was presented either with the hiding place backgrounds different colours or with the covers different colours, and two main results emerged. Infants performed better if they were rotated rather than the table, and they performed better when cover cues were used rather than background cues. In the infant rotation condition with cover cues few infants made an error, whereas in the table rotation condition with background cues, most made an error. In the other two conditions, about half made an error.

The cueing effect is no surprise. It is probably much simpler to keep track of an object when there is a very direct cue to its presence, and it is hard to think of a more direct cue than a distinct cover. However, it is less obvious why performance was better when the infant moved. Bremner suggested that since these infants were just beginning to crawl, they were getting used to finding that a fixed self-referent coding becomes unreliable whenever they move. In the infant movement condition they were moved passively, but even a passive movement may have been enough to prompt them to update their coding of the object's position.

Acredolo (1978) used a comparable method of assessing spatial orientation in larger scale space. Infants were placed in a square room which had windows in the walls to the left and right of the infant (see figure 4.10). The first phase involved training the infant to turn in anticipation of a consistent event at one of the windows. A buzzer was sounded, followed by the appearance of a person at one window, a contingency that was continued until infants reliably turned to the window before the person appeared. Then came the crucial phase. The infant was moved around to the opposite side of the room so that she faced in the opposite direction, and the window that was to the left was now to the right, and vice versa. Then the buzzer was sounded again, and note was taken of where she looked. If infants were to locate the event window correctly, they had to perform some sort of updating of its position relative to them, otherwise they were likely to look to the wrong window.

Acredolo carried out this task in a marked condition, in which the event window was marked by a colourful star pattern, and in an unmarked condition, in which both windows looked the same. She found that six-month-olds in both conditions turned in the same direction after movement, and hence fixated the wrong window. At 11 months, performance was still poor in the unmarked condition, while only half of the infants in the marked condition turned the wrong way, indicating that spatial cues were beneficial at this age. By contrast, at 16 months performance was good in both conditions, so it would seem that by that age infants' spatial orientation is good enough not to need the support of strong direct cues. Subsequently, Acredolo and Evans (1980) found that by presenting even stronger position cues, they could elicit correct updating from the majority of nine- and 11-month-olds. In comparison, the performance of six-month-olds under these conditions was still poor.

Some workers have found that even six-month-old infants are capable of taking account of their own movements (McKenzie, Day and Ihsen, 1984; Rieser, 1979). In both studies, however, the movement was a simple bodily

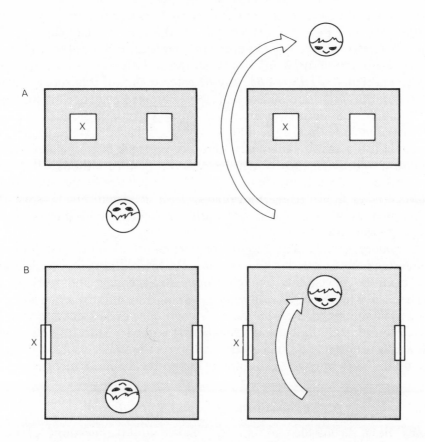

Figure 4.10 Methods used by (A) Bremner (1978b) and (B) Acredolo (1978) to test spatial orientation. Correct performance in both cases involves reorientation to a fixed position after a move. Bremner's dependent measure was search for an object hidden before movement while Acredolo's was visual anticipation of a consistent event, trained before movement. (B) Copyright 1978, American Psychological Association. Reprinted by permission of the author.

rotation without a displacement. In McKenzie, Day and Ihsen's study, infants were trained to anticipate an object movement at a particular locus, and were tested on direction of looking after the chair in which they sat had been rotated. Six- and eight-month-olds showed the ability to fixate the correct location despite body rotations of up to 90 degrees. In contrast, infants of this age do not seem able to take account of 180 degree rotations (Cornell and Heth, 1979), so there are limits to their ability.

It is not yet clear what processes are guiding infant's performance on these tasks. On the one hand, there is evidence that eight-month-olds use landmarks as a guide to orientation, performing better when they are present (Meuwissen and McKenzie, 1987). Additionally, Keating, McKenzie and Day (1986) found that the same age group performed better in a square room than a circular one, presumably benefiting from the spatial features provided by the room corners in the former case. On the other hand, there is evidence that infants can compensate for rotational movements in environments devoid of landmarks. Although an earlier study (Lepecq and Lafaite, 1989) had only detected ability of this sort at around eleven months, Tyler and McKenzie (1990) obtained evidence for successful reorientation in a featureless environment by eight-month-olds. Tyler and McKenzie conclude that, in addition to landmark-based systems, infants are capable of using vestibular information to keep track of body rotation. It is premature to draw such a conclusion, however, since although they used a featureless environment, there was sufficient texture in the surround to produce visual flow during movement. Thus it is entirely possible that infants used visual flow information during movement to keep track of their changing orientation.

In summary, infants of six months are capable of taking account of bodily rotation, as long as it is not too extreme. However, the ability to deal with more complex movements involving both displacement and reorientation appears somewhat later, having been shown at nine months when there are strong spatial cues, and at 16 months when cues are absent. As we shall see, it is quite likely that the developmental sequence starting with coping with bodily rotation and progressing later to rotation plus displacement may have a firm basis in concurrent motor and postural developments.

Active movement and spatial orientation

It may be no coincidence that the ability to take account of bodily movements involving displacement as well as reorientation emerges at around nine months. Infants begin to crawl sometime between six and nine months and it seems plausible that this new-found activity has quite a dramatic effect on their ability to orient in space. Before beginning to crawl they must have plenty of experience of being carried around by their parents, but this experience may not be as effective as that resulting from their own active movements, where visual experiences bear a contingent relation to their activities.

The notion that active experience is important is not new. As well as being an important part of Piaget's theorizing, it has its base in a different theoretical tradition which is best exemplified by a classic study by Held and Hein (1963). They used the method shown in figure 4.11 to equate the visual experience of two kittens, but to give only one of them active experience. Kittens were reared in the dark until capable of locomotion, and were then placed in the apparatus for a three hour period each day. Whenever the active kitten moved or turned, the passive kitten experienced a similar move or turn. After a number of sessions in this apparatus, passive kittens showed defects in spatial orientation that could not be put down to motor impairment, since the two groups were comparable on

Figure 4.11 Held and Hein's method (1963) of giving kittens passive experience. The kitten in the basket cannot bring about its own movements, but every move of the active kitten is reproduced for the passive one. Copyright 1963, American Psychological Association. Reprinted by permission of the author.

measures of motor control. The main measures of spatial ability were visual placing (extension of the paws as the animal is lowered on to as a horizontal surface) and visual cliff avoidance. Passive kittens showed poor visual placing and failed to avoid the deep side of the visual cliff.

This should prompt the question of whether active locomotion is important in infants' development of visual cliff avoidance. In chapter 3 evidence was reviewed indicating that infants only became wary of the visual cliff at around nine months, once they have begun to crawl. One possibility is that crawling leads to unfortunate experiences with drops, but that seems unlikely, given the measures parents take to stop their offspring falling from heights. The alternative that springs from the Held and Hein work is that the onset of crawling permits active exploration of the environment that has a crucial role in 'tuning up' the infant's space perception.

If crawling experience does enhance infants' spatial ability, we would predict that infants who had been crawling longer would show more advanced abilities than infants with little or no crawling experience. But although this hypothesis is straightforward, investigating it is less so. Suppose we test two groups of infants who all started to crawl at about the same age, testing one group immediately after they began to crawl and the other group after they have crawled for a month. Any difference we obtain might be due to differences in age at test, and hence to the infants' general developmental level rather than to the crawling experience as such. Instead, we could hold the test age constant, assigning infants to different experience groups in terms of the age at which they started to crawl. This would be a more conservative test of the hypothesis, since any difference between groups could not be put down to differences relating to the infants' age at testing. But even this step is not enough, as we can see by looking at the growing literature on the relation between locomotion onset and visual cliff avoidance (reviewed by Campos et al., 1982).

Using a heart rate measure, Svejda and Schmid (1979) found that with test age held constant, infants with some locomotor experience showed evidence of wariness, while those who were not yet mobile did not. This looks like good evidence for a causal relationship, but Campos et al. (1982) identified an interpretative problem. Suppose infants who crawl early do so because they are generally more advanced. It is then possible that although age was held constant, infants in the experienced group (who crawled early) performed in a more advanced way not through the experience of crawling but because they were more rapid developers in general. Given this possibility, the issue would be clarified if experience of locomotion could be directly manipulated in a way that has an effect on the visual cliff response, since under these circumstances we could more safely assume a causal relationship. Campos and colleagues achieved this by supplying one group of infants with baby-walkers during their fifth month, subsequently comparing their visual cliff responses with a control group of the same age (Campos et al., 1981). Those with experience in the baby-walker showed a heart rate increase (indicative of wariness) whereas the control group showed a heart rate decrease. It therefore appears that a direct causal link can be shown between locomotor experience and visual cliff avoidance.

Unfortunately, other evidence suggests that this causal link may be complicated by other factors. Richards and Rader (1981) found that age of crawling onset was the main predictor of visual cliff avoidance, but in quite the opposite direction from expectation. Infants who crawled before six and a half months often failed to show visual cliff avoidance, compared to a group of later crawlers who did. This result is in keeping with the notion that the infant has to be sufficiently developed in other ways to interpret the information arising from locomotion. Very early crawlers may not be guided as much by visual information, and hence they may not show development in visually guided movement to the same extent. Probably the safest conclusion is that crawling experience does affect infants' awareness of depth, but only in interaction with their developmental level. If they crawl too early, the experience is not used to sharpen their visual awareness of spatial relations, because they are not sufficiently developed in other ways. What these other ways might be has yet to be shown. Maybe infants have to reach a certain level of perceptual development before they can benefit from visual feedback accompanying active movement. However, this would not explain why very early crawlers showed less advanced visual cliff behaviour than later ones, and Rader, Bausano and Richards (1980) suggest that early crawlers are directed more by tactile than by visual input, a difference that may persist in later crawling. This would result in earlier, tactually guided crawlers not showing the same advances in spatial orientation as later, visually guided crawlers.

Nevertheless, these findings may only apply to very early crawlers, and other results lend support to the notion that, at least for most infants, ability to take account of bodily displacement emerges partly as a result of experience gained through locomotion. If wariness of the visual cliff develops partly as a result of locomotor experience, it seems even more likely that the ability to perform in spatial orientation tasks should as well. After all, crawling actually brings about the sorts of bodily displacements and reorientations that occur in these tasks, whereas we would hope that crawling does not lead to much direct experience of displacement in the vertical plane!

Some studies have investigated this issue by seeing if it makes any difference whether infants move passively or actively in the task itself (Acredolo, Adams and Goodwyn, 1984; Benson and Uzgiris, 1985). Such a comparison can be achieved by adapting the two-position object search task in the way shown in figure 4.12. Infants see an object hidden at one place, but cannot reach it from their initial position because the array is surrounded by transparent screens on three sides. To obtain the object, infants in the *active* condition have to crawl around to the opposite side of the array, from where they can reach the hiding places through the gap in the transparent screen system. This clever adaptation leads infants to execute for themselves movements that were imposed by the experimenter in previous work. Both Acredolo, Adams and Goodwyn (1984) and Benson and Uzgiris found that infants who reoriented actively in this manner, performed significantly better than infants in control conditions who were carried passively round the array.

Other workers have taken the approach used in the visual cliff work, attempting to show a link between length of crawling experience and spatial orientation. So far, the data are sparse, and appear to be contradictory.

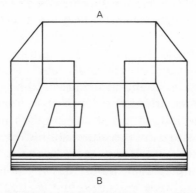

Figure 4.12 Method used by Acredolo, Adams and Goodwyn (1984) to test the effects of active locomotion in a spatial reorientation task. This infant sees the object hidden in one of the containers from position A, but has to locomote to position B before search is possible.

On the one hand, McComas and Field (1984) found no relationship between degree of crawling experience and spatial orientation in the task used by Acredolo (see figure 4.10). However, they did not hold test date or crawling onset age constant, and they compared infants with different degrees of crawling experience rather than experienced crawlers versus non-crawlers, so their negative result may be misleading. In contrast, Bertenthal, Campos and Barrett (1984) showed a positive relationship between locomotor experience and spatial orientation in a version of Acredolo's task. Additionally, Bai and Bertenthal (1992) found a similar relationship using an adaptation of Bremner's task. Interestingly, in the latter study locomotor experience was positively related to performance on the version of the task in which the infant was moved around the array, but was unrelated to the equivalent task in which the array was rotated. This is in keeping with the suggestion (Bremner, 1978b, see page 135) that once infants are capable of locomotion, even passive self movement prompts them to update their coding of stable places in space.

Despite the specificity of the effect just mentioned, it turns out that effects of locomotor experience are not limited to tasks that explicitly measure spatial orientation ability. Horobin and Acredolo (1986) found that infants who had been crawling longer were less likely to make the Piagetian stage IV error. Although this error may have a basis in spatial coding (see Butterworth's arguments, page 130), Kermoian and Campos (1988) found that crawling experience also facilitated the onset of search at a single location. It is not clear how this earlier phenomenon should relate directly to experiences resulting from crawling, and Kermoian and Campos speculate that locomotion may have its effect by facilitating attention to objects and events around the child and consequently speeding development of understanding.

There are clearly many questions in this area that are only just beginning to yield answers, and more research is needed before we will reach a good understanding of the relationships between locomotion and cognitive development, some of which appear to be quite direct while others may be mediated by enhanced attention which results from locomotion.

It is also important not to limit our attention just to the onset of locomotion. In an extension of Held and Hein's work with kittens, Walk (1979) showed that visual attention to surrounding events was enough to enhance depth perception in kittens deprived of locomotor experience. In this respect, the acquisition of the sitting posture in infancy may be an important milestone, since this posture should permit more controlled inspection of the world, and hence more scope for precise information analysis. Before this stage, when infants lie on the floor or sit in a chair, head and body movements are restrained by the support they are receiving. By contrast, once infants sit up they can move their head freely and later they can rotate their trunk to produce a further extension of the visual field. An interesting point is that the sorts of spatial transformations that result from these head and body rotations are just those that infants were

tested on in the study by McKenzie, Day and Ihsen (1984). Infants
to solve these tasks not long after they have achieved the sitting po.
and it is tempting to speculate on a possible causal relationship here. W
we add to this the finding that infants begin to deal with rotation ʲ
displacement not long after they have begun to crawl, we have t..
beginnings of an account of spatial development in which motor and
postural developments have an important causal role. But at present, a
relationship between rotational updating and the achievement of the sitting
posture can only be inferred from the fact that both abilities appear at
about the same time. Clearly we need stronger evidence to support a causal
relationship, evidence that future research may well supply.

Summary

Recent work appears to have established more about spatial orientation in
infancy than about the development of object permanence. This is probably
not surprising, since an abstract concept like permanence is hard to subject
to empirical investigation. The main findings are that spatial orientation
goes through a gradual improvement between the ages of six and 18
months. In the early stages infants are capable of taking account of bodily
rotation but it is some months before they start to take account of
bodily displacement as well, a finding that may fit in with the concurrent
sequence of postural and motor development, leading from control over
body rotation to control over body displacement with the onset of crawling.
The link with crawling is made more likely by two strands of evidence.
First, infants perform better in spatial orientation tasks when they execute
the reorientation themselves, suggesting that they benefit from the richer
feedback accompanying active movement. Secondly, orientation ability
appears to relate to degree of crawling experience, although this effect appears
to occur in interaction with other developmental factors. Finally, and not
too surprisingly, infants benefit from the provision of spatial landmarks,
particularly in the early stages of orientation ability. Many of these issues
were not tackled directly by Piaget, but the high level of performance in
many studies suggests that infants are rather more sophisticated in their
spatial understanding than he suggested.

Imitation

In some respects it is quite a jump from object concepts and spatial
orientation to the topic of imitation. Indeed, we might well find discussion
of imitation in a chapter on social development and early communication,
where it is often put forward as a learning mechanism, or as an index of
social awareness. However, imitation in itself is an important source of
information about infants' understanding, specifically their understanding

of the relationship between self and other people. If an infant imitates the act of an adult, we would be inclined to assume that he or she understood the relationship between his or her own act and the adult's act, no mean achievement in cognitive terms, let alone in terms of its implications for social awareness. For this reason, Piaget (1951) used imitation as another index of cognitive development, claiming that it developed through the same series of stages as other aspects of sensori-motor development, with true imitation only becoming apparent around the end of the second year. In contrast, there have been a number of recent claims that imitation can be observed in very young babies, claims that have important implications for both the cognitive and the social abilities of the young infant. So this topic provides important evidence about cognitive development and also serves as a bridge to our discussion of social development in the next chapter.

Piaget on the development of imitation

The reader can probably guess the kind of account of imitation that Piaget would present. Given that the infant is born with no awareness of the world as distinct from self, or self as distinct from the world, there is no question in Piaget's mind of infants truly imitating external models. He notes behaviour patterns right from birth that might be interpreted as imitation, but he claims that the mechanisms underlying these patterns are much too basic for them to be given the status of imitation. Nevertheless, he identifies these early behaviours as precursors of imitation proper, and links the gradual development of the latter to the elaboration of sensori-motor

Table 4.2 Piaget's stages in the development of imitation

Sensori-motor stage	Level of imitation
I	Apparent imitation through confusion of sounds made by others with sounds accompanying own reflex activity (e.g. crying 'in sympathy')
II	The same as stage I, except this now applies to the infant's acquired behaviours (primary circular reactions). Confusion of sensations accompanying own and others' head movements
III	A link is constructed between seeing others' acts and producing own acts, but still a case of confusion between own acts and others' acts
IV	Imitation through actions that the infant cannot see himself or herself make
V	Imitation through new acts not in infant's prior repertoire
VI	Deferred imitation – true imitation of an act witnessed some time earlier, indicating representation

schemes. Table 4.2 shows the correspondence between the sensori-motor stages and level of imitative behaviour.

The first three stages: preparation for imitation   Piaget notes behaviour even in newborns that might be taken as imitation. The newborn baby, lying quietly in his cot, hears the cries of other infants, and begins to cry 'in sympathy'. But this example does not convince Piaget. He claims that the behaviour arises because of the infant's extreme egocentrism. The infant does not distinguish between the sound of another baby's cry and his own. Due to the tendency to repeat reflexes, the sound stimulates the activity, and the infant cries. During stage II, developments in imitation are related to the development of the primary circular reactions. The infant begins to modify reflexes, so that new sounds and new actions become possible, but imitation still occurs solely through confusion between sounds and visual stimuli produced by others and those produced by the infant. For instance, Piaget notes how at about two months his daughter begins to imitate him moving his head from side to side, and goes on to differentiate between nodding and shaking the head, copying each correctly. He argues that in watching the head movement, she recognizes a visual effect that she obtains when she moves her own head, and this leads her to produce that movement. So despite the apparently convincing nature of these acts, they are still no more than visual or auditory stimulation of a sensori-motor scheme. Part of Piaget's evidence for this lies in the fact that infants only 'imitate' with acts that are already in their repertoire; there is no acquisition of new behaviours through imitation.

During stage III, coordination between looking and acting on objects occurs (see p. 126 above), and this means that infants can extend the range of acts imitated, since the link between acting and seeing the visual result of the act forms a bridge between acting and seeing the visual result of another's actions. However, these activities are still the result of confusion between the acts of others and the acts of self. Also, for this confusion to take place, infants have to be able to see the outcome of both their act and that of the other person. So there is no question in Piaget's mind of infants imitating facial expressions, where they can see the other person's expression but not their own.

Despite this claim, Piaget notes examples of stage II and III infants putting out their tongue in response to the same action by an adult. Since they cannot see themselves doing this, these examples appear to be an embarrassment for Piaget's account, but he dismisses them, claiming that they are cases of *pseudo-imitation* resulting from parental training. He gives little detail, though, of how this training takes place.

Stages IV and V: imitation through unseen actions and new actions   The coordination between schemes characteristic of stage IV (see p. 127) leads to sufficient integration for infants to begin to make a match between movements that they see others make and movements that they can only feel themselves making. From this point on, Piaget would agree that infants are able to imitate the facial expressions of others through a two-stage matching, first across modalities, between the feelings associated with forming a facial expression and the expression itself and secondly, between their facial expression and that of someone else. Again, however, this link and the resulting imitations are based on the common denominator of an action that the infant already makes.

In stage V, through beginning to experiment with action, infants begin to imitate acts of others that they had not previously produced themselves. Piaget gives the following example from his daughter Jacqueline at one year:

> At 1;0 (16) J. discovered her forehead. When I touched the middle of mine, she first rubbed her eye, then felt above it and touched her hair, after which she brought her hand down a little and finally put her finger on her forehead. On the following days she at once succeeded in imitating this gesture, and even found approximately the right spots indicated by the model. (1951, p. 55)

So imitation is no longer a matter of the stimulation of existing acts. Infants watch the model and vary their act of imitation until they find it a satisfactory match.

Stage VI: deferred imitation as evidence for representation The limitation of stage V imitation is that it is an act in direct response to the act of another, and Piaget believes that this does not supply evidence that the infant is capable of mentally representing the acts of others. In stage VI, however, infants can be seen imitating acts that they saw others making some time previously. For instance, Piaget gives the example of one of his children imitating a tantrum thrown by a young visitor the day before. Piaget accepts this as evidence that imitation now has its base in mental representation. As he puts it:

> Imitation is no longer dependent on the actual action, and the child becomes capable of imitating internally a series of models in the form of images and suggestions of actions. (1951, p. 62)

So, just as infants gain the ability to represent objects and spatial relations mentally, they gain the ability to represent the acts of others, deferred imitation being an excellent example of this process of representation in action.

The radical alternative: newborn imitation of facial gestures?

Piaget is quite adamant that imitation is a gradual development. He writes:

There is nothing innate in imitation. The child learns to imitate, and this learning process is particularly obvious in the field of movements he cannot see himself make. (1951, p. 78)

In his view, imitation of facial gestures only occurs towards the end of the first year, once infants have established the cross-modal correspondence between their own faces and the faces of others. But even Piaget notes that at a much earlier age, tongue protrusion occurs, apparently in response to the same action by an adult. The major issue is whether he was right to discard this as trained *pseudo-imitation*. He could be accused of having relegated it to this status because it does not fit his theoretical framework rather than on the basis of direct evidence that it is a trained response.

Consequently, the crucial question is whether facial gestures are imitated under circumstances in which we can rule out the possibility of response learning. It is possible, for instance, that parents present a gesture and reinforce the infant for approximations to it, a process that leads to gradual shaping of accurate imitation. Such an explanation becomes less likely the younger the infant studied, and it also becomes less likely in the case of gestures that as far as we know adults do not generally seek to elicit, such as tongue protrusion.

A number of workers have reported examples of imitation of facial gestures by young infants (e.g. Gardner and Gardner, 1970; Maratos, 1973), but Meltzoff and Moore (1977) performed the first systematic study. The major problem that has to be overcome in tackling this issue with very young infants is that of measurement. When infants are stimulated by social interaction their mouths are in fairly constant motion, and tongue protrusions are frequent. Hence, we have to be able to distinguish between generalized activity and a specific response to a modelled gesture. Also, we have to try to ensure that the experimenter does not reinforce the infant following a particular gesture, to eliminate the possibility that the response is being trained even within the test session. Meltzoff and Moore surmounted the first problem by presenting a set of three different facial gestures (tongue protrusion, lip protrusion and mouth opening) and one manual gesture (sequential finger movements) and looking for responses that were specific to the gestures modelled. A dummy was held in infants' mouths to prevent them from responding until after the model gesture was complete, and close-up video analysis was based on the period following each gesture. Independent judges were asked to rate the infants' gestures in terms of their approximation to each of the ones modelled by the experimenter. The important point here is that the judges were not aware what adult gesture infants were responding to in any of these cases. Judges' ratings showed a significant relationship to the gesture modelled, and Meltzoff and Moore concluded that infants were capable of imitating specific facial gestures (figure 4.13) as well as manual ones. Since the infants in this study were between two and three weeks old, it seems relatively

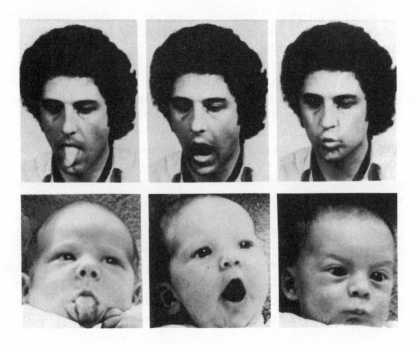

Figure 4.13 Modelled expression and infant's imitation (from Meltzoff and Moore, 1977). Copyright 1977 by the AAAS.

unlikely that these responses could have been learned. However, Meltzoff and Moore (1983a) went on to test infants less than three days old, where we can fairly safely rule out the possibility of learned imitation. In this study they presented only two facial gestures (tongue protrusion and mouth opening) and again they found clear evidence of imitative responses specific to the gestures modelled. Additionally, in a more recent study, Meltzoff and Moore (1989) obtained evidence of neonatal imitation of rotational head movements much like an exaggerated head shake. Thus, they claim that even at birth imitation is not restricted to oral gestures.

Jacobson (1979) replicated these results with infants tested at six, ten and 14 weeks, but noted that other stimuli such as an approaching pen or ball were as likely to elicit tongue protrusion as the facial gesture itself. She suggests that there may be some form of *innate releasing mechanism* (Tinbergen, 1951) at the root of these behaviours, the idea being that infants are innately predisposed to respond in specific ways to a range of visual events with the same basic structure, that of a small object moving towards or away from the infant's mouth. However, subsequent work has yielded rather different and more illuminating results. Abravanel and DeYong (1991) working with five- and twelve-week-olds and Legerstee (1991) working with five- to eight-week-olds obtained evidence of specific imitation of tongue protrusion and mouth opening in response to these gestures modelled by a person, but no evidence when the gestures were simulated by objects. Although Legerstee found that gestures increased in the model condition, they did not match the specific gesture presented. Thus, although presentation of particular object events may well increase infant gestures, this seems to be a different effect from that occurring in the case of gestures modelled by people, where it appears from these data that real imitation occurs.

Fontaine (1984) used a much stricter criterion for imitation in which judges had to count the frequency of specific gestures rather than rate the infants' expressions in terms of their approximation to particular gestures. On this criterion clear evidence for imitation was obtained from three weeks onwards. In contrast, imitation was not observed in younger infants, a result that is maybe not surprising since the response specificity demanded in this study probably requires a degree of motor coordination that is beyond the youngest infants.

A number of other workers have failed to replicate Meltzoff and Moore's basic data (Hayes and Watson, 1981; Koepke et al, 1983; McKenzie and Over, 1983). Such failures are always a worry, but they may simply attest to the elusiveness of the response. Although all these studies claim to be more or less replications of Meltzoff and Moore's methodology, Meltzoff and Moore (1983b) point to a number of methodological differences that could have led to negative results. For instance, they note that care has to be taken not to habituate infants to adult facial gestures immediately before testing. Koepke et al. (1983) did not limit infants' view of adult interaction before the test, and so may not have created the optimal conditions for testing. Meltzoff and Moore also question whether measurement techniques in some studies were sensitive enough to allow detection of subtle responses by the infants. In their 1977 study Meltzoff and Moore took a close-up video that only included the infant's face. Both Koepke et al. (1983) and McKenzie and Over used wide-angle video recording which, in the view of Meltzoff and Moore, is not a sufficiently sensitive measure.

Other workers have managed to obtain imitation of facial gestures by neonates. For instance, Reissland (1988) obtained imitation of lip widening and pursing in a group of newborns in rural Nepal. Additionally, Kaitz, Meschulach-Sarfaty, Auerbach and Eidelman (1988) obtained imitation of tongue protrusion by neonates, although they failed to obtain evidence of imitation of emotional gestures. They put this down to the high salience of tongue protrusion as an action and question whether they detected true imitation. However, given the specificity of and variety of responses obtained by others it seems likely that this was a case of imitation. It makes sense that if imitation exists it should be easier to elicit in the case of frequent well practised actions than in the case of less frequently used actions that are not yet fully coordinated.

On balance, then, it seems reasonable to assume that imitation is a real phenomenon from birth onwards. But how can we explain this ability? Meltzoff and Moore (1985) suggest that the explanation of neonatal imitation in terms of innate stimulus–response connections or *innate releasing mechanisms* is unlikely to be correct. In animal examples the response is not isomorphic with the stimulus, but rather is adapted to it in some way. For instance, egg rolling behaviour in gulls is 'released' by the stimulus of an egg (Tinbergen, 1951). Instead, Meltzoff and Moore take recourse to the recent findings on cross-modal matching in infants, putting forward a model based on *active intermodal mapping*. As they put it:

> *In our view, this early imitation reflects a process of active intermodal mapping in which infants use the equivalences between visually and proprioceptively perceived body transformations as a basis for organizing their responses.* We also posit that imitation, even this early imitation, is mediated by an internal representation of the adult's act. (1985, p. 153; original emphasis)

They interpret evidence of cross-modal matching in early infancy (see chapter 3) as evidence that early perception is 'supramodal', that is, it crosses boundaries between modalities. Hence, from the very beginning, infants can imitate an action that they cannot see themselves make; feeling themselves doing it is equivalent to seeing themselves doing it.

Meltzoff and Moore's claim that newborns *represent* the acts of adults should be considered with care though, since they probably mean something quite different from what Piaget considered as representation. They are not talking about representation in the form of mental images, but in the form of a multi-modal description of events to which infants can match their own actions. Probably, however, their account is not such a radical departure from Piaget's as it would appear. The main factor they stress is the multimodal nature of early perception, and if this ingredient were added to Piaget's theory, it could incorporate the possibility of imitation of facial gestures far earlier. But I suspect that Piaget would still claim this was far from true imitation. Although responses occurred after the gesture was modelled, it is doubtful whether the time between observing and imitation is sufficient to conclude that these are cases of deferred imitation based on a full mental representation of the act.

Nevertheless, even if we can explain neonatal imitation assuming only a relatively modest level of cognitive sophistication, the existence of the imitative ability is likely to have considerable importance for the infant's social development, since it is a ready-made mechanism for acquiring human behaviour. Consequently, the topic will re-emerge in chapter 5. Additionally, Meltzoff and Moore (1992) identify imitation as having a central role in the development of understanding of people as individuals. Their suggestion is that young infants' understanding of people as individuals is poorly developed and that they use imitation as a means of establishing the identity of others, a type of representation through action. Thus, imitation is not simply triggered by adult gestures, it is used as a

means of bolstering infants' representation of the person, just as, accordi
to Piaget, they might manipulate an object in particular ways to establ
its identity more clearly. Certainly, there is evidence that imitation by both
infant and mother is used frequently in social exchanges when the infant
is around a year old (Masur, 1987), and it appears that infants who engage
in a large amount of imitation from birth onwards have a better quality of
relationship with their mothers at three months (Heimann, 1989). However, the bases for these effects are unclear, and the place of imitation in
social development currently remains fairly speculative.

Cognitive precursors of language

Thinking back to chapter 1, it was the question of the origins of language
that prompted what might be called one of the earliest experiments in
developmental psychology, in which James IV of Scotland isolated two
infants from linguistic input to see what language they would develop. And
he reached the firm conclusion that the Hebrew language was innate,
emerging without any exposure to language. It seems inevitable that he
faked his evidence, since there is no evidence that a specific language is
built in in that sense. Nevertheless, language development is the area in
which the nativism–empiricism debate in its original form has stayed alive
longest. On the one hand Chomsky (1968) argued for an innate language
acquisition device, a module separate from the rest of the cognitive system
that ensured that the child acquired the language to which he or she was
exposed. On the other hand, there were those who argued that language
was acquired through imitation and the behaviourist principle of reinforcement (Skinner, 1957).

Additionally, theories have emerged that treat language as a produce of
cognitive development, its emergence waiting upon development of necessary cognitive pre-requisites. Piaget, for instance, claimed that language was
just one aspect of the symbolic function, the development of which
depended on the emergence of representation towards the end of the
sensori-motor period (Piaget, 1967). Recently, a number of workers have
adopted less grand-scale theorizing, investigating links between early language acquisition and specific cognitive developments. The development of
object permanence is one of the areas that has come under scrutiny in this
respect. Additionally, there is growing interest in relationships between
language development and early categorization and concepts. Before looking at this body of work, however, something should be said about the role
of imitation in language acquisition.

Vocal imitation

Although few now subscribe to the notion that language in all its complexity can be explained in terms of imitation, most workers see an important

role for imitation in language development. There is clear evidence that children imitate words and occasionally phrases that they hear from adults. On the other hand, there is also plenty of evidence that many of their multi-word utterances are arrived at through their own constructions, so imitation does not explain most of the fundamental developments in syntactic and semantic development. Nevertheless, Bates and her colleagues identify imitation as one of three pre-requisites for language development (Bates et al., 1979), the other two being means–ends analysis and communicative intent. The notion here is that all three of these of these capacities must reach threshold levels for language to be possible.

Given that neonates imitate facial and manual gestures, one might expect vocal imitation to be present early. Certainly by four months of age, infants show that ability to imitate various vowel sounds (Kuhl and Meltzoff, 1982), although Legerstee (1990) showed that imitation only occurred if infants both heard the sound and saw the model producing it. Thus it appears that there is an important link here with cross-modal integration. Working with infants from nine months old upwards, Poulson and her colleagues found that infants were capable of imitating non-word sounds including vowel-consonant combinations (Poulson et al., 1991). Thus, experimental evidence backs the observational data on language imitation by indicating that the necessary capacity has developed by the time first words begin to emerge (often before the end of the first year).

Object permanence

Working from Piaget's claims about the cognitive origins of language, a number of workers in the seventies suggested a link between object permanence and language (Bloom, 1973; Wales, 1970). The notion behind this was that in order to use words to name objects, infants had to have a well developed concept of permanent objects. However, evidence for such a relationship has been rather hard to come by. Although Corrigan (1978) found a general chronological agreement between the onset of single words and the beginning of stage VI of object permanence, and that the end of stage VI coincided with a vocabulary explosion, she found relatively little evidence of specific links. One suggestive indicator, however, was the fact that words like *allgone* and *more* first appeared at the end of stage VI. These words appeared in the context of object disappearance, and the suggestion was that their use depended on a concept of object permanence. Similarly, Gopnik (1984) found that the use of the term *gone* emerged during stage VI of object permanence development, although somewhat earlier than Corrigan's finding with *allgone*.

The problem here is whether we are dealing with a suggestive coincidence, or with a real relationship. And if it is a real relationship, just what is it that is developing in stage VI that allows progress in language? The conventional story would be that representational ability only emerges at the end of the sensori-motor period, and that this ability is needed for language acquisition. However, we have seen that such an interpretation misrepresents even Piaget's position, in which the beginnings of representation are seen in stage IV. Additionally, given claims by Bower, Baillargeon and others about the early development of knowledge of permanence and awareness of physical reality, it becomes even more difficult to pin down what is happening in terms of object concept development around eighteen months that makes language possible. As we shall see in chapter 5, there are a range of social cognitive abilities that emerge around this time, and it is possible that suggestive links between emergence of terms like *gone* and solution of conventional object permanence tasks are to do with the fact that such terms emerge during activities involving hiding and finding objects, but that these activities appear on the scene for reasons other than development of permanence, reasons such as the negotiation with another over the disappearance and reappearance of an object.

Categorization

One of the disappointments for those seeking a connection between permanence and language was the lack of clear evidence for a specific link between object permanence and object naming. However, it is possible that workers were looking for a link with the wrong aspect of object knowledge. One thing that infants need to know about objects if they are to use naming appropriately is that objects belong to classes, since names generally refer to classes of objects rather than just to specific objects. This consideration has led investigators to look for relationships between categorization skill and language. There is evidence through use of habituation techniques that from three months upwards, infants are capable of forming perceptual discriminations at a category level (Younger and Gotlieb, 1988) and that by around ten months they are capable of dealing with categories in quite sophisticated ways (Younger, 1985; 1990). However, it is not until some time later that infants begin to sort objects into categories spontaneously. Gopnik and Meltzoff (1987) presented infants with objects of two types and found that at around 16 months infants began to group objects of one type into a single category while ignoring the others, whereas by around 17 months, they would exhaustively categorize objects into two categories. They also found that onset of this two-category grouping preceded or coincided with the naming explosion.

In this study, the objects in categories were identical, whereas in real life categories such as *dog* and *cat* contain exemplars that differ in detail while holding general features in common. Thus Gopnik and Meltzoff (1992) looked additionally at a categorization task in which objects in categories varied in some of their details. Although infants generally performed less well at this task than one in which objects within categories were identical, they found that infants who engaged in either form of categorization produced significantly more names than those who used neither. Thus there appears to be reasonably clear evidence of a link between categorization and object naming, particularly the naming explosion towards the end of the second year.

We can, however, ask the same question as in the case of the object permanence studies, that is, if perceptual categorization appears at three months, what is different about spontaneous categorization through sorting that links it to language acquisition? This problem may be solvable by reference to Mandler's (1992) account of the infant's progress from perceptual categories to object concepts. She argues that perceptual categorizations revealed through habituation studies are different from object concepts in the sense that no meanings need be attached to the categories. In perceptual tasks it is sufficient that the infant perceives features that differentiate some objects and are common to others, and it is Mandler's view that these raw categorizations need to go through considerable analysis before they become concepts. Thus, concepts in which classes of objects are linked through common meaning emerge later and support the emergence of language. Possibly, spontaneous sorting is a symptom of this level of knowledge of objects.

There is, however, a good deal more work needed in this area before a clear picture can emerge. At present, the data do not adequately rule out radically different interpretations of the relations between categorization and naming. Could it be, for instance, that the appearance of language imposes structures on the infant's mental processes that bring categorization to the forefront. To disentangle this possibility from others, we need more detailed longitudinal studies to see whether spontaneous categorization leads to categorical naming or vice versa.

We also need to be aware of the view promoted by Bates et al. (1979) that language emergence depends on infants reaching threshold levels in a range of cognitive skills. Although it is not entirely clear that these workers have identified the appropriate skills (like the object permanence case, clear relationships between means–ends skills and language development have been rather elusive), an analysis of this sort is highly plausible. As we shall see in chapter 5, there are a range of social factors that appear to be involved in the emergence of language, and the fact that we are likely to be dealing with multiple causes makes it doubly difficult to obtain evidence for the contribution of individual factors. It appears likely that the most useful analyses of the future will be based on the assumption that infants are in the process of developing multiple skills in different domains (Fischer, 1980), and that while progress in individual domains may develop at times independently, knowledge already established in one domain may be used to assist establishment of knowledge in another domain (Golinkoff and Hirsh-Pasek, 1990). Thus, although we may seek cognitive precursors of language, it also becomes reasonable to seek ways in which progress in language may act back to produce developments in cognition.

Conclusion: relations between perception and cognition

At the beginning of this chapter I mentioned interpretation and representation as two factors that have often been used to differentiate between perception and cognition. On the matter of interpretation, there is growing evidence that quite young infants are capable of responding to complex events. This evidence would lead us to conclude either that the cognitive abilities needed to interpret perception are very early developments, or that perception does not have to be interpreted to make sense. The latter view is advanced by proponents of J. J. Gibson's theory of direct perception, in which the structure of the world is simply 'picked up' by the organism. However, there is a danger of glossing over questions about the structure of the infant's mind through glib use of the phrase 'picked up'. In order to pick up complex information, the infant's perceptual system must be sufficiently complex in itself. Hence, we should avoid the notion that there is nothing to be explained once we agree that perceptual structure exists in the environment ready to be detected. Although the ecological approach has enormous potential, there is a danger that we may underplay the part of the infant in the act of perceiving. However, the long-term conclusion may be that the infant has sophisticated perceptual structures that allow the extraction of information from the environment. If we abandon the old notion that we perceive a series of two-dimensional images and have to build systems to interpret these, the need for a distinction between perception and cognition becomes less obvious.

On the matter of representation, we have Meltzoff and Moore's claim that newborn infants have representational abilities. But these abilities may be very different from the sort Piaget had in mind. They may be no more than the registering of a relationship between a particular perceptual pattern and a particular action pattern, with all the rest explained by the amodal nature of early perception. But if we do not need to invoke representation to explain these abilities, the issue then is rather one of determining to what extent cognition becomes redundant in accounts of infant behaviour.

In the light of all the early competences that the studies in the literature are turning up, another important issue is the question of what actually develops. On the one hand, infants seem very competent in many ways at birth. On the other, they do show enormous changes. How are we now to explain the changes? We can uncover a number of possibilities by looking at specific examples of change in the light of current evidence and theories. Take the example of the relation between locomotion and spatial orientation. Locomotion may act to 'tune up' perception through the added information gained from matching proprioceptive and visual information. Or, taking the Gibsonian view, perception is the active extraction of information. The organism picks up information about the environment from the perceptual flow accompanying its movement and consequently, as the infant's ability to locomote develops, so she encounters new perceptual experiences. Certain properties of the world may only be perceived by a mobile organism.

Where does this leave cognition? Certainly, it would appear that theories of cognitive development must be modified considerably in recognition of the perceptual sophistication of the young infant. But there must still be a place for the construction of cognitive structures. Although infants may well be born able to perceive fairly high level properties of the environment, these properties probably still have to be interpreted for their meaning in relation to infants' developing actions in the environment. Going back to the locomotion example, through moving about in space, infants may discover properties of the world that affect their locomotion. For instance, they may discover that steps impede progress, or that certain surfaces provide better traction than others. The perceptual correlates of these functional properties were perceived in advance, but their implications for infants' actions have to be established through action. Similar discoveries may arise in connection with infants' manual actions on objects; for instance, they may arrive at the general concept of a container through retrieving objects from a variety of places. Additionally, development of new actions, while allowing new scope for functioning in the world, presents new problems that demand solution. For instance, once infants are capable of locomotion they are faced with detour problems, the solutions to which are not provided by perception alone but must be constructed by the infant.

In summary, instead of constructing a three-dimensional world out of almost meaningless sensory input, the infant may be constructing meanings and functions of objects in a ready-made three-dimensional world. This concept of functional knowledge is analogous to Gibson's concept of *affordance*. For instance, in his terms, a flat, solid horizontal surface *affords* locomotion. My argument would be that functions or affordances are developed by the infant through action on the world, and also that new motor skills lead infants to confront new problems, the solutions of which add to their cognitive repertoire. From this viewpoint, infants are busily engaged in working out what the world offers for action rather than what the world is in physical terms.

There is an almost inevitable link with social development here. Infants do not generally act on the world in a solitary fashion, and many of the functions of objects are likely to be constructed with the aid of parental action. Consequently, it is likely that we need to add to conventional constructionism a social form of construction in which the resulting concepts are the joint product of infant and parent. There is exciting potential here for the drawing together of cognitive and social development within a unified developmental framework, something to which we shall return near the end of chapter 5.

5

Social development

Many topics fall under the heading of social development. The most obvious problem for study concerns the formation of the relationship between infant and parents, often referred to as the process of *attachment*. But as soon as we begin to consider the development of social relationships, questions arise that point to the need to investigate this topic in close conjunction with a number of other issues. For instance, a primary requirement for the establishment of a social relationship is the ability to recognize people, and furthermore, to discriminate between one person and another. So we should take account of studies of *person perception*, since their results may have implications for theories of how first relationships are formed. Another topic that is intimately tied up with relationships is *emotion*. Social relationships have a strong emotional component, and if the attachment literature is to be believed, this is particularly true of the relationship between infant and parent. Consequently, it is important to investigate the nature of emotion in early infancy, and also the degree to which emotional development is moulded by the early social relationships themselves. Additionally, we need to know whether infants are capable of detecting emotions in others. Another central aspect of social development is the acquisition of knowledge of self. Self concept relates closely to understanding of others and the two together form the basis for the development of a 'theory of mind', a form of knowledge which emerges largely in early childhood but which has its roots in developments in late infancy.

There is also the whole issue of how interactions develop within these first relationships. Early social interaction is an important topic in its own right and has been investigated in considerable detail. However, parent–infant interaction must also be investigated as a possible social mechanism for development, including development in domains not conventionally thought of as social. In past work there has been a good deal of emphasis on studying the role of social interaction in the development of language, but more recently a number of workers have begun to look at social interaction as a vehicle for general cognitive development.

Despite the range of issues, there is a growing theoretical flavour to work in this area, emphasizing links between them. For this reason, I have resisted the impulse to treat separate topics in separate chapters, with the aim of directing attention to relationships between topics as well as to the topics themselves.

Person perception

It is clear that from very early on, infants treat people differently from objects. Reviewing a range of evidence, Legerstee (1992) concludes that by two months of age infants treat people as social objects, smiling, vocalizing and imitating their actions, whereas they treat objects as things to be looked at and goals for attempted reaching. Additionally, there is evidence that even newborns produce different manual actions in the presence of people versus objects (Rönnqvist and Hofsten, 1993). Thus there is little doubt that they treat people in a special way, and so we must assume that they perceive special properties in people. Many of the building blocks for person perception have already been mentioned in chapters 3 and 4. Until relatively recently, the bulk of work on person recognition has concentrated on vision, tackling the issue of whether infants are capable of recognizing faces. We touched on this in chapter 3, using Fantz's classic work on face preference as a starting point for investigation of more basic issues in perception. Here I shall review the work on face preference and face discrimination that has stemmed from Fantz's studies. Much of this research has been done with two-dimensional 'schematic' faces, but some workers have preferred to use real faces. As we shall see, there is a trade-off between the precise control over stimulus features that schematic stimuli permit, and the direct realism of real faces.

Perception of schematic faces

In chapter 3 it became clear that there were a number of uncontrolled stimulus variables in Fantz's study (1961) that made it impossible to know whether infants' preferences were based on the dimension of 'facedness'. Stimuli also varied in complexity, symmetry and amount of external contour, and the first and last of these factors were shown to be dimensions of preference for young infants. Since then a range of studies has been done in which more careful control has been exercised over these other stimulus variables. For instance, Wilcox (1969) paired a face-like stimulus with a rearranged one which was symmetrical and had the same amount of external countour (figure 5.1).

When these controls were applied, the common finding was that a preference for 'facedness' did not emerge until between four and five months. Haaf (1974) systematically varied both complexity and facial resemblance, and found that while one- to two-month-olds responded purely to complexity, four- to five-month-olds responded to both complexity and

Scrambled   Schematic

Figure 5.1 Face stimuli used by Wilcox (1969) in which normal and scrambled versions were equated for number of pattern elements, symmetry and external contour.

facedness. Thus it appeared that the face perception did not emerge until four months. However, Dannemiller and Stephens (1988) obtained evidence of face preference at three months although not at six weeks. Also, testing one- and two-month-olds, Maurer and Barrera (1981) found no preference for facedness at one month but a clear preference at two months. This seems a convincing demonstration that face perception develops earlier, since they controlled for complexity, symmetry and external contour. The question is why Maurer and Barrera obtained these earlier preferences while other workers failed to do so.

It seems likely that the reason for different results here lies partly with technique. In many studies preference is assessed from differences in total looking time over a series of trials, but presumably habituation reduces this difference as trials proceed. For this reason, duration of first fixation may be a more sensitive measure of preference. But here, Maurer and Barrera point to a further problem. Typically, infants' first fixation of either stimulus is quite long, maybe around 40 seconds. In many studies, trial length is no more than 30 seconds, possibly too short a period for a difference in looking time to emerge. All this points to the need for very careful experimental technique if infants are to be shown at their best. And these are not the only difficulties that make it hard to assess the earliest time of face preference. Maurer (1985) suggests that young infants' known preference for complexity can act to 'damp out' preference for facedness. Even if both stimuli are of equal complexity, their equal attractiveness on that dimension could tend to equate looking time, despite other perceived differences.

Maurer claims, however, that infants younger than two months are unlikely to recognize facial arrangements. In addition to the fact that preferences are rarely obtained below two months, she points out that very young infants rarely scan internal features of patterns. It is plausible that this arises because internal features are hard for the young infant's low acuity visual system to resolve (see chapter 3), and further evidence on this comes from studies showing failure to discriminate stimuli on the basis of internal features. Yet again, however, some workers claim that face preferences can be shown at birth. Goren, Sarty and Wu (1975) found that newborns just minutes old would follow a face-like stimulus further than two others consisting of unnatural arrangements of the same features. Maurer and Young (1983), however, found much less convincing evidence of neonatal face preference. Using a procedure very similar to that used by Goren's group, they obtained only weak evidence of differential following. Infants did show greater following of the face arrangement as compared with one of the other arrangements, but there was no difference between face arrangement and the third unnatural arrangement. They conclude that infants did discriminate between two of the patterns, but the lack of a general face preference suggested that the discrimination was based on some specific featural difference rather than the general dimension of facedness.

In contrast, though, Dziurawiec and Ellis (1986) replicated the result of Goren, Sarty and Wu (1975), so there may be more to early facial recognition than Maurer and Young suggest. Could it be that in order to detect a face preference at birth we need to use stimuli in which the features are in motion? Remember from chapter 3 that, in the case of non-social stimuli, movement of internal features led young infants to discriminate them (Bushnell, 1979). If that were the case we might expect to find earlier preferences in more standard visual preference tasks in which the internal features of the face and comparison stimuli were moved. However, this does not seem to be the explanation. Testing one-, three- and five-month-olds, Johnson, Dziurawiec, Bartrip and Morton (1992) found that inclusion of natural movements of features only enhanced the preferences of the oldest infants, interpreting this as due to the fact that such movements satisfied these infants' more precise specification of a face.

Subsequent work has shown that the effectiveness of the face tracking task declines during the early months. Johnson, Dziurawiec, Ellis and Morton (1991) found that it was effective in eliciting a face preference at one month but not at three or five months. So we have the peculiar finding that one technique elicits a face preference in early infancy only, while another technique elicits a preference from two months onwards. Johnson and Morton (1991) interpret this as due to the fact that the two techniques tap into separate face recognition systems controlled by different parts of the brain. In common with arguments developed in chapter 3 for the case of early pattern preferences, they suggest that infants are born with a specific system for locating and, tracking faces that appear in peripheral vision. In line with Bronson's (1974) account, this function is supported by the midbrain visual system. In contrast, the emergence at two months of face preferences in the visual preferences task reflects the take-over of facial processing by the visual cortex, a system much more geared to learning about faces than simply detecting their presence. It is suggested that these two systems function independently, but that the earlier midbrain system has a role in directing appropriate stimuli to the developing cortical system.

This is an attractive model, since it apparently accounts for the data and provides a neurophysiological underpinning for the processes involved.

However, the neurophysiological side of the model shares some of the problems suffered by Bronson's model, assuming, for instance, that the cortical visual system is non-functional at birth. Additionally, there are continuing questions about whether the newborn preference data unambiguously measure a preference for faces as such. For instance, Kleiner (1990) claims that the data are explicable at a lower level, in similar terms to the linear systems model presented by Banks and Ginsburg (1985). So this continues to be a fascinating area of controversy in which clear conclusions will only emerge as a result of further research.

Discrimination between faces

It is easy to forget that the work reviewed above relates to perception of schematic faces. What makes young infants' capabilities at this particularly impressive is that they appear to be detecting abstract properties of a two-dimensional pattern that correspond to the arrangement of features in real faces. There is something very persuasive about the notion that to find out about everyday face perception we should use real faces rather than two-dimensional abstractions. However a real face is, of course, a much more complex stimulus. It is three-dimensional and it moves. Also, real faces cannot be equated for brightness and stimulus density in the way that manufactured two-dimensional stimuli can, and so difficulties arise in interpreting a discriminative response. On the other hand, there are obvious pay-offs in using real faces when it comes to drawing conclusions about person perception and discrimination. A good balance may be struck in future by more use of laser holography to present controlled 'three-dimensional' stimuli, a method already used by Nelson and Horowitz (1983). However the bulk of current evidence comes from studies in which real faces were used.

The commonest method used to test facial discrimination is to compare infants' responses to the faces of mother versus stranger. Using the preferential looking technique, Carpenter (1974) obtained such a discrimination in infants between two and seven weeks old. There have, however, been several criticisms of this study. Raters were not blind to the stimulus presented, so the possibility of scoring bias cannot be eliminated. Also, only one stranger was used, leading to the possibility that preferential looking might have been based on specific features of the stranger rather than on general mother–stranger discrimination. Maurer and Salapatek (1976) corrected for the second problem by using six different strangers and, testing five-month-olds, they did manage to replicate Carpenter's result. But they reported few fixations to internal features, and concluded that discrimination was based on peripheral features such as differences in chin shape or hairline. Again, however, the observer was not blind to the stimulus being presented, so we should still be a little cautious about the result.

More support for face discrimination by the beginning of the second month comes from a study by Bushnell (1982), in which colour slides of mother and strangers were used instead of real faces. Bushnell habituated five-, 11- and 18-week-olds to five versions of a colour slide of the mother's face, the normal face and four different versions with a feature or features (e.g. eyes, hair, mouth, eyes and hair) obscured. After habituation with each form of face, the equivalent form of a stranger's face was presented and dishabituation measured. Even the youngest group showed significant dishabituation to the stranger's face in the normal condition and when eyes or mouth were obscured. However, there was no dishabituation when the hair was obscured, again suggesting that the discrimination was based on peripheral features such as hairline.

As usual, investigators have gradually worked down to younger and younger infants. Using live faces, Field and co-workers (1982) found that neonates with a mean age of 45 hours showed a reliable preference for their mother's face as opposed to that of a stranger. They also showed that neonates habituated to their mother's face over repeated presentations, so that they eventually looked longer at a stranger's face. The initial preference for the mother is a striking finding, particularly in view of the fact that these infants had only had about four hours' contact with their mother before testing. In this study, models were asked to produce a stimulating expression and unfortunately it is possible that the initial preference occurred because mothers presented particularly stimulating faces when faced with their own new baby. However, it seems unlikely that this explains their result, since Walton, Bower and Bower (1992) obtained a newborn preference for mother's face using computer images of mother's and stranger's face. Since the images were obtained while models looked at a video camera, there is no basis in this case for the mother presenting a more stimulating face than the stranger, who was also a new mother in each case. In addition, Bushnell, Sai and Mullin (1989) replicated Field's finding while controlling olfactory cues, so we can rule out the slight possibility that the discrimination was made throught the sense of smell. Beyond that, however, there is no way of telling what the basis of discrimination was. Previous work suggests that gross features such as hairline are used, however, Walton et al. (1992) went to considerable lengths to match models in gross features such as colouring and hairstyle. And the shift to preference for the stranger's face after habituation to the mother suggests that basic learning processes were at work, so neonates may be able to learn characteristics of faces very rapidly. In one sense then this result is extremely important, indicating that neonates distinguish between mother and strangers, and this finding suggests the need to modify Johnson and Morton's model, in which learning about faces should not take place until about two months. But in another sense it is not very informative, since it tells us nothing directly about the basis on which the discrimination is made. Nevertheless, whatever we ultimately conclude about its basis, the very early appearance of discrimination between mother and stranger is likely to have important implications for early social development. Discrimination may not indicate that newborns recognize their mother as a special social entity, but it certainly forms a perceptual basis on which such knowledge can be built.

Discrimination between voices

As noted in chapter 3, very young infants are capable of distinguishing different speech sounds, so it would not be too surprising if they were shown capable of distinguishing one voice from another. Additionally, I pointed out that in view of the good transmission of sound to the womb, auditory learning might well start some time before birth. This opens up the possibility that infants learn to recognize their mother, even if only her voice, before they are even born. Like the evidence on visual preference at birth, such a process would be another important starting point for the development of social relationships.

DeCasper and Fifer (1980) found that newborn infants preferred their mother's voice over the voice of another baby's mother. These infants were only three days old, and had had only 12 hours' contact with their mothers prior to the study, so how could such a preference have been established? Either it was formed very rapidly (we should be wary of assuming that learning must take a long time), or infants established the preference before they were born. Spence and DeCasper (1982) obtained evidence that supports the second alternative. They asked mothers to repeat a prose passage several times over the several weeks before birth, and found that newborn infants so exposed preferred this passage to an unfamiliar one. This suggests that in addition to simple stimulus detection, the fetus must be capable of encoding speech in sufficient detail to allow discrimination between two passages spoken in the same tone of voice. What makes this phenomenon even more impressive is that a preference is shown for the previously exposed story even if it and the novel story are read by a stranger (DeCasper and Spence, 1986). Thus, the fetus is apparently encoding something about speech patterning that is not just unique to the mother's voice but is general across speakers.

Interestingly, it turns out that although newborns prefer their mother's voice over a female stranger's they show no preference for their father's voice over a male stranger's (DeCasper and Prescott, 1984). However, by the age of two weeks, infants do form such a preference, being more easily soothed by the sound of father's or mother's voice than by the voice of a same-sex stranger (Hulsebus, 1975). This fits in well with DeCasper and Spence's claim that newborn discrimination between mother and stranger is based on specific information about the mother's voice picked up in utero. This learning before birth supports discrimination between mother and stranger at birth, but not between father and stranger, since the fetus is likely to pick up little information about the father's voice prior to birth. It is worth noting that Hulsebus suggests that parents' voices have a specific comforting effect on infants. But as usual we must be cautious about the precise interpretation. It is possible that parents' voices were more salient 'attention-getters', and that crying ceased to allow attention rather than because the voice fulfilled an emotional need.

Thus it would appear that both information about speech patterns that are general across speakers and specific information about the mother's voice is encoded prior to birth. However, none of these studies tells us which characteristics of speech are being encoded. It is known that young infants can distinguish speech on the basis of prosody (intonation contour, timing and rhythm), and these grosser speech characteristics are fairly likely to be transmitted to the womb. Furthermore, the salience of these variables is likely to be enhanced by the fact that parents generally use a special form of speech when addressing infants. The main features of this *motherese* as it has been called are simplified sentence structure and exaggerated intonation patterns. One group of workers (Mehler et al. 1978) found that four- to six-week-old infants showed a preference for maternal over non-maternal speech, but only so long as the intonation pattern was of the sort the mothers used when talking to their baby. Also, using unfamiliar speakers, Fernald (1982) found that four-month-old infants preferred motherese to normal speech, and it appears that this preference was based on the expanded intonation contours present in infant-directed speech (Fernald and Simon, 1984), in particular the exaggerated rising contour at the end of utterances (Fernald and Mazzie, 1991). Pegg, Werker and McLeod (1992) confirmed the preference for infant directed speech over adult directed speech and found that seven-week-olds showed this preference even if the speaker was male. So in this respect the term 'motherese' is something of a misnomer. Most of this sort of work has been done with infants at least a month old, and we would need similar evidence from studies with newborns if intonation contour is to be identified as the basis of newborn and indeed fetal voice perception. Fortunately such evidence now exists, since Cooper and Aslin (1990) found that even two-day-old infants showed a preference for infant-directed over adult-directed speech.

The distinct characteristics of infant-directed speech do not seem to be just a Western phenomenon, since similar alterations in intonation contour and other aspects of prosody appear in languages with very different structures such as Chinese (Grieser and Kuhl, 1988; Papousek, Papousek and Symmes, 1991) and Japanese, as well as a range of other European languages (Fernald, Taeschner, Dunn, Papousek, Boysson-Bardies and Fukui, 1989). This evidence for universality suggests that infant-directed speech is likely to have an important function in adult–infant communication, and it is suggested that, long before words are understood, intonation contour serves as a communicative device that infants are capable of interpreting. Two pieces of evidence lend some support to this view. Firstly, it turns out that adults are capable of interpreting the intent of a message to an infant from intonation contour alone (Fernald, 1989). Secondly, Papousek, Bornstein, Nuzzo, Papousek and Symmes (1990) found that four-month-old infants looked more at a face stimulus if looking resulted in a typical encouraging intonation contour (consisting of a slow pitch change) and less if it resulted in a discouraging contour (consisting of a rapid pitch change). In summary, then, there is a wealth of evidence that very young infants respond selectively to infant-directed speech and the beginnings of evidence that they are able to interpret the communicative intent behind such speech at least in rudimentary ways.

Multisensory discrimination

Although most studies of person discrimination have investigated single modalities, we should be mindful of the fact that people, and parents in particular, rarely present infants with stimulation in only one modality. The bulk of parent–infant interaction is face-to-face and rarely takes place in silence, and so seeing or hearing people alone may be a fairly unnatural event for the infant. Add to this the growing evidence for early intermodal integration, and it becomes important to investigate the infant's perception of people as multimodal stimuli. In chapter 3 I reviewed evidence that infants as young as ten weeks (Dodd, 1979) and certainly by 16 weeks (Spelke and Cortelyou, 1981) are capable of making a match between voice and facial movements. We also know that they will look more at father or mother depending on whose voice is presented (Spelke and Owsley, 1979), and although it looks as if this learned face–voice match may be limited to the case of gross male–female differences, it is again an important building block in multimodal person perception.

Given this evidence, we might expect that person discrimination would be more successful if information was available in more than one modality. Reviewing a whole range of studies, Zucker (1985) concludes that multisensory studies yield stronger evidence for person discrimination within the first 12 weeks. A study aimed specifically at this issue (Field et al., 1984) showed that addition of voice cues aided mother–stranger discrimination by newborns. Although infants showed a visual preference for their mother when only her face was presented, the preference was more marked when voices were presented also. The improvement was not very large, however, and it turned out that only female infants benefited from the addition of auditory information. But there may be no reason to expect large effects from the introduction of multisensory conditions. In addition to allowing detection of mismatches between modalities, cross-modal integration may also make it possible for information from one modality at a time to be quite adequate for person recognition.

Summary

The evidence suggests that infants either begin life equipped with some of the necessary bases for social perception, or they develop them fairly rapidly within the first few months. Recent studies investigating face preferences indicate that we may have to revise our estimate of the earliest age at which these preferences occur, certainly to around two months and probably right back to birth. In addition, other evidence indicates that by three months of age, infants appear to be utilizing quite complex dynamic information to identify people. For instance, Bertenthal, Proffitt, Kramer and Spetner (1987) found that three-month-olds discriminated between dynamic light-point stimuli which either did or did not correspond to an adult body in motion (see figure 5.2), being much slower to habituate to the latter.

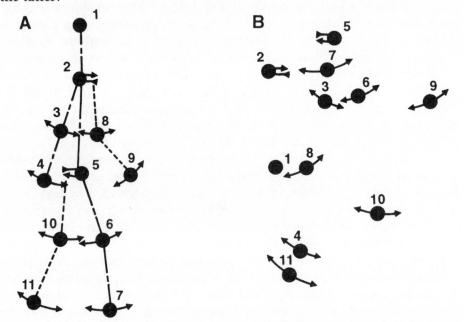

Figure 5.2 The light-point displays used by Bertenthal et al. (1987). Diagram A represents normal walking, while diagram B represents the same set of light-point movements with their relative locations scrambled. © American Psychological Association. Reprinted by permission.

Additionally, Stucki, Kaufmann-Hayoz and Kaufmann (1987) found that three-month-olds were capable of recognizing a human face purely on the basis of movements of a set of points in a way that represented facial movements during face-to-face interaction. These findings suggest that infants identify the human body and face through dynamic relational information of a high level of complexity.

Finally, there is also evidence that within the first few days of life infants begin to discriminate between their mother and a stranger through vision and hearing. Admittedly, most of this evidence says little about the nature of these discriminations; they might be a symptom of very sophisticated person perception or they might simply indicate that infants are able to pick up differences in very basic facial features such as hairline. But all this, added to the evidence on intersensory integration, makes it possible that young infants' capacities for person perception are reasonably well developed. And we can add evidence not discussed in this section, for instance, that newborns discriminate mother from others on the basis of smell (Macfarlane, 1975) and that young infants recognize their mother by the way she handles them (Gekoski, 1974). There is enough evidence here for it to be rather unlikely that the first three months of life really is a period of 'undiscriminating social responsiveness' (Ainsworth, 1973), a conclusion that was at least partly based on old notions about lack of person discrimination in early infancy.

Emotional development

Emotion is a relatively neglected topic, both in infancy and later childhood. There are, of course, reasons for this neglect. For instance, emotions are quite hard to define, let alone measure. These problems multiply when we try to study the emotions of infants, but it is becoming increasingly evident that we must extend our understanding in this area. Even in the case of attachment theory, in which emotion has always been considered central, problems arise over the vagueness of terminology relating to emotion. How, for instance, are we to define and measure the warmth of a relationship, or the strength of attachment, without having fairly clear notions about emotion? In addition, there is a growing view that emotions have an important role in cognitive development. The conventional view that emotions are just an outcome of cognitive activity (for instance, pleasure on successfully solving a problem) is being replaced with the view that emotions also serve as positive or negative forces behind cognitive development itself. In this respect, emotion may determine which aspects of the world are to be approached and which are to be avoided, and consequently which are learned about and which are not.

Past accounts of emotional development

Emotion has not always been as neglected as it is in today's psychology. Darwin (1872) recognized the value of the expression and recognition of emotion as aspects of an evolved communicative system. He claimed that basic facial expressions of emotion were innate, and that although infants had to develop associations between expressions of emotion and the underlying states of mind, perception of emotional expressions was also innate. These assertions were based both on observation of infants and on evolutionary arguments about the adaptive value that such abilities conferred on species whose survival depended on communication and cooperation. Others took broadly similar views. Watson (1930) claimed that the basic emotions of fear, rage and love were innate, and Baldwin (1894) identified the basic emotions as 'a phenomenon of instinct purely'. In most of these accounts, however, considerable development was envisaged. For instance, Baldwin distinguished between emotion as a phenomenon of instinct and emotion as a phenomenon of thought, claiming that the latter only emerged in a sequence of developmental stages.

Within more recent developmental psychology, however, emotion was given little standing. This was partly because many theorists viewed emotion merely as an outcome of cognitive activity. Kagan (1971) suggests that wariness in the presence of an unusual event is the outcome of failure to assimilate the event to current cognitive structures, and Papousek (1967) argues that emotional responses are products of the infant's success or failure in predicting events. Even when emotion was assigned a motivational role in cognitive development, this was at a very general level. For instance, Piaget and Inhelder (1969) admit that every behaviour involves an emotional component which can act as a driving force for cognitive change, but argue that the emotional component does not explain the cognitive component, or vice versa.

With respect to infancy, there was general scepticism in experimental psychology about the existence of emotions as such, which probably led to neglect of the topic. The general view is summed up well by quotes from two developmental texts of the 1950s:

> At first, any stimulus or situation we would think of as likely to lead to an emotional response serves mainly to increase the general activity level of the infant. He gives no sign that he can make any distinction between states we would call anger, fear, or sadness. (Goodenough and Tyler, 1959, pp. 189–90)

In other words, the belief was that the only index of emotion was general level of excitement, and richer interpretations of infant emotion tended to be dismissed out of hand. For example,

> Watson's theory of three innate emotions, rage, fear, and love, is only remembered today as a vivid illustration of anthropomorphic interpretation of infant behavior. (Ausubel, 1958, p. 220)

In contrast though, psychoanalytic theory always accorded a central role to infant emotion. Much of the work to be covered in the section on *attachment* has psychoanalytic roots, and the presence of this work has maintained a link between emotion and social development. Also, growth of interest in ethological perspectives on development led to a renewed emphasis on the adaptive importance of emotions, and workers have seriously begun systematic investigation of the place of emotion in mother–child interaction.

Measurement of infant emotion

If you ask the parents of a young baby whether their child shows emotion, most would say yes without hesitation. Johnson and co-workers (1982) interviewed mothers about their infant's expression of emotion and found that even when the infant was only one month old, the majority of mothers reported emotions of anger, interest and joy. In addition, they found that over half reported fear and about a third, sadness. Of course, we have to be quite cautious about this sort of subjective report. Mothers may be drawing on context to decide what emotion the infant should be feeling rather than actually identifying an emotional expression in face or voice. However, when mothers were questioned in detail about their judgements, they referred frequently to aspects of facial expression or qualities of vocalization that are indicators of these emotions in adults. If these maternal reports are a valid index of infant emotion, we would be likely to conclude that emotions are well differentiated even within the first month. But there is still a good deal of scope for subjective attribution of emotions in everyday parent–infant interaction that reference to facial and vocal expression does not clear up. There is a possibility that parents also use infants' facial expression and vocalization to attribute adult-like emotions to infants who may be feeling nothing of the sort. Consequently, many workers would only be convinced by more objective measures.

Renewed confidence that we can arrive at objective measures of infants' emotional states comes in part from improvements in technique. Ethologists studying facial expression cross-culturally have devised a variety of methods of scoring facial expression in adults that have been adapted for use with infants. Some of these methods are quite complex, being based on the states of a combination of facial muscles. But this means that no judgements have to be made in advance about the significance of the expressions, and also raises the possibility of coding new expressions not previously looked for.

Another important problem concerns the separation of emotional expressions from co-occurring expressions that do not have emotional significance. For instance, we might investigate emotional responses by presenting an emotion eliciting stimulus and looking for appropriate facial expressions in the period following. However, the infant may respond to the stimulus with a transitory expression rapidly replaced by other unrelated expressions, so the stimulus-produced expression could easily be lost among the others. One way around this problem is to ask judges to select the best examples of facial expressions according to prearranged criteria, and then to measure the degree of temporal correspondence between these and the eliciting stimuli.

These methods yield evidence that at least some emotional expressions can be detected in infants. Hiatt, Campos and Emde (1979) presented situations presumed to elicit joy, fear and surprise, and found that 10- to 12-month-old infants produced a high proportion of predicted facial movements in the case of joy and surprise, but not in the case of fear. Stenberg, Campos and Emde (1983) also found strong evidence for anger in seven-month-olds on removal of a biscuit, and Stenberg (1982) noted anger expressions even in one-month-olds when their arms were restrained against their will.

A less time-consuming method is to measure the degree of observer agreement over the meaning of infant facial expressions. Clearly, it is important to control the circumstances under which these judgements are made, to rule out any possibility that judges use the context rather than the expression as the basis for identifying the emotion. One group of workers (Izard et al., 1980) controlled context by asking for judgement of emotion in photographs of young infants' facial expressions, and found that emotions such as surprise, joy, sadness and anger were agreed upon by judges at well above chance level. But again, for reasons outlined above, this does not show that infants are experiencing these emotions.

Finally, some workers have investigated neonates' responses to different tastes. The general finding is that they produce quite different facial responses for positive (sweet) versus negative (sour/bitter) tastes, apparently indicating pleasure and disgust respectively (Steiner, 1974; 1979). Other evidence indicates that in addition to discriminating different intensities of taste stimuli (Crook, 1978), neonates produce facial expressions that range from aversion, through indifference, to acceptance, depending on the intensity of the stimulus (Ganchrow, Steiner and Daher, 1983). We should be cautious, however, in assuming that these expressions can be straight-forwardly interpreted as indicators of emotions like disgust and pleasure. Rosenstein and Oster (1988) showed that neonates produced different expressions for sour, bitter and salty tastes, and that close examination indicated that some components of these expressions did not match adult expressions of disgust, being more akin to expressions normally taken as indicators of interest in older infants.

These studies present at least a starting point for measurement of emotion in infancy, but reliance on facial expression as the sole or main indicator of emotion is problematic, firstly because facial expression is only one way through which emotion is expressed, and secondly because interpretation of facial expression has a strong subjective element. Admittedly, there is some work on vocalization. Much of the earlier work involved categorization of infant cries according to their emotional import (Wolff, 1969), and there is now growing interest in the range of infant vocalizations as indicators of emotional state. For instance, Papousek (1989) has shown that parents of two-month-olds are capable of interpreting the emotional import of a range of vocalizations. However, important as this work is, it again concentrates on just one indicator of emotion. One system known as the *Monadic Phases Coding System* (Tronick, Als and Brazelton, 1980) takes account of information about gaze, posture, vocal and facial expressions, and also looks at the type of activity that the infant is engaged in. This, one would hope, increases the richness of the data by tapping a range of sources of information about emotion, and it appears that this system produces greater inter-observer agreement than a test based on facial expression alone (Matias, Cohn and Ross, 1989). Additionally, a multi-dimensional measure of this sort is more in keeping with recent theoretical accounts that treat emotion as a system for governing functional relationships between infant and environment (Barrett and Campos, 1987; Campos, Campos and Barrett, 1989; see the following section) since this sort of approach demands that emotions be interpreted not simply from facial expressions but in terms of the interaction of a range of infant and environment factors.

Another way around the lack of objectivity may lie in some Japanese work, in which a technique called *infrared telethermography* is being used to measure psychological stress in infants (Mizukami et al., 1990). This technique is based on the finding that stress leads to a drop of skin temperature, and these workers find a significant drop in infants' forehead temperature during brief separations from the mother. Although this sort of technique currently does not permit differentiation between emotions, it offers an objectivity that many of the measures based on facial expression lack.

Theories of emotional development in infancy

Given the difficulty in obtaining objective evidence in this area, much of the theorizing on emotional development is speculative, but as such it provides a fairly rich starting point for further investigation. Theories fall into two broad types, depending upon the degree to which they assume that discrete emotions are experienced by newborns. For instance, Bridges (1930) claimed that emotions were undifferentiated at birth. Neonates only experienced varying levels of excitement, and development took the form of progressive differentiation of emotions as a result of developments in other areas such as cognition. In contrast, Izard (1978) and Sroufe (1979) both claim that some emotions are present at birth, a claim that seems more in keeping with what evidence there is on differentiation of facial expressions in early infancy. Izard and Malatesta (1987) claim that these basic emotions are innate, are well differentiated from birth onwards, and are reflected in innate facial expressions. There is, however, some doubt over the claim about differentiation, since Matias and Cohn (1993) found that in the case of negative expressions there were as many expressions in which two emotions were blended as there were discrete emotional expressions. Thus it would appear that either infants do not experience discrete emotions, or they are unable to express them accurately in facial expressions alone.

The second major issue on which accounts differ concerns the way in which emotional development occurs. Izard, for example, argues that only those emotions required by the neonate are present at birth, with other emotions emerging according to a genetically determined maturational sequence. There is an indirect link with cognitive development here, since cognitive progress leads to changes in the infant's 'lifestyle', which occasion the need for new emotions that emerge at the appropriate time. These synchronies apply to other aspects of development such as the onset of locomotion. Once the infant is mobile, fear becomes an important adaptive response as a preventer of over-ambitious exploration. Despite the fact that later developments of this account recognize growing reciprocal influences between emotion and cognition as development proceeds (Izard and Malatesta, 1987), it is claimed that the emotion system is fundamentally independent of the cognitive system in its origins and major developmental aspects. Emotions simply emerge when they are needed and, if anything, any causal link goes in the opposite direction. For instance, emotions accompanying failure to comprehend new events may act to motivate the child to develop this comprehension.

In contrast, there is a recent approach which, in addition to conceptualizing emotion in a radically different way, does much more to identify multidirectional causal links between emotion, cognition and particularly, social development. Barrett and Campos (1987) conceptualize emotion as a system of processes that govern the functional relationships between infant and environment. Thus emotion acts as a means of achieving environmental goals and of regulating social interaction. In the latter case in particular, social factors are particularly important within the system, since it is through appreciation of social conventions that emotions such as embarrassment and shame come to be experienced. However, an important point is that emotional processes are conceived of in systems theory terms, as made up of the interaction between organismic and environmental features, such that a change in either changes the nature of the process. As they put it, 'The presence of a particular emotion is determined not by documenting a particular type of response, but rather by documenting a particular set of functional relationships between an organism and the environment.' (Barrett and Campos, 1987, p. 556). Although this sounds complex, the gist of it is that we cannot understand emotion simply in terms of the infant's response, but must take account of the contribution of the entire context, physical and social, in which it occurs.

Barrett and Campos identify three different classes of emotion. The *primordial emotions* include disgust and fear, and these types of emotional significance are derived either from the innate tendencies of the infant (for instance, the expression of disgust in response to certain tastes or fear in response to a loud noise), or they are learned through social interaction, in which an ambiguous event may come to elicit fear through communication of this emotion from parents. An example of this can be found in the research on visual cliff avoidance, discussed in chapter 3. Sorce et al. (1981) found that with an intermediate drop, most infants crossed when the mother produced an encouraging face, but none did when she produced a fearful face. The second group, the *concurrent-goal emotions*, which include anger and sadness, relate to the infant's attempts to achieve environmental goals. In this case, the emotional significance of particular states of affairs is determined very much by the goal that the infant is achieving. For example, the presentation of food will promote a positive emotional response from a hungry infant but a negative response from one that is bent on play. In addition, however, emotional significance in relation to particular goals may be communicated socially through parents' reactions during a goal directed activity. The third group are classed the *social emotions*, and include shame, guilt, envy and pride. These also gain their significance in relation to particular goals that the infant is trying to achieve, but in this case the goals are derived from processes of socialization. One way of thinking about this is that in cases such as shame and guilt, the emotion may arise because the infant is guided by a desire that is in conflict with a socialized goal. In the case of pride, the emotion is experienced when a socialized goal is achieved. And in all cases, there is the added ingredient of understanding of others' perceptions, in the sense that shame or pride have to do not just with the act but the fact that it is observed by another.

There are close links between emotional and cognitive development, through the fact that cognitive developments allow infants to interact with and understand the environment more fully, processes that lead in turn to appreciation of the emotional significance of a wider range of situations. For example, the emergence of fear of strangers at around eight months, often taken as an indicator of the first emergence of the general emotion of fear, is really an indicator that the infant's developing perception and understanding of people has made strangers a focus of fear. In addition, infants' methods of coping with emotions change as a result of cognitive and related motor developments. For instance, the young infant can only regulate parental proximity through clinging or giving signs of distress to parents who are out of range. Once infants can crawl, however, they can maintain proximity to parents and distance themselves from objects of fear by their own actions, a development that gives them more direct and immediate control in these situations. Cognitive development also contributes to coping strategies by allowing the infant to predict emotional situations and to avoid them before they develop.

Barrett and Campos see socialization as even more influential on emotional development than cognitive development. As already mentioned, socialization results in new goals and associated emotions: infants learn what is socially appropriate behaviour, and emotions of pride or shame become associated with production of or deviation from this behaviour respectively. Campos et al. (1983) point out that processes of this sort may happen by direct social influence. Mothers respond to their infants' emotions with facial expressions of their own. Very often, their expression corresponds to that of the infant, but in some cases the response differs, depending on the sex of the infant. For instance, when girls show anger, mothers tend to react with an angry expression, but when boys show anger, mothers are more likely to react with knitted brow, apparently indicating sympathy (Malatesta and Haviland, 1982). These asymmetries may serve to mould sex differences in emotional expression towards cultural norms, in this case the norm that anger is a more acceptable response by males than females. Of course, a lot is left unsaid here, since we need to know just what is involved in this moulding process. A behaviourist account would be that anger is maternally reinforced in boys but not in girls. However, given what we know about the infant as an active participant in interactions, the process is likely to be a good deal more complex.

One important point to emerge from consideration of the social processes involved in emotional development is the assumption that, in addition to parents being able to interpret infants' emotions, infants are at least to some extent capable of interpreting the emotions of their parents. However, before being convinced that emotional development is influenced by social processes involving mutual recognition of emotion, we would want to see evidence that infants are capable of detecting the emotions of others.

Perception of emotions in others: early empathy?

In addition to the role it may have in the development of the infant's personal emotions, perception of emotions in others has direct implications for the development of *empathy*. Although the conventional Piagetian view was that the ability to take account of the feelings of others was something that only emerged as a result of cognitive developments in middle childhood, many have disputed this view, and Hoffman (1981) identifies the roots of empathy in neonatal behaviour. Sagi and Hoffman (1976) noted that newborns often begin to cry at the sound of another infant's cry, calling this *empathic arousal*. Hoffman claims that this is a very rudimentary form of empathy, and that its further development depends upon cognitive developments such as object permanence. However, the recent growth of evidence for perceptual competence in early infancy should lead us to entertain the possibility that in this area, as in others, the young infant's ability has been underestimated. As we shall see, some recent studies suggest that young infants derive information about others' emotions directly from perception. Such findings have exciting implications for our understanding of the roots of empathy, since perception of emotion appears to be unique in giving direct access to the states of mind of others.

This topic leads us back to methods very similar to those used to study face recognition and face discrimination. Instead of asking whether infants are capable of discriminating between different faces, the question is whether they can discriminate between different emotional expressions. Early findings suggested that this ability did not begin to emerge until around five months. Ahrens (1954) presented schematic drawings of faces with various expressions, and measured infants' spontaneous responses to them. Before five months there was no evidence of infants responding differently to different expressions, and clear reactions such as distress or avoidance when presented with a frowning face did not appear until eight months.

Quite predictably, many of the more recent investigations adopted visual preference or habituation techniques. Young-Browne, Rosenfeld and Horowitz (1977) used an habituation method to test three-month-olds' discrimination between happy, sad and surprised expressions. Using photographs of faces as stimuli, they found that surprise was discriminated from both other expressions, but that happy and sad were not discriminated. Also, Barrera and Maurer (1981) tested three-month-olds' discrimination between photographs of smiling and frowning faces by habituating them to one and testing for dishabituation to the other. They found that infants readily discriminated these expressions both when the model was their mother and when she was a stranger.

Instead of looking at infants' ability to discriminate different expressions, Kuchuk, Vibbert and Bornstein (1986) tested their ability to discriminate different intensities of the same expression. They found that three-month-old infants showed a preference for a smiling face over a neutral one and that the strength of the preference increased as the smile became more intense. This suggests highly accurate discrimination between different levels of the same expression, rather an unexpected result given the failure of Young-Browne, Rosenfeld and Horowitz (1977) in showing discrimination between happy and sad expressions. This may be another example of how workers are gradually becoming more skilled at detecting more subtle discriminations in early infancy.

There are problems with studies of this sort, in which discrimination is the sole measure. True, infants are showing evidence of discrimination between some expressions, but we cannot tell whether they are discriminating facial expression as such, or whether they are responding on the basis of a specific feature, such as a wide open mouth in the case of the surprise expression. Discrimination at this lower level does not amount to perception of emotion, although it might be an important precursor of it.

One way of testing the generality of the discrimination is to see whether it persists despite introduction of other differences between faces, for instance, changes in the person modelling the expression. Nelson and Dolgin (1985) habituated seven-month-olds to photographs of three different models showing the same expression (happiness or fear), and tested for novelty preference when infants were faced with photographs of a new model showing the familiar and the novel expression. They found that discrimination between happy and fearful faces occurred despite changes in the identity of the model, and, using a similar technique Caron, Caron and Myers (1982) obtained generalized discrimination between happy and surprised faces. Thus by this age at least, we can say that infants' discrimination is based on more than specific featural differences. Of course, this does not rule out the possibility that these discriminations are based on differences in a single feature, such as mouth or eyes, and it appears that it is only after seven months that infants begin to identify the emotional tone in expressions that differ in terms of the appearance of specific features. The evidence here is that ten-month-olds but not seven-month-olds are capable of treating two positive expressions (surprise and happiness) as similar while discriminating them from negative expressions such as fear (Ludemann, 1991).

Thus despite the evidence pointing to early sensitivity to emotional expression, many workers conclude that perception of emotion is a relatively late development. Although Nelson (1985) agrees that quite young infants are capable of discriminating on the basis of some of the facial features that distinguish different emotions, he suggests that 'the perception of facial expressions as expressions does not develop until the second half of the first year' (p. 111). He also concludes that recognition of emotion is still quite rudimentary at two years (Nelson, 1987). A fairly similar view is presented by Klinnert and co-workers (1983), who identify four developmental levels on which infants perceive facial expressions. The first is characterized by lack of any consistent discrimination between emotional expressions, and lasts for about the first six weeks. Once at the second level, which lasts from six weeks to about five months, infants are capable of discriminating between facial expressions without necessarily understanding their emotional significance. In contrast, at the third level, infants respond with expressions that match those of the model, and Klinnert et al. suggest that what is involved here is a form of 'emotional resonance' in which the infant directly experiences the other person's emotions. Infants function at this level between the ages of five and nine months, whereupon they progress to a final level in which they appreciate that the emotions of others are directed to particular targets in the environment. This final step relates to the general phenomenon of social referencing, and allows infants to use the facial expressions of others to guide their acts.

This general account, like Nelson's, is pessimistic about the young infant's ability to perceive emotions. But recent work suggests that these theorists may have underestimated infants' ability by claiming that they initially discriminate only in terms of specific features. Kestenbaum and

Nelson (1990) showed that if a specific feature normally denoting an emotion was prominent (their example was visible teeth as in a smile) seven-month-olds would use this feature as a basis of discrimination even when it did not indicate a difference in emotion, but that if the feature was absent, they showed evidence of discrimination on the basis of the emotional significance of the facial expressions. Interestingly, this only occurred provided the faces were presented upright, whereas discrimination on the basis of a single feature occurred whatever the stimulus orientation. It appears that infants are responding to a facial configuration which only makes sense when it is upright.

Another study using a rather different technique suggests that at least by seven months infants are extracting the emotional significance of some facial expressions. Phillips, Wagner, Fells and Lynch (1990) found that if seven-month-old infants were presented with a pair of facial expressions depicting joy and sadness and at the same time were exposed to a vocalization denoting either joy (ascending tone) or sadness (descending tone), they attended more to the face that matched the auditory tone in emotional import. This ability to identify a match across modalities strongly suggests that infants are capable of discriminating at the level of emotional significance rather than just in terms of surface features.

Surprisingly little work has been done on infants' perception of emotion in vocal expression. What work there is suggests that discrimination of vocally expressed emotion appears somewhat earlier than discrimination of facial emotions. For instance, Walker-Andrews and Grolnick (1983) found that five-month-olds discriminated happy and sad vocal expressions. It should be noted, however, that these workers presented a static matching facial expression along with the vocalization, so the discrimination may have depended on multi-modal information. Subsequently, Walker-Andrews and Lennon (1991) indicated the importance of multi-modal information, showing that five-month-olds could discriminate vocal expressions of emotion only when an appropriate facial expression was presented in parallel. This, however, rather than indicating a limitation of young infants' ability, suggests that they are well tuned to pick up emotion in situations that approximate more to real life, in which emotion is typically conveyed by tone of voice as well as facial expression. Soken and Pick (1992) suggest that infants form the correspondence between visual and vocal expressions through the common rhythm of the sound and facial movements, having shown that infants were capable of discriminating emotional expressions on the basis of dynamic point light patterns corresponding to the formation of facial expressions.

A point to bear in mind is that many of the arguments developed in this area are based on evidence from infant perception of two-dimensional patterns. For instance, Klinnert et al. (1983) use the fact that young infants fail to scan or discriminate internal features of patterns to argue that they are unlikely to be responsive to expressions, since these reside in the internal features of the face. However, we should be wary of drawing too much from infants' responses to two-dimensional stimuli. The nose, eyes and mouth on real faces are not internal features in the same sense as they are in two-dimensional representations; they are all external features of a three-dimensional object. Secondly, the features of a real face are dynamic. This is likely to make them better elicitors of attention (as Bushnell found with inanimate stimuli: see chapter 3), or it may actually be the dynamic information during formation of an expression that the infant uses to detect the expression.

If there is anything in this notion, young infants should discriminate emotions better when presented with real faces. Early work, however, suggested that this was not so. For instance, Spitz and Wolf (1946) found no evidence of differences in spontaneous reactions to different facial expressions by infants of between two and six months old. More recent evidence has changed the story though. Using live faces, Field and her colleagues employed a number of methods to investigate discrimination of emotions by neonates (Field et al., 1982). Using the usual sort of habituation–dishabituation method, they found that neonates discriminated between happy, sad and surprised expressions. They also found that infants' fixation patterns differed depending upon the expression modelled. They looked predominantly at the mouth in the case of happy and sad expressions, but alternated between mouth and eyes more in the case of the surprised expression. Field et al. suggest that this difference arises because most information for happiness and sadness is carried in the mouth, whereas it is carried in eyes and mouth in the case of surprise.

Note, however, that neither the discrimination data nor the visual fixation data need indicate that the infant perceives emotion. Only one model was used, so discrimination could have been based on a specific difference in some feature. Also, the differences in looking patterns could have been determined by the increased salience of wide eyes in the surprised expression. But Field et al. (1982) took a third measure, the outcome of which appears to rule out these alternatives. Judges were asked to guess from the infant's face alone which gesture was being produced by the model, and in the case of all gestures they guessed at levels above chance, a finding later replicated even with pre-term neonates (Field et al., 1983). Apparently, infants did not merely discriminate different expressions; they produced matching expressions themselves (see figure 5.3). This phenomenon looks very similar to other forms of neonatal imitation (Meltzoff and Moore, 1977), in which it is assumed that infants are attempting to produce an expression that matches the model's. But there is an alternative possibility. Instead of setting out to imitate, infants may be perceiving the emotion in the model and responding 'empathically' with the same emotion, producing a matching expression as a result. This raises the possibility that, contrary to the view advanced by Klinnert et al. (1983), 'emotional resonance' may exist at birth.

Using the emotions of others to guide action: social referencing

While perception of emotion in others appears to be possible very early in infancy, according to current evidence, the ability to use the emotional signals of others to guide action appears somewhat later. This process is known as *social referencing*, and we have already seen a good example of it in the visual cliff study by Sorce and colleagues, in which it was shown that infants faced with an intermediate drop were likely to cross if the mother produced an encouraging face but did not cross if she produced a fearful face (Sorce, et al., 1981). In general, the phenomenon is seen in cases in which infants are unsure how to act, circumstances under which they will look to their parents for cues. Hornik and Gunnar (1988) investigated this in a relatively natural situation in which infants of 12 and 18 months encountered a rabbit in a cage for the first time. Social referencing appeared in the form of looks towards the mother and then towards the rabbit, accompanied by questioning facial or vocal expressions. Mothers provided affective information through facial expressions and tone of voice. In the early phase of the encounter, wary infants engaged in more social referencing than bold infants, presumably because they had stronger doubts about how to act.

A number of studies have looked specifically at the effects of parental emotional signals on infants' behaviour. One of the problems that workers have faced is that, rather than carrying information about how to act on a specific object, a show of positive or negative emotion by a parent may simply have a general encouraging or discouraging effect on actions of all sorts. However, Hornik, Risenhoover and Gunnar (1987) obtained data that effectively rule out this possibility. Working with 12-month-olds, they found that maternal negative expressions produced a lasting reduction in infants' frequency of play with and proximity to the specific toy present when the expression was produced, but did not affect play with other toys in a free play situation. Thus, the effect could not be explained as a general suppression of action. They also obtained similar but less marked effects with positive expressions.

Although quite young infants look towards their parents when the latter are making emotional expressions, it appears that they do not immediately use what they see to guide action. Investigating social referencing by infants between six and 22 months old, Walden and Ogan (1988) found that infants below ten months of age looked more to parents when they produced a positive expression, whereas older ones looked more when they produced a fearful expression. Also, it was only from ten months onwards that parental expression modified infants' investigation of toys. Possibly infants have to go through a period of learning that there are relationships between objects in the world and parental expressions before they can use the latter to guide their actions towards objects. Interestingly, infants who are at an age at which they are able to use parental expressions to guide actions appear to be particularly distressed if they receive conflicting emotional messages from each parent, this situation having a stronger negative effect than a consistent negative signal (Hirshberg, 1990). This suggests that conflicting signals are quite stressful for infants who have just gained the ability to interpret parental emotional signals.

Summary

Research on infant emotion has quite a way to go before anything like a clear picture emerges. There is rather a lack of evidence on expression of emotion in very young infants, but quite firm evidence of well-differentiated expressions from seven months on. In the case of perception of emotions, much of the theory is guided by indirect evidence from other areas of study, or from work with two-dimensional stimuli. Because of this, there is a danger that the young infant's ability is seriously underestimated, and the results of recent studies with neonates suggest that at least some rudimentary ability to perceive and respond to basic emotions is present at birth. Since infants are responding with appropriate expressions, this evidence also suggests that differentiated emotions are experienced as well as perceived at birth. These findings should have direct implications for theories of empathy development. The newborn's mirroring of adult emotional expressions provides at least a perceptual–motor basis for well-differentiated empathic responding. It seems relatively unlikely that infants are simply imitating expressions without any direct link to emotional experience, and it is rather more likely that infants are sensitive to adults' emotions, and that the matching facial expression is the result of this. If this is the correct interpretation, we are left with the conclusion that empathic responding to a range of emotions is present at birth. In this respect, Hoffman may have underestimated the sophistication of initial empathic responding.

In addition, we should consider the possiblity that a social mechanism for emotional development may operate right from birth. Given the infant's responsiveness to the emotions of others, the mother's emotional responses both to infant and to external events may be an important source of information used by infants as they develop the more complex blended emotions that appear in later months. It is not just infants who match the emotional expressions of adults; parents 'mirror' the emotional expressions of their infant (Murray and Trevarthen, 1985). There may be a vital added ingredient on the parental side, since it seems likely that part of this parental mirroring process is based on adult assumptions about how someone should feel in a given situation. Hence, adults may actually be amplifying the infant's emotion, effectively saying 'this is how you should be feeling', information which the infant picks up and gradually incorporates into a more complex emotional system. While this sort of suggestion

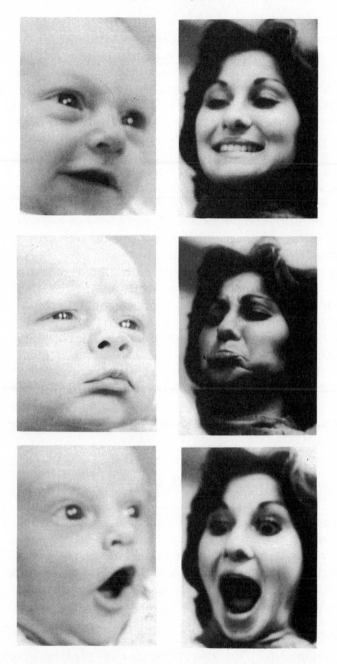

Figure 5.3 Modelled and matching expressions of adult and neonate (from Field et al., 1982. Copyright 1982 by the AAAS).

is currently quite speculative, it is in keeping with other arguments that we shall encounter in the section on parent–infant interaction, and so I shall return to it again there.

Knowledge of self and others and the roots of a theory of mind

Development of a concept of self has been recognized as a fundamental aspect of social development, it being claimed that such knowledge is necessary in order to identify oneself as human and to interact meaning-fully with other humans (Lewis, 1990). Evidence about the development of a self concept in infancy has, however, proved hard to obtain, and as we shall see, much of the theorizing in this area is fairly speculative. Additionally, the small amount of evidence that exists is not always unambiguously indicative of the infant's self concept. However, there now does seem to be some progress on the empirical front, particularly in relation to ecological theories of self perception, and this area appears set to be of particular importance in the future.

An additional reason for attributing central importance to development of the self concept is that, in parallel with the infant's understanding of others, it forms the basis from which understanding of the working of the mind develops. That is, higher level understanding of self involves the ability to reflect on one's own mental processes. Similarly, higher levels of understanding of others involves the ability to reflect upon their mental states. This is just the sort of ability that interests those who work on the general topic of 'theory of mind' which, although mainly based in studies of children older than two years, is now recognized as having its roots in developments in understanding of self and others taking place during infancy.

Development of a concept of self

According to Piaget (1954), development of understanding of self as an object in space is a relatively late development, lagging behind development of understanding of other objects. As indicated in chapter 4, the self is treated effectively as the centre of the infant's physical world, and although progress occurs in development of self understanding from sensori-motor stage IV onwards, it is only in stage VI that infants gain the representational ability to effectively step outside self to view it in the same way as any other object in space.

Much of the data initially gathered supported the notion that the self concept develops late. The main technique adopted by investigators involved observing infants' reactions to their own image and images of objects in a mirror. The general finding is that during the large part of the first year infants treat the mirror as an object of interest, touching it and looking behind it, at times almost treating it as if it were another infant with whom to interact, whereas older infants progressively show more ability to identify mirror images as reflections of self or other objects. The most commonly accepted evidence for self recognition in mirror tasks has been some form of behaviour related to self. For instance, infants who touch their nose on seeing in the mirror that it has a spot of rouge on it (see figure 5.4) are credited with self recognition, similarly, infants who name themselves on seeing their image (Amsterdam, 1972). These abilities appear to emerge at around 18 months, although some have found naming to emerge later (Bertenthal and Fischer, 1978). Other measures include looking towards an object above or behind them on seeing it in the mirror, the rationale here being that they are recognizing the image as representing self and using self as referent for the object's position in space (Bigelow, 1981). The range of tasks used, however, has led to disagreement over the age at which self recognition emerges, since different tasks yield different ages for success.

Figure 5.4 The rouge test of selfrecognition.

One solution to this problem suggested by Bertenthal and Fischer (1978) is to treat the various tasks as measuring different stages in the development of a self concept. Testing children between six and 24 months old, they confirmed that the initial response to a mirror image of self involves behaviour directed to the mirror alone. In addition, they found that the ability to locate objects from mirror images emerged before the ability to direct actions to self or to refer to self. Rather than choose one of these measures as the single criterion for self recognition, Bertenthal and Fischer interpret them as indicative of the stages of development of self recognition, basing the developmental sequence on increasing cognitive complexity of

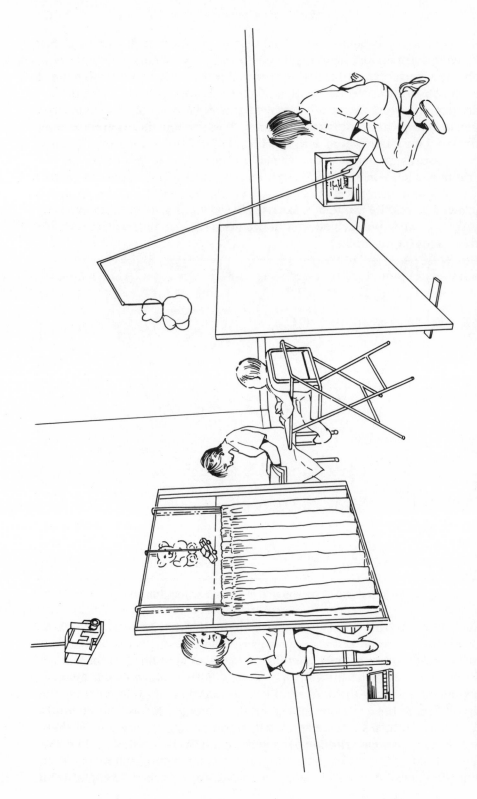

Figure 5.5 The setup used by Robinson et al. (1990) to investigate infants' ability to locate a target from its mirror image. In this case, the curtain is drawn over the lower part of the mirror, so the infant does not have access of an image to self.

the tasks. For instance, mirror directed behaviour is simpler than object or self directed behaviour, and the ability to relate objects to self comes prior to the ability to identify disparities between the mirror image and how self normally appears in the mirror.

There is, however, reason to question whether all these tasks measure self recognition. In particular, tasks involving object localization have come under scrutiny. Robinson et al., (1990) found that localization of an object from its mirror image was unaffected by whether or not the infant's own image was available in the mirror (see figure 5.5). Thus, since the infant's image is not used as referent, it is questionable whether such a task tells us anything about self recognition, although it does raise interesting questions about infants' spatial abilities. Such a conclusion is in keeping with a study by Priel and de Schonen (1986) carried out with a group of infants with no previous experience with mirrors. They found that perform-ance of self recognition tasks such as the 'rouge task' and self naming did not change with additional experience with mirrors, whereas performance of the object location task did. Thus the latter task appears to be one in which the infant has to learn spatial rules, and the finding obtained by Robinson and colleagues would suggest that these spatial rules do not depend on use of self image as a referent. Finally, a study by Johnson (1983) showed that many behaviours taken to be indicative of self recognition occurred at the same frequency in one- to two-year-old infants whether they were shown video sequences of their own image or that of another infant. Many infants even used their own name to label the other infant's image. The only exception was response on the 'rouge test' which was very infrequent when presented with the image of another infant. These studies thus suggest that most of the measures used in mirror tasks are suspect, and that the 'rouge test' is probably the only reliable indicator of the later stages of development of self recognition.

Despite the difficulty in obtaining experimental evidence on the topic, theories about the development of the self concept abound. Most accounts would have it that self awareness begins very early in infancy, although in a very different form from its later manifestations. For instance, there is a popular distinction between detection of direct information about self and the ability to refer to or reflect upon self. For instance, Lewis (1991) refers to these as *subjective* versus *objective* self awareness respectively, and argues that while aspects of subjective self awareness are present from birth, objective self awareness emerges around the middle of the second year.

Many of the arguments for the existence of direct information about self in early infancy are influenced by Gibson's theory of direct perception. For instance, Samuels (1986) suggests that infants pick up information which directly specifies their body boundaries, and that visual flow patterns during bodily movement specify the identity of the body in space. He also points to the fact that parts of the infant's nose and brow are always in the visual field, giving rise to perception of self. However, accounts of this sort leave the reader with the feeling that although these sources of information are likely to be important, much is left to be done in providing a convincing account of precisely in what way they necessarily specify a self. Probably more convincing arguments relate to recognition of intermodal correspondences during movement, in particular the correspondences between proprioceptive and visual information about limb movement. Bahrick and Watson (1985) showed that five-month-olds discriminated between a video display of their own concurrent leg movements and a display of themselves making a different set of movements, looking longer at the unrelated movement sequence. This suggests that they detect something amiss when proprioceptive and visual information do not match. If this is so, then we might expect them to use this sort of information as a means of specifying self. In everyday life infants have plenty of visual experience of their own limbs in motion, and the correspondence between the pattern of their acts and the resulting visual sensations may help to specify a 'visual self'. It appears that such intersensory correspondences continue to be important in self recognition in older infants, since Bigelow (1981) found that self recognition as indicated, for instance, by naming of an image of self, developed first when there was a correspondence between self and image movement and later when, for instance, the image was static.

There is an interesting link here with evidence on gender identity in infancy. Lewis and Brooks-Gunn (1979) identify gender identity as an important aspect of the self concept, and argue that awareness of gender is present at ten months, based on the fact that infants presented with photographs of a male and female infant look longer at the same sex photograph. Kujawski and Bower (1993) investigated the importance of movement information in this phenomenon by presenting ten- to 14-month-olds with light-point displays of male and female babies walking and running. Infants showed a looking preference for the same sex infant under these conditions, indicating that quite abstract information about movement was sufficient basis for discrimination and, according to Kujawski and Bower, identification of the like-self infant. This is an amazing finding, but links well with the suggestions above pointing to self movement as an important source of information about self.

Another source of information identified as important in early self perception is that derived from social interactions. Neisser (1991) distinguishes between an *ecological self*, specified by information such as visual flow during movement, and an *interpersonal self* specified by information derived from social interaction. The latter information includes perception of the fact that the interaction partner's behaviour is directed to the position of self, a position also specified by ecological information, and the fact that the infant's behaviour produces systematic effects on the partner's behaviour. According to Neisser, both of these 'selves' are directly perceived on the basis of information available in the environment. However, he also recognizes a *representational self* which develops in the second year and which corresponds to the level of self concept others have argued is reflected in mirror recognition tasks.

In summary, the area of self concept is a difficult one, both theoretically and empirically. Early studies appeared to indicate that a self concept did not emerge until around the middle of the second year. However, much of the evidence on which these claims were based has been questioned, and only the 'rouge task' emerges relatively unscathed. Recent theoretical developments, stimulated particularly by Gibson's theory of direct perception, recognize the presence of self perception within the first year, but this involves perception of self rather than the ability to refer to or reflect upon self, something which emerges during the second year. It should be noted, however, that not all theorists would accept that the early, perceptually based, sources of information give rise to true information about self. For example Case (1991) argues that knowledge of self cannot be simply perceived, but must be constructed mentally. Thus, controversy continues, and a good deal more research must be done before a clear picture emerges in this area.

Concepts of self and others as the foundations of a theory of mind

In the first section of this chapter, we encountered a range of evidence showing that quite young infants are well equipped to perceive people and that even from birth they behave differently to people versus objects. Additionally, in the second section evidence was presented indicating that infants are capable of detecting the emotions of others. These abilities may well have a similar status to the earlier forms of self awareness just discussed. That is, much of the information may be directly perceived and may not depend on mental representation. At a higher level it seems likely that there are even closer parallels between representation of self and others. Certainly, many theorists have identified close links, although often from opposing standpoints. For instance, Kohut (1977) suggests that infants construct their self knowledge from their knowledge of others, whereas Piaget (1951) claims that knowledge of others follows developmentally from knowledge of self, and really develops rather late. What evidence there is suggests that knowledge of self and knowledge of others develop along similar courses, although in particular domains of ability one leads the other and vice versa (Pipp, Fischer and Jennings, 1987).

It has also been argued that representations of both self and others are necessary precursors for important aspects of social development. Lewis (1990) claims that we must distinguish between social interaction, which even very young infants engage in, and social relationships, which entail both knowledge of self and other within the relationship. Thought of in this way, a relationship involves a special form of interaction in which the individuals modify their contributions on the basis of assessment of the other's mental and emotional state. This effectively takes us into the realms of theory of mind research, since this is aimed at investigating a particular aspect of knowledge of self and others, knowledge of the 'mental self' and 'mental other'.

Many forms of evidence have been used to support the view that infants understand something about the mental processes of others. For instance, it appears that quite young infants know something about other people as perceivers. Butterworth and Cochran (1980) showed that even six-month-olds were able to locate the target of their mother's gaze, provided the target was within their visual field. And in the following twelve months this ability becomes increasingly precise and extends to targets that are not in the visual field. Additionally, during the second year, infants begin to understand the conditions under which objects will be invisible to another person, and by two years will orient a picture appropriately for an adult viewer (Lempers, Flavell and Flavell, 1977).

There are also a set of phenomena that can be observed in natural interactions which have implications for the infant's understanding of the mental states of others. Dunn (1991) notes that in the second year, infants can be observed comforting others or showing concern for them, evidence that they are aware of others' emotional states. And of course we have already covered evidence of social referencing, in which infants' perception of their mothers' emotional state modifies their actions. Dunn also notes that infants begin to use deceit during the second year. Since deceit is directed towards misleading the adult, in other words, changing their beliefs, there is an assumption that infants must have an awareness of adults as possessors of beliefs. Additionally, during their second year, infants engage in pretend play, and by the age of two this includes the ability to take on the role of another person. This appears to go beyond imitation of another person's behaviour and suggests some ability to understand that person's mental processes.

Teasing is another activity that is identified quite early in infancy. Reddy (1991) claims that this activity is specifically aimed at changing the emotional state of the other and, as such, implies the ability to represent the emotions of the other. A typical example of teasing is withdrawal of a proffered object just before the parent grasps it, but Reddy also identifies more complex cases, for example:

Rebecca (11 months) Mother playing recorder, not specifically *to* Rebecca, who takes it away from her. M allows her, not thinking about reasons for Rebecca's action. Rebecca laughs, then gives it back to M. M takes it, laughing, and then resumes playing the tune. Rebecca reaches out and takes it again, laughing. M allows her. Rebecca then gives it back with a 'wicked grin'. M laughs 'because it was so obvious that she was teasing'. (1991, p. 145)

Although it has been shown that parents also tease their infants (Nakano and Kanaya, 1993; Trevarthen, 1989), Reddy concludes that it is unlikely that infants simply learn adult teasing routines, because the adult recipients of infant teasing appear to be genuinely affected by the event and not just engaged in a reversal of a well known routine.

In a similar way, Camaioni (1992) identifies intentional communication as a tool for manipulating the attention of others with regard to objects or events. She also assumes that the ability to manipulate the attention of others implies the ability to represent their attentional states, and thus assumes that the emergence of intentional communication during the second year indicates the emergence of the theory of mind. Also, Bretherton and Beeghly (1982) note that during their second year infants begin to use terms to refer to mental states, and that these terms are frequent by the beginning of the third year, with reference to self states somewhat ahead of reference to the states of others. This sort of evidence is also used as a basis for the argument that infants understand the minds of others, and Bretherton and Beeghly argue that preverbal infants have an implicit theory of mind which becomes explicit as they master the relevant aspects of language.

While most workers would concede that these phenomena give us important information about infants' developing awareness of other people, many would not interpret them as evidence that infants possess a theory of mind as such. For instance, Wellman and Woolley (1990) claim that possession of a theory of mind involves the knowledge that self and others have mental representations of the world that are used as a guide for action. In this respect, they distinguish between knowledge of desires and knowledge of beliefs, claiming that although desires are internal states they are not representations. Thus showing a knowledge of the desires of another does not constitute a theory of mind. In contrast, beliefs are mental representations of the world, and so a knowledge of the beliefs of another does constitute a theory of mind. Wellman and Woolley provide evidence that two-year-olds can answer questions about other people's desires, whereas it is only at three years that they can do so for people's beliefs. Additionally, when referring either to self or others, two-year-olds use only desire terms like 'want' while three-year-olds extend this to belief terms like 'think' and 'know' (Wellman, 1991).

In contrast, Leslie (1988) claims that pretence play exhibited by infants in their second year involves the ability to represent beliefs, and so he concludes that this ability is present early. Furthermore, he claims that infants understand causality in everyday action sequences. However, he suggests that infants and young children are incapable of coordinating representation of belief with causality, so that they do not appreciate how beliefs guide action. This ability emerges around four years and constitutes progress to a fully fledged theory of mind. In some ways, this is close to Astington and Gopnik's (1991) account, in which a true knowledge of mental representations only emerges at five years, once children are capable of understanding the way in which beliefs and desires lead to intentions and in turn to actions.

This takes us beyond the period of infancy and so a full discussion is beyond the scope of this book. I summarize some of the arguments here, however, to give a flavour of the controversy surrounding the topic, since this undoubtedly affects the interpretations placed on relevant infant phenomena. There is a tendency on the part of some to play down the significance of the infant findings, claiming that these do not indicate a theory of mind. However, two points are important. Firstly, the distinctions developed with regard to what is and what is not a theory of mind are subtle and complex, and their investigation requires fairly contrived experimental techniques that generally involve questioning children about the beliefs of others. As Dunn (1991) points out, although these techniques yield the sort of experimental rigour required, there is a serious danger that they underestimate young children's ability, since rather than assessing infants' knowledge of people in everyday reality, testing takes place in artificial situations often involving toy people or stories about imaginary people. Additionally, as Camaioni points out, the strong reliance on verbal response is problematic, since it is not easy to know if a particular limitation reflects lack of knowledge or lack of the relevant vocabulary.

Secondly, there appears to be rather little to be gained from discussing precisely when children possess a theory of mind, particularly since definitions differ. Instead it would seem more profitable to analyse the naturalistic phenomena and experimental evidence across the age range from infancy through to early childhood with the aim of providing an account of the development of knowledge of the mind from its earliest stages. To an extent this is already happening, but when this standpoint is more widely adopted, it should be possible to set the phenomena in infancy in developmental relationship with the findings emerging at four or five years and thus provide an all too rare link between research in infancy and early childhood.

Attachment: the first relationships

Research on the development of attachment has a different flavour from most of the rest of infancy research. This is partly because the work in this area has different theoretical roots, being heavily influenced by psychoanalytic theory. According to Freudian theory, adult personality characteristics can be traced to early fixations in ego development, for instance, compulsiveness was taken to be due to fixation in the anal stage (hence the label 'anal personality'). Furthermore, these fixations take place as a result of particular parental practices in areas like feeding and toilet training, and so it was claimed that the way parents treated their offspring could have an important role in determining whether the individual developed a normal personality in later years.

Another way in which work on attachment stands out is in its applied emphasis. The psychoanalytic stress on the importance of early patterns of care, and later the ethological emphasis on the importance of early *imprinting* experiences, alerted practitioners to the need to attend more closely to factors in infancy contributing to later mental wellbeing. Although the initial emphasis was on aspects of physical care, largely through Bowlby's influence emphasis shifted to social and emotional factors. These issues were particularly relevant to those caring for children denied a normal family upbringing, who were faced with a range of questions concerning the adequacy of different types of substitute care.

Most work focuses primarily on the mother–infant relationship, about which two major questions arise. First, how is the relationship between infant and mother formed and maintained? Secondly, what is the importance of this relationship for the infant's development in other spheres? Bowlby (1953) claimed, 'what is believed to be essential for mental health is that an infant and young child should experience a warm, intimate, and continuous relationship with his mother' (p. 13). If this statement is correct, the early mother–child relationship is absolutely crucial. However, more recent work has taken a more analytic line (Rutter, 1981). Is continuity of care crucial for the formation of attachments, or is the quality of the relationship more important? How can we define quality of interaction so as to distinguish between good and bad relationships? Apart from tackling these issues, workers have also continued to investigate the relation between early attachment and later development. For obvious ethical reasons, it is difficult to carry out well-controlled experimental studies in this area, and the bulk of the data arise from naturally occurring cases of 'maternal deprivation'. As we shall see, this makes isolation of crucial variables hard, since deprivation generally occurs in several forms simultaneously and is accompanied by other unsettling life events. When care has been taken to account for these other variables, the frequent conclusion is that the link between early attachment and later personality is less strong than Bowlby concluded.

The formation of attachments: Bowlby's theory

Early theories generally explained attachment as functioning to satisfy some sort of innate need or *drive*. For instance, the child's tie with his or her mother arose to satisfy the need to cling to objects or to suck. Some theories seem almost mystical. For instance, one notion was that in attachment behaviour infants were attempting to satisfy a craving to return to the womb. Until the early 1950s the favoured explanation was *secondary drive theory*. According to this, attachment to the mother was simply a means to an end, the end being the infant's basic needs, particularly food. The primary drive was towards satisfaction of basic needs, and the secondary drive was attachment to the mother *in order* to satisfy these needs. This theory received a severe blow, however, from Harlow's findings with infant monkeys (1961), in particular, the finding that when given the choice between an artificial 'mother' made of comfortable cloth and one made of wire that offered milk, young monkeys chose the former and became attached to it rather than the one that presented sustenance.

This finding is more in line with the notion that attachment satisfies the need to cling, but Bowlby was unimpressed by all these theories, in which needs were more or less manufactured to explain the infant's behaviour. Consequently, he developed a theory in which attachment behaviour was more precisely defined as a system that had evolved to increase the infant's chances of survival.

The evolutionary basis for attachment behaviour As well as being influenced by psychoanalytic thinking, Bowlby (1969) drew on concepts from evolutionary biology. In particular, he was influenced by the ethological work of Hinde (1963, 1966) and Tinbergen (1951), work which stressed the importance of instinctive *imprinting* phenomena through which the young of various species were observed to form early attachments to parents. The main evidence for these attachments was the young animal's tendency to maintain proximity to the imprinted object wherever it moved. Bowlby maintained this emphasis, claiming that various forms of *attachment behaviours* occurred during infancy, having the function of maintaining proximity between infant and mother.

Bowlby's theory embodies a number of concepts drawn from biology and systems theory. First, he stresses the notion that attachment behaviour has evolved as an important survival mechanism. The tendency to maintain proximity to adults affords protection against predators and presumably reduces the likelihood of the infant's becoming separated from the adult or adults upon whom he or she depends for survival. Bowlby argues that we can only understand this mechanism by reference to the primeval human environment. This is because changes in the relatively recent history of humanity have been too great and too rapid for evolutionary mechanisms to keep up. Hence Bowlby argues that the innate systems that we see emerging in infancy today are adaptations to the human *environment of evolutionary adaptedness* of the past, and may in some respects be poorly suited to present day environments.

Bowlby uses systems theory to explain how parent–infant proximity is maintained. The key concept is that of a control system which has the function of monitoring some variable and maintaining it within set limits. A simple example is a feedback system such as a room thermostat, in which the system monitors room temperature and responds to fluctuations by cutting the heating system in or out so that the change is counteracted. More sophisticated servo systems constantly monitor the difference between actual and required states and produce a response proportionate to the degree of difference. In the case of attachment behaviour, the variable monitored is distance between mother and infant. If this distance increases beyond acceptable levels, particular behaviours are activated that have the effect of bringing the distance back within acceptable bounds. In Bowlby's words, 'the child's tie to his mother is a product of the activity of a number of behavioural systems that have proximity to mother as a predictable outcome' (1969, p. 223).

Expanding on this concept, Bowlby distinguishes between adaptive behaviours that are goal-corrected (in the servo system sense) and those that are not. In early infancy, crying generally ensures the approach of parents if they are out of range. However, crying may be triggered by factors such as hunger or discomfort, and so although the outcome may be proximity, we cannot say that the behaviour was directed at that goal. Even when crying is triggered by parental absence, initially it is not modified depending upon distance between parent and infant, and so it cannot be said to be goal-corrected in the full sense. In contrast, once infants can crawl, they will monitor their mother's movements, and crawl at rates and in directions that ensure continuing proximity. For Bowlby, this is a true example of goal-corrected attachment behaviour.

Bowlby stresses the point that these systems are not directed at maintaining proximity with any adult. As the infant develops, attachment behaviour becomes increasingly directed at one person in particular, and although other attachments are formed, there is always one attachment, normally with the infant's mother, that is probably qualitatively different from other attachments. This aspect of attachment is often referred to as *monotropy*.

Another aspect of the theory that comes directly from ethological theory is the notion that there is a sensitive period during which attachments are easily formed. The onset of this period is determined mainly by perceptual factors; infants cannot direct attachment behaviour selectively until they can discriminate parents from others. The sensitive period is brought gradually to an end by the onset of wariness of strangers, and the outcome is that infants who do not form an attachment before this point will find it progressively harder to do so as time goes on.

In the account developed so far, there is little reference to feelings of emotion, and Bowlby is reluctant to identify a direct causal relation between emotion and attachment behaviour. Instead, he suggests that feelings of emotion, like other conscious experiences, are products of the infant's appraisal of the degree to which the behavioural system is succeeding in maintaining the set goal. Unacceptable separation from mother may result in feelings of anxiety, whereas recognition that proximity has been achieved may result in feelings of security. So emotional experiences are only important as concomitants of attentive monitoring, and Bowlby sees no evidence that they are directly causal of attachment behaviour. In this sense, his argument has more in common with the views of Kagan (1971) and Papousek (1967) than more recent views that attribute a causal role to emotion (Barrett and Campos, 1987).

The development of attachment behaviour   Bowlby describes a range of early activities that can be termed attachment behaviours because they serve to increase or maintain proximity between mother and infant. Examples are crying, grasping, smiling and babbling. Crying serves to bring the mother to the infant and grasping serves to maintain close contact. Smiling and babbling enhance social interaction and hence help to ensure that the mother stays close. Part of Bowlby's account concerns the way in which these behaviours become selectively directed to one person. The argument here is that infants cannot initially discriminate between people and can only begin to be selective in their attachments once their perceptual abilities have developed sufficiently. This aspect of Bowlby's theory needs modification in the light of recent evidence on person perception reviewed in the earlier part of this chapter.

Bowlby describes four phases in the development of attachment behaviour, summarized as follows:

Phase I (birth to 8/12 weeks)	Infant orients and responds in characteristic way to people but has little or no ability to discriminate between people.
Phase II (8/12 to 24/30 weeks)	Infant orients and responds preferentially to one figure (usually the mother).
Phase III (24/30 weeks to 2/3 years)	Onset of locomotion leads infant to make active attempts to maintain proximity to attachment figure.
Phase IV (2/3 years on)	Child begins to discern the mother's goals and needs and begins to take account of them in acting as a partner in the relationship.

In phase I, which lasts at least for the first eight weeks, infants behave in special ways towards people, for instance they orient to people, soon beginning to smile and babble in their presence. They may also stop crying on seeing a face or hearing a voice. But, because of their very limited ability to discriminate between people, they show no selectivity in these responses, directing them to mother and perfect stranger alike. During phase II, however, these behaviours become progressively more marked when the mother is the focus of attention, although they are still produced to a lesser extent in the presence of others. In both of these phases, attachment behaviour consists solely of signals that serve to bring adults closer, and their success depends upon activity by the adult. During phase III, the onset of locomotion allows the infant to take a direct role in maintaining proximity through fully fledged goal-corrected behaviour. Also, wariness of strangers begins to develop, a factor that strengthens the selectivity of social responsiveness. By this point, some people are likely to have been selected as subsidiary attachment figures, but those that have not will be treated with increasing wariness. Cognitive developments during this phase lead to the infant reaching a better understanding of people as independent and enduring objects, and this means that attachment behaviours can be directed towards an absent goal. Finally, in phase IV the infant begins to reach an awareness of the mother's own goals and the way she achieves them. This allows the development of a partnership in which both infant and mother take account of each other's feelings and motives in formulating their behaviour to each other. This, according to Bowlby, is a relatively late development, occuring only after infancy has ended.

It must be remembered that Bowlby based much of this account on the evidence of the day, which presented the young infant as perceptually and cognitively immature. More recent evidence and theory presents the infant in a different light, and there are a number of ways in which Bowlby's theory has to be modified. For instance, there is growing evidence for person discrimination and selective social responsiveness in early infancy that casts doubt on some of his claims about the young infant's deficiencies in this area. Also, the conventional Piagetian account of object concept development was much more strongly adhered to in the 1960s than it is now, and some workers would claim that people should be understood as permanent objects a good deal earlier than phase III. Additionally, as already noted, there is evidence derived from use of telethermography indicating that infants as young as two months old show stress at the absence of their mothers (Mizukami, et al., 1990), evidence for the presence of the sort of selective attachment that is assumed to depend on developments in object permanence formerly assumed to occur at about seven or eight months. Nevertheless, many aspects of the account, such as the shift during development towards the infant having direct goal-corrected control over proximity, remain valid.

Bowlby claimed that the primary function of attachment behaviour was protection from predators, and one might be tempted to conclude that in the environment of today it would matter little whether or not infants formed firm attachments. However, there are several reasons why attachment may still be vital. First, although the primary function of early attachment may be largely redundant today, Bowlby argued that there were close links between the quality of early relationships and the individual's ability to form relationships in later childhood and adulthood. Hence, failure to form an attachment in infancy would lead to social problems in later life. This issue will be explored further in the section on maternal deprivation. Secondly, Bowlby points out how proximity to a mother figure enhances the infant's chances of learning through interaction with her.

Finally, although attachment behaviours are the antithesis of exploration, the notion is that the establishment of an attachment provides a secure base from which the infant can explore novel environments. Thus a behaviour which in itself appears to be the very opposite of exploration leads in turn to good conditions for production of the more outgoing behaviours that progressively take over as the child becomes more independent. The need to be able to explain the relationship between attachment and later independence has led many workers to measure attachment in terms of its security.

Measuring security of attachment: Ainsworth's 'strange situation'

Early measures of strength of attachment were generally derived from single behaviours such as separation protest or proximity seeking, or maybe the proportion of smiles directed to mother as opposed to strangers. These measures cast attachment in a rather negative light, it being easy to interpret them as indicators of dependency rather than security. More recently, a more thorough assessment method was devised that has proved more satisfactory (Ainsworth et al., 1978). Rather than relying on single measures, the security of infants' attachment is assessed on the basis of their responses to a variety of events presented in a standard setting, the 'strange situation'.

Ainsworth's test lasts about 25 minutes and consists of eight different episodes (see tables 5.1, 5.2) from which it is possible to assess the infant's response to being in a strange situation either alone, with mother, with stranger, or with both. In addition, the coming and going of the mother during the session allows the infant's response to separation and reunion to be assessed. After a brief introduction (episode 1), the second episode is used to assess the infant's security in the presence of the mother. The third episode is used to assess the infant's response to a stranger when the mother is present. Then episode 4 is used to measure the infant's response to the departure of the mother, and the degree to which the stranger is able to comfort him or her, and in episode 5 the infant's response to the return of the mother is assessed. Then response to separation and reunion are assessed again, this time with the slight variation that the infant is initially left alone (episode 6) but is then joined by the stranger (episode 7) and then finally by the mother (episode 8). Although all episodes apart from the first one last three minutes, those in which the mother is absent are curtailed if the infant becomes too distressed.

By using a combination of measures taken at different points in the session, Ainsworth claims it is possible to classify all infants into one of three broad groups in terms of the security of their attachment to mother. Group A infants are labelled *anxious–avoidant*. Although they may not be particularly happy in the strange situation and may cry in the absence of their mother, they do not seek proximity with her, and actively avoid contact during reunion episodes. They do not react very differently to strangers, and may even appear to prefer them to their mother. Group B

Table 5.1 Phases of the strange situation

Number of episode	Persons present	Duration	Brief description of action
1	Mother, baby and observer	30 sec.	Observer introduces mother and baby to experimental room, then leaves
2	Mother and baby	3 min.	Mother is non-participant while baby explores: if necessary, play is stimulated after 2 min.
3	Stranger, mother and baby	3 min.	Stranger enters. Min. 1: stranger silent. Min. 2: stranger converses with mother. Min. 3: stranger approaches baby. After 3 min. mother leaves unobtrusively
4	Stranger and baby	3 min.[a] or less	First separation episode. Stranger's behaviour is geared to that of baby
5	Mother and baby	3 min.[b] or more	First reunion episode. Mother greets and comforts baby, then tries to settle him again in play. Mother then leaves, saying 'bye-bye'
6	Baby alone	3 min.[a] or less	Second separation episode
7	Stranger and baby	3 min.[a] or less	Continuation of second separation. Stranger enters and gears her behavior to that of baby
8	Mother and baby	3 min.	Second reunion episode. Mother enters, greets baby, then picks him up. Meanwhile stranger leaves unobtrusively

[a] Episode is curtailed if the baby is unduly distressed.
[b] Episode is prolonged if more time is required for the baby to become reinvolved in play.
Source: Ainsworth et al., 1978.

infants are labelled *secure*. They are at ease in the strange situation as long as the mother is present, using her as a secure base for exploration. They may cry in her absence and seek proximity and contact with her on her return, but they soon settle down happily after the reunion. They also show a marked preference for the mother over a stranger. Group C infants are labelled *anxious–ambivalent* because they show a combination of positive and negative reactions to their mother. Before separation they seek contact with her to such an extent that exploration of the environment may be

Table 5.2 Classifications of infant attachment

Classification	Descriptor	Classification criteria[a]					
		Proximity seeking	Contact maintaining	Proximity avoiding	Contact resisting	Crying
A (2 subgroups)	Avoidant	Low	Low	High	Low	Low (pre-separation), high or low (separation), low (reunion)
B (4 subgroups)	Secure	High	High (if distressed)	Low	Low	Low (Pre-separation), high or low (separation), low (reunion)
C (2 subgroups)	Ambivalent	High	High (often pre-separation)	Low	High	Occasionally (pre-separation), high (separation), moderate to high (reunion)

[a] Based on reunion episodes 5 and 8 in table 5.1 typical of the group as a whole; subgroups differ in non-reunion episodes and to some extent in reunion behaviour. See Ainsworth et al. (1978) for detailed classification instructions.

Source: Waters, 1978. © The Society for Research in Child Development, Inc.

inhibited, and on separation they are likely to become very upset. On the other hand, contact may be actively resisted, particularly during a reunion episode. This tendency towards physical resistance of the caretaker's approaches has led to this group being frequently referred to by the alternative term *anxious-resistant*.

In samples of infants born to middle-class families in the United States, the majority of infants (approximately 65 per cent) are classified as securely attached, whereas between 15 and 20 per cent fall into the other two categories. The significance of such a classification depends very much upon its stability over time. For example, there is little to be gained from a classification that depends upon the infant's mood at the time of testing. Consequently, a good deal of research has been directed to the issue of test–retest stability. Some studies show high stability in classification over time. For instance, Waters (1978) showed almost perfect agreement between infants' strange situation classification at 12 and 18 months, and Antonucci and Levitt (1984) found a good degree of consistency between seven months and 13 months. On the other hand, other studies (for instance, Ainsworth et al., 1978) show less consistency over time.

Although we would be unhappy with a classification that depended entirely on the infant's mood at the time of testing, we should bear in mind the likelihood that at least some attachments change in quality over time. If, for example, infants have unsettling experiences at home their quality of attachment may be changed for the worse. One group of workers (Vaughn et al., 1979) point to this as an explanation of instability of classification in a subset of their infants. There were more reports of unsettling family events in the case of infants changing from secure classification to insecure than there were in the case of infants who were classified as secure on both occasions. So there does seem to be evidence that, given stable home circumstances, the strange situation measures show good stability over time.

Despite this evidence, there is still something paradoxical about the way security is measured largely in terms of proximity seeking and maintenance on the mother's return. Although other measures such as degree of exploration are mentioned in the classification, they seem to take second place to behaviours directed towards the mother. So, there is still a need for independent evidence that this classification scheme, however stable, actually measures a positive characteristic indicative of security in the wider world. One study supplies fairly direct evidence on this. Cassidy (1986) found that infants classified as securely attached not only showed more exploration of the environment but showed superior abilities in negotiating obstacles and generally finding their way around. Thus there seems to be a link between mother-directed behaviour and the infant's ability to learn about the environment. As Cassidy puts it, 'A baby who has built up an image of the mother as both physically and emotionally available is free to attend to other aspects of the environment', a point that emphasizes the possibility of a link between attachment security and cognitive development.

An infant who is constantly preoccupied with the whereabouts of his or her mother may as a consequence fail to learn about other aspects of the environment.

A further case in which the presence of the mother may form a secure base appears in infants' responses to strangers. Here again is a case in which primary emphasis is placed on developing wariness of strangers, and yet wariness must presumably be balanced by a positive tendency to affiliate with new people if the infant is to develop satisfactory social relations beyond the immediate family. Bohlin and Hagekull (1993) found that ten- to 13-month-olds confronted with a stranger showed a heart rate increase (indicating wariness) when their mother was absent, but when she was present showed a heart rate decrease (indicating interest) at least in the initial phase of the stranger approach. Additionally, this heart rate decrease was most marked in the more sociable infants. They conclude that the infant's reaction to strangers is determined by two opposing tendencies, wariness and affiliation. When the mother is present, the security she provides may permit affiliation to predominate over wariness. Additionally, it is possible that older infants may look to the mother for emotional signals, assuming that in the absence of negative signals wariness is unnecessary.

If there are important links between quality of attachment and other aspects of development, these should be revealed in correlations between attachment and other measures of behaviour, both in infancy and beyond. A whole range of studies have looked for relations with various measures of social and cognitive function. Some workers have looked for links with cognitive development. For instance, Bell (1970) found that only securely attached infants consistently developed person permanence before object permanence, and Bretherton et al. (1979) found that they showed more advanced tool use than other attachment groups. Other workers have looked for links with aspects of social behaviour or personality, both during infancy and later. For instance, Sroufe (1983) found that infants classified as securely attached at 18 months were at four years rated more highly by their teachers on a number of positive characteristics such as popularity, resilience and independence. One review of the evidence (Lamb et al., 1984) concludes that there is clear evidence of a link between strange situation classification and a variety of aspects of later behavioural adjustment. But these authors also point out that these relationships only hold when family circumstances remain stable, so there is no magical guarantee that a securely attached infant will become a well-adjusted child.

Probably one of the most controversial issues surrounding attachment as measured by the strange situation relates to Bowlby's claim that the formation of a secure attachment is a universal biological tendency. According to such a view, the majority of infants should exhibit secure attachment and those that do not may be assumed to have failed to develop an optimum relationship. However, early cross-cultural comparisons revealed

distributions that differed markedly from the 'American norm'. For instance, a German study revealed a majority of anxious–avoidant infants
(Grossmann, Grossmann, Huber and Wartner, 1981), while an Israeli
study (Sagi, et al., 1985) and a Japanese study (Takahashi, 1986) both
revealed a higher proportion of insecure–resistant infants than obtained in
the US, although in these cases secure attachments dominated.

As further evidence has accrued, however, these cross-cultural differences have been shown to be less striking than they initially appeared.
IJzendoorn and Kroonenberg (1988) showed that in addition to cross-
cultural differences there were wide intra-cultural differences in the proportions of the three attachment types, with the intra-cultural variation about
one and a half times larger than the cross-cultural variation. They also
showed that when data were pooled across studies in each culture separately, while the relative proportions of the two types of insecure attachment
varied between cultures, secure attachments always predominated, although not always so much as in the case of the initial US studies. We are
left, however, with the finding that distinct cross-cultural differences exist,
although not in as marked a form as the initial German study suggested.
These differences have led some workers to conclude that the strange
situation is not an appropriate measure of attachment in some cultures. For
instance, Takahashi (1990) suggests that the standard procedure induces
too much stress in Japanese infants, since the norm in that country is to
avoid stress and separation during infancy rather than to teach infants to
deal with it. The question is then whether we can explain the larger
intra-cultural differences in similar terms. That is, are there inter-cultural
differences that make the strange situation a poor test of attachment except
in sub-sections of the culture to which it is particularly adapted, or do these
differences arise from differences in quality of parenting within a culture?
A third possibility is that these data indicate that there is no such thing as
a universal tendency to become attached in a particular way. Probably the
solution to this debate lies not in taking any one of these stances to the
exclusion of others, but in developing an account based on the assumption
that while universal biological tendencies may exist these are liable to be
modified by cultural factors (IJzendoorn and Tavecchio, 1987). Thus,
although there appears to be a general tendency to seek attachment, this
may be converted relatively early into independence in cultures in which it
is the norm to foster this, but may remain reflected as dependence for
longer in cultures in which mothers maintain proximity and take steps to
reduce the stress that goes along with formation of independence. Additionally, these differences in parenting styles may well relate adaptively to
differences between cultures in the requirements placed on individuals with
respect to independence etc. Thus at least when considering attachment
across cultures we should probably abandon the notion that there is a
single correct style of parenting or even that an insecure attachment is
inevitably poorer than a secure attachment.

Maternal sensitivity and security of attachment   Ainsworth claims that the security of attachment depends upon the mother's sensitivity to the infant. Mothers of insecurely attached infants are either rejecting or insensitive to the infant's social overtures, whereas mothers of securely attached infants respond rapidly and positively to their infants and engage in more face-to-face contact. This analysis puts responsibility for the infant's normal development firmly at the mother's door. Those mothers who do not respond appropriately to their infant's signals do not provide the reassuring indicators that the infant needs in order to form a secure attachment. Support for this notion comes from a variety of sources. For instance, Belsky, Rovine and Taylor (1984) found that both over-responsive and under-responsive mothering was related to insecure attachments, and Smith and Pederson (1988) found that mothers of securely attached infants were more sensitive to their infants' needs. They also appeared to know more about their infants and to enjoy interacting with them more than mothers of insecurely attached infants (Pederson, Moran, Sitko, Campbell, Ghesquire and Acton, 1990). Additionally, Isabella (1993) found that mothers of securely attached infants were more sensitive in their responses and less rejecting than mothers of insecurely attached infants. Furthermore, mothers of anxious–resistant infants tended to be rejecting only when the infant was very young, which suggests that this form of insecurity may result from inconsistencies in maternal response over the developmental period. Most of these measures are taken during the first year, however it appears that late in infancy, more symbolic play is engaged in between mother and infant in the case of securely attached infants (Slade, 1987).

Thus, a range of studies suggest a relationship between style of parenting and type of attachment. As Campos et al. (1983) point out, however, differences in maternal behaviour may in themselves be partly due to the infant's characteristics. A mother may be unresponsive because her infant is unresponsive, and so correlations between maternal responsiveness and security of attachment need not indicate that the direction of causality runs from mother to infant. There is some evidence, however, which suggests that quality of attachment may be at least partly determined by the mother's characteristics. For instance, Izard, Haynes, Chisholm and Baak (1991) found that, among other things, maternal personality traits predicted the form of the infant's attachment. Despite this, however, it seems likely that the formation of attachment is determined by a fairly complex interaction between characteristics of infant and mother. It seems clear that the way the mother interacts with her infant affects the quality of attachment. In addition to the mother's own predispositions, however, it seems inevitable that the way her infant behaves will influence her style of response.

Infant temperament and security of attachment   If differences in mothers' interactional style influence the quality of infant attachment, it seems obvious to ask whether individual differences between infants bear a relationship to attachment. As we know from chapter 2, infants show differences in temperament at birth which persist in the months that follow, and there has been considerable controversy over whether infant temperament is an important factor in predicting the type of attachment that the infant will form. While some workers such as Kagan (1984) have argued that temperament is an important factor, others have argued that it is of minor importance in predicting attachment (Sroufe, 1985). Some recent evidence tends to indicate that although infant temperament may affect the infant's behaviour in the strange situation, it does not affect their overall classification. For instance, Belsky and Rovine (1987) suggest that infant temperament affects how infants demonstrate security or insecurity but does not affect their classification, and while finding no link between temperament and attachment security, Vaughn and his colleagues (Vaughn, et al., 1989) found that certain negative emotional behaviours in the strange situation were related to temperament. On the other hand, some studies do claim to show effects on attachment security. For instance, Calkins and Fox (1992) showed that infants' temperament at two days, as measured by their response to withdrawal of a dummy, predicted whether these infants would be securely or insecurely attached. Additionally, Vaughn, et al. (1992) obtained modest relationships between temperament and attachment. Vaughn and his colleagues claim that there is necessarily some overlap between measures of temperament and attachment, since both are a means of assessing emotional response in the infant, and they suggest that the focus should be on diagnosing the relative contribution of individual and social factors in determining infants' emotional responses, rather than on establishing whether or not there is a relationship between temperament and attachment.

Possibly we also need to adopt this approach in the analysis of maternal responsiveness, and indeed we may have to go a step further to measure the degree to which maternal and infant emotional and interactional styles mesh, relating this to security of the relationship. There is already evidence that the form of attachment at one year can be predicted from the quality of the interaction between mother and infant, those interactions showing greatest synchrony between one and nine months being predictive of secure attachment, while those showing asynchrony predicting insecure attachments (Isabella, Beisky and von Eye, 1989; Isabella and Belsky, 1991). The tendency, however, is still to look for and hence to interpret the sources of synchrony or asynchrony in terms of maternal sensitivity. But it has been shown that both maternal personality and infant temperament affect the quality of interaction (Fish, Stifter and Belsky, 1993). Also, as we shall see in the section *Early communication: parent–infant interaction*, there is evidence that interactional synchrony is contributed to by both partners in the exchange. Thus it may be most realistic to consider security of attachment as determined by the way maternal and infant variables interact. Those whose emotional and cognitive styles mesh early in development may be more likely to develop secure relationships than those whose styles clash.

The other side of the coin: the mother's attachment to her infant

So far the analysis has concentrated purely on how infants become attached to their parents, but it is commonly believed that normal mother–infant relations rely also on the mother becoming firmly attached to her infant. This seems a perfectly sensible supposition, and indeed during the 1970s there was a good deal of research based on the notion that mother to infant bonding occurred rather like animal imprinting during a critical period immediately following birth. Initially there seemed to be good evidence for this. For example, Klaus and Kennell (1976) found that a group of mothers given extra contact with their infant within the first few days were more strongly attached at one month and even two years later. However, others have had difficulty in replicating the long-term effect. For instance, Whiten (1977) found that any differences between extra contact and normal contact mothers had disappeared by two months.

A number of workers even claimed that early skin-to-skin contact served to enhance the bonding process. For instance, Hales et al. (1977) found that mothers given skin contact reported being more strongly attached to their infant one month later. However, there are problems with both this sort of study and those on extended contact. Campos et al. (1983) point out that investigators and parents were aware of the predicted effect of contact, with the consequence that the results may attest to the power of suggestion rather than the presence of a real relationship, and they conclude that there is at best weak evidence for the importance of skin contact in mother–infant bonding. In fact, Slukin, Herbert and Slukin (1983) claim that there is no evidence to support a rapid imprinting process of any sort, concluding instead that the mother's bond to her infant develops gradually over a matter of weeks. Thus, if early skin-to-skin contact has any effect, it is probably because it 'helps to get the mother–infant relationship off to a good start' (Maccoby and Martin, 1983) rather than because it is involved in some rapid imprinting process on the maternal side. One study, however, showed that physical contact over a period of months resulting from use of a soft baby carrier led to an increase in maternal responsiveness and a dramatic increase in the frequency of secure attachments in a group of low socio-economic status mother–infant dyads (Anisfeld, et al., 1990). However, although these workers conclude that close contact of this sort has a direct effect on maternal responsiveness, they also conclude that there is a direct effect on the infant, since the increase in maternal responsiveness did not appear to be enough to explain the very large increase in the number of securely attached infants.

Such a modification of our view of the process of mother–infant bonding does not mean that we should conclude it has a lesser role in the formation of a happy relation between infant and mother. Rather it points to the likelihood that we will not fully understand the process of attachment by considering it from one side alone. It seems realistic to consider the process as a two-way one in which the attachment of mother to infant and of infant to mother may be facilitated or obstructed by the degree to which the characteristics of the two partners mesh or fail to mesh in their early interactions. There is growing evidence that quality of interaction is an important determinant of a secure relationship. For instance, Antonucci and Levitt (1984) identify measures relating to quality of interaction as the most stable indicators of attachment quality. Many of the paradoxes in the attachment literature may be eliminated in future by focusing in detail on the form of the mother–infant relationship. In this way it may be possible to relate security on both sides to the degree to which mother and infant have adapted to each other's styles of interaction.

Maternal deprivation

Up till now we have focused on theories of how parent–infant attachments develop under normal conditions of care. However, the most controversial aspects of Bowlby's writing were the claims he made about the consequences of either a lack or a loss of maternal care. In his view, formation and maintenance of a strong attachment with a single mother figure was essential for the current and later mental health of the child. The claim was that a range of personality and behavioural problems were likely to result in later life if a satisfactory attachment was not formed during infancy. Also, if an attachment, once formed, was disrupted through separation from the mother figure, there would at least be severe emotional effects on the infant for the duration of the separation, and the likelihood of permanent damage increased the longer the separation continued. Although Bowlby was inclined to the conclusion that the effects of temporary separation from the mother were less severe if this happened in the first six months, before a specific attachment had begun to form, he noted that separation during these early months might interfere with the process of attachment formation, and so might have equally severe effects that could go unnoticed because young infants showed no immediate emotional reaction to separation.

In short, maternal deprivation occuring in the early months could interfere with the initial formation of an attachment, and deprivation occurring in later months could lead to disruption of an existing attachment. In Bowlby's view either of these effects could have long-term consequences, and he documented many cases in which deprivation of maternal care had led to severe problems such as mental retardation, delinquency and *affectionless psychopathy* in later life (Bowlby, 1953). He conceded that these effects could be reversed or minimized by return to the mother or by the prompt supply of adequate substitute care, but he was sharply critical of most forms of care other than adoption or fostering, in which the infant was supplied with a replacement single mother–figure. Here he made probably his most controversial claim, that 'children thrive better in bad homes than in good institutions' (1953, p. 78). However, he did add that the truth of this statement depended on just how bad the home was and just how good the institution, a point that his critics often fail to mention.

While this qualification makes Bowlby's statement less controversial, it leaves us largely in the dark as to what constitutes a good institution or a poor home, and more recent analyses of the problem have attempted to do much more to isolate the factors that are needed for adequate care, whether it be in the home or in an institution. Questions have also been asked about the strength of the evidence on which Bowlby bases his claims about the long-term effects of maternal deprivation. Human deprivation can only be studied where it occurs naturally, and in nature events seldom occur in isolation. Often, for instance, separation from the mother is the outcome of other factors, such as when family disharmony leads to an infant being taken into care. In this case, are the long-term effects due to the separation, the preceding disharmony, or both? For ethical reasons it is impossible to resolve this sort of issue through experiment, and we are left with the alternative of assessing the effect of separation under as many different circumstances as possible. In this way it is possible to reach some conclusions about the relative contribution of separation versus other accompanying factors. This sort of analysis underlies a number of extensive discussions of the topic (Clarke and Clarke, 1976; Rutter, 1981; Schaffer, 1971), and in all cases the conclusions about the effects of maternal deprivation are less pessimistic than Bowlby's. Here I shall provide only a brief summary of conclusions about the severity of short and long-term effects of deprivation, and the factors that contribute to them.

Short-term effects Rutter (1981) classifies as 'short-term' those effects of deprivation that either result immediately or over a short period following the experience, and as 'long-term' those effects that appear some years later. In the case of an infant who for one reason or another is separated from mother and family there is a typical reaction sequence that most workers agree upon. First, infants display acute distress which cannot be easily alleviated by caretakers (sometimes called the period of protest). Then they enter a phase of general misery and apathy (the period of despair), but eventually they enter a final phase in which they appear content and seem to be no longer concerned by the absence of their parents (the period of detachment). Fortunately, it turns out that this reaction, although common, is far from inevitable. A number of factors effect its intensity or even whether it occurs at all.

First, Rutter points out that this very intense reaction to separation is more usual in the case of a child entering hospital, circumstances very different from those surrounding a separation when a child goes to visit relatives, or maybe remains in the home while his or her mother is absent. The hospitalized child has to cope with a new environment and maybe painful treatment in addition to separation from parents. Consequently, it is possible that the distress reaction is caused by entry into a strange environment rather than by separation from the mother. This conclusion is supported by the finding that distress on separation is greater in a strange environment than in a familiar one (Ross et al., 1975). This, however, cannot be the whole story, since infants admitted to hospital with their mother show less distress than those admitted alone (Fagin, 1966). So we must conclude that at least two factors influence the intensity of separation distress, the separation itself and the strangeness of the environment.

Another issue is whether separation from the mother is the crucial factor. When the infant goes into hospital unaccompanied, he or she is separated from the whole family, not just the mother. Possibly what the infant misses is the whole set of experiences surrounding family life – the familiar environment, familiar people and a family routine. Clearly, these aspects of the situation are difficult to disentangle, but two pieces of evidence help to build a tentative picture of the way different factors interact. First, the presence of a familiar person other than the mother may also reduce distress in a strange situation. For instance, distress is reduced if the child is accompanied by a sibling on entry to a residential nursery (Heinicke and Westheimer, 1965). Secondly, children show much less distress if they are placed in a family environment similar to their own (Robertson and Robertson, 1967). Thus it appears that two types of link with previous family life, either the continuing presence of someone in the family, or continuity of the structure of family life with new people, may reduce the child's feelings of isolation.

This does not mean that any familiar person is as good as the mother. Although presence of some other member of the family may alleviate distress on separation from the mother, the alleviation is not complete. Similarly, even in the best conditions of fostering, where the family structure is familiar, some initial distress is still present. Hence, separation from the mother may still be a crucial aspect of the experience. It is possible, for instance, that presence of a familiar person comforts the infant because the person acts as a reminder of the mother rather than as a true substitute. This issue can only be resolved by looking at the degree to which attachment is specific to the mother (see Monotropy, mothers and fathers, p. 188 below).

Long-term effects Although we would wish to reduce short-term effects of separation to a minimum, it is even more important to assess the extent to which an early experience of this sort might have long-term consequences. It would be easier to accept short-term effects if we knew that they were easily reversed, with no likely long-term consequences. On this issue, later evaluations were much more positive than Bowlby's. Here I shall concentrate on two commonly postulated long-term effects of deprivation, namely mental retardation and defects of personality or behaviour.

Evidence that deprivation leads to mental retardation came from studies of institutionalized children showing retardation in language and cognition (e.g. Tizard, 1969). However, there is evidence that when institutional care involves a good quality of stimulation, no intellectual impairment is found, even if the style of care is rather impersonal (Tizard and Tizard, 1971). In addition, there is evidence that children with a large number of siblings generally show poorer intellectual development than those with few siblings, presumably because parents have less time to spend with each individual.

Having isolated stimulation as a crucial variable, the question then becomes whether it is perceptual or social stimulation that is important. Casler (1968) argued that the former was crucial, and that mothering was really just a matter of providing essential perceptual stimulation. Alternatively, it is possible that lack of social stimulation could have an indirect influence on intellectual development. For instance, depression resulting from emotional deprivation could lead to poorer intellectual progress. Rutter (1981) argues that while both sensory and social stimulation are important for normal intellectual development, both these factors can be dissociated from attachment. Lack of linguistic stimulation will lead to backwardness in language just as lack of perceptual stimulation leads to intellectual backwardness, but it is quality of stimulation that matters rather than the presence or absence of a strong infant–adult relationship.

One of the primary sources of evidence regarding the effects of deprivation on later personality and behaviour is the link between broken homes and delinquency (Rutter, 1981). The link seems strong, but it is not immediately clear whether it is the inadequacy of care leading up to separation or the separation itself that is the crucial factor. The test is to compare the incidence of delinquency following different types of separation experience in which family discord was either present or absent beforehand. Such comparison suggests that it is the experience leading up to separation that is crucial. Rutter reviews a number of studies comparing delinquency rates between children separated through death of their mother and children separated as a result of family discord, all of which found increased rates of delinquency in the latter group alone.

Another question is whether long-term problems result from the failure of the normal development of attachment, or through separation from someone to whom an attachment had been formed. Rutter points to evidence that infants institutionalized early are more likely to show subsequent personality problems than those institutionalized late (Pringle and Clifford, 1962), and interprets this as support for the notion that long-term problems result from failure to form attachment rather than from its subsequent disruption. The argument here is that infants admitted to an institution in their early months had not had time to form an attachment, suffering accordingly, whereas infants admitted later had established an attachment before admission and so showed no long-term problems.

Rutter concludes that there are long-term effects of early life experiences, but that these stem primarily from a lack rather than a loss of normal family experience. Undoubtedly there are some forms of early social experience that can have dramatic effects on the infant's emotional and cognitive state, both in the short and the long term. However, few of these effects can be attributed exclusively to deprivation of care from the infant's own mother. What seems to be important is the quality of stimulation, and some sense of continuity. Generally these may be supplied by the mother, but relationships with other members of the family may be equally important or may become more important as the infant develops. Probably, therefore, the phrase *maternal deprivation* should be replaced by something more appropriately general, such as *social deprivation*, remembering even then that this deprivation is made up of many facets, perceptual and cognitive as well as emotional.

Monotropy, mothers and fathers

The fact that the presence of a member of the family other than the mother may reduce distress raises the question of whether there is anything special about the mother–infant relationship. Is Bowlby correct in claiming that this relationship is unique, or do infants in fact make multiple attachments of similar quality to a number of family members? Studying infants longitudinally, Schaffer and Emerson (1964) found that although the majority of infants formed their initial attachment to one particular person, almost a third of the sample had formed multiple attachments in which it was hard to discern one preferred individual. Also, the breadth of attachment increased rapidly with age so that by 18 months the great majority of infants had developed attachments to more than one person. Consequently, Schaffer (1971) claims 'The concept of "monotropy", suggested by Bowlby . . . is thus not borne out by the facts'. Instead, he suggests that although initial attachments are usually to one person, it is the social situation that determines this. Good care from more than one person is likely to lead to multiple attachments, and the infant will be none the worse for this.

At 18 months, almost half of infants showed stronger attachment to someone other than the mother, usually the father, despite the fact that the mother spent more time caring for the infant. So even when a primary attachment is identifiable, it need not be to the mother. Schaffer and Emerson (1964) conclude that it is the quality of stimulation rather than its duration that determines the strength of attachment. Lamb (1977) found that between 15 and 24 months, boys in particular showed a preference for their father. At earlier ages the common finding is that infants show no preference for either mother or father on measures of attachment in unstressful settings (Feldman and Ingham, 1975; Willemsen et al., 1974), but if a more sensitive assessment is made by presenting infants with a choice of both parents in a stressful setting, they choose the mother (Lamb, 1976a). Campos et al. (1983) propose that instead of the term 'monotropy' we should consider the possibility that there is a hierarchy of attachments in the early months, with the mother generally at the top. They note, however, that this may be a short-lived phenomenon, given the common reversals of preference in later months.

Contrary to popular belief, some studies have shown that fathers are often just as emotionally involved or 'engrossed' in the birth of their child as mothers (Greenberg and Morris, 1974; Parke and O'Leary, 1976), and it also appears that they can be equally responsive to their infant (Parke and Sawin, 1980). However, we have to distinguish between potential capability and the usual state of affairs, since Belsky, Gilstrap and Rovine (1984) found that as a general rule mothers provided much more stimulation and care than fathers. This was confirmed by Ninio and Rinott (1988) who found that in a sample of Israeli families fathers spent on average about 45 minutes per day with their infants. They also found that fathers attributed lower levels of competence to their infants than mothers did and that this difference was most marked in the case of fathers who were least involved in the care of their infants.

Nevertheless there is evidence that fathers provide qualitatively different stimulation, supplying short periods of intense stimulation and engaging in more physical play than mothers (Lamb, 1976b). In contrast, mothers provide more predictable and placid interaction, often linked with care-taking, and they give more verbal stimulation (Pedersen et al., 1979). These differences may be largely the result of conventional family patterns in which the mother is usually the main caretaker, a supposition which is supported by the fact that differences in style are often altered if the mother is employed. Working mothers stimulate their infants more intensely and engage in more play than non-working mothers (Pedersen, Cain and Zaslow, 1982), suggesting that when taken out of their usual caretaking role they react more like fathers. Also, going back to Ninio and Rinott's work, fathers who are highly involved in infant care attribute levels of competence to their infants that compare closely to their wives' ratings. So we may conclude with reasonable safety that, apart from obvious areas like giving birth and breast-feeding, there are no clearly established biological or psychological reasons for singling out the mother as the only adequate caretaker.

However, we should not underrate the strength of social convention in maintaining the normal predominance of care by the mother. Although the convention is gradually changing towards more paternal involvement in child care, Lewis (1986) points out how strongly parental roles are still determined by society's conventional attitudes and by patterns of employment. Even parents who set out to equalize or reverse roles often return to conventional patterns after a short period (Russell, 1983), so although fathers make perfectly good caretakers, the pressures to conform to conventional patterns determine that true role reversal or equal role sharing still happen relatively rarely.

Predictability and security

Again the conclusions from the literature on deprivation point to the importance of considering the quality of the infant's early experience rather than simply the presence or absence of a mother figure. It seems reasonable to conclude that perceptual stimulation from adults is an important factor in perceptual development. On the social side, however, it is not clear how we should define adequate stimulation. In the past, this has been defined in terms of the 'warmth' or 'loving nature' of the interaction, but these concepts are vague. A more measurable property of a relationship is the degree of predictability existing between the signals of the infant and the responses of the mother (and maybe vice versa). Lamb (1981) suggests that securely attached infants have mothers who respond to their signals in a predictable manner. So maybe a major factor contributing to the security that infants feel is the degree to which they can predict the behaviour of those who care for them.

A range of findings would be accounted for by such a model, particularly if we extend its scope beyond the immediate mother–infant relationship. First, this could explain why newborns in special care units settle down into a steady daily routine more rapidly if cared for by only a few nurses. Presumably the more caretakers there are, the more unpredictable is the response to a particular signal by the infant. Of course, there is no need to assume that the infant is actively trying to predict the caretaker's response. It could be the case that consistent caretaking simply provides a framework into which the infant can fit. However, Lamb suggests that infants begin to construct expectations about the behaviour of others very early, maybe within the first two months.

This sort of model might also explain why infants' initial attachment is normally preferentially directed to one person. The more people involved, the less easy it should be to predict the response to a particular signal. Additionally, it explains why infants provided with day care commencing prior to their first birthday are more likely to be classified as 'insecure-avoidant' than other groups (Barglow, Vaughn and Molitor, 1987; Belsky and Rovine, 1988), since these infants have to predict the responses of the caretaker as well as parents. However, it is worth noting that Chase-Lansdale and Owen (1987) found no evidence of this sort in a sample of families in which the mother had returned to work before the infant was six months old. It appears that insecurity is less likely to result if caretaking commences in the early months, before the infant has formed a full attachment to the mother (Lamb, Sternberg and Prodromidis, 1992). Thus it is unlikely that predictability on its own will explain all the phenomena. Other factors such as the infant's ability to form representations of other people are also likely to be influential.

Nevertheless, the predictability model has good deal of potential for providing at least a basis for some of the phenomena and, as Lamb argues, degree of predictability may be a useful way of measuring parental sensitivity and of distinguishing parenting styles that do or do not lead to secure attachments. It is probably necessary to add a developmental dimension to this model. Although predictability may lead to security, total predictability is likely to lead to stagnation. There is evidence from the non-social sphere pointing to the fact that infants become rapidly bored when presented with events over which they have total control, but that they will work to master a contingency over which their control is not perfect (Bower, 1982). Also, if we want to relate security of attachment to security in later life, we have to build in a fair degree of tolerance of unpredictability, at least in the case of older children. After all, people differ in their predictability, and no one is totally predictable. Consequently, the developmental model could be of the following form. Initially infants require a high degree of predictability in their social environment if they are to feel secure. Hence, they are likely to seek the company of one person who produces relatively predictable responses to their signals. As they develop, however, they begin to tolerate more unpredictability, so they can develop close relations with more people without feeling overwhelmed by the differences in their responses.

If there is anything in this model, the recipe for caretaking would be to start by giving the infant as much predictability in social interaction as possible but, bearing in mind that the end result has to be someone who can deal with the unpredictable wider world, to decrease predictability gradually by allowing new people to share in caretaking as the infant grows older.

Summary

Bowlby's theory of the development of attachment requires revision on a number of counts. First, at a theoretical level his claim that selective attachments cannot form within the early months requires revision in the light of evidence of early social discrimination. If attachments do not form in the early months it is not because the infant does not possess the relevant perceptual abilities. Secondly, he seems to have overstated the short- and long-term effects of maternal deprivation. Thirdly, the infant's attachment to the mother may often be initially stronger than other attachments, but it does not appear to be unique. More recent work emphasizes the quality of the relationship, rather than the adult involved, as a major factor determining security of attachment. In addition, predictability of the parent's response to the infant is a promising way of measuring the quality of the relationship.

Early communication: parent–infant interaction

The emphasis in previous sections on the importance of rich social interaction for normal development leads us on naturally to look at parent–infant interaction as a major focus of study in itself. If the quality of interaction is so important, who determines this quality? Are we dealing with something very much like adult interaction, with both partners contributing to the timing and flow of events? Or is initial control of the interaction solely in the adult's hands, with any appearances of interaction just a matter of the adult fitting in around the infant's asocial vocalizations? A casual glance at a mother and young infant interacting might lead us to favour the first alternative. Even when infants are quite young, mother–infant interaction takes place in a smooth, coordinated way (Lieven, 1978; Winnicott, 1965), with each partner taking their turn. But equally, we might be tempted towards the second interpretation, since the infant does not appear to be communicating anything sensible. Maybe he or she is just vocalizing at random, or under the stimulation of the mother, and the sequencing of events is actually due to the mother's skill in weaving her vocalizations around those of her infant.

But the evidence presented earlier in this chapter should alert us to the possibility that even very young infants are far more active controllers of interaction than this view suggests. Infants appear to be sensitive to the emotional expressions of others, they are sensitive to the synchrony between the auditory and visual aspects of adult's vocalizations, and many of the claims about neonatal imitation or matching of facial expressions can be used to suggest that they perceive others as social beings and can respond with some form of resonance to their emotional state. There are enough pointers here to suggest that infants may be socially aware, and hence capable of taking an active part in interaction, from a very early age.

A look at the literature on parent–infant interaction does not lead us immediately to a clear choice between these alternatives, since workers differ widely in the degree to which they attribute social awareness and control of interaction to the young infant. There are many facets of social interaction, and rather than attempting to cover them all, I shall concentrate primarily on the issue of control over initiation and turn-taking.

Neonatal pre-adaptations and the structure of early communication

A primary feature of social interaction is its periodicity. Interactions are initiated and terminated, and during vocal exchanges, partners take turns to vocalize while the other partner maintains silence. Brazelton (1979) suggests that the basic rhythm inherent in newborn behaviour constitutes an important precursor for communication. In particular, the 'burst-pause' sequence occurring in sucking may provide a ready-made structure for early interactions. The mother appears to interpret pauses in sucking as cues for her to interact by rocking her infant, initiating face-to-face interaction and speaking (Kaye and Brazelton, 1971), and so the first social interactions begin. Kaye (1977) extends this argument to suggest that the presence of these natural rhythms is a great asset from the mother's point of view, since their simplicity and regularity allow her to learn quite rapidly to anticipate her infant's behaviour and to respond appropriately. In turn her consistent response constitutes a predictable pattern for the infant.

Brazelton is not suggesting that the neonate has a completely passive role in these early exchanges. It appears that he or she will pause from sucking for longer if the mother fails to respond socially, so there seems to be a very early expectation that particular events should fill these pauses. In addition, Brazelton claims that in a number of ways neonates are equipped for social interaction. For instance, they are capable of controlling their own state, maintaining it at the optimal attentive level necessary for successful inter-action. Also, they are particularly attentive to social stimuli such as face and voice. As Brazelton puts it,

> When the stimulus is the human voice, the neonate not only searches for the observer's face, but when he finds it, his face and eyes become wide, soft and eager, and he may even crane his neck, lifting his chin gently towards the source of the voice. (1979, p. 83)

Although the conclusion is that the infant is preadapted for communica-tion, the view emerging here is that it is mainly the mother's skill in fitting her interaction into the infant's natural activity patterns that gives rise to the impression that both are engaged in communication. Even when it comes to the communicative exchanges that develop during the first half year, Kaye concludes that the smoothness of interaction is due more to the mother's skill than the infant's.

In contrast, Trevarthen (1969) claims that infants are born with the ability to communicate. In his view, young infants display both *subjectivity*, the ability 'to *show* by coordinated acts that purposes are being consciously regulated' (1969, p. 322), and *intersubjectivity*, the ability to adapt their own purposeful activities to the subjectivity of others. Thus, intersubjectiv-ity involves both acting intentionally and taking account of others' inten-tions and mental states in forming these acts (note here that Trevarthen appears to be attributing to young infants what some would recognize as a rudimentary theory of mind). Through close analysis of videotape of mother–infant interaction, Trevarthen identifies a range of manual and facial gestures that have much in common with adult gestures used during conversation, and he concludes that infants show an innate intention to speak. *Prespeech* takes the form of movements of lips and tongue which, it is claimed, are precursors of the movements used in adult articulation. These movements appear when the infant is in intense face-to-face inter-action with the mother and so, in addition to being similar to adult gestures, they are produced in the appropriate communicative context.

Some workers are sceptical of these claims, and it would be easy to conclude that the gestures of infant and adult are only linked because both individuals possess the same facial musculature. Thought of in this way, the fact that infants produce gestures similar to those of adults is less surprising; they simply can do nothing else given the facial muscles at their command. But this does not explain why prespeech occurs under appropri-ate circumstances, when infants are in face-to-face interaction with their mother. Also, if the mother becomes unresponsive during a face-to-face exchange, the infant makes vigorous attempts to regain her participation (Murray and Trevarthen, 1985). For Trevarthen, these activities are clearly intentional attempts to re-initiate communication. Indeed, he is of the view that the infant has a more dominant role in controlling the interaction than the mother, even at two or three months.

One way of resolving the issue of whether we are dealing with a two-sided interaction in early exchanges is to look in detail at the contin-gencies between infant's and mother's behaviour. If the mother is control-ling the interaction by fitting her contribution into the infant's random silences, there should be a strong contingency between the infant's termina-tion of an utterance and the mother's commencement of an utterance. But it would take considerable skill for the mother to predict exactly when her infant is about to vocalize again, so we would expect the transition from mother's vocalization to infant's vocalization to be less smooth, possibly with a longer pause or with a period during which both partners are vocalizing at once. There is some evidence in favour of this interpretation. For instance, Schaffer, Collis and Parsons (1977) found that 'speaker-switch' pauses were much shorter when the switch was from infant to mother than when it was in the other direction. In addition, mothers keep their utterances quite brief with plenty of pauses between them, and Schaffer (1984) concludes from all this that turn-taking is mainly control-led by the mother skilfully fitting in around the infant's utterances.

Schaffer does suggest a minor role for infants in turn-taking, pointing to the possibility that they may suppress vocalization during attention to the speech of another. In so doing, infants take their turn, but as part of an attentional activity rather than because they understand the rules of turn-taking. If such a mechanism were operating consistently, we would expect simultaneous vocalization by mother and infant to be rare. But there is some disagreement between studies on this. One study (Stern et al., 1975) found that simultaneous vocalization was the rule rather than the exception in the early months, whereas Schaffer (1984) cites a number of studies in which simultaneous vocalizations were rare.

It is worth noting, though, that Stern et al. see simultaneous vocalization as a different mode of communication rather than failed sequential vocalization. They believe that both *coactive* (simultaneous) and *alternating* modes exist but that the former predominates in the early months. It also appears that the mode adopted depends on the form of the interaction. Coaction is most frequent during high arousal, such as during games, whereas the alternating mode appears more during quieter face-to-face interaction. This observation suggests that suppression of vocalization may occur under specific communicative circumstances that are closer to those arising between adults when information is being conveyed. So although Schaffer may be correct in suggesting that infants maintain silence to attend, this tendency may well be limited to particular types of communication, and so may reflect a specific communicative adaptation. There is, however, reason to question whether the coactive mode is as pronounced as Stern suggests. Ginsburg and Kilbourne (1988) confirmed the existence of an initial phase around two to three months during which simultaneous vocalization was dominant, but found that it was rapidly replaced within about four weeks by the alternating mode.

Although several pieces of evidence are in keeping with the notion that the infant does little to control the interaction, the evidence is often rather indirect, showing, for example, that the mother is better than the infant at some aspects of timing. This should not be taken as evidence that the infant plays no active part in the sequence. For instance, the fact that the speaker-switch pause from mother to infant is longer than from infant to mother might simply attest to generally slower reaction time by the infant rather than an absence of responsiveness to turn-taking cues. A more direct measure would be to look for infant responses that are contingent on specific turn-taking cues from the mother. Adopting this approach, Mayer and Tronick (1985) found that three-month-old infants were responsive to their mother's cues, but only when three or four were combined. Thus, if the mother signalled the end of her contribution by a combination of gestures – head movements, hand movements and specific intonation patterns – infants interpreted this as a cue to vocalize. It would appear then that infants do actively take turns in communication, but that the mother has to make her turn-taking cues very clear if they are to get the message that it is their turn.

Also, there is some evidence that mothers use their infant's responsiveness as a communicative cue. Murray and Trevarthen (1986) had mothers and two-month-old infants interact via a video relay, both normally and under conditions in which the video picture reaching the mother from the infant was delayed. Despite the fact that infants were equally responsive in the two conditions, mothers' speech became more negative and less infant-related under the delay condition, and they reported the feeling that they were not communicating successfully. Presumably this happens because the delay condition creates the impression that the infant's acts are no longer related to the mother's, something that mothers interpret as communication failure. On the basis of this, Murray and Trevarthen conclude that infants have direct control over the course of communication through the way they respond to the mother's communicative acts.

Recent evidence using sophisticated analyses of changes in both partners' behaviour indicates that both infant and parent act together to regulate turn-taking. Cohn and Tronick (1988) found that at three and nine months infants and mothers had approximately equal influence on the other's behaviour, while at six months there was actually a tendency for infants to have the dominant influence. One should not conclude, however, that mother–infant interaction runs as smoothly as adult interaction. Tronick and Cohn (1989) found that although coordination improved between three and nine months, even at later ages there was still a high degree of miscoordination. Additionally, in some ways the pattern of infant–parent interaction may be less sophisticated than some had thought. For instance, Stern (1974) suggested that maternal gaze directed to the infant enhances the likelihood that the infant will look towards the mother and reduces the likelihood that he or she will look away. However, Messer and Vietze (1988) pointed towards problems in previous coding systems used to measure this phenomenon, and failed to obtain clear effects of this sort when using a system in which these faults had been rectified. Nevertheless, the balance of evidence suggests that from an early age both infant and parent are active partners in interactions. The difficulty remains in specifying just in what way one influences the other and vice versa.

Developmental changes in parent–infant communication

Whether or not we conclude that the young infant has true communicative abilities, there are some marked changes in the form of parent–infant communication during the first two years. Some of these changes relate to the infant's developing abilities in other spheres, such as perception and motor skill. Parents, however, recognizing changes in the infant's behaviour, adapt their own behaviour in ways that they feel are appropriate. Consequently, to understand fully the development of communication, we need to look at both individuals in the pair. The infant is changing rapidly, but the adult is also changing in response, and the adult's interpretation of the infant's behaviour will affect the form of the interaction and may be an important developmental force in itself.

Schaffer (1984) describes five different stages of communicative development occurring within the first two years.

Stage 1: the immediate post-birth period During the first two months the main focus of social behaviour is the establishment of the infant's basic biological processes, such as sleep patterns and feeding patterns. As indicated in the previous section, the infant's contribution is limited to the display of biological rhythms, which the parent comes to predict and respond to consistently. Hence, during this period, the main development is behavioural predictability on both sides.

Stage 2: two to four months   As a result of early perceptual developments infants become much more attentive to the external world. This is particularly true of people, and infants begin to engage in frequent face-to-face visual contact. It is as if their predominant concern has become seeking out and learning about people. Adults treat these face-to-face episodes as interactions, and it is during this period that we begin to see the turn-taking in vocal interaction discussed in the previous section.

Stage 3: five to seven months   As infants gain increased control over manipulation of objects, attention shifts from people to objects. Parents recognize this shift by basing their interactions around objects, but the infant is not initially able to shift attention from object to person at all readily, let alone engage in social activity over objects. So in this period it is still mainly adults who maintain the social interaction. At this point, due to the infant's increased interest in objects, the task has become to establish *topic sharing*, something which may be established, among other ways, by either partner following the other's line of gaze or their pointing. However, although a good deal of mutual gaze occurs, Schaffer concludes that this is mainly a matter of parents interpreting the infant's line of gaze rather than the reverse. Infants have an interest in both people and objects, but are incapable of coordinating these interests because their skills in the two areas develop separately until they reach a sufficient level of mastery for their coordination (see Bruner, 1973). This may be to make a slight underestimate of infants' ability, however. Although there is little evidence that infants below nine months are able to interpret an adult's pointing (Murphy and Messer, 1977), Butterworth and Cochran (1980) have shown that six-month-olds are capable of following the mother's line of regard provided the focus is within the subject's visual field.

Stage 4: eight to 16 months   The onset of this stage is marked by a radical reorganization of infants' social cognition, taking place between eight and ten months. An important factor at the root of this transformation is their new-found ability to coordinate disparate events in space and time. This leads to assimilation of physical objects to social events that allows infants to engage in interaction over objects. Also, Schaffer invokes the Piagetian concept of *decentration* to describe how infants come to understand social interaction not just in terms of their own actions, but as a coordinated sequence in which each partner has an active role in bringing about an outcome that infants can predict. Infants understand that a dialogue has to be maintained by both partners and that roles in the interaction can be exchanged. Tied up in all this is the development of an understanding of intentionality; infants begin to understand how their acts communicate to others and modify their efforts in accordance with feedback from the other person. The sum of all these steps forward is a much more symmetrical pattern of social interaction in which, for the first time, the infant can be said to be a more or less equal partner.

Stage 5: from 18 months on The final transition comes through the development of symbolic representation. As infants begin to understand that words can stand for things, interactions become less tied to the here-and-now of specific objects. Schaffer also suggests that the acquisition of symbolic representation allows infants to gain new social skills, such as the ability to reflect on the behaviour of self or others. As a consequence, social behaviour becomes much more planned and self-conscious than before. This period is also marked by the emergence of the first efforts at verbal communication, the starting point of language development.

This sequence of development presents the infant as an asocial being in the early months. True interactions do not begin to emerge until around eight months, and developments before then are put down to changes in perceptual, motor and cognitive abilities, which themselves are fostered by the parent's responsiveness to the infant's current state. According to Schaffer, all psychological abilities develop in a social context in which the parent supports the infant's efforts. But only once the appropriate cognitive level is reached can it be said that the infant is acting socially. So although there is a strong social component to the developmental process, this comes initially from the parental side of the dyad and the last thing to develop in the infant is social awareness itself.

It is worth making a comparison with Trevarthen's theory here. In one respect, there is agreement. Trevarthen also points to a major transition at around eight or nine months. As he puts it,

> The most important feature of the new behaviour at 9 months is . . . its systematically combining of interests of the infant in the physical, privately-known reality near him, and his acts of communication addressed to persons. A deliberately sought sharing of experiences about events and things is achieved for the first time. (Trevarthen and Hubley, 1978, p. 184)

Like Schaffer, Trevarthen finds that before nine months infants are incapable of combining their actions on objects with their actions towards people. But in other respects, his account is quite different. He claims that the young infant has the capacity for intentional communication (prespeech), for self reflection and for knowing and using objects, and the limitation is simply that he or she cannot combine these activities. In contrast, the older infant is able to combine these activities, and the resulting interaction over objects Trevarthen names *secondary intersubjectiv-ity*, since it involves 'a deliberately sought sharing of experience about events and things'. (Trevarthen and Hubley, 1978, p. 184). So there is agreement on the separation of early social and object skills, but Trevar-then sees the infant as socially competent from birth, whereas Schaffer sees social competence emerging late on in the first year to some extent as a result of the coordination of social and manipulative skills.

There is another respect in which the two accounts differ. While Schaf-fer's model is based heavily on perceptual and cognitive developments, Trevarthen identifies emotion as having a strong influence on interaction. Murray and Trevarthen (1985) showed how if during an interaction the mother assumes a blank face, the infant will make strenuous attempts to reinitiate the interaction, and when these fail, will show clear signs of distress. This is not an isolated finding, having been noted in earlier work and replicated in a number of studies since. For instance Lamb, Morrison and Malkin (1987) found that infants between one and seven months of age showed distress and tension when confronted with an unresponsive adult. It is worth noting that this 'still face' procedure generally also involves cessation of interaction through touch and voice, and so it is not immediately clear that it is the facial expression that has the primary effect on infants. However, Gusella, Muir and Tronick (1988) obtained the usual response to a still face with six-month-olds when they viewed their mother on video with the sound turned down. Thus by this age the still face alone is sufficient to prompt a response. Toda and Fogel (1993) looked in detail at the nature of infants' responses to the still face procedure, finding that these changed with age. Although both three- and six-months-olds showed less smiling and looked away from the mother more, the older group engaged in more manipulation of objects, apparently as a way of dealing with the stress of the situation. It is not clear in these studies that infants were making attempts to re-initiate interaction, and this raises the issue of whether they are responding simply to an unusual show of neutral emotion by the parent or to the disruption of the normal interaction sequence. The second alternative appears most likely, since Murray and Trevarthen found that distress did not arise if interaction was broken off through the inter-ruption of another adult, so it seems that the infant has quite precise expectations about the affective responses that should be forthcoming during interaction, and can also distinguish normal breaks in communica-tion from abnormal ones. According to their account, infants from the very beginning are attempting to establish emotional relationships with adults. Infants detect features of the mother's behaviour and interpret them as indicators of her emotional state. In addition, they regulate their own state to match her's, and produce expressions that she can interpret in emotional terms. In other words, within interactions there is a close coordination between behaviour of mother and infant that indicates a good awareness of each other's emotions. In support of this, Mundy, Kasari and Sigman

(1992) found evidence at 20 months for higher displays of positive emotion during joint attention than during other mother–infant behaviours. Thus, they suggest that in addition to their relevance for development of cognitive skills, situations involving joint attention are liable to be important in transmission of emotion between partners.

Some workers would doubt whether the data demand such a rich interpretation, but in the light of recent evidence on the perception of emotion by young infants, it would be unwise to neglect the contribution of emotional awareness to early interaction patterns. If infants are capable of perceiving emotions in others, it would be strange if this information did not take a central role in social interaction, which is, after all, an activity that is full of emotion on both sides. The problem for future study is to determine the actual level of emotional awareness possessed by young infants, a tricky empirical problem.

This points us to a general problem with the literature in this area, namely that accounts based on very similar data differ widely in the degree to which they attribute social awareness to young infants. It is not clear how to provide a direct empirical test that would provide a choice between 'richer' interpretations like Trevarthen's and more cautious ones like Schaffer's. However, maybe a strong preoccupation with identifying the infant's ability leads us away from the central issue. Many workers argue that we should concentrate on the dyad rather than on the infant as the developing unit. From this point of view, it matters less whether or not there are social intentions behind the infant's acts; the crucial point is that parents treat these acts *as if* they were intentional. Workers like Lock (1980) and Newson (1979) adopt the philosophical stance of Macmurray (1961) to argue that it is this parental predisposition to treat their offspring as intentional beings that leads eventually to their becoming intentional beings.

Parent–infant interaction as a developmental process

Parent–infant interaction and development of knowledge

We have already covered evidence suggesting that parent–infant interaction is a rich source of information, not just about other people but about how to act in the world. For instance, we saw how mothers respond to their infants' emotions with emotional reactions of their own that may either encourage or discourage their infant's response. Although this evidence was presented in the context of development of gender differences, Bretherton (1992) suggests that these maternal responses provide the infant with knowledge of which emotional response is appropriate and which inappropriate in a given situation. Additionally, we saw how infants faced with an ambiguous situation look to their parents for emotional signals that will tell them how they should feel about a particular object or event. Although this *social referencing* phenomenon has conventionally been analysed for its significance for the infant's emotional development, there seems no reason to assume that such a process stops there. One example of social referencing was that in which the mother's emotional expression is used by infants to guide their actions on the visual cliff (Sorce et al., 1981), and so it seems likely that infants learn both how they should feel about a particular situation and how they should act. Feinman (1992) adopts a broad concept of social referencing, defining it as, '. . . a process in which one person utilises another person's interpretation of the situation to formulate her own interpretation of it . . .' (1992, p. 4). According to this definition, the other person's interpretation may be indicated through emotional signals and through actions. For instance, an infant may be reassured about a new toy through the parent's encouraging signals, and may also be given information as to what can be done with the toy by parental demonstration. Thus, during interactions, parents consciously teach their infant about the world. But at the same time, probably largely unwittingly, they provide a wealth of emotional cues that help the infant to interpret the world in emotional terms. As Feinman puts it, 'In referencing, one person serves as a base of information for another and, in so doing, facilitates the other's efforts to construct reality' (1992, p. 4).

Some workers feel that the term 'social referencing' should be restricted to the processes by which emotional signals are interpreted (see, for example, Campos, 1983). However, it would seem arbitrary to adopt a more restricted definition. Additionally, this broad definition coincides well with the general approach in which the infant is portrayed as acquiring knowledge through processes of social construction. This approach stems primarily from the work of Vygotsky (1962) and is based on the notion that development is not a solitary process but rather one in which parent and infant collaborate.

There are many examples of the way in which, either unwittingly or wittingly, adults support infants' strivings to understand the world. Firstly, the parents' actions on objects appear to act as a direct model for infants. Hofsten and Siddiqui (1993) showed that six- and 12-month-old infants imitated their mothers' acts, not just in general but in specific relation to the objects acted upon. Thus, if infants had seen one object shaken, they tended to shake it, while if they had seen another object banged on the table, they tended to do the same with it. This was an experimental study in which the acts modelled bore an arbitrary relation to the objects acted upon. However, the same principle is likely to apply in everyday situations, providing infants with information about how objects are to be used.

Another source of information is provided by parental analysis of objects and tasks. Lock and his colleagues indicate how during interaction over a toy or a picture, the mother will label salient parts, thus segmenting a complex object or picture into its elements (Lock et al., 1989). Their argument is that this activity provides infants with a framework through which they can organize their perception and understanding of the world. Additionally, Rogoff (1990) points out how mothers' tendency to label objects for infants is liable to help them to categorize the objects that they encounter. Another function of parental support is to simplify the task for the infant, and Rogoff shows how parents will often draw comparisons between a new task and activities with which the infant is already familiar. By so doing, they help infants to bring current knowledge to bear on new problems and thus make solution possible through use of existing skills.

The structuring provided by parents is often described as scaffolding or framing, and it is easy to reach the conclusion that the process here is one sided, with parents providing a rigid framework upon which infants hang their cognitive structures. At first sight, such an analysis seems plausible, since parents have already developed knowledge of the world whereas infants have yet to develop it. However, it is more realistic to view the whole process as involving adjustment on both sides. For instance, Rogoff and her colleagues conclude that social referencing is not a one sided process in which infants interpret parents' signals, arguing instead that both partners have their own goals in an interaction and that they both use social referencing to negotiate with their partner (Rogoff et al., 1992). Thus, the mother is also engaged in interpreting her infant's emotional signals as indicators of his or her interpretation of the situation, and this activity meshes with that of her infant in determining the outcome of the interaction. Working at a different level of analysis, Fogel (1990) argues that in simple activities such as transferring an object from infant to mother, the mother's part in the activity is continuously adjusted to her infant's activity. As he puts it, '... the action of each individual is organized in part by the action of the other' (p. 77), and the suggestion is that it is only through the contribution of both that the action is successful. Thus, for instance, the infant's initial difficulty in letting go of the object is overcome in part by the form of the mother's act. This is not a matter of the mother blatantly extracting the object from the infant's continuing grasp; her contribution is much more subtle, so that one can neither say that the infant released the object nor that the mother took it. Instead the object is transferred as a result of a subtle meshing of the partners' actions and would not happen successfully through the efforts of one partner alone. For Fogel, this is an example of the need for dynamic systems theory (discussed in chapter 2) as a framework for analysing social behaviour, since the structure of the act cannot be said to be supplied by one or other individual but rather is a property of the whole interactional system of which the individuals are a part. Indeed, for the same sorts of reason, Fogel and Thelen (1987) argue that such an analysis has advantages over more conventional theories in explaining a range of phenomena in infant communicative development.

Once the analysis shifts to investigation of mutual rather than one sided influence, a number of links with other topics fall into place. The bulk of evidence for social referencing appears from the end of the first year onwards, which is no surprise since the process depends upon the emergence of joint attention to an object. In this respect there is a close link with Trevarthen's concept of *secondary intersubjectivity*, in which partners have a mutual awareness of each other's experience and seek to communicate intentionally about their joint focus. Such an ability in turn implies the beginnings of a theory of mind, and Bretherton puts social referencing in the general context of the processes by which an 'interfacing of minds' takes place between parent and infant through intentional communication on both sides.

A parental role in the development of intentional communication

The problem of how infants gain the ability to communicate intentionally is an issue in itself. Again, this is a case in which it has been argued that infants receive vital support from parents, and so the development of intention tends to be viewed as the product of joint efforts of parent and infant. The fundamentals of the likely process can be found in Newson's (1979) claim that 'human babies become human beings because they are treated as if they already were human beings' (p. 208). Newborns are biologically programmed to emit behaviour in discrete 'chunks', and in that sense they are adapted for communication (cf. Brazelton, 1979). Equally, the infant's parents have a natural tendency to attribute social significance to these early behaviours, and these two facts together lead to the eventual development of intentional communication. Chappell and Sander (1979) suggest very much the same thing. Neonates emit 'signals' that reflect their state, but these signals are not directed towards anyone. However, parents treat the signs as if they were directed to them, and hence elevate them to the status of intentional communication.

This argument is very appealing, but on first sight it smacks a little of magic. Although parents may well impute intentions to infants, it is not immediately clear how such treatment leads in the long run to infants' actually acting in an intentional manner. What we need here is evidence for a process through which this is accomplished.

Lock (1980) has done most to uncover such a process. His model draws on two of the fundamental principles of Vygotsky's theory of development (1962). The first is that before an infant can subject a *function* (ability) to intentional control, he or she must already be capable of exercising the function. The second is that any function appears in the child's development on two planes successively, first on the social plane between infant and parents, and then on the psychological plane within the child. Vygotsky calls these the *intermental plane* and *intramental plane* respectively, and this second principle satisfies the requirements of the first, since a function is first 'possessed' on the intermental plane and later comes under intentional personal control at the intramental plane. The main point with respect to parent–infant interaction is that abilities are initially possessed by the parent–infant dyad, and are only later possessed by the infant as an individual.

The question is still, of course, how we get from the intermental to the intramental plane. On the basis of detailed longitudinal observation of three infants, Lock describes how a range of abilities gradually come under the infant's intentional control. A prime example is crying. Initially, the infant's cry signals a need, but in Lock's view there is no question of the infant crying in order to communicate this need to another, indeed the infant may not initially know what the need is. However, from the outset, the mother treats the cry as a communicative act by seeking to satisfy the need. This may be done on a trial-and-error basis until the baby stops crying, the cue that the need has been met.

Later, crying occurs under circumstances that suggest it is being brought under voluntary control. For instance, the infant will cry on seeing a desired object (e.g. a drink), and crying is terminated promptly once the desired goal (being given a sip) is achieved. In other examples, crying is terminated as soon as the mother picks up the desired object, before the infant even receives it. These examples suggest that the cry is now being used quite competently to influence the behaviour of another, and Lock suggests that the transition from crying as an involuntary response to crying as an intentional communicative act occurs as a result of the infant's mother treating the former as if it were the latter.

How this happens becomes clearer when we consider another example, that of the infant's behaviour on being picked up. In this case the behaviour is acquired, unlike crying which is already in the repertoire of the newborn. Lock suggests that acquisition occurs in the following steps. Initially, the infant makes no response to being picked up, so as the mother places her arms under the infant's armpits and lifts, the infant's arms are raised passively. The next step is that the infant turns this movement into an active anticipatory one; when the mother approaches he raises his arms ready to be picked up. Later, it becomes unnecessary that the mother approach and bend down; the infant recognizes certain contexts, such as meal preparation in which a pick-up is ultimately a part, and will arm-raise in anticipation. At all these stages, however, arm-raising is still a response to a specific set of events, and the final step occurs when the infant realizes that the action has communicative significance, that is, that it can be used to influence the behaviour of another. According to Lock, this occurs through the mother treating the infant's action as a request rather than an anticipation, the evidence being that she picks up her infant in response to the arm-raise when she had no prior intention to do so. Consequently, that action becomes intentional within the dyad (intermentally) and this leads ultimately to it becoming internalized by the infant as an intentional act.

It is still a little hard to see how the infant realizes that he or she has influenced the mother's behaviour. From the infant's point of view, she approached, and the usual thing happened. Maybe the infant learns through making anticipatory errors, arm-raising and then realizing that the mother was not approaching in the usual manner preceding a pick-up, but then finding that she picked him up all the same. In general, infants may learn a good deal about the effects of their acts through mismatches on one side or another. For instance, Lock gives the following example (see figure 5.6):

> Mary is holding a grate-tidy brush in her right hand and a shovel in her left hand. She has been waving the shovel around for a few moments. In doing this she turns to her mother (1–2) and brings the shovel round to hold it upright in front of her near her mother (3–4). She turns to look at mother, and they smile at each other (5). In doing this the shovel topples in her grip so that it is pointed towards mother. Mother interprets this fortuitous event as Mary offering her the shovel, and moves her right arm to take it (5–6). Mary was not intending to give the shovel away (at this time she cannot give objects ...) and turns away from mother to continue waving the shovel about at the same time that mother attempts to take the shovel (6). Mother relaxes her arm into her lap and Mary goes on playing (7). (1980, p. 64)

Maybe it is in this sort of situation that infants come to realize that their acts influence the behaviour of others. A whole set of acts that do not have social significance for the infant may become intentionally social through the infant noting their effects on the mother and then beginning to use them to produce this effect. But the infant only notes that there is an effect on the mother because the mother's response is initially out of harmony with the infant's activity. In the pick-up example, the mother's response was always a part of the behaviour, and so it should be harder for the infant to detect that he or she influences the mother's behaviour, but in other cases maternal interpretations may be particularly informative.

Summary: the parents' role in the social construction of reality

In the section on attachment we encountered claims about the importance of maternal sensitivity for secure attachment. And we covered many examples of parents showing sensitivity to their infant's acts, and some examples of infants showing sensitivity to parents. Terms like 'emotional resonance' and 'matching behaviour' have cropped up, stressing the similarity between parental and infant acts. As one group have put it,

> There is a process that occurs between parents and infants which allows the infant to perceive *how* he is perceived. In this process parents non-verbally 'reflect back' to the infant his own experiences. (Stern et al., 1985, p. 249)

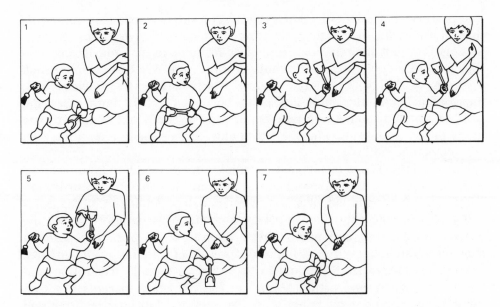

Figure 5.6 An interaction sequence between mother and child (after Lock, 1980).

But the question here is how it helps the infant to have his experiences reflected back; to be told 'you feel like this' adds nothing when you already feel 'like this'. The answer may be that there is more here than simple reflection. Discussing the phenomenon, Kaye says 'It is never a perfect match, always a variation, in the direction of an individual's personal style, a learner's incompetence or an instructor's agenda' (1979, p. 199). Hence 'you feel like this' is more 'this is how you should feel'. In cases of emotional 'mirroring' it is likely that the mother's expression is the product of her adult interpretation of the infant's emotion rather than an exact imitation. Consequently, the infant is faced with an adult model of the emotion that he or she should be feeling in the situation. This harmonizes well with the literature on social referencing, in which it is claimed that adults provide emotional interpretations of situations that infants find ambiguous.

There may also be scope for learning in situations in which there is a complete emotional mismatch between infant and mother. Stern et al. (1985) discuss the phenomenon of *affect attunement*, in which both partners apparently have direct access to the emotional states of the other and behave in an empathic manner. They identify an important role for this phenomenon in the infant's acquisition of a sense of self. However, it again seems vital that if the infant is to learn from the parent's attunements these must present something new. This can happen in the way discussed above, through parents amplifying rather than simply mirroring. However, it is also possible that infants benefit as much from the affect mis-attunements that Stern et al. also note. Mis-attunements may often occur because parents interpret their infant's responses in adult terms, and in so doing they present a good model for infants to learn from. We can compare such a process with Lock's example above, in which Mary is provided with information about the adult interpretation of her act. In both cases, the adult is providing something new because he or she is not *totally* attuned to the infant, and it is this newness that may provide the infant with a vital developmental foothold.

This of course is not to say that parents' primary role is to be unattuned to their infant. First of all, sensitivity and attunement appear to be important for the formation of a secure relationship. Additionally, for interaction to run smoothly there must exist common assumptions about the focus of interaction and each other's intentions. So although parental misinterpretations may be an important source of information for infants, constant misinterpretation could be expected to lead to frustration and breakdown of the interaction. Also, in cases in which parents are seen 'tutoring' their infant by analysing situations and labelling features and objects, it seems inevitable that the parent's efforts will be more successful if they are governed by an understanding of the infant's current abilities. Vygotsky (1962) points to a distinction between what an infant is capable of in solitary activity and more advanced levels that he or she can reach in collaboration with an adult, labelling the latter as the *zone of proximal development*. According to this account, the adult's role is to provide support to allow infants to act beyond their individual capability. To be successful in this the adult's activities must be closely attuned to the infant's capabilities, since input that is directed beyond the zone of proximal development will be ineffective. An example of this can be seen in the way many mothers simplify their infant-directed speech at the time when their infant is beginning to comprehend words (Murray, Johnson and Peters, 1990). At the same time, however, it is important that the adult aims slightly beyond the infant's individual level. It is not clear that parents do this deliberately, however a combination of sensitivity to the infant's abilities and a natural tendency to place adult interpretations on situations and behaviour may lead to parental behaviour that, while not above infants' heads, is sufficiently ahead of their individual competence to ensure that they are constantly challenged and drawn forward.

The beginnings of language

Since infancy is conventionally thought of as the period of development before the emergence of language, a section on language development might seem out of place. However, there are at least two reasons for saying something about language here. First, infants often begin to produce recognizable words before the end of the first year and are generally producing two-word utterances by the end of the second year, so language is on the scene well before infancy ends. Secondly, many of the phenomena already discussed, such as the development of intentional communication, are seen as crucial precursors of spoken language, so our discussion would be incomplete without some mention of early language. There is a vast literature on language, so I shall be very selective in my review, only covering topics in early language that have close links with the material in the earlier parts of this chapter. As such, the emphasis here is primarily social, and the reader should keep in mind the evidence on cognitive precursors of language discussed near the end of chapter 4.

From early communication to language

Lock (1980) argues that infants have acquired the fundamentals of language before they have properly begun to use words. We saw in the previous section how the infant's acts, initially responses to an internal state or to external events, become intentional communicative acts through the fact that parents treat them as such. Following this step, Lock describes how gestures become combined. For instance, the infant begins to cry to attract attention and then to point to direct attention to what he or she wants. At first these gestures are produced sequentially, but later they are produced simultaneously. According to Lock, communication of this sort both conveys information (I want X) and involves reference (point at X). From his point of view, there is little difference between a gestural combination of this sort and the child actually saying the name of the object in a tone of voice that indicates to parents that he or she wants it.

Gestural combinations are occurring frequently by the beginning of the second year, and by this time the infant may well have begun to produce words. However, Lock observes that early lexical development proceeds along a separate path from communicative development. Words initially appear in play simply as part of the whole activity and without seeming to convey information. It is only several months later that they begin to appear within communicative episodes, and then they are embedded within the gestural system that the infant has developed by that time. It is as if the use of words in play leads the infant to understand that words can refer to objects, with the consequence that he or she then progressively uses words to replace indicative gestures such as pointing. Nothing new has taken place on the communicative front, and Lock argues that language is really just a complex system that makes explicit the communicative function that existed between people prior to the acquisition of words and grammar. There may be reason to question whether words are initially treated separately from gestural communication, since Morford and

Goldin-Meadow (1992) found that very early in language development infants used words in combination with gestures and could also understand gestures in combination with speech and when used as a substitute for speech. However, this does not weaken Lock's main point about the gestural system being a ready-made framework for language.

Halliday (1979) puts forward a view that has much in common with Lock's. Studying the development of his son Nigel, he identified many language-like properties in the child's very early communication. Initially, acts are directed at objects or people, and the infant's aim is to obtain the object or to gain the person's attention. Soon, however, these acts are combined in a way that gives them symbolic meaning. For instance, the infant touches the object gently while looking at the adult, a combination that the adult interprets as 'I want that'. In Nigel's case, these gestural 'acts of meaning' were all replaced by vocal ones by the age of ten months, and by 11 months he had developed twelve distinct elements in his vocal *proto-language*. These fall into four categories according to their semantic function:

1 Instrumental (e.g., 'I want that').
2 Regulatory (e.g., 'Do that again').
3 Interactional (e.g., 'Let's be together').
4 Personal (e.g., 'I like that').

So before the end of the first year Nigel is using a fairly extensive semantic system based on these 'acts of meaning'. Again we have a theory in which many of the major aspects of language are developed before the infant begins to speak.

Thinking back to Lock's views about the shared nature of early knowledge, we might ask whether these abilities are really possessed by the infant. Does Nigel really intend to communicate these meanings or is it a matter of the adults interpreting his acts as conveying these meanings? Halliday does point out that language creation is a social process which is only successful because adults interpret the infant's acts as carrying meaning. His theoretical framework, while not so explicit on the nature of the social developmental processes, therefore appears to be compatible with Lock's account.

Bates and her colleagues have looked closely into the relationships between gesture and language (Bates et al., 1989). They find evidence in keeping with the view that gestural and language systems have common roots. Also, these appear to be treated almost as a single symbolic system, since infants may have a gesture for one thing and a word for another, but rarely duplicate by having a word and a gesture for the same thing. However, they suggest that some proportion of the relation between gestural system and language may arise from the fact that parents' verbal input during symbolic play enhances the likelihood of certain gestural activities. In other words, the infant's comprehension of adult speech promotes development of particular symbolic gestures, but since language production follows comprehension, production of the relevant language follows production of the gesture. This gives the appearance of gesture leading to language, when in fact it was language comprehension that led to gesture. Thus, later in development, in addition to the direct progression suggested by Lock, it appears that language may feed back to enrich the gestural system.

First words

The age at which the first word is produced varies widely from child to child. For instance, Bates (1979) found that some infants produced their first word at nine months, whereas Barrett and his colleagues found that some did not speak until 16 months (Barrett et al., 1986). There is a growing view that words are not generally used first in a *referential* manner, that is, to refer to objects or actions. Instead, many words are produced in specific contexts and, rather than referring to a specific object, a word is associated in some way with the whole activity (Barrett, 1986). This finding is in keeping with Lock's observation that early words appeared first in play situations, and although some workers find first words appearing outside play, the common factor seems to be the association between general context and the word rather than between a specific object or action and the word.

In addition to these context-bound words, Barrett (1989) notes the parallel emergence of another group that are produced in a range of contexts, and appear to refer to the infant's internal state. These words can actually be viewed as communicative, since they indicate something about internal state. By contrast, since the context-bound words are just part of the general activity and do not refer to specific objects or actions, they do not appear to have any communicative role.

A number of authors (e.g. McShane, 1979; Nelson, 1983) have suggested that infants begin by using words in a non-referential manner, only later gaining a general insight into their referential function and going on to use them to refer to objects and events. Barrett (1989) disagrees with this view, pointing both to the fact that some state-related words appear to be used referentially from the start, and the fact that context-bound words do not all begin to be used referentially at the same point in development. Instead, *decontextualization* seems to be a gradual process, occurring word by word over an extended period.

According to Barrett, decontextualization is not simply a matter of learning that a word refers to an object instead of to a general context in which the word occurs. Underlying the change, important cognitive developments are going on. The notion is that many of the infant's early concepts of the world, rather than being object-related, are undifferentiated representations of frequently occurring events in the infant's social world. As a result, words are related to these representations of social contexts rather than to specific objects. Barrett suggests that infants begin to differentiate these event representations into components such as people, objects and acts. Through this process, and through observing the occasions on which adults use particular words, infants construct a prototype for the object or event to which the word refers. In this connection, Baldwin (1991) has shown that infants are capable of using adults' nonverbal cues as means of identifying what a word refers to.

However, as already noted, Barrett finds that some words are used referentially from the start, and as development proceeds, the infant's lexicon is increasingly supplemented by such words. In addition, some infants show more referential use of first words than others. This would suggest that understanding of reference is a separate development from word acquisition, with the former following the latter in some infants, and preceding it in others. But an alternative is that all words are used referentially from the start, and that the difference between cases lies in what the word refers to. If it refers to a general context, then it does not actually communicate anything to other people, whereas if it is used across contexts to apply to an object or act, it does communicate.

Barrett suggests that the transition towards the end of the second year from one-word to two-word utterances occurs first of all through infants' beginning to produce single words sequentially, and secondly through a reduction in the delay between individual words so that they appear as a pair. As evidence for the idea that sequential use of single words is a precursor of the two-word stage, Barrett cites findings that the intonation pattern of the first word in a successive single-word utterance was the same as that in the corresponding two-word utterance, and different from that when the word occurred alone (Branigan, 1979). This suggests that even at the successive single-word stage, the infant is using some principle of word combination. Barrett suggests that the infant arrives at general rules for word combination by noting the common combinations across a range of sequential single-word utterances. Once these rules are abstracted, true rule-generated two-word utterances emerge, with the explicit link between the words reflected in the smooth production of a phrase with little delay between elements.

Once infants enter the two-word phase they are well into the construction of grammar. The rules by which they combine words are the subject of considerable research and controversy, and this whole topic is beyond the scope of this book, particularly since the development of grammar takes place largely in the period beyond infancy. But before leaving the topic of language development, it is worth taking a brief excursion into the issue of early differences in language style. This is important not just in order to dispel the notion that all infants develop language in the same way, but also because looking at individual differences brings language development within the theoretical framework discussed earlier in this section. If development is not simply a matter of the infant constructing a rule system, and is rather a product of both the efforts of infant and parents, differences in parental style are likely to be reflected in differences in infant's style. In particular, differences in early language acquisition and use may relate to differences in the way parents interact with their infant in the social contexts in which first words are formed.

The influence of parental style on early communication and language

Barrett points out that not all infants arrive at two-word utterances in the way described above, noting that some infants first produce words in combinations and later break down these *formulas* or *amalgams* into their constituents (Barrett, 1989) A good deal of controversy has surrounded this distinction. On the one hand, it has been argued that formulas are a linguistic 'dead end' since they resist analysis into their components (Brown and Hanlon, 1970). On the other hand, it has been argued that use of formulas reflects a different route into language, there being no good evidence that infants using formulas early on show slower vocabulary development (Pine and Lieven, 1990). The suggestion is that formulas are not organized collections of separate words, but that infants using them progress to true multiword utterances through differentiation rather than through integration of single words into grammatical strings (Barrett, 1989). On balance, the assumption that formula use reflects a different route into language rather than a poorer linguistic strategy appears to have stronger support.

This difference may be traced to another distinction that has been pointed to within the one-word stage. Nelson (1973) suggests that each infant's early language style lies on a continuum between two extremes. *Referential* infants tend to concentrate on object naming, requesting or referring to objects. In contrast, *expressive* infants use more personal names, and words referring to actions or social situations. These infants also show frequent use of multiword amalgams of the sort to which Barrett refers, particularly of the sort that are useful in directing others. In summary, referential infants appear to use words to focus interaction on objects, whereas expressive infants use words to refer to the interaction itself.

Another way of thinking about this distinction is presented by Bates (1979). She identifies 'style 1 infants' as those who concentrate on part-whole analysis and who are consequently good at extracting the relation between single words and specific referents. In contrast, 'style 2 infants' are those who concentrate on wholistic processing, using words or often unanalysed phrases as general strategies for communication without analysing the components of the utterances with reference to specific elements of the situation to which they refer. Style 1 can be roughly equated with Nelson's referential style, and style 2 with her expressive style.

Identifying different styles is interesting in itself, but it yields the question of why individual infants should rely more on one strategy than another. Service (1984) suggests that there may be a link between the infant's language style and general aspects of the way the mother engages in interaction. Observing the whole sequence of events involved in mothers picking up their baby, she noted two different maternal styles. *Symbolic* mothers tend to break their acts down into well-marked components that have a clear role as communicative symbols, for instance, they approach their infant, offer outstretched arms until they have the infant's attention (often marking this further by vocalizations like 'Do you want to come up?'), and finally complete the pick-up provided the infant shows compliance. In contrast, *functional* mothers simply approach and scoop up their infant without marking the act into components.

Differences of this sort also appear in play. The symbolic mothers tend to give fewer objects to their infant than the functional mothers, but spend a large amount of time pointing to the components of the objects. Again, they appear to be breaking things down for their infant in a way that the other group do not, although this time it is the physical world rather than the social that they are analysing.

These maternal differences appear to be reflected in differences in the way infants behave. Infants of symbolic mothers begin to respond to pick up offers with adjustive arm movements earlier than infants of functional mothers, and later they tend to make pick-up requests that look particularly symbolic, using much more definite 'marked arm raising'. In contrast, the other group show less definite arm movements mixed with leaning towards the mother, as if the action is more a direct attempt to get to her than a symbolic request.

The general notion is that these differences in the way mothers treat their infants have a direct effect on the infant's communicative (and cognitive) style which persist into later development. Hence, at the onset of language, infants of symbolic mothers become Nelson's 'referential' infants, and those of functional mothers become 'expressive'. The reader may feel that the linkup here is not entirely obvious, since it is not clear why functional mothering should lead to expressive infants. However, the problem may lie with Nelson's classification, since Lieven, Pine and Barnes (1992) argue that variations in infant language style are best described in terms of differences in the kinds of units that infants initially extract from the language they are exposed to. They found that the clearest distinction was to be made in terms of the relative frequency of single common nouns versus phrases, basically whether infants tended to use single words or formulas. One might assume that symbolic mothers' tendency to break up situations into their elements would provide the structure through which infants could break up accompanying maternal language into single elements, and that infants not provided with such a structure would be more likely to extract whole phrases. We can wonder also whether there may be a link here with Barrett's concept of decontextualization. As he points out, some infants show less context-dependent word use early in development than others, a difference that may also be traced to maternal style. All language development occurs within a social context, and whether the infant first uses the word as an adjunct to that general context or to refer to a particular object or event occurring in that context may depend on whether the mother has analysed the whole social and physical situation into its components. Thus it may turn out that both context-dependent single word use and use of formulas are partly determined by parental style. Two points need to be noted, however. Firstly, it is hard to escape the implication that symbolic mothers in some way do a better job than functional mothers. However, as Lieven et al. (1992) point out, high dependence on phrases does not disadvantage infants in later language development. Thus, although symbolic parents may provide their infants with an analysis of the world, either this analysis is not very important for language development or infants of functional mothers arrive at such an analysis through their own efforts. Secondly, there is a tantalizing question of how these differences in maternal style come about. Although the common assumption is that they are part of the mother's pre-existing style, Yoder and Kaiser (1989) suggest that maternal style is at least in part a response to infant style, as the mother adapts her interaction to a form that works well with her infant.

Ending this chapter on such a note makes it evident how great a need there is for investigation of the role of parent–child interaction in not just the development of social abilities, but in the development of perception and cognition as well. If parents have the important role in their infant's general development that is being suggested here, then we must look again at theories of cognitive development such as Piaget's, in which infants are portrayed as single-handed constructors of reality. If current theories on the social roots of knowledge are correct, infants could not do this without considerable help from their friends. Even if infants are shown to be capable of constructing some aspects of understanding in their own solitary investigation of the world, it seems clear that quite important differences in the way infants develop relate to the type of pre-structuring of the social and physical world that they receive from adults.

Conclusion

This chapter has presented more diversity of subject matter and of theoretical stances than have earlier ones. Nevertheless, a number of themes have emerged. First, there is the accumulation of evidence on infants' person perception, pointing to the possibility that they are at least partly socially aware from birth. This view re-emerged in the sections on emotion and social interaction. Again there is evidence that infants are aware of the emotions of adults and respond with matching emotions during interactions. There is also evidence that young infants have some skills as communicators, making early parent–infant interaction less one-sided than might be assumed.

However, not even those favouring the richest interpretations of early behaviour claim that young infants are so socially advanced that nothing remains to be developed. We encountered evidence indicating development in infants' knowledge of self and others. Much of the evidence suggests that important progress in these abilities occurs between the beginning and the middle of the second year, involving a transition from a perceptual/ecological to a representational basis for this knowledge. At the same time, we see emergence of social referencing, with clear evidence of infants using parental interpretation of situations to influence their emotional responses and actions. It seems likely that all these phenomena are underpinned by cognitive developments that allow infants to represent self and others.

Another major focus of the chapter was consideration of the processes through which parents support their infant's development. There is a good deal of stress on a form of 'oneness' between infant and parent as a source of security in the infant. For instance, Lamb (1981) suggests that predictability in interactions is a major factor leading to secure attachments. Parents of securely attached infants are those who monitor their infant's needs and respond in a consistent manner. Also Stern et al. (1985) stress the importance of affect attunement for emotional development. However, it emerged later that unpredictability might be a potent mechanism for development. If parents misinterpret or reinterpret infants' acts in terms of adult norms, they give infants unique access to adult models of the world, precisely because their acts were not predicted from the infant's stance, indicating a dissonance between infant and adult. It may well be that there is a continuous tension between the security value of predictable acts understood and the information value of new information yet to be assimilated. As noted already, complete predictability is likely to lead to stagnation, but too much unpredictability may lead to an emotional insecurity that stands in the way of learning.

All this relates to a growing emphasis on the importance of a parental contribution to the infant's development in cognitive as well as social spheres. Our understanding of the developmental mechanisms by which parents contribute to development is in its early stages, but the approach has promise both as a general principle of development and through its potential ability to explain individual differences in early development.

6

Research, theory and images of infancy

At the beginning of chapter 1, I said that one of the aims of this book was to show how recent research had changed our images of infancy. The role of this chapter is to pull together the findings and theoretical issues that have emerged chapter by chapter, attempting in the process to produce an image of infancy that incorporates the diversity of current evidence.

Important strands of evidence emerged from each of the four main chapters, where work was described that both advances our basic knowledge of what infants are capable of, and contributes to theory on the nature of early abilities and the processes behind their development. The main theme to emerge is that young infants are more competent than previous accounts recognized, and this early competence must force a change in models of how infants develop. Despite its good points, Piagetian constructionism did not recognize the degree of early competence that more recent studies have revealed, and the main alternative theory now being used to explain recent data is Gibson's ecological theory of perception (1979). While Piaget's theory was discussed in depth in chapter 4, so far I have only summarized Gibson's theory (chapter 1). A fuller discussion is therefore contained in this chapter as a preliminary to presenting an overall summary view of infancy.

Although the reader may have come this far with the impression that different workers have very different images of infancy, I shall suggest that there are common themes running through current thinking, and that these themes can be brought together to form a model of infancy that incorporates not only the strong parts of both Piaget's and Gibson's accounts, but also notions about the social construction of reality (Macmurray, 1961). In line with ecological theories and in particular, dynamic systems theory, I shall argue that to understand infant development, the unit of study must be the infant–environment system rather than just the infant. Such a model has some implications for the way we perform our research, and so at the end of this chapter I shall return to the issue of methodology discussed in chapter 1, with some suggestions of ways in which our empirical approaches need to be modified in light of our changing views of the nature of infancy.

Major themes

Physical and motor development

Two important themes emerged from the discussion of physical and motor development in chapter 2. The first relates to the growing evidence for developmental processes operating *before* birth, through which the fetus actively adapts to the environment of the womb. This evidence means we must re-evaluate the nature of newborn abilities. Rather than being genetically specified innate reflexes, some of these at least (for instance, the stepping reflex) may in fact be adaptations to the womb which developed in that environment through the active participation of the fetus (Prechtl, 1984), much in the way that it is claimed many abilities are developed after birth.

Additionally, this story was supplemented by evidence in chapter 3 pointing to auditory learning in the womb, so we can add perceptual learning to the processes occurring before birth. It would be going too far, however, to suggest that all newborn abilities have developed in this way. For instance, although there is considerable scope for auditory development based on sensory input before birth, there is no scope for this in the case of pattern vision, since if any illumination reaches the womb it is bound to be diffuse and unpatterned. Consequently, we have to conclude that some newborn abilities have developed without the aid of specific stimulation, and it is hard to see how active fetal participation could have a direct influence on these processes. In the case of some other abilities, however, we have to do away with the notion that fetal development involves an automatic unfolding process, one in which behaviours appear in a genetically determined maturational way. Although there must be a component of genetic determination in all these changes, the degree to which the activity of the fetal organism and the properties of the fetal environment have a part to play in the developmental process differs according to the behaviour or ability in question, and in some cases it certainly seems likely that these factors have a vital role in developments occurring well before birth.

A second issue emerging from chapter 2 has more to do with the *nature* of newborn behaviours than with their origins. There is growing evidence for newborn behaviours that look qualitatively different from those conventionally classified as reflexes. For instance, there is Bower's evidence for primitive visually guided reaching at birth (Bower, Broughton and Moore, 1970a; Bower, Dunkeld and Wishart, 1979), with the claim that this behaviour is guided rather than simply triggered by visual stimuli. Although we are far from a complete understanding of the full extent of newborn capacities, there is growing evidence that newborns are far more sophisticated than hitherto imagined, and we must entertain the possibility that the neonate's behaviour, however poorly executed, contains elements of intentional skilled action previously only attributed to older infants.

Unfortunately, not all workers have managed to obtain evidence for early reaching, but part of the reason for this may lie with the temporary disappearance of many neonatal behaviours shortly after birth. Whatever the reasons for this disappearance, and the reappearance of the behaviours in modified form some months later, the phenomenon presents an important problem for those studying early development. Workers failing to obtain evidence of behaviours such as reaching may sometimes have failed because they did not test infants early enough after birth. In summary then, both in their developmental origins and their form, many newborn behaviours appear to be more like behaviours developing later in infancy than was previously thought. However, they are particularly elusive, often disappearing shortly after birth, and we are still a long way from understanding the relationship between them and the more fully formed behaviours that emerge later. Significant steps forward have been made, however, through the application of *Dynamic Systems Theory* as a framework for explaining development of motor abilities in infancy.

Perceptual development

The major point arising directly from the evidence on perceptual development covered in chapter 3 was that young infants possess a whole range of perceptual capacities that were unsuspected ten or 20 years ago. Many aspects of pattern perception and perception of three-dimensional properties of the world can either be detected at birth or quite soon after. Auditory capacities are also well developed and there is growing evidence for cross-modal perception in early infancy.

The notion that the infant's own activities are instrumental in the developmental process re-emerged in this field of discussion, with the suggestion that early visual preferences were a result of infants' directing visual attention to the patterns that provided optimum stimulation for their developing visual system.

While it is relatively easy to explain some of the basic phenomena in perception in terms of underlying neural mechanisms, this sort of account rapidly becomes less helpful as we progress to the more impressive phenomena in early perception. Consequently, accounts of early perception of the third dimension and early cross-modal perception tend to be based on perceptual theories such as Gibson's which avoid recourse to neural mechanisms. As already indicated, the major thrust of Gibson's theory is that the properties of the world can be directly perceived from the structure of the stimulation reaching the organism, particularly the dynamic structure emerging as the organism moves. Other workers such as Bower have extended parts of the Gibsonian argument to suggest that early perception deals with the high level abstract properties of stimulation, abstract to the extent of not even being tied to specific modalities.

In one sense, Gibson's approach dodges the major issue of the perceptual structures necessary for direct perception, and there is clearly much to be done to uncover the full complexity of 'pre-wired' perceptual structures that must underlie early perception. But the account still has major implications for our notions of development in infancy, particularly those relating to cognitive development, since the suggestion is that many properties of the world can be perceived directly without the need for cognitive interpretation. This issue became a theme of the chapter on cognitive development itself.

Cognitive development and Piaget

In the discussion of cognitive development in chapter 4 one major issue concerned the contrasting views of Piaget and some more recent theorists on the nature of infant cognition. While Piaget argued that concepts of space and object permanence were gradually constructed by infants during their first two years, a range of workers have since presented evidence to suggest that quite young infants have an objective awareness of the world, including an awareness of the permanence of objects. The same state of affairs was discovered when we looked at infant imitation. Again, there is growing evidence for imitation of facial gestures even in neonates.

Much of the more recent evidence, for example on the object concept, is obtained in highly structured laboratory settings, and the fact remains that infants do not show the same awareness of object permanence in more obviously purposive behaviour, such as object search. This led to questions about whether some of the experimental data obtained from young infants really do indicate objective understanding of reality. Many years earlier Piaget drew a distinction between discriminating different distances and actually understanding the third dimension as a systematic set of inter-relationships in depth, claiming that the former developed early while the latter was only constructed gradually. From this it is fair to conclude that much of the recent evidence would not satisfy Piaget's criteria for understanding.

This brings the distinction between perception and cognition into central focus. In general, the term *perception* is used to describe more basic processing of sensory information, while *cognition* is used in describing capacities that in one way or another go beyond direct processing of sensory input. In fact, stronger forms of the perception–cognition distinction are based on the notion that perception has little meaning until it is interpreted by cognitive structures. An obvious example here is Piaget's theory, according to which infants only gradually reach an objective understanding of the world through development of sensori-motor structures that interpret perceptual input. But given the growing body of evidence that perception supplies objective information about the world directly, it is necessary to reevaluate the perception–cognition distinction, either redefining it or, in the extreme, discarding it altogether.

One issue that continues to emerge from most theories, however, is that of the relation between perception and action. Even if an objective world is directly perceived, it is clear that infants have much to learn about how to act appropriately in accordance with their perceptions. At least in this realm it seems evident that infants actively modify their actions to adapt them to perceptual input, and the result may be the development of cognitive structures that permit the infant to act appropriately in a world that was objectively perceived from the start. In other words, cognitive structures may not function to supply infants with knowledge of the objective structure of the world, but they may be needed at a higher level as infants attempt to discover the implications of that structure for their own actions.

In the end, it may be largely arbitrary whether we label abilities as perceptual or cognitive, but there is still a clear distinction to be drawn between abilities with which infants enter the world and abilities that they develop later. There appears to be a range of newborn capacities for perceiving high level properties of things and people, and in the case of imitation, even to make a match between the structure of external stimulation and the structure of the infant's own acts. Given this state of affairs, my suggestion was that infants do not need to develop concepts of the objective nature of space and the permanence of objects, since these properties are picked up directly by perception. Instead, infants have to develop concepts of how the world can be used. In other words, they have to attach meaning to perception. Finally, it was suggested that this was a task in which they received considerable support from parents, and so there was likely to be a strong social component in this developmental process.

Social development

Chapter 5 reviewed a range of impressive evidence on early perception of people, extending even to perception of their emotions and the production of matching facial expressions. Therefore it seems the story about early direct perception may usefully be extended to properties of people as well as things.

However, there was also plenty of evidence of infants developing more sophisticated emotional responses and acquiring communication skills and language during the months and years that follow. It was here that the role of social interaction as a developmental process became more explicit, with the notion that infants become more like adults because parents interpret their acts in adult terms. For instance they develop intentional communication because parents from the beginning interpret infants' acts as if they were intentional.

This notion was extended to suggest a general role for adults as presenters of appropriate stimulation for development. There is nothing new in the idea that adult stimulation has a role in development, but the notion here is that it is the very adult nature of this stimulation that makes it appropriate. Although adults make special efforts to adapt their speech and mode of interaction to suit their infant, their contribution, although simplified, is still essentially that of an adult human. By responding in adult ways to infants' acts, and by using objects in adult ways, parents provide infants with a rich variety of social information on which to feed. Hence, infants are far from the solitary constructors of understanding that the Piagetian image suggests.

It is of note that in the social realm important changes appear to be taking place between the end of the first year and the middle of the second year. For instance, infants begin to use parental emotional signals to guide their action, they gain an understanding of self at a representational level, and some would argue, they acquire a basic theory of the minds of others. However, these changes have to be set in the context of evidence for very early perception of aspects of self and others. Thus, as in the case of the infant's knowledge of the physical world, these developments appear to be a matter of constructing meanings to attach to perception. In this case, the developmental process is based in interactions with adults, and the meanings arrived at are cultural rather than related to personal activity. However, to be fully able to benefit from social interaction, infants have to come to understand others as mental entities. This indicates the interweaving of social and cognitive development, since possibly this more than anything else calls for the need to form mental representations.

Conceptualizing development: direct perception and constructed understanding

J. J. Gibson and the ecological approach to visual perception

The first general principle in Gibson's account (1979) is that the unit of study should not be the organism in isolation from its environment. He argues that we should look instead at the organism–environment system, since looking at either on its own is liable to be misleading. Accounting for perception purely in terms of the perceptual structures of the organism leads to the mistaken notion that there must be a system that reconstructs objective structure out of subjective experience, mistaken because from this stance we ignore the degree to which the structure is actually present in the environment ready to be picked up. But similarly, trying to define the perceptual structure available in the environment by aiming to define an objective physical environment is liable to mislead, since the environmental structures that the organism actually detects depend in themselves on the structure and activities of the organism.

There are two senses in which this is true. First, much of the structure of the environment is only picked up from the dynamic flow of information generated by movement, so we are likely to identify the form of some of the structures perceived by looking at how animals move. Secondly, higher level properties of the environment (which Gibson calls *affordances*) only have meaning in relation to the characteristics and habits of the organism in question. For instance, water 'affords' swimming for animals that can swim but drowning for those that cannot, and a flimsy surface affords support for light animals but not for heavier ones.

It is easy to trivialize Gibson's account by picking on these examples as nothing more than statements of the obvious. But what is radical about Gibson's account is not the statements themselves but their proposed implications for our thinking about perception. He argues that these *affordances*, like other aspects of environmental structure, are directly perceived. As the animal moves through its habitat it receives a rich flow of information which directly specifies the structures of the environment and the relevance of these structures for the animal's activities.

This argument has important implications for issues in infant development. Take, for example, understanding of objects and spatial relations. The claim is that as an organism moves through its environment an optical flow results which directly specifies the relationship between objects; the optical flow is more rapid for near objects than for further ones, and is more rapid the further the objects are radially from the direction of motion. In addition, far objects are progressively occluded by near ones, and Gibson argues that this dynamic event is directly perceived as one object going behind another, not as a two-dimensional phenomenon on the retina that has to be interpreted as such by higher structures. As a consequence, the continued existence of the occluded object is directly perceived even once it has gone out of sight (cf. Bower's evidence in chapter 3).

This last point may seem rather strong, since in effect the claim is that we perceive objects that we cannot see. It is relatively easy to accept the notion that a progressive occlusion is directly perceived as one object going behind another; an object going out of sight in this way does so in a perfectly lawful manner, with its surface progressively occluded by the other object at a perceived boundary. However, the conventional view would be that such perception comes to a stop when the object goes out of sight, with some inferential or representational process needed to specify the object's continued existence.

The notion that such representational processes are unnecessary for the detection of permanence becomes more plausible, however, in the light of another key point in Gibson's account. He claims that perception should be treated as a dynamic process occurring over time, and in so doing he dismisses the notion of static retinal images as the basis of perception. Instead of attempting to explain how we see movement by integrating a series of 'snap-shots' of reality, the problem if anything is how we ever manage to extract frozen views from the dynamic flow. This explains why it makes sense to claim that the organism perceives objects that are out of sight. The point is that since perception is a continuous process over time, an object's presence can be as well specified by its past history as by present perception. In summary, perception is not just about the here and now; a stationary object's position in space is determined by the stimulation arising from it over time and not at any particular moment. So if it is occluded by another object the dynamic perceptual process continues to specify its existence. This argument is extended to moving objects that go out of sight. In this case the object's trajectory is perceived over time, and the dynamic process serves to 'fill in' any gaps in the trajectory when the object is out of sight.

This approach largely does away with a distinction between perception and cognition. As Gibson puts it,

> To perceive the environment and to conceive it are different in degree but not in kind. One is continuous with the other. Our reasons for supposing that seeing something is quite unlike knowing something comes from the old doctrine that seeing is having temporary sensations one after another at the passing moment of present time, whereas knowing is having permanent concepts stored in memory. (1979, p. 258)

And of course this is the very definition of seeing that Gibson discards. He does admit that there are aspects of human knowing that might be called cognitive because they 'are not strictly perceptual' (1979, p. 260). For instance, he notes how *tacit* knowledge derived from perception can become explicit once the person can put this knowledge into words, and also how this verbal information can be used as a source of knowledge in itself. However, it still only acts as a supplement to perception, and a large part of everyday activity is guided by knowledge derived directly from perceptual stimulation.

The theory of direct perception and development in infancy

In contrast to Piaget's account, the theory of direct perception carries the implication that there is no need for infants to construct concepts of reality in order to understand the world in objective terms. As E. J. Gibson puts it, 'I do not believe that it is essential to invent mechanisms for assembling what we know we actually *do* perceive. . . . There is structure in the array, relational information that does not have to be pieced together because, like truth, it is already there' (1977, p. 157). Perception is objective from the start, itself amounting to understanding, and development is a matter of progressive abstraction of information from the world through a process of increased differentiation of environmental structure (Gibson, 1977). There certainly seems to be growing evidence in keeping with this view. Data reviewed in chapter 3 indicated that newborns perceive objects rather than retinal images (the shape constancy work) and that quite young infants perceive depth and show size constancy. In addition, evidence was presented in chapter 4 that infants of five months and probably a good deal younger detect the continued existence of hidden objects. Finally chapter 5 detailed evidence that newborns perceive and respond to the emotions of others. All these early abilities point to the young infant as a competent perceiver of objective properties of the world right from birth. In terms of ecological theory we could say that infants are born adapted to pick up aspects of the physical and social structure of their environment.

There are, however, a number of qualifications that need to be applied if this view is to fit the facts of infancy, and I shall introduce these as assumptions to be built into the model presented in the next section. First, there are bound to be some constraints on the efficiency of early information pick-up. We know, for instance, that the perceptual systems are not fully developed at birth, in particular, low visual acuity will limit the degree of detail that the infant can pick up. However, from the point of view of direct perception, this may not be such a constraint as it seems. The notion is that infants need to pick up very general properties of stimulation (what J. J. Gibson calls perceptual invariants) rather than specific pattern details. Bower has adapted this notion to suggest that young infants pick up the very abstract properties of stimulation, and it is actually possible that poor acuity aids this process through filtering out the specifies of fine pattern detail.

A more important constraint from the point of view of direct perception is the infant's initial lack of motor and locomotor control. According to J. J. Gibson's theory, perception is an activity that involves the whole organism, and he lays stress on the degree to which information is picked up from the dynamic perceptual flow resulting from the organism's movement. According to this view, young infants' information pick-up should be significantly limited by their inability to locomote.

These considerations apart, however, the implication is that the infant's task in development is simply the progressive pick-up of perceptual structure and its affordances for action. An account of development purely in terms of direct perception would thus suggest that infants should only be constrained by their inability to act, and to some extent by the immaturity of their perceptual systems. There would really be little or no place for cognition during infancy, since all the infant needs to know can be derived from perception, and development could be conceptualized simply as the progressive pick-up of new affordances.

A role for constructionism – individual and social

The Gibsonian account seems too extreme in one respect at least. Although infants may well perceive the three-dimensionality of the world, and even the identity of objects temporarily out of view, they can only discover the full scope of what the world offers through acting on it, initially in a trial-and-error manner. My suggestion is that affordances are constructed through action in much the way Piaget envisaged, the difference being that instead of constructing concepts of the objective nature of the world, they construct functional concepts about how human beings can use the world.

In addition to redefining the nature of early concepts in the light of what can be directly perceived, this account has to be extended into the social domain in two ways. First, infants are not solitary constructors of these concepts of human action. They are given considerable help by parents, partly through the way they break down global aspects of the perceived world into components for joint attention, and partly through the way their adult actions present a model of how human beings act on specific features of the world, for instance, how they use particular objects as containers of other objects, or in general how they use specific objects for specific purposes. Secondly, although infants appear to be able to perceive many properties of people directly, they still have to extend this *social* knowledge, and to learn how to utilize it in social interaction and communication. Here parents have a crucial role in drawing the infant forward by presenting adult models of communication and by constantly interpreting the infant's acts as if they were intentional acts of communication.

Thus, according to this view, construction still has a vital role to play in development, albeit in the acquisition of functional knowledge rather than understanding of the physical properties of the world. But in addition to the Piagetian view of the individual infant as constructor of his or her world, we need to add the model of the infant as a partner in the social construction of reality (MacMurray, 1961), a model in which knowledge is constituted jointly through the activities and interpretations of infant and parents (see Lock, 1980; chapter 5 of this volume).

A model of development in infancy

If we bring together the data and theoretical points summarized so far, the following outline model of infant development emerges.

The infant is born able to pick up aspects of the objective structure of reality. This structure is very general in form and can be picked up through a variety of sensory channels. For instance, the location of an event relative to the infant can be picked up through sight or sound, and one version of this argument would have it that young infants do not even discriminate between the same information coming in through different sensory channels. Consequently, one aspect of development concerns the gradual differentiation of these global abstract properties of stimulation into more detailed specific features (Bower, 1989). This process may occur in part in a relatively simple way, the gradual improvement in the resolution of the sensory channels making it possible to pick up more fine detail in sensory information. However, it is not clear how this process would lead to differentiation between sensory channels, so if Bower's account is correct, it is likely that an important differentiation process underlies early perceptual development.

The finer tuning of perception taking place in the early months will have other specific implications. For instance, although young infants may be capable of perceiving the general properties that specify a face, their perceptual resolution may not be sufficient to permit discrimination between specific faces in terms of subtle pattern differences. So although very young infants appear to discriminate between people, this is likely to happen on the basis of gross differences such as hairline (Bushnell, 1982). Also, perceptual limitations may have implications for the infant's knowledge about permanence of objects. Although young infants perceive many disappearance sequences as one object moving behind another, poor acuity may set limits to the events that can be perceived in this way. Small differences in depth may not be resolved, and so young infants may not be capable of perceiving the movement of one object behind another for what it is if the separation between object and occluder is too small (Neilson, 1977). In general, the ability to segregate closely placed objects as separate entities may be constrained by acuity limits rather than by conceptual limitations.

In addition, however, infants are actively engaged in making sense of the world, and in this respect the developmental process is likely to be more in line with Piagetian theory. The primary difference concerns the nature of early concepts. Because the objective properties of reality can be directly perceived, the infant has no need to construct concepts about the physical nature of reality. But he or she does have to construct relationships between environmental structure and human action. In this respect, this account also departs from J. J. Gibson's by claiming that affordances have to be constructed through action on the world. Rather than being properties of the world, affordances are relationships between environmental features and the infant's activities. Thus they are not there to be picked up: on the development of new activities the infant has to construct categories of objects and events that relate in particular ways to these actions. In other words, to perception of the world has to be added meaning in relation to action. Additionally, new motor abilities, while offering new scope for exploration of the world and manipulation of objects in it, always present new problems for solution. For example, the onset of locomotion brings with it the need to solve detour problems. It is assumed that solution of these problems occurs through mental activity. Also, since solution results in more elaborate mental representations of space, problem solution in itself is an important contributor to cognitive development.

One of the fundamental problems in infancy involves determination of the way in which knowledge is represented. Mandler (1988) draws a distinction between implicit procedural knowledge embedded in sensorimotor procedures and explicit conceptual knowledge. It is possible that much of the infant's knowledge of the relationships between perception and action is of the former sort, picked up through acting and learning from action. On the other hand, problem-solving requires planning in advance of action, and so must involve mental processes that are at least separable from action and are probably conscious. We should also be aware of the possibility that it is during problem-solving that new relationships between action and perceptual features are discovered. Thus, although the knowledge gained may be largely procedural, the prime developmental driving force may be located in mental activity.

There are two other differences between this model and Piagetian constructionism. First, the construction process is viewed in a different manner. In Piaget's theory, the role of construction is firmly in the infant's hands; the infant constructs reality from action on the world, and the environment's role is just to be there to be acted upon. In the sense that there would be no development without an environment, the environment has a *permitting* role in development, but it does not have a *determining* role. In contrast, the current model draws on the ecological emphasis on the infant–environment system as the subject for study, to assign a stronger role to environmental structure in determining the course of development. The developmental process is envisaged as a constant interplay between the structure of the infant's knowledge and the structure of the world. At any point in development the infant's cognitive state determines the environmental features attended to, features that present specific problems the solution of which leads the infant to a new state of knowledge. This in turn leads to attention to new environmental features, and so the cycle repeats itself. The main difference between this and the conventional constructionist view is that environmental structure has a specific determining role in the course of development, and the consequence is that we may be able to explain the course of development partly through looking at the environmental structures that become the focus of the infant's attention at particular points in development.

The second difference is that this model recognizes a strong social component to the construction process. The outline above presents the infant as a solitary constructor of knowledge, and it is assumed that a good deal of knowledge of the physical world is achieved through this process. However, it is assumed that this process is supplemented by a form of social construction that occurs when infant and parents interact over objects. In chapter 5 we saw how some parents in particular go to great lengths to break down the world into relevant components for the benefit of their infant, and in this process they may simplify the infant's task by making the structure of reality more explicit. It is likely that these solitary and social processes can substitute for each other, so that infants of parents who do less of this environment analysis are left to do more of the work on their own.

Of course, the parents' contribution to development is doubly important in the case of the construction of social understanding. Here, parents and other adults provide a great deal of the structure of human action ready made. Infants are supplied with information on the way humans act in the social and physical world through observing and interacting with adults, and in these cases development may be more a matter of picking up human patterns than constructing them totally unaided, a guided reinvention process (Lock, 1980) rather than a solitary effort.

A key question concerns the level at which adult input contributes to infant knowledge. On the one hand, adult efforts to break down the world into relevant parts may act primarily at a perceptual level, imposing structures on infants' perception but leaving it for infants to construct meanings in relation to this way of structuring the world. On the other hand, infants may be able to attribute meaning directly, by seeing how adults use objects. However, some would argue that to do the latter depends on the infant being able to represent the adult as an individual and to understand the causal relationship between intentions and activities, abilities that appear to emerge during the second year. In this respect, the acquisition of socially transmitted cultural meaning may come somewhat later than the acquisition of meaning in relation to personal activity, and may well depend on relatively high level representations of others.

There is, however, a particular difficulty in interpreting data on interaction between infants and parents. Vygotsky's (1962) account of the social construction of reality contains the fundamental principle that knowledge is first possessed between people, in this case between infant and parent, and later becomes possessed by the infant as an internal psychological structure. If this is the case, it is not easy to draw conclusions about the abilities possessed by infants from evidence of their competence in interaction. As noted in chapter 5, a successful collaboration between parent and infant should lead to the latter performing beyond the level at which he or she could perform individually. It is thus not a simple matter to extract a measure of individual competence, particularly in the case of abilities that are normally only seen in social interaction.

Implications for further research on cognitive development

The model outlined above provides a general framework for thinking about infant development, and in a sense is no more than a set of suggested processes based on relationships between infant and the physical and social world. I have attempted to draw together a range of findings and lines of thought, with the intention of showing that a coherent image of infancy can still be constructed despite the diversity of data and views. As such, the model is by no means comparable to more detailed theories such as Piaget's, and needs to be 'filled out' by a detailed description of the processes involved. In this respect, *dynamic systems theory* is likely to prove particularly important. As indicated in chapter 2, the key principles of this approach are that complex systems are self organizing, and that development involves progression through a series of stable states, with progress determined by forces acting either from within or outside the organism. Thus, in a similar general way, a change in leg weight may promote a new locomotion pattern, the onset of locomotion may lead to a new way of organizing space, and in parent–infant interaction, a change in either partner's behaviour may lead to a new level of interaction. The main point is that in each case, the new development is an emergent property of the relevant system under study rather than a property of the infant alone, such as a cognitive structure. Adoption of such an approach provides important challenges to how we conceptualize psychological processes. However, I believe that such an approach should not be seen as a replacement for current ways of thinking about infant development. Instead, I believe that it constitutes an important means of implementing many of the notions already current in developmental psychology. For instance, it appears to hold potential for filling in the detail of process currently lacking in Gibsonian developmental psychology, and it appears directly applicable to the Vygotskian principle that knowledge is initially possessed by the parent and infant together rather than by the individual infant. It is undoubtedly a powerful tool for sharpening up our conceptualizations of development, but it is not a replacement for them.

It is, of course, important that in addition to changing our reconceptualizations of the developmental processes, we take note of the implications of these reconceptualizations for how we carry out our research. There is much that could be said on this topic, but I will focus on just two issues here. First, the general model that I have outlined assumes that at all points in development the infant's cognitive level determines those aspects of the environment to be treated as problems, and that solution of these problems constitutes the next step in construction of knowledge. If this is so, there will be a precise link between the structure of these problems and the type of knowledge that develops next (which in turn determines the next set of environmental problems), and so part of the the key to the course of development lies in the basic invariant structure of the infant's everyday environment. Infants do not develop in the way they do just because of some internal construction process. They develop in this way as much because of the structure of the problems they encounter at different points in the sequence.

Consequently, while laboratory studies may measure infant ability or potential very well, it is unlikely that the developmental processes themselves can be measured solely in the laboratory, since the causal factors are as much in the infant's environment as in his or her mind. Thus we need to supplement laboratory study of perception and cognition with home-based study, not only moving our experiments out of the laboratory, but tackling different questions as well. Take, for example, the development of spatial abilities. Instead of being content to trace the development of general spatial reference systems through laboratory investigation, we need to focus also on the structure of the home environment that the infant uses, and on the activities that infants generally engage in at home which necessitate particular spatial systems. Looking at these issues may give us important clues as to why development proceeds in the way that it does, since to some extent abilities may be developed when the nature of the infant's transactions with the environment make them necessary rather than because of the actions of some mysterious developmental process hidden within the infant.

This by no means indicates that we should abandon conventional laboratory investigation. The laboratory still offers greater experimental control over a range of variables. In addition, we need parallel laboratory investigation to test the generality of abilities uncovered in the home environment. One possibility is that infants initially develop systems of orienting that are tied to the specific structure of their own home, systems that do not immediately generalize to orientation in novel spaces. An alternative is that they immediately pick up the general spatial properties of their surroundings (see Bower, 1989), and so are as capable of orienting in novel surroundings as in familiar ones. To test these alternatives we need to set up laboratory studies in which infants are faced with both a novel environment, and one in which particular aspects of spatial structure can be manipulated systematically.

Secondly, we need to be more aware of the fact that the experiment itself is a social interaction in which the infant may be trying as much to identify the experimenter's intentions as to understand the physical task (Fischer and Jennings, 1981). For instance, in object search studies is the infant trying to understand the object's movements or the social structure of the interaction over the task materials? This sort of issue has come to prominence in work with older children, and the evidence on infants' social awareness makes it clear that it should be a central concern in infancy research as well.

Another aspect of this issue fits into what has just been said about the contribution of environmental structure. Many early 'abilities' are only detected in highly structured experimental settings, and we can ask to what extent the ability appears here because the experimenter is pre-structuring the problem for the infant. In the extreme, it can be suggested that some experimental studies tell us more about the cleverness of the experimenter than about the cleverness of the infant. However, we must conclude that they always tell us a little about both. On the one hand, it is true that infants only show some abilities under extremely structured conditions, and in this respect we might conclude that their mental structures are not as mature as the experimental evidence suggests. But on the other hand, we have to assume a good deal about infants' mental organization in order to explain their ability even under these well-structured conditions. The lesson to be learned is that in experiments, just as in more naturalistic investigation, we need to attend to the props and the rest of the cast of actors as well as to the individual performer. Not only may this allow us to interpret the results of experiments more realistically, but we may also discover a good deal more about cognitive development through analysing the structure of early social interactions over objects. This presents a considerable challenge to the ingenuity of the researcher, for as already indicated, an implication of Vygotsky's theory is that it is by no means simple to draw conclusions about the infant's ability from data on social interaction, or for that matter from the experiment once it is recognized as a social negotiation between infant and investigator.

References

Abramson, A. S. and Lisker, L. 1970: Discriminability along the voice continuum: cross language tests. *Proceedings of the Sixth International Congress of Phonetic Sciences*. Prague: Academia.

Abravanel, E. and DeYong, N. 1991: Does object modeling elicit imitative-like gestures from young infants? *Journal of Experimental Child Psychology*, 52, 22–40.

Acredolo, L. P. 1978: Development of spatial orientation in infancy. *Developmental Psychology*, 14, 224–34.

Acredolo, L. P., Adams, A. and Goodwyn, S. W. 1984: The role of self-produced movement and visual tracking in infant spatial orientation. *Journal of Experimental Child Psychology*, 38, 312–27.

Acredolo, L. P. and Evans, D. 1980: Developmental changes in the effects of landmarks on infant spatial behavior. *Developmental Psychology*, 16, 312–18.

Adams, R. J. 1987: Visual acuity from birth to five months as measured by habituation: a comparison to forced-choice preferential looking. *Infant Behavior and Development*, 10, 239–44.

Adams, R. J., Maurer, D. and Davis, M. 1986: Newborns' discrimination of chromatic from achromatic stimuli. *Journal of Experimental Child Psychology*, 41, 267–81.

Ahrens, S. R. 1954: Beitrage zur entwicklung des physiognomie und mimiker-kennes [Contributions on the development of physiognomy and mimicry recognition]. *Zeitschrift fur Experimentelle und Angewandte Psychologie*, 2, 412–54.

Ainsworth, M. D. S. 1973: The development of infant–mother attachment. In B. M. Caldwell and H. N. Ricciuti (eds), *Review of Child Development Research* vol. 3. Chicago: University of Chicago Press.

Ainsworth, M. D. S., Blehar, M., Waters, E. and Wall, E. 1978: *Patterns of Attachment*. Hillsdale, NJ: Erlbaum.

Aitken, S. and Bower, T. G. R. 1982: Intersensory substitution in the blind. *Journal of Experimental Child Psychology*, 33, 309–23.

Allen, J. 1978: 'Visual acuity development in human infants up to six months of age'. Unpublished doctoral dissertation, University of Washington.

Amsterdam, B. 1972: Mirror self image reactions before age two. *Developmental Psychobiology*, 5, 297–305.

Anisfeld, E., Casper, V., Nozyee, M. and Cunningham, N. 1990: Does infant carrying promote attachment? An experimental study of the effects of increased physical contact on the development of attachment. *Child Development*, 61, 1617–27.

Antonucci, T. C. and Levitt, M. J. 1984: Early prediction of attachment security: a multivariate approach. *Infant Behavior and Development*, 7, 1–18.

Apgar, V. 1953: A proposal for a new method of evaluation of the newborn infant. *Current Research in Anesthesia and Analgesia*, 32, 260–7.

Aronson, E. and Rosenbloom, S. 1971: Space perception in early infancy: perception within a common auditory-visual space? *Science*, 186, 649–50.

Arterberry, M. E., Bensen, A. S. and Yonas, A. 1991: Infants' responsiveness to static-monocular depth information: a recovery from habituation approach. *Infant Behavior and Development*, 14, 241–51.

Ashmead, D. H., Clifton, R. K. and Perris, E. E. 1987: Precision of auditory localization in human infants. *Developmental Psychology*, 23, 641–7.

Ashmead, D. H., Davis, D. L., Whalen, T. and Odom, R. D. 1991: Sound localization and sensitivity to interaural time differences in human infants. *Child Development*, 62, 1211–26.

Ashmead, D. H. and McCarty, M. E. 1991: Postural sway of human infants while standing in light and dark. *Child Development*, 62, 1276–87.

Aslin, R. N. 1977: Development of binocular fixation in human infants. *Journal of Experimental Child Psychology*, 23, 133–50.

—— 1981: Development of smooth pursuit in human infants. In D. F. Fisher, R. A. Monty and J. W. Senders (eds), *Eye Movements: cognition and visual perception*. Hillsdale, NJ: Erlbaum.

Aslin, R. N., Pisoni, D. B. and Jusczyk, P. W. 1983: Auditory development and speech perception in infancy. In M. M. Haith and J. J. Campos (eds), *Infancy and Developmental Psychobiology* (vol. II of P. H. Mussen (ed.), *Handbook of Child Psychology*), 4th edn. New York: Wiley.

Aslin, R. N. and Salapatek, P. 1975: Saccadic localization of peripheral targets by the very young human infant. *Perception and Psychophysics*, 17, 293–302.

Astington, J. W. and Gopnik, A. 1991: Developing understanding of desire and intention. In A. Whiten (ed.), *Natural theories of mind: evolution, development and simulation of everyday mindreading*. Oxford: Blackwell.

Atkinson, J. and Braddick, O. J. 1981: Acuity, contrast sensitivity and accommodation in infancy. In R. N. Aslin, J. R. Alberts and M. R. Petersen (eds), *The Development of Perception: psychobiological perspectives*: v.ol. 2. *The visual system*. New York: Academic Press, 245–77.

Atkinson, J., Hood, B., Wattam-Bell, J., Anker, S. and Tricklebank, J. 1988: Development of orientation discrimination in infancy. *Perception*, 17, 587–95.

Atkinson, J., Hood, B., Wattam-Bell, J. and Braddick, O. 1992: Changes in infants' ability to switch visual attention in the first three months of life. *Perception*, 21, 643–53.

Ausubel, D. P. 1958: *Theory and Problems of Child Development*. New York: Grune and Stratton.

Bahrick, L. E. 1988: Intermodal learning in infancy: learning on the basis of two kinds of invariant relations in audible and visible events. *Child Development*, 59, 197–209.

Bahrick, L. E. 1992: Infants' perceptual differentiation of amodal and modality-specific audio-visual relations. *Journal of Experimental Child Psychology*, 53, 180–99.

Bahrick, L. E. and Watson, J. S. 1985: Detection of intermodal proprioceptive-visual contingency as a potential basis of self-perception in infancy. *Developmental Psychology*, 21, 963–73.

Bai, D. L. and Bertenthal, B. I. 1992: Locomotor status and the development of spatial search skills. *Child Development*, 63, 215–26.

Baillargeon, R. 1986: Representing the existence and the location of hidden objects: object permanence in six- and eight-month-old infants. *Cognition*, 23, 21–41.

—— 1987a: Object permanence in 3.5- and 4.5-month-old infants. *Developmental Psychology*, 23, 655–64.

—— 1987b: Young infants' reasoning about the physical and spatial properties of a hidden object. *Cognitive Development*, 2, 179–200.

Baillargeon, R. and DeVos, J. 1991: Object permanence in young infants: further evidence. *Child Development*, 62, 1227–46.

Baillargeon, R. and Graber, M. 1987: Where's the rabbit? 5.5-month-old infants' representation of the height of a hidden object. *Cognitive Development*, 2, 375–92.

Baillargeon, R. and Graber, M. 1988: Evidence of location memory in eight-month-old infants in a nonsearch AB task. *Developmental Psychology*, 24, 502–11.

Baillargeon, R., Needham, A. and DeVos, J. 1992: The development of young infants' intuitions about support. *Early Development and Parenting*, 1, 69–78.

Baillargeon, R., Spelke, E. S. and Wasserman, S. 1985: Object permanence in five-month-old infants. *Cognition*, 20, 191–208.

Baldwin, D. A. 1991: Infants' contribution to the achievement of joint reference. *Child Development*, 62, 875–90.

Baldwin, J. M. 1894: *Mental Development in the Child and the Race*. London: Macmillan.

Ball, W. and Tronick, E. 1971: Infant responses to impending collision: optical and real. *Science*, 171, 818–20.

Banks, M. S. 1980a: Infant refraction and accommodation. *International Ophthalmology Clinics*, 20, 205–32.

—— 1980b: The development of visual accommodation during early infancy. *Child Development*, 51, 646–66.

Banks, M. S. and Ginsburg, A. P. 1985: Infant visual preferences: a review and new theoretical treatment. *Advances in Child Development and Behavior*, 19, 207–46.

Banks, M. S. and Salapatek, P. 1981: Infant pattern vision: a new approach based on the contrast sensitivity function. *Journal of Experimental Child Psychology*, 31, 1–45.

—— 1983: Infant visual perception. In M. M. Haith and J. J. Campos (eds), *Infancy and Developmental Psychobiology* (vol. II of P. H. Mussen (ed.), *Handbook of Child Psychology*), 4th edn. New York: Wiley.

Barglow, P. Vaughn, B. E. and Molitor, N. 1987: Effects of maternal absence due to employment on the quality of infant–mother attachment in a low-risk sample. *Child Development*, 58, 945–54.

Barrera, M. E. and Maurer, D. 1981: The perception of facial expressions by the three-month-old. *Child Development*, 52, 203–6.

Barrett, J. H. W. 1982: Prenatal influences on adaptation in the newborn. In P. Stratton (ed.), *Psychobiology of the Human Newborn*. Chichester: Wiley.

Barrett, K. and Campos, J. J. 1987: Perspectives on emotional development: II. A functionalist approach to emotions. In J. Osofsky (ed.), *Handbook of infant development*, 2nd edn. 555–8. New York: Wiley.

Barrett, M. D. 1986: Early semantic representations and early word usage. In S. A. Kuczaj and M. D. Barrett (eds), *The Development of Word Meaning*. New York: Springer-Verlag.

—— 1989: Early language development. In A. Slater and J. G. Bremner (eds), *Infant Development*. London: Erlbaum.

Barrett, M. D., Harris, M., Jones, D. and Brookes, S. 1986: Linguistic input and early context-bound word use. In *Proceedings of the Child Language Seminar 1986*. Department of Psychology, University of Durham.

Bates, E. 1979: *The Emergence of Symbols: cognition and communication in infancy.* New York: Academic Press.

Bates, E., Benigni, L., Bretherton, I., Camaioni, L. and Volterra, V. 1979: *The emergence of symbols: cognition and communication in infancy.* New York: Academic Press.

Bates, E., Thal, D., Whitesell, K., Fenson, L. and Oakes, L. 1989: Integrating language and gesture in infancy. *Developmental Psychology*, 25, 1004–19.

Bayley, N. 1969: *Bayley Scales of Infant Development.* New York: The Psychological Corporation.

Bell, M. A. and Fox, N. A. 1992: The relations between frontal brain electrical activity and cognitive development during infancy. *Child Development*, 63, 1142–63.

Bell, S. M. 1970: The development of the concept of the object and its relationship to infant–mother attachment. *Child Development*, 41, 291–312.

Belsky, J., Gilstrap, B. and Rovine, M. 1984: The Pennsylvania infant and family development project, I: stability and change in mother–infant and father–infant interaction in a family setting at one, three, and nine months. *Child Development*, 55, 692–705.

Belsky, J. and Rovine, M. J. 1988: Nonmaternal care in the first year of life and the security of infant–parent attachment. *Child Development*, 59, 157–67.

Belsky, J., Rovine, M. and Taylor, D. G. 1984: The Pennsylvania infant and family development project, III: the origins of individual differences in infant–mother attachment: maternal and infant contributions. *Child Development*, 55, 718–28.

Benson, J. B. and Uzgiris, I. C. 1985: Effect of self-initiated locomotion on infant search activity. *Developmental Psychology*, 21, 923–31.

Berkeley, G. 1709: *A New Theory of Vision.* Reprinted in Everyman's Library (1963), London: Dent and Sons.

Bernard, J. and Sontag, L. W. 1947: Fetal reactivity to tonal stimulation: a preliminary report. *Journal of Genetic Psychology*, 70, 205–10.

Bertenthal, B. I. 1985: 'Some indirect effects of early crawling experience on perceptual, cognitive, and affective development.' Paper presented at the 8th Biennial Meeting of The International Society for the Study of Behavioural Development, Tours, France.

Bertenthal, B. I. and Bai, D. L. 1989: Infants' sensitivity to optical flow for controlling posture. *Developmental Psychology*, 25, 936–45.

Bertenthal, B. I., Campos, J. and Barrett, K. 1984: Self-produced locomotion: an organizer of emotional, cognitive and social development in infancy. In R. Emde and R. Harmon (eds), *Continuities and discontinuities in development* 175–210. New York: Plenum Press.

Bertenthal, B. I., Campos, J. J. and Haith, M. M. 1980: Development of visual organisation: the perception of subjective contours. *Child Development*, 51, 1072–80.

Bertenthal, B. I. and Fischer, K. W. 1978: The development of self-recognition in the infant. *Developmental Psychology*, 14, 44–50.

Bertenthal, B. I., Proffitt, D. R., Kramer, S. J. and Spetner, N. B. 1987: Infants' encoding of kinetic displays varying in relative coherence. *Developmental Psychology*, 23, 171–8.

Bigelow, A. E. 1981: The correspondence between self and image movement as a cue to self-recognition for young children. *Journal of Genetic Psychology*, 139, 11–26.

Bjork, E. L. and Cummings, E. M. 1984: Infant search error: stage of concept development or stage of memory development. *Memory and Cognition*, 12, 1–19.

Blakemore, C. and Cooper, G. F. 1970: Development of the brain depends on the visual environment. *Nature*, 228, 477–8.

Bloom, L. 1973: *One word at a time*. The Hague: Mouton.

Blurton-Jones, N. G. 1972: Characteristics of ethological studies of human behaviour. In N. G. Blurton-Jones (ed.), *Ethological Studies of Child Behaviour*. Cambridge: Cambridge University Press.

Bohlin, G. and Hagekull, B. 1993: Stranger wariness and sociability in the early years. *Infant Behavior and Development*, 16, 53–67.

Boller, K. and Rovee-Collier, C. 1992: Contextual coding and recoding of infants' memories. *Journal of Experimental Child Psychology*, 53, 1–23.

Bornstein, M. H. 1975: Qualities of color vision in infancy. *Journal of Experimental Child Psychology*, 19, 401–19.

Bornstein, M. H., Ferdinandsen, K. and Gross, C. G. 1981: Perception of symmetry in infancy. *Developmental Psychology*, 17, 82–6.

Bornstein, M. H., Kessen, W. and Weiskopf, S. 1976: Color vision and hue categorization in young human infants. *Journal of Experimental Psychology, Human Perception and Performance*, 2, 115–29.

Bornstein, M. H. and Krinsky, S. J. 1985: Perception of symmetry in infancy: the salience of vertical symmetry and the perception of pattern wholes. *Journal of Experimental Child Psychology*, 39, 1–19.

Bornstein, M. H., Krinsky, S. J. and Benasich, A. A. 1986: Fine orientation discrimination and shape constancy in young infants. *Journal of Experimental Child Psychology*, 41, 49–60.

Bornstein, M. H. and Sigman, M. D. 1986: Continuity in mental development in infancy. *Child Development*, 57, 251–74.

Borovsky, D. and Rovee-Collier, C. 1990: Contextual constraints on memory retrieval at six months. *Child Development*, 61, 1569–83.

Boswell, S. L. 1976: Young children's processing of asymmetrical and symmetrical patterns. *Journal of Experimental Child Psychology*, 22, 309–18.

Bower, T. G. R. 1964: Discrimination of depth in premotor infants. *Psychonomic Science*, 1, 368.

—— 1966: The visual world of infants. *Scientific American*, 215, 80–92.

—— 1967: The development of object-permanence: some studies of existence constancy. *Perception and Psychophysics*, 2, 411–18.

—— 1972: Object perception in infancy. *Perception*, 1, 15–30.

—— 1974: *Development in Infancy*. San Francisco: Freeman.

Bower, T. G. R. 1975: Infant perception of the third dimension and object concept development. In L. B. Cohen and P. Salapatek (eds), *Infant Perception: from sensation to cognition*, vol. 2: *perception of space, speech and sound*. New York: Academic Press.

—— 1977a: Comment on Yonas et al. 'Development of sensitivity to information for impending collision'. *Perception and Psychophysics*, 21, 281–2.

—— 1977b: Blind babies see with their ears. *New Scientist*, 73, 255–7.

—— 1982: *Development in Infancy*. 2nd edn. San Francisco: Freeman.

—— 1989: The perceptual world of the newborn child. In A. Slater and G. Bremner (eds), *Infant Development*. London: Erlbaum.

Bower, T. G. R., Broughton, J. M. and Moore, M. K. 1970a: Demonstration of intention in the reaching behavior of neonate humans. *Nature*, 228, 679–81.

—— 1970b: Infant responses to approaching objects: an indicator of response to distal variables. *Perception and Psychophysics*, 9, 193–6.

—— 1971: The development of the object concept as manifested by changes in the tracking behavior of infants between seven and 20 weeks of age. *Journal of Experimental Child Psychology*, 11, 182–93.

Bower, T. G. R., Dunkeld, J. and Wishart, J. G. 1979: Infant perception of visually presented objects. *Science*, 208, 1137–8.

Bower, T. G. R. and Paterson, J. G. 1973: The separation of place, movement and time in the world of the infant. *Journal of Experimental Child Psychology*, 15, 161–8.

Bower, T. G. R. and Wishart, J. G. 1972: The effects of motor skill on object permanence. *Cognition*, 1, 165–72.

Bowlby, J. 1951: *Maternal Care and Mental Health*. Geneva: World Health Organization.

—— 1953: *Child Care and the Growth of Love*. Harmondsworth: Penguin Books.

—— 1969: *Attachment*. London: Hogarth Press.

Boynton, R. M. 1979: *Human Color Vision*. New York: Holt, Rinehart and Winston.

Brackbill, Y. 1971: Cumulative effects of continuous stimulation on arousal level in infants. *Child Development*, 42, 17–26.

Braddick, O., Atkinson, J., French, J. and Howland, H. C. 1979: A photorefractive study of infant accommodation. *Vision Research*, 19, 1319–30.

Braddick, O., Wattam-Bell, J. and Atkinson, J. 1986: Orientation-specific cortical responses develop in early infancy. *Nature*, 320, 617–19.

Branigan, G. 1979: Some reasons why successive single word utterances are not. *Journal of Child Language*, 6, 411–21.

Brazelton, T. B. 1973: *Neonatal Behavioral Assessment Scale* (Clinics in Developmental Medicine, 50). London: Heinemann.

—— 1979: Evidence of communication during neonatal behavioral assessment. In M. Bullowa (ed.), *Before Speech: the beginning of interpersonal communication*. Cambridge: Cambridge University Press.

Bremner, J. G. 1978a: Spatial errors made by infants: inadequate spatial cues or evidence for egocentrism? *British Journal of Psychology*, 69, 77–84.

—— 1978b: Egocentric versus allocentric coding in nine-month-old infants: factors influencing the choice of code. *Developmental Psychology*, 14, 346–55.

—— 1985: Object tracking and search in infancy: a review of data and a theoretical evaluation. *Developmental Review*, 5, 371–96.

Bremner, J. G. and Bryant, P. E. 1977: Place versus response as the basis of spatial errors made by young infants. *Journal of Experimental Child Psychology*, 23, 162–71.

Bremner, J. G. and Knowles, L. S. 1984: Piagetian stage IV errors with an object that is directly accessible both visually and manually. *Perception*, 13, 307–14.

Brennan, W. M., Ames, E. W. and Moore, R. W. 1966: Age differences in infants' attention to patterns of different complexity. *Science*, 151, 354–6.

Bretherton, I. 1992: Social referencing, intentional communication, and the interfacing of minds in infancy. In S. Feinman (ed.), *Social referencing and the social construction of reality in infancy*. 57–78, New York: Plenum.

Bretherton, I., Bates, E., Benigni, L. Camaioni, L. and Volterra, V. 1976: Relationships between cognition, communication, and quality of attachment. In E. Bates, L. Benigni, I. Bretherton, L. Camaioni and V. Volterra (eds), *The Emergence of Symbols: cognition and communication in infancy*. New York: Academic Press.

Bretherton, I. and Beeghly, M. 1982: Talking about internal states: the acquisition of an explicit theory of mind. *Developmental Psychology*, 18, 906–21.

Bridges, K. M. 1930: A genetic theory of the emotions. *Journal of Genetic Psychology*, 37, 514–27.

Bronson, G. W. 1974: The postnatal growth of visual capacity. *Child Development*, 45, 873–90.

—— 1990: Changes in infants' visual scanning across the two- to fourteen-week age period. *Journal of Experimental Child Psychology*, 49, 101–25.

—— 1991: Infant differences in rate of visual encoding. *Child Development*, 62, 44–54.

Brookman, K. E. 1980: 'Ocular accommodation in human infants.' Unpublished doctoral dissertation. Indiana University (cited by Banks and Salapatek, 1983).

Brown, I. 1973: 'A study of object permanence.' Unpublished BSc. thesis, University of Edinburgh (cited by Bower, 1982).

Brown, K. W. and Gottfried, A. W. 1986: Cross-modal transfer of shape in early infancy: is there reliable evidence? In L. P. Lipsitt and C. Rovee-Collier (eds), *Advances in infancy research*, 4, 171–81, Norwood, NJ: Ablex.

Brown, R. and Hanlon, C. 1970: Derivational complexity and order of acquisition in child speech. In J. R. Hayes (ed.), *Cognition and the development of language*. pp. 11–54, New York: Wiley.

Bruner, J. S. 1973: Organization of early skilled action. *Child Development*, 44, 1–11.

Bruner, J. S. and Koslowski, B. 1972: Visually preadapted constituents of manipulatory action. *Perception*, 1, 3–14.

Bryant, P. E., Jones, P., Claxton, V. and Perkins, G. M. 1972: Recognition of shapes across modalities by infants. *Nature*, 240, 303–4.

Bullinger, A. 1990: Posture control during reaching. In H. Bloch and B. I. Bertenthal (eds), *Sensory-motor organisations and development in infancy and early childhood*. Dortrecht: Kluwer.

Bushnell, I. W. R. 1979: Modification of the externality effect in young infants. *Journal of Experimental Child Psychology*, 28, 211–29.

—— 1982: Discrimination of faces by young infants. *Journal of Experimental Child Psychology*, 33, 298–308.

Bushnell, I. W. R., McCutcheon, E., Sinclair, J. and Tweedie, M. E. 1984: Infants' delayed recognition memory for colour and form. *British Journal of Developmental Psychology*, 2, 11–17.

Bushnell, I. W. R., Sai, F. and Mullin, J. T. 1989: Neonatal recognition of the mother's face. *British Journal of Developmental Psychology*, 7, 3–15.

Butterworth, G. 1974: 'The development of the object concept in human infants.' Unpublished DPhil. thesis, University of Oxford.

—— 1975: Object identity in infancy: the interaction of spatial location codes in determining search errors. *Child Development*, 46, 866–70.

—— 1977: Object disappearance and error in Piaget's stage IV task. *Journal of Experimental Child Psychology*, 23, 391–401.

—— 1983: Structure of the mind in human infancy. In L. P. Lipsitt (ed.), *Advances in Infancy Research*, vol. 2. Norwood: Ablex.

Butterworth, G. and Castillo, M. 1976: Coordination of auditory and visual space in newborn human infants. *Perception*, 5, 155–60.

Butterworth, G. E. and Cicchetti, D. 1978: Visual calibration of posture in normal and motor retarded Down's syndrome infants. *Perception*, 7, 513–25.

Butterworth, G. E. and Cochran, E. 1980: Towards a mechanism of joint visual attention in human infancy. *International Journal of Behavioural Development*, 3, 253–72.

Butterworth, G. E. and Hicks, L. 1977: Visual proprioception and postural stability in infancy: a developmental study. *Perception*, 6, 255–62.

Butterworth, G. and Hopkins, B. 1988: Hand-mouth coordination in the new-born baby. *British Journal of Developmental Psychology*, 6, 303–14.

Butterworth, G., Jarrett, N. and Hicks, L. 1982: Spatio-temporal identity in infancy: perceptual competence or conceptual deficit. *Developmental Psychology*, 18, 435–49.

Calkins, S. D. and Fox, N. A. 1992: The relations among infant temperament, security of attachment, and behavioral inhibition at twenty-four months. *Child Development*, 63, 1456–72.

Camaioni, L. 1992: Mind knowledge in infancy: the emergence of intentional communication. *Early Development and Parenting*, 1, 15–22.

Campos, J. J. 1983: The importance of affective communication in social referencing: a commentary on Feinman. *Merrill-Palmer Quarterly of Behavior and Development*. 28, 445–470.

Campos, J. J., Barrett, K. C., Lamb, M. E., Goldsmith, H. H. and Stenberg, C. 1983: 'Socioemotional development', In M. M. Haith and J. J. Campos (eds), *Infancy and Developmental Psychobiology* (vol. II of P. H. Mussen (ed.), *Handbook of Child Psychology*). 4th edn. New York: Wiley.

Campos, J. J., Campos, R. G. and Barrett, C. K. 1989: Emergent themes in the study of emotional development and emotional regulation. *Developmental Psychology*, 25, 394–402.

Campos, J., Langer, A. and Krowitz, A. 1970: Cardiac responses on the visual cliff in prelocomotor human infants. *Science*, 170, 195–6.

Campos, J., Svejda, M., Bertenthal, B., Benson, N. and Schmid, D. 1981: 'Self-produced locomotion and wariness of heights: new evidence from training studies.' Paper presented at the meeting of the Society for Research in Child Development, Boston, Mass.

Campos, J. J., Svejda, M. J., Campos, R. G. and Bertenthal, B. 1982: The emergence of self-produced locomotion: its importance for psychological development in infancy. In D. Bricker (ed.), *Intervention with At-risk and Handicapped Infants*. Baltimore, Md: University Park Press.

Caron, A. J., Caron, R. F. and Carlson, V. R. 1979: Infant perception of the invariant shape of objects varying in slant. *Child Development*, 50, 716–21.

Caron, A. J., Caron, R. F. and Myers, R. S. 1982: Abstraction of invariant face expressions in infancy. *Child Development*, 53, 1008–15.

Carpenter, G. C. 1974: Mother's face and the newborn. *New Scientist*, 61, 742–4.

Case, R. 1991: Stages in the development of the young child's first sense of self. *Developmental Review*, 11, 210–30.

Casler, L. 1968: Perceptual deprivation in institutional settings. In G. Newton and S. Levine (eds), *Early Experience and Behavior*. Springfield: Thomas.

Cassidy, J. 1986: The ability to negotiate the environment: an aspect of infant competence as related to quality of attachment. *Child Development*, 57, 331–7.

Castillo, M. and Butterworth, G. E. 1981: Neonatal localisation of a sound in visual space. *Perception*, 10, 331–8.

Cernoch, J. M. and Porter, R. H. 1985: Recognition of maternal axillary odors by infants. *Child Development*, 56, 1593–8.

Chappell, P. F. and Sander, L. W. 1979: Mutual regulation of the neonatal–maternal interactive process: context for the origins of communication. In M. Bullowa (ed.), *Before Speech: the beginning of interpersonal communication*. Cambridge: Cambridge University Press.

Chase-Lansdale, P. L. and Owen, M. T. 1987: Maternal employment in a family context: effects on infant–mother and infant–father attachments. *Child Development*, 58, 1505–12.

Chomsky, N. 1968: *Language and Mind*. New York: Harcourt Brace Jovanovich.

Clarke, A. M. and Clarke, A. D. B. 1976: *Early Experience: myth and evidence*. London: Open Books.

Clifton, R., Perris, E. and Bullinger, A. 1991: Infants' perception of auditory space. *Developmental Psychology*, 27, 187–97.

Clifton, R. K., Morrongiello, B. A., Kulig, J. W. and Dowd, J. M. 1981a: Newborns' orientation towards sound: possible implications for cortical development. *Child Development*, 53, 833–8.

—— 1981b: Developmental changes in auditory localization in infancy. In R. N. Aslin, J. R. Alberts and M. R. Petersen (eds), *Development of Perception: psychobiological perspectives*, vol. 1. *Audition, somatic perception and the chemical senses*. New York: Academic Press.

Cohen, L. B., Diehl, R. L. Oakes, L. M. and Loehlin, J. C. 1992: Infant perception of /aba/ versus /apa/: building a quantitative model of infant categorical discrimination. *Developmental Psychology*, 28, 261–72.

Cohen, L. B. and Oakes, L. M. 1993: How infants perceive a simple causal event. *Developmental Psychology*, 29, 421–33.

Cohen, L. B. and Younger, B. A. 1984: Infant perception of angular relations. *Infant Behavior and Development*, 7, 37–47.

Cohen, S. E. 1974: Developmental differences in infants' attentional responses to face–voice incongruity of mother and stranger. *Child Development*, 45, 1155–8.

Cohn, J. F. and Tronick, E. Z. 1988: Mother–infant face-to-face interaction: influence is bidirectional and unrelated to periodic cycles in either partner's behavior. *Developmental Psychology*, 24, 386–92.

Colombo, J., Mitchell, D. W., Coldren, J. T. and Freeseman, L. J. 1991: Individual differences in infant visual attention: are short lookers faster processors or feature processors? *Child Development*, 62, 1247–57.

Colombo, J., Mitchell, D. W., O'Brien, M. and Horowitz, F. D. 1987: The stability of visual habituation during the first year of life. *Child Development*, 58, 474–87.

Condry, S. M., Haltom, M. and Neisser, U. 1977: Infant sensitivity to audio-visual discrepancy: a failure to replicate. *Bulletin of the Psychonomic Society*, 9, 431–2.

Connolly, K. and Bruner, J. 1974: *The Growth of Competence*. London: Academic Press.

Cook, M., Field, J. and Griffiths, K. 1978: The perception of solid form in early infancy. *Child Development*, 49, 866–9.

Cook, M., Hine, T. and Williamson, A. 1982: The ability to see solid form in early infancy. *Perception*, 11, 677–84.

Cooper, R. P. and Aslin, R. N. 1990: Preference for infant–directed speech in the first month after birth. *Child Development*, 61, 1584–95.

Cornell, E. H. and Heth, C. D. 1979: Response versus place learning by human infants. *Journal of Experimental Psychology, Human Learning and Memory*, 5, 188–96.

Corrigan, R. 1978: Language development as related to stage six object permanence development. *Journal of Child Language*, 5, 173–89.

Courage, M. L. and Adams, R. J. 1990: The early development of visual acuity in the binocular and monocular peripheral fields. *Infant Behavior and Development*, 13, 123–8.

Crassini, B. and Broerse, J. 1980: Auditory–visual integration in neonates: a signal detection analysis. *Journal of Experimental Child Psychology*, 29, 144–55.

Crook, C. K. 1978: Taste perception in the newborn infant. *Infant Behavior and Development*, 1, 52–69.

Cruikshank, R. M. 1941: The development of visual size constancy in early infancy. *Journal of Genetic Psychology*, 58, 327–51.

Cummings, E. M. and Bjork, E. L. 1983: Persevertion and search on a five-choice visible displacement hiding task. *Journal of Genetic Psychology*, 142, 283–91.

Dannemiller, J. L. 1989: A test of color constancy in nine- and 20-week-old human infants following simulated illumination changes. *Developmental Psychology*, 25, 171–84.

Dannemiller, J. L. and Hanko, S. A. 1987: A test of color constancy in four-month-old human infants. *Journal of Experimental Child Psychology*, 44, 255–67.

Dannemiller, J. L. and Stephens, B. R. 1988: A critical test of infant pattern preference models. *Child Development*, 59, 210–16.

Darwin, C. 1872: *The Expression of the Emotions in Man and Animals*. Chicago: University of Chicago Press, 1975.

Dawes, G. S. 1973: Revolutions and cyclical rhythms in prenatal life: fetal respiratory movements. *Pediatrics*, 51, 965–71.

Day, R. H. and McKenzie, B. E. 1973: Perceptual shape constancy in early infancy. *Perception*, 2, 315–20.

—— 1977: Constancies in the perceptual world of the infant. In W. Epstein (ed.), *Stability and Constancy in Visual Perception: mechanisms and process*. New York: Wiley.

—— 1981: Infant perception of the invariant size of approaching and receding objects. *Developmental Psychology*, 17, 670–7.

Dayton, G. O. and Jones, M. H. 1964: Analysis of characteristics of fixation reflexes in infants by use of direct current electrooculography. *Neurology*, 14, 1152–6.

DeCasper, A. J. and Fifer, W. 1980: Of human bonding: newborns prefer their mothers' voices. *Science*, 208, 1174–6.

DeCasper, A. J. and Prescott, P. A. 1984: Human newborns' perception of male voices: preference, discrimination and reinforcing value. *Developmental Psychobiology*, 17, 481–91.

DeCasper, A. J. and Spence, M. J. 1986: Prenatal maternal speech influences newborns' perception of speech sounds. *Infant Behavior and Development*, 9, 133–50.

Delorme, A., Frigon, J. Y. and Lagacé, C. 1989: Infants' reactions to visual movement of the environment. *Perception*, 18, 667–73.

Dewan, E. M. 1969: The programming (P) hypothesis for REMS. *Physical Science Research Papers*, 388.

Diamond, A. 1988: Abilities and neural mechanisms underlying AB performance. *Child Development*, 59, 523–7.

—— 1990: The development and neural bases of memory functions as indexed by the AB and delayed response tasks in human infants and infant monkeys. In A. Diamond (ed.), *The development and neural bases of higher cognitive functions*. New York: New York Academy of Sciences Press, 267–317.

DiFranco, D., Muir, D. W. and Dodwell, P. C. 1978: Reaching in very young infants. *Perception*, 7, 385–92.

Dineen, J. T. and Meyer, W. J. 1980: Developmental changes in visual orienting behavior to featural versus structural information in the human infant. *Developmental Psychobiology*, 13, 123–30.

Dobson, V. 1976: Spectral sensitivity of the two-month infant as measured by the visually evoked cortical potential. *Vision Research*, 16, 367–74.

Dodd, B. 1979: Lipreading in infants: attention to speech presented in- and out-of-synchrony. *Cognitive Psychology*, 11, 478–84.

Dunn, J. 1991: Understanding others: evidence from naturalistic studies of children, in A. Whiten (ed.), *Natural theories of mind: evolution, development and simulation of everyday mindreading*. Oxford: Blackwell.

Dunst, C. J., Brooks, P. H. and Doxsey, P. A. 1982: Characteristics of hiding places and the transition to stage IV performance in object permanence tasks. *Developmental Psychology*, 18, 671–81.

Dziurawiec, S. and Ellis, H. D. 1986: 'Neonates' attention to face-like stimuli: Goren, Sarty and Wu (1975) revisited.' Paper presented at the Annual Conference of the Developmental Psychology Section of the British Psychological Society, Exeter.

Eaton, W. O. and Saudino, K. J. 1992: Prenatal activity level as a temperament dimension? Individual differences and developmental functions in fetal movement. *Infant Behavior and Development*, 15, 57–70.

Eilers, R. E., Gavin, W. J. and Oller, D. K. 1982: Cross-linguistic perception in infancy: early effects of linguistic experience. *Journal of Child Language*, 9, 289–302.

Eimas, P. D. 1975: Speech perception in early infancy. In L. B. Cohen and P. Salapatek (eds), *Infant Perception: from sensation to cognition*, vol. 2. *Perception of space, speech and sound*. New York: Academic Press.

—— 1985: Some constraints on a model of infant speech perception. In J. Mehler and R. Fox (eds), Neonates Cognition: beyond the blooming buzzing confusion. Hillsdale, NJ: Erlbaum.

Eimas, P. D., Siqueland, E. R., Jusczyk, P. W. and Vigorito, J. 1971: Speech perception in infants. *Science*, 171, 303–6.

Ellis, H. D. and Young, A. W. 1988: Are faces special? In A. W. Young and H. D. Ellis (eds), *Handbook of Research on Face Processing*. Amsterdam: North Holland.

Evans, W. F. 1973: 'The stage IV error in Piaget's theory of object concept development.' Unpublished dissertation, University of Houston.

Fagan, J. F., III. 1973: Infants' delayed recognition memory and forgetting. *Journal of Experimental Child Psychology*, 16, 424–50.

Fagan, J. F. and McGrath, S. K. 1981: Infant recognition memory and later intelligence. *Intelligence*, 5, 121–30.

Fagan, J. F. and Singer, L. T. 1983: Infant recognition memory as a measure of intelligence. In L. P. Lipsitt (ed.), *Advances in Infancy Research*, vol. 2. Norwood: Ablex.

Fagin, C. M. R. N. 1966: *The Effects of Maternal Attendance during Hospitalization on the Post-hospital Behavior of Young Children: a comparative study*. Philadelphia: Davis.

Fantz, R. L. 1961: The origin of form perception. *Scientific American*, 204, 66–72.

—— 1963: Pattern vision in newborn infants. *Science*, 140, 296–7.

—— 1966: Pattern discrimination and selective attention as determinants of perceptual development from birth. In A. H. Kidd and J. L. Rivoire (eds), *Perceptual Development in Children*. London: University of London Press.

Fantz, R. L., Fagan, J. F. and Miranda, S. B. 1975: Early visual selectivity as a function of pattern variables, previous exposure, age from birth and conception, and expected cognitive deficit. In L. B. Cohen and P. Salapatek (eds), *Infant Perception: from sensation to cognition*. vol. I. *Basic visual processes*. New York: Academic Press.

Fantz, R. L. and Miranda, S. B. 1975: Newborn infant attention to form of contour. *Child Development*, 46, 224–8.

Fantz, R. L., Ordy, J. M. and Udelf, M. S. 1962: Maturation of pattern vision in infants during the first six months. *Journal of Comparative and Physiological Psychology*, 55, 907–17.

Feinman, S. 1992: In the broad valley: an integrative look at social referencing. In S. Feinman (ed.), *Social referencing and the social construction of reality in infancy*. pp. 3–14, New York: Plenum.

Feldman, S. and Ingham, M. 1975: Attachment behavior: a validation study in two age-groups. *Child Development*, 46, 309–30.

Fernald, A. 1982: *Acoustic determinants of infant preference for 'motherese'*. (Doctoral dissertation, University of Oregon). *Dissertation Abstracts International*, 43, 545B.

—— 1989: Intonation and communicative intent in mothers' speech to infants: is the melody the message? *Child Development*, 60, 1497–510.

Fernald, A. and Mazzie, C. 1991: Prosody and focus in speech to infants and adults. *Developmental Psychology*, 27, 209–21.

Fernald, A. and Simon, T. 1984: Expanded intonation contours in mothers' speech to newborns. *Developmental Psychology*, 20, 104–13.

Fernald, A., Taeschner, T., Dunn, J., Papousek, M., Boysson-Bardies, B. de and Fukui, I. 1989: A cross-language study of prosodic modifications in mothers' and fathers' speech to preverbal infants. *Journal of Child Language*, 16, 477–501.

Ferrandez, A. M. and Pailhous, J. 1986: From stepping to adaptive walking: modulations of an automatism. In H. T. A. Whiting and M. G. Wade (eds), *Themes in Motor Development*. Dordrecht: Nijhoff.

Field, J. 1976: Adjustment of reaching behavior to object distance in early infancy. *Child Development*, 47, 304–8.

—— 1977: Coordination of vision and prehension in young infants. *Child Development*, 48, 97–103.

Field, J., Muir, D., Pilon, R., Sinclair, M. and Dodwell, P. 1980: Infants' orientation to lateral sounds from birth to three months. *Child Development*, 51, 295–8.

Field, T., Cohen, D., Garcia, R. and Greenberg, R. 1984: Mother–stranger face discrimination by the newborn. *Infant Behavior and Development*, 7, 19–26.

Field, T., Woodson, R., Cohen, D., Greenberg, R., Garcia, R. and Collins, K. 1983: Discrimination and imitation of facial expressions by term and preterm neonates. *Infant Behavior and Development*, 6, 485–90.

Field, T., Woodson, R., Greenberg, R. and Cohen, D. 1982: Discrimination and imitation of facial expressions by neonates. *Science*, 218, 179–81.

Fischer, K. W. 1980: A theory of cognitive development: the control and construction of hierarchies of skills. *Psychological Review*, 87, 477–531.

Fischer, K. W. and Jennings, S. 1981: The emergence of representation in search: understanding the hider as an independent agent. *Developmental Review*, 1, 18–30.

Fish, M., Stifter, C. A. and Belsky, J. 1993: Early patterns of mother–infant dyadic interaction: infant, mother, and family demographic antecedents. *Infant Behavior and Development*, 16, 1–18.

Fogel, A. 1990: Sensorimotor factors in communicative development. In H. Bloch and B. I. Bertenthal (eds), *Sensory-motor organisations and development in infancy and early childhood*. pp. 75–88, Dordrecht: Kluwer.

Fogel, A. and Thelen, E. 1987: The development of expressive and communicative action in the first year: reinterpreting the evidence from a dynamic systems perspective. *Developmental Psychology*, 23, 747–61.

Fontaine, R. 1984: Imitative skills between birth and six months. *Infant Behavior and Development*, 7, 323–33.

Fontaine, R. and Pieraut le Bonniec, G. 1988: Postural evolution and integration of the prehension gesture in children aged four to ten months. *British Journal of Developmental Psychology*, 6, 223–33.

Freeman, N. H., Lloyd, S. and Sinha, C. G. 1980: Infant search tasks reveal early concepts of containment and canonical usage of objects. *Cognition*, 8, 243–62.

Freud, S. 1940: *An Outline of Psychoanalysis*. New York: Norton (1949).

Friedman, S. 1972: Habituation and recovery of visual response in the alert human newborn. *Journal of Experimental Child Psychology*, 13, 339–49.

Ganchrow, J. R., Steiner, J. E. and Daher, M. 1983: Neonatal facial expressions in response to different qualities and intensities of gustatory stimuli. *Infant Behavior and Development*, 6, 473–84.

Gardner, J. and Gardner, H. 1970: A note on selective imitation by a six-week-old infant. *Child Development*, 41, 1209–13.

Gekoski, M. 1974: 'Changes in infant quieting to mother or stranger over the first six months.' Unpublished masters thesis, Rutgers University.

Ghim, H. R. 1990: Evidence for perceptual organization in infants: perception of subjective contours by young infants. *Infant Behavior and Development*, 13, 221–48.

Gibson, E. J. 1977: How perception really develops: a view from outside the network. In D. LaBerge and S. J. Samuels (eds), *Basic Processes in Reading: perception and comprehension*. Hillsdale, NJ: Erlbaum.

Gibson, E. J. and Walk, R. D. 1960: The 'visual cliff'. *Scientific American*, 202, 64–71.

Gibson, E. J. and Walker, A. S. 1984: Development of knowledge of the visual-tactual affordances of substances. *Child Development*, 55, 453–60.

Gibson, J. J. 1966: *The Senses Considered as Perceptual Systems*. Boston: Houghton Mifflin.

—— 1979: *The Ecological Approach to Visual Perception*. Boston: Houghton Mifflin.

Ginsburg, G. P. and Kilbourne, B. K. 1988: Emergence of vocal alternation in mother–infant interchanges. *Journal of Child Language*, 15, 221–35.

Goldberg, S. 1976: Visual tracking and existence constancy in five-month-old infants. *Journal of Experimental Child Psychology*, 22, 478–91.

Golinkoff, R. M. and Hirsh-Pasek, K. 1990: Let the mute speak: what infants can tell us about language acquisition. *Merrill-Palmer Quarterly*, 36, 67–91.

Goodenough, F. L. and Tyler, L. E. 1959: *Developmental Psychology*. 3rd edn. New York: Appleton Century Crofts.

Gopnik, A. 1984: The acquisition of *gone* and the development of the object concept. *Journal of Child Language*, 11, 273–92.

Gopnik, A. and Meltzoff, A. 1987: The development of categorization in the second year and its relation to other cognitive and linguistic developments. *Child Development*, 58, 1523–31.

—— 1992: Categorization and naming: basic-level sorting in eighteen-month-olds and its relation to language. *Child Development*, 63, 1091–103.

Gordon, B. 1972: The superior colliculus of the brain. *Scientific American*, 227(6), 72–82.

Goren, C., Sarty, M. and Wu, P. 1975: Visual following and pattern discrimination of face-like stimuli by newborn infants. *Pediatrics*, 56, 544–9.

Gottlieb, G. 1976: The roles of experience in the development of behavior and the nervous system. In G. Gottlieb (ed.), *Neural and Behavioral Specificity*. Academic Press: New York.

—— 1983: The psychobiological approach to development. In M. M. Haith and J. J. Campos (eds), *Infancy and Developmental Psychobiology* (vol. II of P. H. Mussen (ed.), *Handbook of Child Psychology*), 4th edn. New York: Wiley.

Granrud, C. E. 1986: Binocular vision and spatial perception in four- and five-month-old infants. *Journal of Experimental Psychology, Human Perception and Performance*, 12, 36–49.

Granrud, C. E. and Yonas, A. 1984: Infants' perception of pictorially specified interposition. *Journal of Experimental Child Psychology*, 37, 500–11.

Gratch, G., Appel, K. J., Evans, W. F., LeCompte, G. K. and Wright, N. A. 1974: Piaget's stage IV object concept error: evidence of forgetting or object conception. *Child Development*, 45, 71–7.

Greenberg, M. and Morris, N. 1974: Engrossment: the newborn's impact upon the father. *American Journal of Orthopsychiatry*, 44, 520–31.

Grieser, D. L. and Kuhl, P. K. 1988: Maternal speech to infants in a tonal language: support for universal prosodic features in motherese. *Developmental Psychology*, 24, 14–20.

Grimwade, J. C., Walker, D. W., Bartlett, M., Gordon, S. and Wood, C. 1971: Human fetal heart rate change and movement in response to sound and vibration. *American Journal of Obstetrics and Gynecology*, 109, 86–90.

Grossmann, K. E., Grossmann, K., Huber, F. and Wartner, U. 1981: German children's behavior towards their mothers at 12 months and their fathers at

18 months in Ainsworth's strange situation. *International Journal of Behavioral Development*, 4, 157–81.

Gusella, J. L., Muir, D. and Tronick, E. Z. 1988: The effect of manipulating maternal behavior during an interaction on three- and six-month-olds' affect and attention. *Child Development*, 59, 1111–24.

Haaf, R. 1974: Complexity and facial resemblance as determinants of response to facelike stimuli by five- and 10-week-old infants. *Journal of Experimental Child Psychology*, 18, 480–7.

Hales, D., Lozoff, B., Sosa, R. and Kennell, J. 1977: Defining the limits of the maternal sensitive period. *Developmental Medicine and Child Neurology*, 19, 454–61.

Halliday, M. A. K. 1979: One child's protolanguage. In M. Bullowa (ed.), *Before Speech: the beginning of interpersonal communication*. Cambridge: Cambridge University Press.

Harlow, H. F. 1961: The development of affectional patterns in infant monkeys. In B. M. Foss (ed.), *Determinants of Infant Behaviour*, vol. 1. London: Methuen.

Harris, P. and Macfarlane, A. 1974: The growth of the effective visual field from birth to seven weeks. *Journal of Experimental Child Psychology*, 18, 340–8.

Harris, P. L. 1973: Perseverative errors in search by young infants. *Child Development*, 44, 28–33.

—— 1974: Perseverative search at a visibly empty place by young infants. *Journal of Experimental Child Psychology*, 18, 535–42.

—— 1983: Infant cognition. In M. M. Haith and J. J. Campos (eds), *Infancy and Developmental Psychobiology* (vol. II of P. H. Mussen (ed.), *Handbook of Child Psychology*), 4th edn. New York: Wiley.

Hartlep, K. L. and Forsyth, G. A. 1977: Infants' discrimination of moving and stationary objects. *Perceptual and Motor Skills*, 45, 27–33.

Hayes, L. A. and Watson, J. S. 1981: Neonatal imitation: fact or artifact? *Developmental Psychology*, 17, 655–60.

Haynes, H., White, B. L. and Held, R. 1965: Visual accommodation in human infants. *Science*, 148, 528–30.

Hebb, D. O. 1949: *Organization of Behavior*. New York: Wiley.

Heimann, M. 1989: Neonatal imitation, gaze aversion, and mother–infant interaction. *Infant Behavior and Development*, 12, 495–505.

Heinicke, C. M. and Westheimer, I. J. 1965: *Brief Separations*. London: Longman.

Held, R. and Hein, A. 1963: Movement produced stimulation in the development of visually guided behavior. *Journal of Comparative and Physiological Psychology*, 56, 872–76.

Hendrickson, A. and Kupfer, C. 1976: The histogenesis of the fovea in the macaque monkey. *Investigative Opthalmology*, 15, 746–56.

Hepper, P. G. 1992: Fetal psychology: an embryonic science. In J. G. Nijhuis (ed.), *Fetal behaviour: developmental and perinatal aspects*. Oxford: Oxford University Press.

Hiatt, S., Campos, J. and Emde, R. N. 1979: Facial patterning and infant emotional expression: happiness, surprise, and fear. *Child Development*, 50, 1020–35.

Hillier, L., Hewitt, K. L. and Morrongiello, B. A. 1992: Infants' perception of illusions in sound localization: reaching to sounds in the dark. *Journal of Experimental Child Psychology*, 53, 159–79.

Hinde, R. A. 1963: The nature of imprinting. In B. M. Foss (ed.), *Determinants of Infant Behaviour*, vol. 2. London: Methuen.

Hinde, R. A. 1966: *Animal Behavior: a synthesis of ethology and comparative psychology*. New York: McGraw Hill.

—— 1983: Ethology and child development. In M. M. Haith and J. J. Campos (eds), *Infancy and Developmental Psychobiology* (vol. II of P. H. Mussen (ed.), *Handbook of Child Psychology*), 4th edn. New York: Wiley.

Hirshberg, L. 1990: When infants look to their parents: II. Twelve-month-olds' response to conflicting parental emotional signals. *Child Development*, 61, 1187–91.

Hofer, M. A. 1981: *The Roots of Human Behavior*. San Francisco: Freeman.

Hoffman, M. L. 1981: Perspectives on the difference between understanding people and understanding things: the role of affect. In J. H. Flavell and L. Ross (eds), *Social Cognitive Development: frontiers and possible futures*. Cambridge: Cambridge University Press.

Hofsten, C. von 1980: Predictive reaching for moving objects by human infants. *Journal of Experimental Child Psychology*, 30, 369–82.

—— 1982: Eye-hand coordination in newborns. *Developmental Psychology*, 18, 450–61.

—— 1984: Developmental changes in the organisation of prereaching movements. *Developmental Psychology*, 20, 378–88.

—— 1990: Development of manipulation action in infancy. In H. Bloch and B. I. Bertenthal (eds), *Sensory-motor organisations and development in infancy and early childhood*. Dordrecht: Kluwer.

Hofsten, C. von and Fazel-Zandy, S. 1984: Development of visually guided hand orientation in reaching. *Journal of Experimental Child Psychology*, 38, 208–19.

Hofsten, C. von, Kellman, P. and Putaansuu, J. 1992: Young infants sensitivity to motion parallax. *Infant Behavior and Development*, 15, 245–64.

Hofsten, C. von and Lindhagen, K. 1979: Observations on the development of reaching for moving objects. *Journal of Experimental Child Psychology*, 28, 158–73.

Hofsten, C. von and Rönnqvist, L. 1988: Preparation for grasping an object: a developmental study. *Journal of Experimental Psychology: Human Perception and Performance*, 14, 610–21.

Hofsten, C. von and Siddiqui, A. 1993: Using the mother's actions as a reference for object exploration in six- and 12-month-old infants. *British Journal of Developmental Psychology*, 11, 61–74.

Hood, B. and Willatts, P. 1986: Reaching in the dark to an object's remembered position: evidence for object permanence in five-month-old infants. *British Journal of Developmental Psychology*, 4, 57–65.

Hooker, D. 1952: *The Prenatal Origin of Behavior*. Lawrence: University of Kansas Press.

Hornik, R. and Gunnar, M. R. 1988: A descriptive analysis of infant social referencing. *Child Development*, 59, 626–34.

Hornik, R., Risenhoover, N. and Gunnar, M. 1987: The effects of maternal positive, neutral, and negative affective communications on infant responses to new toys. *Child Development*, 58, 937–44.

Horobin, K. and Acredolo, L. 1986: The role of attentiveness, mobility history, and separation of hiding sites on stage IV search behavior. *Journal of Experimental Child Psychology*, 41, 114–27.

Hulsebus, R. C. 1975: 'Latency of crying cessation: measuring infants' discrimination of mothers' voices.' Paper presented at the Meeting of the American Psychological Association, Chicago (cited by Zucker, 1985).

—— 1981: 'Father discrimination two weeks after birth.' Paper presented at the Meeting of the Southeastern Psychological Association, Atlanta (cited by Zucker, 1985).

Humphrey, G. K., Humphrey, D. E., Muir, D. W. and Dodwell, P. C. 1986: Pattern perception in infants: effects of structure and transformation. *Journal of Experimental Child Psychology*, 41, 128–48.

Humphrey, T. 1969: Reflex activity in the oral and facial area of human fetuses. In J. F. Bosma (ed.), *Oral Sensation and Perception*. Springfield, Ill.: Thomas.

Ianniruberto, A. 1985: 'Prenatal onset of motor patterns.' Paper presented to Conference on Motor Skill Acquisition in Children. NATO Advanced Study Institute, Maastricht, Netherlands.

IJzendoorn, M. H. van and Kroonenberg, P. M. 1988: Cross-cultural patterns of attachment: a meta-analysis of the strange situation. *Child Development*, 59, 147–56.

IJzendoorn, M. H. van and Tavecchio, L. W. C. 1987: The development of attachment theory as a Lakatosian research program: philosophical and methodological aspects. In L. W. C. Tavecchio and M. H. van IJzendoorn (eds), *Attachment in social networks: contributions to the Bowlby-Ainsworth attachment theory*. 3–31, Amsterdam: North Holland.

Illick J. E. 1976: Child rearing in 17th century England and America. In L. de Mause (ed.), *The History of Childhood*. London: Souvenir Press.

Illingworth, R. S. 1973: *Basic Developmental Screening: 0–2 years*. Oxford: Blackwell Scientific.

Isabella, R. A. 1993: Origins of attachment: maternal interactive behavior across the first year. *Child Development*, 64, 605–21.

Isabella, R. A. and Belsky, J. 1991: Interactional synchrony and the origins of infant–mother attachment: a replication study. *Child Development*, 62, 373–84.

Isabella, R. A., Belsky, J. and Eye, A von 1989: Origins of infant–mother attachment: an examination of interactional synchrony during the infant's first year. *Developmental Psychology*, 25, 12–21.

Izard, C. E. 1978: On the ontogenesis of emotions and emotion-cognition relationships in infancy. In M. Lewis and L. Rosenbloom (eds), *The Development of Affect*. New York: Plenum.

Izard, C. E., Haynes, O. M., Chisholm, G. and Baak, K. 1991: Emotional determinants of infant–mother attachment. *Child Development*, 62, 906–17.

Izard, C. E., Huebner, R., Risser, D, McGinness, G. and Dougherty, L. 1980: The young infant's ability to produce discrete emotion expressions. *Developmental Psychology*, 16, 132–40.

Izard, C. E. and Malatesta, C. Z. 1987: Perspectives on emotional development I: differential emotions theory of early emotional development. In J. Osofsky (ed.), *Handbook of infant development*, 2nd edn. 555–8, New York: Wiley.

Jacobson, S. W. 1979: Matching behavior in the young infant. *Child Development*, 50, 425–30.

Jeffrey, W. 1968: The orienting reflex and attention in cognitive development. *Psychological Review*, 75, 323–34.

Jersild, A. T. 1955: *Child Psychology*. 4th edn. London: Staples Press.

Johnson, D. B. 1983: Self-recognition in infants. *Infant Behavior and Development*, 6, 211–22.

Johnson, M. H., Dziurawiec, S., Bartrip, J. and Morton, J. 1992: The effects of movement of internal features on infants' preferences for face-like stimuli. *Infant Behavior and Development*, 15, 129–36.

Johnson, M. H., Dziurawiec, S., Ellis, H. and Morton, J. 1991: The tracking of face-like stimuli by newborn infants and its subsequent decline. *Cognition*, 40, 1–21.

Johnson, M. H. and Morton, J. 1991: *Biology and cognitive development: the case of face recognition*. Oxford: Blackwell.

Johnson, W., Emde, R. N., Pannabecker, B., Stenberg, C. and Davis, M. 1982: Maternal perception of infant emotion from birth through 18 months. *Infant Behavior and Development*, 5, 313–22.

Jones, S. S. and Raag, T. 1989: Smile production in older infants: the importance of a social recipient for the facial signal. *Child Development*, 60, 811–18.

Jusczyk, P. W. and Derrah, C. 1987: Representation of speech sounds by young infants. *Developmental Psychology*, 23, 648–54.

Jusczyk, P. W., Rosner, B. S., Cutting, J. E., Foard, F. and Smith, L. B. 1977: Categorical perception of non-speech sounds by two-month-old infants. *Perception and Psychophysics*, 21, 50–4.

Kagan, J. 1971: *Change and Continuity in Infancy*. New York: Wiley.

—— 1984: *The nature of the child*. Cambridge MA: Harvard University Press.

Kaitz, M., Meschulach-Sarfaty, O., Auerbach, J. and Eidelman, A. 1988: A re-examination of newborns' ability to imitate facial expressions. *Developmental Psychology*, 24, 3–7.

Karmel, B. Z. and Maisel, E. B. 1975: A neuronal activity model for infant visual attention. In L. B. Cohen and P. Salapatek (eds), *Infant Perception: from sensation to cognition*, vol. I. *Basic visual processes*. New York: Academic Press.

Kaye, K. 1977: Toward the origin of dialogue. In H. R. Schaffer (ed.), *Studies in Mother–Infant Interaction*. New York: Academic Press.

—— 1979: Thickening thin data: the maternal role in developing communication and language. In M. Bullowa (ed.), *Before Speech: the beginning of interpersonal communication*. Cambridge: Cambridge University Press.

Kaye, K. and Brazelton, T. B. 1971: 'Mother–infant interaction in the organization of sucking'. Paper presented at the meeting of the Society for Research in Child Development, Minneapolis.

Keating, M. B., McKenzie, B. E. and Day, R. H. 1986: Spatial localization in infancy: position constancy in a square and circular room with and without a landmark. *Child Development*, 57, 115–24.

Kellman, P. J. and Spelke, E. R. 1983: Perception of partly occluded objects in infancy. *Cognitive Psychology*, 15, 483–524.

Kermoian, R. and Campos, J. J. 1988: Locomotor experience: a facilitator of spatial cognitive development. *Child Development*, 59, 908–17.

Kestenbaum, R. and Nelson, C. A. 1990: The recognition and categorisation of upright and inverted emotional expressions by seven-month-old infants. *Infant Behavior and Development*, 13, 497–511.

Kestenbaum, R., Termine, N. and Spelke, E. S. 1987: Perception of objects and object boundaries by three-month-old infants. *British Journal of Developmental Psychology*, 5, 367–83.

Kisilevsky, B. S. Muir, D. W. and Low, J. A. 1992: Maturation of human fetal responses to vibroacoustic stimulation. *Child Development*, 63, 1497–508.

Klaus, M. and Kennell, J. 1976: *Maternal–Infant Bonding*. St. Louise: Mosby.

Kleiner, K. A. 1990: Models of neonates' preferences for facelike patterns: a response to Morton, Johnson and Maurer. *Infant Behavior and Development*, 13, 105–8.

Klinnert, M., Campos, J. J., Sorce, J., Emde, R. N. and Svejda, M. 1983: Emotions as behavioral regulators: social referencing in infancy. In R. Plutchik and H. Kellerman (eds), *Emotions in Early Development*, vol. 2. *The Emotions*. New York: Academic Press.

Koepke, J. E., Hamm, M., Legerstee, M. and Russell, M. 1983: Neonatal imitation: two failures to replicate. *Infant Behavior and Development*, 6, 97–102.

Kohut, H. 1977: *The restoration of self*. New York: International Universities Press.

Kuchuk, A., Vibbert, M. and Bornstein, M. H. 1986: The perception of smiling and its experimental correlates in three-month-old infants. *Child Development*, 57, 1054–61.

Kuhl, P. K. and Meltzoff, A. N. 1982: The bimodal perception of speech in infancy. *Science*, 218, 1138–41.

Kuhl, P. K. and Miller, J. D. 1978: Speech perception by the chinchilla: identification functions for synthetic VOT stimuli. *Journal of the Acoustical Society of America*, 63, 905–17.

Kuhl, P. K. and Padden, D. M. 1982: Enhanced discriminability at the phonetic boundaries for the voicing feature in macaques. *Perception and Psychophysics*, 32, 542–50.

Kujawski, J. H. and Bower, T. G. R. 1993: Same-sex preferential looking during infancy as a function of abstract representation. *British Journal of Developmental Psychology*, 11, 201–9.

Lamb, M. E. 1976a: Effects of stress and cohort on mother– and father–infant interaction. *Developmental Psychology*, 12, 435–43.

—— 1976b: Interaction between eight-month-old children and their fathers and mothers. In M. E. Lamb (ed.), *The Role of the Father in Child Development*. New York: Wiley.

—— 1977: The development of mother–infant and father–infant attachments in the second year of life. *Developmental Psychology*, 13, 637–48.

—— 1981: The development of social expectations in the first year of life. In M. E. Lamb and L. R. Sherrod (eds), *Infant Social Cognition: empirical and theoretical considerations*. Hillsdale, NJ: Erlbaum.

Lamb, M. E., Morrison, D. C. and Malkin, C. M. 1987: The development of infant social expectations in face-to-face interaction: a longitudinal study. *Merrill-Palmer Quarterly of Behavior and Development*, 33, 241–54.

Lamb, M. E., Sternberg, K. J. and Prodromidis, M. 1992: Nonmaternal care and the security of infant–mother attachment: a reanalysis of the data. *Infant Behavior and Development*, 15, 71–83.

Lamb, M. E., Thompson, R. A., Gardner, W. P., Charnov, E. and Estes, D. 1984: Security of infantile attachment as assessed in the strange situation: its study and biological interpretation. *Behavioral and Brain Sciences*, 7, 127–47.

Landers, W. F. 1971: The effect of differential experience on infants' performance in a Piagetian stage IV object concept task. *Developmental Psychology*, 5, 48–54.

Leahy, R. L. 1976: Development of preferences and processes of visual scanning in the human infant during the first three months of life. *Developmental Psychology*, 12, 250–4.

Lécuyer, R. 1989: Habituation and attention, novelty and cognition: where is the continuity? *Human Development*, 32, 148–57.

Lee, D. N. and Aronson, E. 1974: Visual proprioceptive control of standing in human infants. *Perception and Psychophysics*, 15, 529–32.

Lee, D. N. and Lishman, J. R. 1975: Visual proprioceptive control of stance. *Journal of Human Movement Studies*, 1, 87–95.

Legerstee, M. 1990: Infants use multimodal information to imitate speech sounds. *Infant Behavior and Development*, 13, 343–54.

—— 1991: The role of person and object in eliciting early imitation. *Journal of Experimental Child Psychology*, 51, 423–33.

—— 1992: A review of the animate-inanimate distinction in infancy: implications for models of social and cognitive knowing. *Early Development and Parenting*, 1, 59–67.

Lempers, J. D., Flavell, E. R. and Flavell, J. H. 1977: The development in very young children of tacit knowledge concerning visual perception. *Genetic Psychology Monographs*, 95, 3–53.

Lepecq, J. C. and Lafaite, M. 1989: The early development of position constancy in a no-landmark environment. *British Journal of Developmental Psychology*, 7, 289–306.

Leslie, A. M. 1984a: Infant perception of a manual pick-up event. *British Journal of Developmental Psychology*, 2, 19–32.

—— 1984b: Spatiotemporal continuity and the perception of causality in infants. *Perception*, 13, 287–305.

—— 1988: Some implications of pretence for mechanisms underlying the child's theory of mind. In J. W. Astington, P. L. Harris and D. R. Olson (eds), *Developing theories of mind*. Cambridge: Cambridge University Press.

Lewis, C. 1986: The role of the father in the human family. In W. Slukin and M. Herbert (eds), *Parental Behaviour*. Oxford: Blackwell.

Lewis, M. 1990: Social knowledge and social development. *Merrill-Palmer Quarterly of Behavior and Development*, 36, 93–116.

Lewis, M. 1991: Ways of knowing: objective self-awareness or consciousness. *Developmental Review*, 11, 231–43.

Lewis, M. and Brooks-Gunn, J. 1979: *Social cognition and the acquisition of self*. New York: Plenum.

Lewkowicz, D. J. 1985: Bisensory response to temporal frequency in four-month-old infants. *Developmental Psychology*, 21, 306–17.

—— 1992: Infants' response to temporally based intersensory equivalence: the effect of synchronous sounds on visual preferences for moving stimuli. *Infant Behavior and Development*, 15, 297–324.

Liberman, A. M., Harris, K. S., Hoffman, H. S. and Griffith, B. C. 1957: The discrimination of speech sounds within and across phoneme boundaries. *Journal of Experimental Psychology*, 54, 358–68.

Lieven, E. V. M. 1978: Conversations between mothers and young children: individual differences and their possible implication for the study of language learning. In N. Waterson and C. Snow (eds), *The Development of Communication*. London: Wiley.

Lieven, E. V. M., Pine, J. M. and Barnes, H. D. 1992: Individual differences in early vocabulary development: redefining the referential-expressive distinction. *Journal of Child Language*, 19, 287–310.

Lindsay, R. 1728: *The history of Scotland from 21 February, 1436 to March 1565, from the most authentick and most correct manuscripts. To which is added a contribution, by another hand till August, 1604* (ed. R. Freebairn). Edinburgh.

Lishman, J. R. and Lee, D. N. 1973: The autonomy of visual kinaesthetics. *Perception*, 2, 287–94.

Lloyd, S. E., Sinha, C. G. and Freeman, N. H. 1981: Spatial reference systems and the canonicality effect in infant search. *Journal of Experimental Child Psychology*, 32, 1–10.

Lock, A. 1980: *The Guided Reinvention of Language*. London: Academic Press.

Lock, A., Service, V., Brito, A. and Chandler, P. 1989: The social structuring of infant cognition. In A. Slater and G. Bremner (eds) *Infant Development*. pp. 243–72, Hove: Lawrence Erlbaum Associates.

Locke, J. 1690: 'Essay concerning human understanding.' In P. Nidditch (ed.), (1975): Oxford: Clarendon Press.

Lockman, J. J., Ashmead, D. H. and Bushnell, E. W. 1984: The development of anticipatory hand orientation during infancy. *Journal of Experimental Child Psychology*, 37, 176–86.

Lucero, M. A. 1970: Lengthening of REM sleep duration consecutive to learning in the rat. *Brain Research*, 20, 319–22.

Ludemann, P. M. 1991: Generalized discrimination of positive facial expressions by seven- and ten-month-old infants. *Child Development*, 62, 55–67.

Maccoby, E. E. and Martin, J. A. 1983: Socialization in the context of the family: parent–child interaction. In E. M. Hetherington (ed.), *Socialization, Personality and Social Development*, (vol. IV of P. H. Mussen (ed.), *Handbook of Child Psychology*), 4th edn. New York: Wiley.

Macfarlane, A. 1975: Olfaction in the development of social preferences in the human neonate. In *Parent–Infant Interaction* (CIBA Foundation Symposium 33). Amsterdam: Elsevier.

Macmurray, J. 1961: *Persons in Relation*. London: Faber and Faber.

Madison, L. S., Madison, J. K. and Adubato, S. A. 1986: Infant behavior and development in relation to fetal movement and habituation. *Child Development*, 57, 1475–82.

Malatesta, C. and Haviland, J. 1982: Learning display rules: the socialization of emotion expression in infancy. *Child Development*, 53, 991–1003.

Mandler, J. M. 1988: How to build a baby: on the development of an accessible representational system. *Cognitive Development*, 3, 113–36.

Mandler, J. 1992: How to build a baby: II conceptual primitives. *Psychological Review*, 99, 587–604.

Maratos, O. 1973: 'The origin and development of imitation in the first six months of life.' Unpublished PhD thesis, University of Geneva.

Marean, G. C., Werner, L. A. and Kuhl, P. K. 1992: Vowel categorization by very young infants. *Developmental Psychology*, 28, 396–405.

Martin, R. M. 1975: Effects of familiar and complex stimuli on infant attention. *Developmental Psychology*, 11, 178–85.

Masur, E. F. 1987: Imitative exchanges in a social context: mother–infant matching behavior at the beginning of the second year. *Merrill-Palmer Quarterly of Behavior and Development*, 33, 453–72.

Mathew, A. and Cook, M. 1990: The control of reaching movements by young infants. *Child Development*, 61, 1238–57.

Matias, R. and Cohn, J. F. 1993: Are max-specified infant facial expressions during face-to-face interaction consistent with differential emotions theory? *Developmental Psychology*, 29, 524–31.

Matias, R., Cohn, J. F. and Ross, S. 1989: A comparison of two systems that code infant affective expression. *Developmental Psychology*, 25, 483–9.

Maurer, D. 1985: Infants' perception of facedness. In T. M. Field and N. A. Fox (eds), *Social Perception in Infants*. Norwood, NJ: Ablex.

Maurer, D. and Adams, R. J. 1987: Emergence of the ability to discriminate a blue from a gray at one month of age. *Journal of Experimental Child Psychology*, 44, 147–56.

Maurer, D. and Barrera, M. 1981: Infants perception of natural and distorted arrangements of a schematic face. *Child Development*, 52, 196–202.

Maurer, D. and Salapatek, P. 1976: Developmental changes in the scanning of faces by young infants. *Child Development*, 47, 523–7.

Maurer, D. and Young, R. 1983: Newborns' following of natural and distorted arrangements of facial features. *Infant Behavior and Development*, 6, 127–31.

Mayer, N. K. and Tronick, E. Z. 1985: Mothers' turn-giving signals and infant turn-taking in mother–infant interaction. In T. M. Field and N. A. Fox (eds), *Social Perception in Infants*. Norwood, NJ: Ablex.

McCall, R. B. and Carriger, M. S. 1993: A meta-analysis of infant habituation and recognition memory performance as predictors of later IQ. *Child Development*, 64, 57–79.

McComas, J. and Field, J. 1984: 'Does crawling experience affect infants' emerging spatial orientation abilities?' Paper presented at the Fourth International Conference on Infant Studies, New York.

McDonnell, P. M. 1975: The development of visually guided reaching. *Perception and Psychophysics*, 18, 181–5.

McGraw, M. B. 1945: *The neuromuscular maturation of the human infant*. New York: Columbia University Press.

McGurk, H. 1974: Visual perception in young infants. In B. Foss (ed.), *New Perspectives in Child Development*. Harmondsworth: Penguin.

McGurk, H. and Lewis, M. M. 1974: Space perception in early infancy: perception within a common auditory-visual space? *Science*, 186, 649–50.

McIlwain, H. 1970: Metabolic adaptation in the brain. *Nature*, 226, 803.

McKenzie, B. E. and Day, R. H. 1972: Object distance as a determinant of visual fixation in early infancy. *Science*, 178, 1108–10.

—— 1976: Infants' attention to stationary and moving objects at different distances. *Australian Journal of Psychology*, 28, 45–51.

McKenzie, B. E., Day, R. H. and Ihsen, E. 1984: Localization of events in space: young infants are not always egocentric. *British Journal of Developmental Psychology*, 2, 1–9.

McKenzie, B. E. and Over, R. 1983: Young infants fail to imitate facial and manual gestures. *Infant Behavior and Development*, 6, 85–95.

McKenzie, B. E., Skouteris, H., Day, R. H., Hartman, B. and Yonas, A. 1993: Effective action by infants to contact objects by reaching and leaning. *Child Development*, 64, 415–29.

McKenzie, B. E., Tootell, H. E. and Day, R. H. 1980: Development of visual size constancy during the first year of human infancy. *Developmental Psychology*, 16, 163–74.

McShane, J. 1979: The development of naming. *Linguistics*, 17, 879–905.

Mebert, C. J. 1989: Stability and change in parents' perceptions of infant temperament; early pregancy to 13.5 months postpartum. *Infant Behavior and Development*, 12, 237–44.

Mehler, J., Bertoncini, J., Barriere, M. and Jassik-Gerschenfeld, D. 1978: Infant recognition of mother's voice. *Perception*, 7, 491–7.

Meicler, M. and Gratch, G. 1980: Do five-month-olds show object conception in Piaget's sense? *Infant Behavior and Development*, 3, 265–82.

Meltzoff, A. N. and Borton, R. W. 1979: Intermodal matching by human neonates. *Nature*, 282, 403–4.

Meltzoff, A. N. and Moore, M. K. 1977: Imitation of facial and manual gestures by human neonates. *Science*, 198, 75–8.

—— 1983a: Newborn infants imitate adult facial gestures. *Child Development*, 54, 702–9.

—— 1983b: The origins of imitation in infancy: paradigm, phenomena, and theories. In L. P. Lipsitt (ed.), *Advances in Infancy Research*, vol. 2. Norwood, NJ: Ablex.

—— 1985: Cognitive foundations and social functions of imitation and intermodal representation in infancy. In J. Mehler and R. Fox (eds), *Neonate Cognition: beyond the blooming buzzing confusion*. Hillsdale, NJ: Erlbaum.

—— 1989: Imitation in newborn infants: exploring the range of gestures imitated and the underlying mechanisms. *Developmental Psychology*, 25, 954–62.

—— 1992: Early imitation within a functional framework: the importance of person identity, movement and development. *Infant Behavior and Development*, 15, 479–505.

Mendelson, M. and Haith, M. M. 1976: The relation between audition and vision in the human newborn. *Monographs of the Society for Research in Child Development*, 41, 1–61.

Messer, D. J. and Vietze, P. M. 1988: Does mutual influence occur during mother–infant social gaze? *Infant Behavior and Development*, 11, 97–110.

Meuwissen, I. and McKenzie, B. E. 1987: Localization of an event by young infants: the effects of visual and body movement information. *British Journal of Developmental Psychology*, 5, 1–8.

Milewski, A. E. 1976: Infants' discrimination of internal and external pattern elements. *Journal of Experimental Child Psychology*, 22, 229–46.

—— 1979: Visual discrimination and detection of configurational invariance in three-month infants. *Developmental Psychology*, 15, 357–63.

Milewski, A. E. and Siqueland, E. R. 1975: Discrimination of color and pattern novelty in one-month human infants. *Journal of Experimental Child Psychology*, 19, 122–36.

Miranda, S. B. and Fantz, R. L. 1974: Recognition memory in Down's Syndrome and normal infants. *Child Development*, 45, 651–60.

Mizukami, K., Kobayashi, N., Ishii, T. and Iwata, H. 1990: First selective attachment begins in early infancy: a study using telethermography. *Infant Behavior and Development*, 13, 257–71.

Moffitt, A. R. 1973: Intensity discrimination and cardiac reaction in young infants. *Developmental Psychology*, 8, 357–9.

Mohn, G. and van Hof-van Duin, J. 1985: Preferential looking acuity in normal and neurologically abnormal infants and pediatric patients. *Documenta Ophalmologica*, Special Issue.

Moon, C., Bever, T. G. and Fifer, W. P. 1992: Canonical and non-canonical syllable discrimination by two-day-old infants. *Journal of Child Language*, 19, 1–17.

Moon, C. and Fifer, W. P. 1990: Syllables as signals for two-day-old infants. *Infant Behavior and Development*, 13, 377–90.

Moore, M. K., Borton, R. and Darby, B. L. 1978: Visual tracking in infants: evidence for object identity or object permanence? *Journal of Experimental Child Psychology*, 25, 183–98.

Moore, M. K. and Meltzoff, A. N. 1978: Object permanence, imitation and language development in infancy: towards a neo-Piagetian perspective on communication and cognitive development. In F. D. Minifie and L. L. Lloyd (eds), *Communicative and Cognitive Abilities: early behavioral assessment*. Baltimore: University Park Press.

Morford, M. and Goldin-Meadow, S. 1992: Comprehension and production of gesture in combination with speech in one-word speakers. *Journal of Child Language*, 19, 559–80.

Morrongiello, B. A. 1988: The development of auditory pattern perception skills. In C. Rovee-Collier and L. P. Lipsitt (eds), *Advances in infancy research*. vol. 5. Norwood, NJ: Ablex.

Morrongiello, B. A., Fenwick, K. D. and Chance, G. 1990: Sound localization acuity in very young infants: an observer-based testing procedure. *Developmental Psychology*, 26, 75–84.

Morrongiello, B. A., Hewitt, K. L. and Gotowiec, A. 1991: Infants' discrimination of relative distance in the auditory modality: approaching versus receding sound sources. *Infant Behavior and Development*, 14, 187–208.

Morrongiello, B. A., and Rocca, P. T. 1987: Infants' localization of sounds in the median vertical plane: estimates of minimum audible angle. *Journal of Experimental Child Psychology*, 43, 181–93.

Muir, D. and Field, J. 1979: Newborn infants orient to sounds. *Child Development*, 50, 431–6.

Muller, A. A. and Aslin, R. N. 1978: Visual tracking as an index of the object concept. *Infant Behavior and Development*, 1, 309–19.

Mundy, P., Kasari, C. and Sigman, M. 1992: Nonverbal communication, affective sharing, and intersubjectivity. *Infant Behavior and Development*, 15, 377–81.

Munsinger, H. and Weir, M. W. 1967: Infants' and young children's preference for complexity. *Journal of Experimental Child Psychology*, 5, 69–73.

Murphy, C. M. and Messer, D. J. 1977: Mothers, infants and pointing: a study of a gesture. In H. R. Schaffer (ed.), *Studies of Mother–Infant Interaction*. London: Academic Press.

Murray, A. D., Johnson, J. and Peters, J. 1990: Fine-tuning of utterance length to preverbal infants: effects on later language development. *Journal of Child Language*, 17, 511–25.

Murray, L. and Trevarthen, C. 1985: Emotional regulation of interactions between two-month-olds and their mothers. In T. M. Field and N. A. Fox (eds), *Social Perception in Infants*. Norwood, NJ: Ablex.

—— 1986: The infant's role in mother–infant communications. *Journal of Child Language*, 13, 15–29.

Nakano, S. and Kanaya, Y. 1993: The effects of mothers' teasing: do Japanese infants read their mothers' play intention in teasing? *Early Development and Parenting*, 2, 7–17.

Neilson, I. 1977: 'A reinterpretation of the development of the object concept in infancy.' Unpublished PhD thesis, University of Edinburgh.

Neisser, U. 1991: Two perceptually given aspects of the self and their development. *Developmental Review*, 11, 197–209.

Nelson, C. A. 1985: The perception and recognition of facial expressions in infancy. In T. M. Field and N. A. Fox (eds), *Social Perception in Infants*. Norwood, NJ: Ablex.

—— 1987: The recognition of facial expressions in the first two years of life: mechanisms of development. *Child Development*, 58, 889–909.

Nelson, C. A. and Dolgin, K. 1985: The generalized discrimination of facial expressions by seven-month-old infants. *Child Development*, 56, 58–61.

Nelson, C. A. and Horowitz, F. D. 1983: The perception of facial expressions and stimulus motion by two- and five-month-old infants using holographic stimuli. *Child Development*, 54, 868–77.

Nelson, K. 1973: Structure and strategy in learning to talk. *Monographs of the Society for Research in Child Development*, 38 (1–2, serial no. 149).

—— 1983: The conceptual basis for language. In T. B. Seiler and W. Wannenmacher (eds), *Concept Development and the Development of Language*. Berlin: Springer-Verlag.

Newson, J. 1979: The growth of shared understandings between infant and caregiver. In M. Bullowa (ed.), *Before Speech: the beginning of interpersonal communication*. Cambridge: Cambridge University Press.

Newson, J. and Newson, E. 1963: *Infant Care in an Urban Community*. London: Allen and Unwin.

Nijhuis, J. G. 1992: The third trimester. In J. G. Nijhuis (ed.), *Fetal behaviour: developmental and perinatal aspects*. Oxford: Oxford University Press.

Ninio, A. and Rinott, N. 1988: Fathers' involvement in the care of their infants and their attributions of cognitive competence to infants. *Child Development*, 59, 652–63.

Norcia, A. M. and Tyler, C. W. 1985: Spatial frequency sweep VEP: visual acuity during the first year of life. *Vision Research*, 25, 1399–408.

Oakes, L. M. and Cohen, L. B. 1990: Infant perception of a causal event. *Cognitive Development*, 5, 193–207.

Olsho, L. W. 1984: Infant frequency discrimination. *Infant Behavior and Development*, 7, 27–35.

Oppenheim, R. W., Pittman, R., Gray, M. and Maderdrut, J. L. 1978: Embryonic behavior, hatching and neuromuscular development in the chick following a transient reduction of spontaneous motility and sensory input by neuromuscular blocking agents. *Journal of Comparative Neurology*, 179, 619–40.

Palmer, C. 1989: The discriminating nature of infants' exploratory actions. *Developmental Psychology*, 25, 885–93.

Panneton, R. and DeCasper, A. 1982: Newborns are sensitive to temporal and behavioral contingencies. Paper presented to the International Conference on Infant Studies, Austin, Texas.

Papousek, H. 1967: Experimental studies of appetitional behaviour in human newborns and infants. In H. W. Stevenson, E. H. Hess and H. L. Rheingold (eds), *Early Behavior*. New York: Wiley.

—— 1969: Individual variability in learned responses in human infants. In R. J. Robinson (ed.), *Brain and Early Behavior*. London: Academic Press.

—— 1977: The development of learning ability in infancy. In G. Nissen (ed.), *Intelligence, learning and learning disturbances*. New York: Springer-Verlag.

Papousek, M. 1989: Determinants of responsiveness to infant vocal expression of emotional state. *Infant Behavior and Development*, 12, 507–24.

Papousek, M., Bornstein, M. H., Nuzzo, C., Papousek, H. and Symmes, D. 1990: Infant responses to prototypical melodic contours in parental speech. *Infant Behavior and Development*, 13, 539–45.

Papousek, M., Papousek, H. and Symmes, D. 1991: The meanings of melodies in motherese in tone and stress languages. *Infant Behavior and Development*, 14, 415–40.

Parke, R. D. and O'Leary, S. 1976: Father–mother–infant interaction in the newborn period: some findings, some observations and some unresolved issues. In K. Riegel and J. Meacham (eds), *The Developing Individual in a Changing World*, vol. 2. *Social and environmental issues*. The Hague: Moulton.

Parke, R. D. and Sawin, D. B. 1980: The family in early infancy: social interactional and attitudinal analyses. In F. A. Pedersen (ed.), *The Father–Infant Relationship: observational studies in a family context*. New York: Praeger.

Parmelee, A. H. and Sigman, M. D. 1983: Perinatal brain development and behavior. In M. M. Haith and J. J. Campos (eds), *Infancy and Developmental Psychobiology* (vol. II of P. H. Mussen (ed.), *Handbook of Child Psychology*), 4th edn. New York: Wiley.

Paulson, G. and Gottlieb, G. 1968: Developmental reflexes: the reappearance of fetal and neonatal reflexes in aged patients. *Brain*, 91, 37–52.

Pêcheux, M. G. and Lécuyer, R. 1989: A longitudinal study of visual habituation between three, five and eight months of age. *British Journal of Developmental Psychology*, 7, 159–69.

Pêcheux, M. G., Lepecq, J. C. and Salzarulo, P. 1988: Oral activity and exploration in one-two-month-old infants. *British Journal of Developmental Psychology*, 6, 245–56.

Pederson, D. R., Moran, G., Sitko, C., Campbell, K., Ghesquire, K. and Acton, H. 1990: Maternal sensitivity and the security of infant–mother attachment: a q-sort study. *Child Development*, 61, 1974–83.

Pedersen, F. A., Cain, R. and Zaslow, M. 1982: Variation in infant experience associated with alternative family roles. In L. Laosa and I. Sigel (eds), *The Family as a Learning Environment*. New York: Plenum.

Pedersen, F. A., Yarrow, L., Anderson, B. and Cain, R. L. 1979: Conceptualization of father influences in the infancy period. In M. Lewis and L. Rosenbloom (eds), *The Social Network of the Developing Infant*. New York: Plenum.

Peeples, D. R. and Teller, D. Y. 1975: Color vision and brightness discrimination in two-month-old human infants. *Science*, 189, 1102–3.

Pegg, J. E., Werker, J. F. and McLeod, P. J. 1992: Preference for infant–directed over adult-directed speech: evidence from seven-week-old infants. *Infant Behavior and Development*, 15, 325–45.

Pettersen, L., Yonas, A. and Fisch, R. O. 1980: The development of blinking in response to impending collision in preterm, full term, and postterm infants. *Infant Behavior and Development*, 3, 155–65.

Phillips R. D., Wagner, S. H., Fells, C. A. and Lynch, M. 1990: Do infants recognize emotion in facial expressions?: categorical and 'metaphorical' evidence. *Infant Behavior and Development*, 13, 71–84.

Piaget, J. 1951: *Play, Dreams and Imitation in Childhood*. London: Heinemann.

—— 1952: *The Origins of Intelligence in the Child* (trans. M. Cook). New York: Basic Books (originally published in French 1936).

—— 1954: *The Construction of Reality in the Child* (trans. M. Cook). New York: Basic Books (originally published in French, 1936).

—— 1967: Language and thought from the genetic point of view. In D. Elkind (ed.), *Psychological Studies*. New York: Random House.

Piaget, J. and Inhelder, B. 1969: *The Psychology of the Child*. New York: Basic Books.

Pieraut-Le Bonniec, G. 1985: From visual-motor anticipation to conceptualization: reaction to solid and hollow objects and knowledge of the function of containment. *Infant Behavior and Development*, 8, 413–24.

Pine, J. M. and Lieven, E. V. M. 1990: Referential style at thirteen months: why age-defined cross-sectional measures are inappropriate for the study of strategy differences in early language development. *Journal of Child Language*, 17, 625–31.

Pineau, A. and Streri, A. 1990: Intermodal transfer of spatial arrangement of the component parts of an object in infants aged four to five months. *Perception*, 19, 795–804.

Pipp, S., Fischer, K. and Jennings, S. 1987: Acquisition of self- and mother knowledge in infancy. *Developmental Psychology*, 23, 86–96.

Pomerantz, J. R. 1977: Pattern goodness and speed of encoding. *Memory and Cognition*, 5, 235–41.

Powlson, C. L., Kymissis, E. Reeve, K. F., Andrectos, M. and Reeve, L. 1991: Generalized vocal imitation in infants. *Journal of Experimental Child Psychology*, 51, 267–79.

Prather, P. and Spelke, E. S. 1982: *Three-month-old infants' perception of adjacent and partly occluded objects*. Paper presented at the International Conference on Infant Studies, Austin, Texas.

Pratt, K. C. 1946: The neonate. In L. Carmichael (ed.), *Manual of Child Psychology*. New York: Wiley.

Prechtl, H. F. R. 1974: The behavioural states of the newborn infant (a review). *Brain Research*, 76, 1304–11.

—— 1977: *The Neurological Examination of the Full Term Newborn Infant*. Clinics in Developmental Medicine, no. 63. London: Heinemann.

—— 1981: The study of neural development as a perspective of clinical problems. In K. J. Connolly and H. F. R. Prechtl (eds), *Maturation and Development: biological and psychological perspectives*. London: Heinemann.

—— 1984: Continuity and change in early neutral development. In H. F. R. Prechtl (ed.), *Continuity of Neural Function from Prenatal to Postnatal Life*. Oxford: Blackwell Scientific Publications.

—— 1986: Prenatal motor development. In M. G. Wade and H. T. A. Whiting (eds), *Motor Development in Children: aspects of coordination and control*. Dordrecht: Nijhoff.

Priel, B. and de Schonen, S. 1986: Self-recognition: a study of a population without mirrors. *Journal of Experimental Child Psychology*, 41, 237–50.

Pringle, M. L. K. and Clifford, L. 1962: Conditions associated with emotional maladjustment among children in care. *Educational Review*, 14, 112–23.

Querleu, D. and Renard, K. 1981: Les perceptions auditives du foetus humain. *Medicine et Hygiene*, 39, 2102–10.

Quinn, P. C., Burke, S. and Rush, A. 1993: Part-whole perception in early infancy: evidence for perceptual grouping produced by lightness similarity. *Infant Behavior and Development*, 16, 19–42.

Rader, N., Bausano, M. and Richards, J. E. 1980: On the nature of the visual cliff avoidance response in human infants. *Child Development*, 51, 61–8.

Rader, N., Spiro, D. J. and Firestone, P. B. 1979: Performance on a stage IV object-permanence task with standard and nonstandard covers. *Child Development*, 50, 908–10.

Rader, N. and Stern, J. D. 1982: Visually elicited reaching in neonates. *Child Development*, 53, 1004–7.

Reddy, V. 1991: Playing with others' expectations: teasing and mucking about in the first year. In A. Whiten (ed.), *Natural theories of mind: evolution, development and simulation of everyday mindreading*. Oxford: Blackwell.

Regal, D. M. and Salapatek, 1982: 'Eye and head coordination in human infants. Paper presented at the meeting of the Association for Research in Vision and Ophthalmology, Sarasota, Florida.

Reissland, N. 1988: Neonatal imitation in the first hour of life: observations in rural Nepal. *Developmental Psychology*, 24, 464–9.

Richards, J. E. and Rader, N. 1981: Crawling-onset age predicts visual cliff avoidance in infants. *Journal of Experimental Psychology, Human Perception and Performance*, 7, 382–7.

Rieser, J. 1979: References systems and the spatial orientation of six month old infants. *Child Development*, 50, 1078–87.

Robertson J. and Robertson, J. 1967: 'Young children in brief separation: I. Kate, aged two years five months in fostercare for twenty-seven days.' Tavistock Child Development Research Unit (cited by Rutter, 1981).

Robinson, J. A., Connell, S., McKenzie, B. E. and Day, R. H. 1990: Do infants use their own images to locate objects reflected in a mirror? *Child Development*, 61, 1558–68.

Rochat, P. 1987: Mouthing and grasping in neonates: evidence for the early detection of what hard or soft substances afford for action. *Infant Behavior and Development*, 10, 435–49.

—— 1989: Object manipulation and exploration in two- to five-month-old infants. *Developmental Psychology*, 25, 871–84.

Rogoff, B. 1990: *Apprenticeship in thinking: cognitive development in social context*. Oxford: Oxford University Press.

Rogoff, B., Mistry, J., Radziszewska, B. and Germond, J. 1992: Infants' instrumental social interaction with adults. In S. Feinman (ed.), *Social referencing and the social construction of reality in infancy*, 323–48, New York: Plenum.

Rönnqvist, L. and Hofsten, C. von 1993: Neonatal finger and arm movements as determined by a social and an object context. *Early Development and Parenting*, 2, in press.

Rose, D. H. and Slater, A. M. 1983: Infant recognition memory following brief stimulus exposure. *British Journal of Developmental Psychology*, 1, 221–30.

Rose, S. A. 1988: Shape recognition in infancy: visual integration of sequential information. *Child Development*, 59, 1161–76.

Rose, S. A., Gottfried, A. W. and Bridger, W. H. 1983: Infants' cross-modal transfer from solid objects to their graphic representations. *Child Development*, 54, 686–94.

Rosenstein, D. and Oster, H. 1988: Differential facial responses to four basic tastes in newborns. *Child Development*, 59, 1555–68.

Ross, G., Kagan, J., Zelazo, P. and Kotelchuck, M. 1975: Separation protest in infants in home and laboratory. *Developmental Psychology*, 11, 256–7.

Rovee-Collier, C. 1987: Learning and memory in infancy. In J. D. Osofsky (ed.), *Handbook of infant development*, 2nd edn. New York: John Wiley.

Ruff, H. 1984: Infants' manipulative exploration of objects: effects of age and object characteristics. *Developmental Psychology*, 20, 9–20.

Ruff, H. A. and Halton, A. 1978: Is there directed reaching in the human neonate? *Developmental Psychology*, 14, 425–6.

Russell, G. 1983: *The Changing Role of Fathers*. Milton Keynes: Open University Press.

Rutter, M. 1981: *Maternal Deprivation Reassessed*, 2nd edn. Harmondsworth: Penguin Books.

Sagi, A. and Hoffman, M. 1976: Empathic distress in the newborn. *Developmental Psychology*, 12, 175–6.

Sagi, A., Lewkowicz, K. S., Shoham, R., Dvir, R. and Estes, D. 1985: Security of infant–mother, father, metapelet attachments among kibbutz-reared Israeli children. In I. Bretherton and E. Waters (eds), Growing points of attachment theory and research. *Monographs of the Society for Research in Child Development*, 50 (1–2, Serial no. 209), 257–75.

Salapatek, P., Bechtold, A. G. and Bushnell, E. W. 1976: Infant visual acuity as a function of viewing distance. *Child Development*, 47, 860–3.

Salapatek, P. and Kessen, W. 1966: Visual scannings of triangles by the human newborn. *Journal of Experimental Child Psychology*, 3, 155–67.

—— 1973: Prolonged investigation of triangles by the human newborn. *Journal of Experimental Child Psychology*, 15, 22–9.

Samuels, C. A. 1986: Bases for the infant's developing self-awareness. *Human Development*, 29, 36–48.

Scarr, S. and Salapatek, P. 1970: Patterns of fear development during infancy. *Merrill-Palmer Quarterly of Behavior and Development*, 16, 53–90.

Schaffer, H. R. 1971: *The Growth of Sociability*. Harmondsworth: Penguin Books.

—— 1984: *The Child's Entry into a Social World*. London: Academic Press.

Schaffer, H. R., Collis, G. M. and Parsons, G. 1977: Vocal interchange and visual regard in verbal and preverbal children. In H. R. Schaffer (ed.), *Studies in Mother–Infant Interaction*. London: Academic Press.

Schaffer, H. R. and Emerson, P. E. 1964: The development of social attachments in infancy. *Monographs of the Society for Research in Child Development*, 29, no. 94.

Schmuckler, M. A. and Gibson, E. J. 1989: The effect of imposed optical flow on guided locomotion in young walkers. *British Journal of Developmental Psychology*, 7, 193–206.

Schneider, B. A. and Trehub, S. E. 1985: Behavioral assessment of basic capabilities. In S. E. Trehub and B. A. Schneider (eds), *Auditory Development in Infancy*. New York: Plenum.

Schwartz, A., Campos, J. and Baisel, E. 1973: The visual cliff: cardiac and behavioral correlates on the deep and shallow sides at five and nine months of age. *Journal of Experimental Child Psychology*, 15, 86–99.

Self, P. A. and Horowitz, F. D. 1979: The behavioral assessment of the neonate: an overview. In J. D. Osofsky (ed.), *Handbook of Infant Development*. New York: Wiley.

Service, V. 1984: Maternal styles and communicative development. In A. Lock and E. Fisher (eds), *Language Development*. London: Croom Helm.

Shotter, J. and Newson, J. 1982: An ecological approach to cognitive development: implicate orders, joint action and intentionality. In G. Butterworth and P. Light (eds), *Social Cognition: studies of the development of understanding*. Brighton: Harvester.

Sigman, M. and Parmelee, A. H. 1974: Visual preferences of four-month-old premature and full-term infants. *Child Development*, 45, 959–65.

Simoneau, K. and Decarie, T. G. 1979: Cognition and perception in the object concept. *Canadian Journal of Psychology*, 33, 396–407.

Skinner, B. F. 1957: *Verbal Behavior*. New York: Appleton-Century-Crofts.

Skouteris, H., McKenzie, B. E. and Day, R. H. 1992: Integration of sequential information for shape perception by infants: a developmental study. *Child Development*, 63, 1164–76.

Slade, A. 1987: Quality of attachment and early symbolic play. *Developmental Psychology*, 23, 78–85.

Slater, A. M. 1989: Visual memory and perception in early infancy. In A. Slater and G. Bremner (eds), *Infant Development*. Hillsdale, NJ: Erlbaum. 43–72.

Slater, A. M. 1990: Infant development: the origins of competence. *The Psychologist: Bulletin of the British Psychological Society*, 3, 109–13.

Slater, A. M. and Findlay, J. M. 1972: The measurement of fixation position in the newborn baby. *Journal of Experimental Child Psychology*, 14, 349–64.

—— 1975: Binocular fixation in the newborn baby. *Journal of Experimental Child Psychology*, 20, 248–73.

Slater, A. M., Mattock, A. and Brown, E. 1990: Newborn infants' responses to retinal and real size, *Journal of Experimental Child Psychology*, 49, 314–22.

Slater, A. M., Mattock, A., Brown, E. and Bremner, J. G. 1991: Form perception at birth: Cohen and Younger (1984) revisited. *Journal of Experimental Child Psychology*, 51, 395–406.

Slater, A. M. and Morison, V. 1985: Shape constancy and slant perception at birth. *Perception*, 14, 337–44.

Slater, A. M., Morison, V. and Rose, D. 1982: Visual memory at birth. *British Journal of Psychology*, 73, 519–25.

—— 1983: Perception of shape by the new-born baby. *British Journal of Developmental Psychology*, 1, 135–42.

Slater, A. M., Morison, V. and Somers, M. 1988: Orientation Discrimination and cortical function in the human newborn. *Perception*, 17, 597–602.

Slater, A. M., Morison, V., Somers, M., Mattock, A., Brown, E. and Taylor, D. 1990: Newborn and older infants' perception of partly occluded objects. *Infant Behavior and Development*, 13, 33–49.

Slater, A. M., Morison, V., Town, C. and Rose, D. 1985: Movement perception and identity constancy in the new-born baby. *British Journal of Developmental Psychology*, 3, 211–20.

Slater, A. M., Rose, D. and Morison, V. 1984: New-born infants' perception of similarities and differences between two- and three-dimensional stimuli. *British Journal of Developmental Psychology*, 2, 287–94.

Slukin, W., Herbert, M. and Slukin, A. 1983: *Maternal Bonding*. Oxford: Blackwell.

Smith, D. W. 1976: *Recognizable patterns of human malformation: genetic, embryological aspects*. 2nd edn. Philadelphia: W. B. Saunders Company.

Smith, P. B. and Pederson, D. R. 1988: Maternal sensitivity and patterns of infant–mother attachment. *Child Development*, 59, 1097–101.

Soken, N. H. and Pick, A. D. 1992: Intermodal perception of happy and angry expressive behaviors by seven-month-old infants. *Child Development*, 63, 787–95.

Sokol, S. 1978: Measurement of infant visual acuity from pattern reversal evoked potentials. *Vision Research*, 18, 33–40.

Sokolov, E. N. 1963: *Perception and the Conditioned Reflex*. New York: Macmiilan.

Sorce, J., Emde, R. N., Campos, J. J. and Klinnert, M. 1981: 'Maternal emotional signaling: its effect on the visual cliff behavior of one-year-olds.' Paper presented at the Meeting of the Society for Research in Child Development, Boston.

Spelke, E. S. 1976: Infants' intermodal perception of events. *Cognitive Psychology*, 8, 553–60.

—— 1979: Perceiving bimodally specified events in infancy. *Developmental Psychology*, 15, 626–36.

—— 1981: The infant's acquisition of knowledge of bimodally specified events. *Journal of Experimental Child Psychology*, 31, 279–99.

—— 1985: Perception of unity, persistence, and identity. In J. Mehler and R. Fox (eds), *Neonate Cognition; beyond the blooming buzzing confusion*. Hillsdale, NJ: Erlbaum.

Spelke, E. S., Breinlinger, K., Macomber, J. and Jacobson, K. 1992: Origins of knowledge. *Psychological Review*, 99, 605–32.

Spelke, E. S. and Cortelyou, A. 1981: Perceptual aspects of social knowing: looking and listening in infancy. In M. E. Lamb and L. R. Sherrod (eds), *Infant Social Cognition: empirical and theoretical considerations*. Hillsdale, NJ: Erlbaum.

Spelke, E. S. and Owsley, C. J. 1979: Intermodal exploration and knowledge in infancy. *Infant Behavior and Development*, 2, 13–24.

Spence, M. J. and DeCaspar, A. J. 1982: 'Human fetuses perceive maternal speech.' Paper presented at the meeting of the International Conference on Infant Studies, Austin, Texas.

Spitz, R. and Wolf, K. 1946: The smiling response: a contribution to the ontogenesis of social relations. *Genetic Psychology Monographs*, 34, 57–125.

Spitz, R. A. 1965: *The First Year of Life*. New York: International Universities Press.

Sroufe, L. A. 1979: Socioemotional development. In J. Osofsky (ed.), *Handbook of Infant Development*. New York: Wiley.

—— 1983: Individual patterns of adaptation from infancy to preschool. In M. Perlmutter (ed.), *Development of Policy Concerning Children with Special Needs: Minnesota Symposia on Child Psychology*, vol. 16. Hillsdale, NJ: Erlbaum.

—— 1985: Attachment classification from the perspective of infant–caregiver relationships and infant temperament. *Child Development*, 56, 1–14.

Starr, A., Amlie, R. N., Martin, W. H. and Sanders, S. 1977: Development of auditory function in newborn infants revealed by auditory brainstem potentials. *Pediatrics*, 60, 831–9.

Steiner, J. E. 1974: Innate discriminative human facial expressions to taste and smell stimuli. *Annals of the New York Academy of Science*, 237, 229–33.

—— 1979: Human facial expressions in response to taste and smell stimulation. In H. Reese and L. P. Lipsitt (eds), *Advances in Child Development and Behavior*, 13. New York: Academic Press.

Stenberg, C. 1982: 'The Development of Anger Facial Expressions in Infancy.' Unpublished doctoral dissertation, University of Denver (cited by Campos et al., 1983).

Stenberg, C., Campos, J. J. and Emde, R. 1983: The facial expression of anger in seven month old infants. *Child Development*, 54, 178–84.

Stern, D. N. 1974: Mother and infant at play: the dyadic interaction involving facial, vocal, and gaze behaviors. In M. Lewis and L. A. Rosenblum (eds), *The effects of the infant on its caregiver*, 187–232, New York: Wiley.

Stern, D. N., Hofer, L., Haft, W. and Dore, J. 1985: Affect attunement: the sharing of feeling states between mother and infant by means of intermodal fluency. In T. M. Field and N. A. Fox (eds), *Social Perception in Infants*. Norwood: Ablex.

Stern, D. N., Jaffe, J., Beebe, B. and Bennett, S. J. 1975: Vocalizing in unison and in alternation: two modes of communication within the mother–infant dyad. *Annals of the New York Academy of Science*, 263, 89–100.

Stifter, C. A. and Fox, N. A. 1990: Infant reactivity: physiological correlates of newborn and five-month temperament. *Developmental Psychology*, 26, 582–8.

Stoffregen, T. A., Schmuckler, M. A. and Gibson, E. J. 1987: Use of central and peripheral optical flow in stance and locomotion in young walkers. *Perception*, 16, 113–9.

Stratton, P. 1982: Newborn individuality. In P. Stratton (ed.), *Psychobiology of the Human Newborn*. Chichester: Wiley.

Streri, A. 1987: Tactile discrimination of shape and intermodal transfer in two- to three-month-old infants. *British Journal of Developmental Psychology*, 5, 213–20.

Streri, A. and Pêcheux, M. G. 1986: Tactual habituation and discrimination of form in infancy: a comparison with vision. *Child Development*, 57, 100–4.

Stucki, M., Kaufmann-Hayoz, R. and Kaufmann, F. 1987: Infants' recognition of a face revealed through motion: contribution of internal facial movement and head movement. *Journal of Experimental Child Psychology*, 44, 80–91.

Sullivan, J. W. and Horowitz, F. D. 1983: Infant intermodal perception and maternal multimodal stimulation: implications for language development. In L. P. Lipsitt (ed.), *Advances in Infancy Research*, vol. 2. Norwood: Ablex.

Suter, S., Suter, P. S. and Crow, C. D. 1991: Infant and adult grating acuity estimated by VEPs and heart-rate change. *Infant Behavior and Development*, 14, 365–82.

Svejda, M. and Schmid, D. 1979: 'The role of self-produced locomotion in the onset of fear of heights on the visual cliff.' Paper presented at the Meeting of the Society for Research in Child Development, San Francisco.

Swaab, D. F., Honnebier, M. B. O. M. and Mirmiran, M. 1992: Development of the central nervous system. In J. G. Nijhuis (ed.), *Fetal behaviour: developmental and perinatal aspects*. Oxford: Oxford University Press, 75–90.

Takahashi, K. 1986: Examining the strange situation procedure with Japanese mothers and 12-month-old infants. *Developmental Psychology*, 22, 265–70.

—— 1990: Are the key assumptions of the 'strange situation' procedure universal? A view from Japanese research. *Human Development*, 33, 23–30.

Tamis-LeMonda, C. S. and Bornstein, M. H. 1989: Habituation and maternal encouragement of attention in infancy as predictors of toddler language, play, and representational competence. *Child Development*, 60, 738–51.

Teller, D. Y., Peeples, D. R. and Sekel, M. 1978: Discrimination of chromatic from white light by two-month-old human infants. *Vision Research*, 18, 41–8.

Thelen, E. 1984: Learning to walk: ecological demands and phylogenetic constraints. In L. P. Lipsitt and C. Rovee-Collier (eds), *Advances in Infancy Research*, vol. 3. Norwood, NJ: Ablex.

Thelen, E. and Fisher, D. M. 1982: Newborn stepping: an explanation of a 'disappearing' reflex. *Developmental Psychology*, 18, 706–15.

Thelen, E., Skala, K. D. and Kelso, J. A. S. 1987: The dynamic nature of early coordination: evidence from bilateral leg movements in young infants. *Developmental Psychology*, 23, 179–86.

Thelen, E. and Ulrich, B. D. 1991: Hidden skills: a dynamic systems analysis of treadmill stepping during the first year. *Monographs of the Society for Research in Child Development*, 56 (1).

Tinbergen, N. 1951: *The Study of Instinct*. Oxford: Oxford University Press.

Tizard, J. 1969: The role of social institutions in the causation, prevention and alleviation of mental retardation. In C. Haywood (ed.), *Socio-Cultural Aspects of Mental Retardation*. New York: Academic Press.

Tizard, J. and Tizard, B. 1971: The social development of two-year-old children in residential nurseries. In H. R. Schaffer (ed.), *The Origins of Human Social Relations*. London: Academic Press.

Toda, S. and Fogel, A. 1993: Infant response to the still-face situation at three and six months. *Developmental Psychology*, 29, 532–8.

Touwen, B. 1976: *Neurological Development in Infancy*. London: Spastics International and Heinemann.

Trehub, S. E. 1976: The discrimination of foreign speech contrasts by infants and adults. *Child Development*, 47, 466–72.

Trehub, S. E., Schneider, B. A. and Endman, M. 1980: Developmental changes in infants' sensitivity to octave-band noises. *Journal of Experimental Child Psychology*, 29, 282–93.

Trevarthen, C. 1969: Communication and cooperation in early infancy: a description of primary intersubjectivity. In M. Bullowa (ed.), *Before Speech: the beginnings of interpersonal communication*. Cambridge: Cambridge University Press.

—— 1989: Signs before speech. In T. A. Sebeok and J. Umiker-Sebeok (eds), 689–755, New York: Mouton de Gruyter.

Trevarthen, C. and Hubley, P. 1978: Secondary intersubjectivity: confidence, confiding and acts of meaning in the first year. In A. Lock (ed.), *Action, Gesture and Symbol: the emergence of language*. London: Academic Press.

Tronick, E. Z., Als, H. and Brazelton, T. B. 1980: Monadic phases: a structural descriptive analysis of infant–mother face-to-face interaction. *Merrill-Palmer Quarterly of Behavior and Development*, 26, 3–24.

Tronick, E. Z. and Cohn, J. F. 1989: Infant–mother face-to-face interaction: age and gender differences in coordination and the occurrence of miscoordination. *Child Development*, 60, 85–92.

Turkewitz, G., Birch, H. G., Moreau, T., Levy, L. and Cornwell, A. C. 1966: Effect of intensity of auditory stimulation on directional eye movements in the human neonate. *Animal Behaviour*, 14, 93–101.

Tyler, D. and McKenzie, B. E. 1990: Spatial updating and training effects in the first year of human infancy. *Journal of Experimental Child Psychology*, 50, 445–61.

Ulvund, S. E. 1983: The canonicality effect in search for the hidden object. *Scandinavian Journal of Psychology*, 24, 149–51.

Uzgiris, I. C. and Lucas, T. C. 1978: Observations and experimental methods in studies of object concept development in infancy. In G. P. Sackett (ed.),

Observing Behavior, vol. I. *Theory and Applications in Mental Representation*. Baltimore: University Park Press.

Vaughn, B., Egeland, B., Sroufe, L. A. and Waters, E. 1979: Individual differences in infant–mother attachment at twelve and eighteen months: stability and change in families under stress. *Child Development*, 50, 971–5.

Vaughn, B. E., Lefever, G. B., Seifer, R. and Barglow, P. 1989: Attachment behavior, attachment security, and temperament during infancy. *Child Development*, 60, 728–37.

Vaughn, B. E., Stevenson-Hinde, J., Waters, E., Kotsaftis, A., Lefever, G. B., Shouldice, A., Trudel, M. and Belsky, J. 1992: Attachment security and temperament in infancy and early childhood: some conceptual clarifications. *Developmental Psychology*, 28, 463–73.

Vries, J. I. P. de 1992: The first trimester. In J. G. Nijhuis (ed.), *Fetal behaviour: developmental and perinatal aspects*. Oxford: Oxford University Press.

Vygotsky, L. S. 1962: *Thought and Language*. Cambridge, Mass.: MIT Press.

Walden, T. A. and Ogan, T. A. 1988: The development of social referencing. *Child Development*, 59, 1230–40.

Wales, R. J. 1970: Comparing and contrasting. In J. Morton (ed.), *Biological and social factors in psycholinguistics*. London: Logos Press.

Walk, R. D. 1968: Monocular compared to binocular depth perception in human infants. *Science*, 162, 473–5.

—— 1979: Depth perception and a laughing heaven. In A. D. Pick (ed.), *Perception and its Development: a tribute to Eleanor J. Gibson*. New York: Wiley.

Walker-Andrews, A. S. and Gibson, E. J. 1986: What develops in bimodal perception? In L. P. Lipsitt and C. Rovee-Collier (eds), *Advances in infancy research*, 4, 171–81, Norwood, NJ: Ablex.

Walker-Andrews, A. S. and Grolnick, W. 1983: Infants' discrimination of vocal expressions. *Infant Behavior and Development*, 6, 491–8.

Walker-Andrews, A. S. and Lennon, E. 1991: Infants' discrimination of vocal expressions: contributions of auditory and visual information. *Infant Behavior and Development*, 14, 131–42.

Walton, G. E., Bower, N. J. A. and Bower, T. G. R. 1992: Recognition of familiar faces by newborns. *Infant Behavior and Development*, 15, 265–9.

Waters, E. 1978: The reliability and stability of individual differences in infant–mother attachment. *Child Development*, 49, 483–94.

Watson, J. B. 1930: *Behaviorism*. Chicago: University of Chicago Press.

Weiss, M. J., Zelazo, P. R. and Swain, I. U. 1988: Newborn response to auditory stimulus discrepancy. *Child Development*, 59, 1530–41.

Wellman, H. M. 1991: From desires to beliefs: acquisition of a theory of mind. In A. Whiten (ed.), *Natural theories of mind: evolution, development and simulation of everyday mindreading*. Oxford: Blackwell.

Wellman, H. M. and Woolley, J. D. 1990: From simple desires to ordinary beliefs: the early development to everyday psychology. *Cognition*, 35, 245–75.

Werker, J. F. and Tees, R. C. 1984: Cross-language speech perception: evidence for perceptual reorganization during the first year of life. *Infant Behavior and Development*, 7, 49–63.

Werner, H. 1948: *Comparative Psychology of Mental Development*. New York: International Universities Press.

Werner, L. A. and Gillenwater, J. M. 1990: Pure-tone sensitivity of two- to five-week-old infants. *Infant Behavior and Development*, 13, 355–75.

White, B. L. 1971: *Human Infants: experience and psychological development*. Englewood Cliffs, NJ: Prentice-Hall.

White, B. L., Castle, P. and Held, R. 1964: Observations on the development of visually directed reaching. *Child Development*, 35, 349–64.

Whiten, A. 1977: Assessing the effects of perinatal events on the success of the mother–infant relationship. In H. R. Schaffer (ed.), *Studies in Mother–Infant Interaction*. London: Academic Press.

Whiting, H. T. A. 1984: *Human motor actions: Bernstein reassessed*. Amsterdam: North Holland.

Wickelgren, L. W. 1967: Convergence in the human newborn. *Journal of Experimental Child Psychology*, 5, 74–85.

Wiesel, T. N. and Hubel, D. H. 1965: Comparison of the effects of unilateral and bilateral eye closure on cortical unit responses in kittens. *Journal of Neurophysiology*, 28, 1029–40.

Wilcox, B. M. 1969: Visual preferences of human infants for representations of the human face. *Journal of Experimental Child Psychology*, 7, 10–20.

Willatts, P. 1979: Adjustment of reaching to a change in object position by young infants. *Child Development*, 50, 911–13.

Willemsen, E., Flaherty, D., Heaton, C. and Ritchey, G. 1974: Attachment behavior of one-year-olds as a function of mother versus father, sex of child, session and toys. *Genetic Psychology Monographs*, 90, 305–24.

Winnicott, D. W. 1965: *The Maturational Process and the Facilitating Environment*. London: Hogarth.

Wishart, J. G. 1979: 'The development of the object concept in infancy.' Unpublished PhD thesis, University of Edinburgh.

Wolff, P. H. 1963: Observations of the early development of smiling. In B. M. Foss (ed.), *Determinants of Infant Behaviour*, vol. 2. London: Methuen.

—— 1969: The natural history of crying and other vocalizations in early infancy. In B. Foss (ed.), *Determinants of Infant Behaviour*, vol. 4. London: Methuen.

—— 1973: The classification of states. In L. J. Stone, H. T. Smith and L. B. Murphy (eds), *The Competent Infant: Research and Commentary*. New York: Basic Books.

Yoder, P. J. and Kaiser, A. P. 1989: Alternative explanations for the relationship between maternal verbal interaction style and child language development. *Journal of Child Language*, 16, 141–60.

Yonas, A., Arterberry, M. E. and Granrud, C. E. 1987: Four-month-old infants' sensitivity to binocular and kinetic information for three-dimensional-object shape. *Child Development*, 58, 910–17.

Yonas, A., Bechtold, A. G., Frankel, D., Gordon, F. R., McRoberts, G., Norcia, A. and Sternfels, S. 1977: Development of sensitivity to information for impending collision. *Perception and Psychophysics*, 21, 97–104.

Yonas, A. and Granrud, C. E. 1985: Development of visual space perception in young infants. In J. Mehler and R. Fox (eds), *Neonate Cognition: beyond the blooming buzzing confusion*. Hillsdale, NJ: Erlbaum.

Yonas, A., Granrud, C., Arterberry, M. and Hanson, B. 1986: Distance perception from linear perspective and texture gradients. *Infant Behavior and Development*, 9, 247–56.

Young-Browne, G., Rosenfeld, H. and Horowitz, F. 1977: Infant discrimination of facial expressions. *Child Development*, 48, 555–62.

Younger, B. 1985: The segregation of items into categories by ten-month-old infants. *Child Development*, 56, 1574–85.

—— 1990: Infant categorisation: memory for category-level and specific item information. *Journal of Experimental Child Psychology*, 50, 131–55.

Younger, B. and Gotlieb, S. 1988: Development of categorization skills: changes in the nature or structure of infant form categories? *Developmental Psychology*, 24, 611–19.

Zelazo, P. R. 1976: From reflexive to instrumental behavior. In L. P. Lipsitt (ed.), *Developmental Psychobiology: the significance of infancy*. Hillsdale, NJ: Erlbaum.

Zimmerman, J., Stoyva, J. and Metcalf, D. 1970: Distorted visual feedback and augmented REM sleep. *Psychophysiology*, 7, 298.

Zucker, K. J. 1985: The infant's construction of his parents in the first six months of life. In T. M. Field and N. A. Fox (eds), *Social Perception in Infants*. Norwood, NJ: Ablex.

Name Index

Name index

Subject Index